# Seeing Between the Pixels

**Springer**
Berlin
Heidelberg
New York
Barcelona
Budapest
Hongkong
London
Mailand
Paris
Santa Clara
Singapur
Tokio

*Christine Strothotte née Helms* is on the scientific staff of the Faculty of Mechanical Engineering at the Otto-von-Guericke University of Magdeburg, Germany and is a fellow of the Humboldt Foundation. She was born in 1968 and raised in the former East Germany. She studied Computer Science at the Technical University of Dresden and the Otto-von-Guericke University of Magdeburg, completing her Dipl.-Ing. degree in 1990. She earned a doctorate in Computer Science in Magdeburg in 1994, specializing in computer simulation.

*Thomas Strothotte* is Professor of Computer Science and Chairman of the Department of Simulation and Graphics at the Otto-von-Guericke University of Magdeburg, Germany. Born in 1959 and raised in Canada, he was educated in Vancouver (British Columbia), Montréal (Québec), and Waterloo (Ontario). He holds a B.Sc. (1980) in Physics and an M.Sc. (1981) in Computer Science from Simon Fraser University, and a Ph.D. (1984), also in Computer Science, from McGill University. He has worked in teaching and research as a computer scientist at INRIA Rocquencourt, the University of Stuttgart (where he completed a *Habilitation* degree in 1989), the IBM Scientific Center in Heidelberg and the Free University of Berlin. He moved to Magdeburg in October 1993, where he served as the Dean of his faculty from 1994 to 1996. He is presently a Vice President of the university.

Christine Strothotte
Thomas Strothotte

# Seeing Between the Pixels

Pictures in Interactive Systems

Foreword by Steven K. Feiner

With 235 Figures, 52 in Color
and 19 Tables

 Springer

Dr.-Ing. Christine Strothotte
Otto-von-Guericke University of Magdeburg
Faculty of Mechanical Engineering
Universitätsplatz 2, D-39106 Magdeburg, Germany
e-mail: tine@isg.cs.uni-magdeburg.de

Prof. Dr. Thomas Strothotte
Otto-von-Guericke University of Magdeburg
Faculty of Computer Science
Universitätsplatz 2, D-39016 Magdeburg, Germany
e-mail: tstr@isg.cs.uni-magdeburg.de

CR Subject Classification (1991): I.3.6, I.3.4, H.5.2, H.1.2, I.2.4

Library of Congress Cataloging-in-Publication Data
Strothotte, Christine, 1968-
    Seeing between the pixels: pictures in interactive systems/
  Christine Strothotte, Thomas Strothotte: forword (sic) by Steven K.
Feiner.
        p.      cm.
    Includes bibliographical references and index.
    ISBN-13:978-3-642-64370-5      e-ISBN-13: 978-3-642-60361-7
    DOI: 10.1007/978-3-642-60361-7
    1. Computer graphics.    2. Interactive computer systems.    3. Image
processing--Digital techniques.   I. Strothotte, Thomas, 1959-  .  II. Title.
T385.S79915    1997
006.6´01´9--dc21                              97-40255
                                              CIP

ISBN-13: 978-3-642-64370-5        e-ISBN-13: 978-3-642-60361-7
DOI: 10.1007/978-3-642-60361-7

© Springer-Verlag Berlin Heidelberg 1997
Softcover reprint of the hardcover 1st edition 1997

Typesetting: Data conversion by perform, Heidelberg
Cover design: Künkel + Lopka, Ilvesheim
SPIN 10502208                    45/3142 – 5 4 3 2 1 0

**Dedicated to Günter Strothotte**
**1926 – 1992**

# Foreword

Pictures are at the heart of how we communicate with computers, emblematic of our current fascination with multimedia and web-based computing. Nevertheless, most of us know far less about pictures and the way in which they work than we know about the text that often accompanies them. In an attempt to understand pictures, perhaps the most fundamental question we can ask is, "What is a picture?" What is it that objects as diverse as icons, bar charts, paintings, and photographs have in common that makes us refer to all of them as pictures? And what is it about pictures that convinces us to use them instead of, or in addition to, text?

We often talk about how pictures "depict" things. But, even the process of depiction seems to differ from one picture to another. On a computer, we may use a paint system to guide a virtual brush over the screen, a video camera to capture a live image, a spreadsheet to automatically generate a corresponding bar chart, or a rendering system that models the interactions of synthetic lights, objects, and cameras. Is there some underlying property that these processes all share?

Computer scientists are used to thinking of pictures in terms of their representation: an array of pixels, a list or hierarchy of graphics primitives, or even a program written in a language such as PostScript. But these descriptions capture only the form in which a picture is encoded for computer display. Might there be something deeper that we can ask about what it means to be a picture? For example, how do pictures do what they do? Or, for that matter, what exactly is it that they do? And how can we make pictures and picture-making programs better at doing it?

Christine and Thomas Strothotte address these issues in this book, in which they examine the place of pictures in computing systems. They provide a wealth of information on the psychological interpretation of pictures, on semiotics, and on design. To put pictures in perspective, they have constructed a classification system that is based in part on how a picture is used. Their taxonomy ranges from *presentational pictures*, which show things that we can see, to *abstract-graphical pictures*, which show abstractions of things that we cannot see, to *pictograms*, whose abstractions stand for more than they show.

Throughout, they stress the notion that a picture's human viewer brings something extremely important to the table in pictorial communication: In addition to the information explicitly communicated by a picture, there is also information that is added by the viewer through the inevitable, but often unpredictable, process of reasoning. Furthermore, they emphasize that use of pictures in computer systems is a two-party game, played by both the computer and the viewer. And if we let the viewer play, then the computer must also be able to interpret and respond to the viewer's input, which requires that the computer have some understanding of the pictures that it presents. The idea that the computer needs to understand something about its pictures is crucial. The authors discuss systems in which this understanding is provided by the viewer, who conveys her analyses back to the computer in a formal language, as well as ones in which the computer generates pictures from its own underlying knowledge about what is to be conveyed.

As static 2D images give way to dynamic 3D ones, and interactive virtual worlds become part of our everyday experience, we are building a future in which pictures play an increasingly fundamental role. As this happens, the questions that this book explores are becoming ever more important.

New York, August, 1997                     Steven K. Feiner
                                            Department of Computer Science
                                            Columbia University

# Preface

*Image science* is a new, emerging discipline concerned with various aspects of the production, use and analysis of pictures. The area has its roots in most fields of scholarly endeavor. Among these are:

- *physics*, where new optical systems are being developed,
- *materials science*, where new materials are being developed with special optical properties,
- *medicine*, involving both new ways of treating visual impairments as well as new techniques for visualizing processes going on in the human body,
- *philosophy*, which studies what pictures actually are,
- *education*, studying learning with pictures,
- *psychology*, studying processes by which humans understand pictures, and last but not least,
- *computer science*, involving image recognition, image synthesis, and human-computer interaction.

Various different terms are being used for degree programs within this general area, for example Imaging Science, Visual Science, Image Engineering, and Computational Visualistics (the latter at the University of Magdeburg).

This book aims at making a contribution to the area of image science by studying pictures – and to a certain extent also language – from a computer scientist's point of view. Our focus is on computer models, their presentation on the computer screen, and viewers' reaction in the form of input. Computer representations of data, and conversions between these, are at the heart of our analysis. Our aim is to further the computational study of pictures to the point where they can be used in dialogue systems as a medium of expression, like language.

One of the central themes of the book is the reasoning process of the recipient of a piece of information during a dialogue, be the recipient the computer or the user. This implies a study of what a user ascertains when viewing a pictorial presentation. Further, it implies that we must endow the machine with the capability of interpreting user input as regards such presentations. We coin the terms *transmitted* and *transputed* information to help sort out what is really happening with respect to reasoning processes when information flows via the human-computer interface. Our interpretation of this flow of information enables us to lift human-computer interaction beyond the barrier posed by the mere conveying of facts between the computer and its user.

Through our approach we complement the work of other disciplines concerned with pictures. For example, we draw on the results of psychologists, who concentrate on the analysis of human understanding of pictures; while there is no evidence that human understanding of pictures is different when viewers see such pictures on the computer screen, we as computer scientists must come to terms with the viewers' reaction in the form of new input to the computer. We also draw on the results of graphic designers, who themselves tend to leave the reader a great deal of freedom. This freedom is no doubt necessary for designers to be able to use their creativity but this tends to make it difficult for others, especially computer scientists, to encode their results directly in effective algorithms.

The book has been written to bring structure into an active research area. To this end, it is intended for the following groups of persons:

- *Computer scientists* interested in research combining the areas of computer graphics and human-computer interaction. On the one hand, the book describes one of the major areas of current research activities. On the other hand, it is suitable for researchers new to the field to identify interesting problems to work on. Thus, for example, graduate students can gain inspiration for their thesis work by reading the book. To this end, it has been used by the authors as reading material for graduate courses on human-computer interaction.

- *Developers of sophisticated applications.* Engineers will benefit from browsing in the book and reading selected portions as a source of insight into new ways of using pictures to communicate information to users.

- *Researchers from other disciplines interested in pictures*, like the natural sciences and engineering, art history, design, psychology, and education. Such researchers will gain insight into how computer scientists view and work with pictures.

The material we present is intended as a source of inspiration for those defining user or system requirements and designing or implementing picture-based interactive systems. We often draw on and analyze pictures in printed materials (for example dictionaries), even if today's commercially available systems often do not offer such pictures. Our assumption is that in the coming years, pictures will become increasingly available and will be in need of structuring. Hence we suggest structures for data which themselves will only gradually become available with time.

While our main thrust is to generate ideas for how pictures can be integrated into interactive systems, we also go into details of algorithms so that the implementation-oriented reader has enough information at his or her disposal to write programs which use pictures in innovative and advanced ways. We discuss a variety of applications, with a concentration in technical subjects, for example in the documentation of technical systems and in visualizations of computer simulations.

## Background

The book is an product of the authors' research and teaching in the area of dialogue systems. Recent years have witnessed a continually rising interest in computer graphics and graphical interaction within the computer science community. We have amassed primarily recent results, both from the scientific community at large as well as from the authors' own laboratories. We cannot claim that the book contains an exhaustive account of the literature; instead, it is designed to be readable and interesting by highlighting what the authors consider to be important advances in the field.

## Quotations

Many authors today round out their publications with quotations by important persons who made interesting remarks bearing some relation to the text at hand. In this book, we have chosen to draw on the pictorial work of our ancient forefathers, who in millennia past left their mark on life through drawings in caves and on stones. These form the oldest recordings of information known to mankind. Not much is really known about such graphics, their meaning being a matter of interpretation on the basis of contextual knowledge. In this sense they are in keeping with an overall theme of this book, which emphasises the reasoning process of the recipient of an image on the basis of his or her current knowledge.

## How to Read this Book

The book can be read sequentially from start to finish, but is also designed so that the reader can pick and choose, depending on his or her own interests. Chapter 1 is an introduction which is useful to set the stage for the approach we have taken. Any potential reader who is not sure if the book is for him or her should definitely read Chapter 2, where the importance of the relationship between pictures and language is analyzed in a variety of application areas. Chapter 3 is also important, as it defines the classification of pictures used throughout the book. Chapter 4 is recommended for anyone who is interested in the psychological processes involved when users look at pictures on the computer screen. While it is not absolutely necessary for understanding the rest of the book, it is nonetheless highly recommended. Chapter 5 by contrast is a must, since the terms it introduces (transmitted and transputed information) are used throughout the book to explain the nature of the information flow between users and computers.

The three central parts of the book (Chapters 6 to 9, 10 to 13 and 14 to 17, respectively) can be read independently of one another. Chapters 8 and 9 form a sequence, but otherwise the chapters are modular so that they can be read in any order or skipped.

The concluding Chapters 18 and 19 should be read by anyone interested in the social aspects of pictures in computing systems and anyone wishing to think seriously about what he or she is really doing when using pictures in human-computer interaction.

## Acknowledgements

The authors gratefully acknowledge the assistance and influence of their academic mentors over the years, particularly Brian Funt, Rul Gunzenhäuser, Peter Lorenz, and Dietrich Ziems. Without their patient understanding over many years, the ideas encoded within this book would not have been able to flourish.

As the work on this book was spread over several years, many persons have contributed directly or indirectly to its completion. Most important have been the authors' colleagues in Berlin and Magdeburg, joint papers with many of whom form the basis of ideas appearing in the book. Among these are in particular Jürgen Emhardt, Ralf Helbing, Axel Hoppe, Martin Kurze, Maria Labarta, Kathrin Lüdicke, Bernhard Preim, Andreas Raab, Lars Reichert, Alf Ritter, Michael Rüger, Jutta Schumann, and Stefan Schlechtweg. A number of persons were of assistance with specific Chapters: Oliver R. Scholz (Chapter 3), Klaus Sachs-Hombach (Chapters 3 and 19), Bernd Weidenmann (Chapter 4), and Pete Wright (Chapter 5).

The authors are indebted to Kate Sturrock and Ute Lau for helping with formulations to make the text read smoothly, to Petra Janka for diligently handling the copyright issues relating to the figures, to Tobias Isenberg for assisting with drawing figures, and to Petra Specht for expertly taking care of all other administrative matters. Thanks also to Grit Sehmisch for painstakingly making all the final corrections to the text and for doing the formatting.

Finally, the expert advice and guidance of the staff at Springer-Verlag in Heidelberg is gratefully acknowledged, particularly J. Andrew Ross for copy-editing and patiently proofreading the manuscript, Peter Strasser for producing, and Hans Wössner for publishing the book.

Magdeburg, August 1997                  *Christine Strothotte, Thomas Strothotte*

# Table of Contents

**Part VI**
**Epilogue**

# Preliminaries

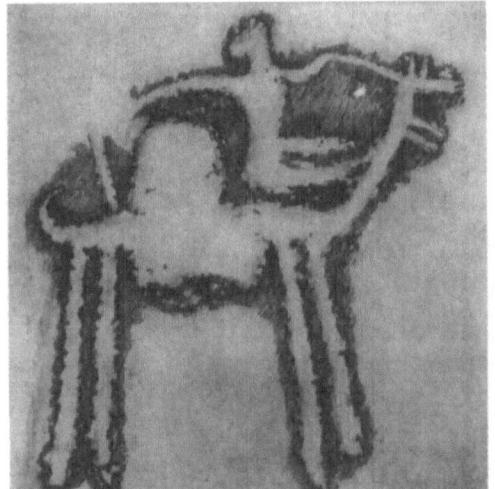

*Camel Rider*
Fezzan, Central Sahara Desert, Africa

# Chapter

# 1

# Introduction

Computer graphics today is a field surrounded by an aura of perfection. Sophisticated tools have been developed for constructing data structures within a computer which describe the geometry of objects in a precise way. The resultant models form the input to renderers, which produce visualizations of the objects. These visualizations are, in turn, generally intended to mimic the task of a camera. Thus it is possible to generate images synthetically which resemble photographs of real scenes with such exactness that only a trained eye can tell the images apart. Even very complex scenes can be generated convincingly (Figure 1.1).

Computer-generated pictures, however, are not the only vehicle for conveying information between computers and users. Command languages still form the basis of much of the interaction. Operating systems such as UNIX and MS-DOS are line-oriented in their input and output. To move such systems more into the realm of pictorial interaction, graphical user interfaces tend to emphasize the pictorial nature of the computer screen by presenting information in two dimensions. However, allowing certain commands to be issued by direct manipulation of pictograms cannot completely hide the underlying language base. Operating systems as well as most application programs routinely use

**Figure 1.1:** Synthetically generated image of a sunflower field
(Prusinkiewicz and Lindenmayer 1990)

dialogue boxes containing mainly text to convey to users what options or parameters are available, at the same time giving them the opportunity to choose among these.

Natural language dialogue systems are also alternatives to graphical interaction. A great deal of research effort has gone into such systems over the last three decades, although few products have emerged that actually make use of the technology. Nonetheless, significant progress has been made on knowledge representation and processing in connection with natural language systems (IJCAI 1995).

Pictures are typically used in particular situations in which a complete presentation can be prepared in advance; motion pictures – movies – are a prime example. The more *interaction* which is enabled in a system, the more the communication shifts away from pictures to a formal or natural language of one kind or another. Graphical user interfaces fall into this latter category too, since graphical symbols on the screen tend to be in a one-to-one correspondence with symbols of a formal command language. This applies to both the users' perspective (graphical symbols are usually designed to represent a particular word) and the machines' perspective (graphical manipulations cause command-like functions to be called and executed).

Where does this leave the state of the art in interaction techniques with respect to pictures and language? To what extent are graphical user interfaces really presenting *pictures* to users, and to what extent do they actually form a language of interaction? When the user of a graphical interface looks at the computer screen, is he or she really looking at a picture? If so, where are the thousand words which the old proverb promises? If he or she is looking at a photorealistic image on the screen with the feeling that the picture is indeed saying a thousand or more words to him or her, are these words represented somewhere within the machine? If not, where do they come from? Can the ability to use pictures to convey words not represented within the machine somehow be harnessed to take human-computer interaction to a new level of sophistication, in which information is conveyed without it being represented explicitly in a knowledge base?

If, on the other hand, the many words a picture conveys to a user are indeed represented within the machine, how is it possible that these are conveyed in a pixel-based (possibly photorealistic) image? How can the machine ensure an adequate encoding? Does a small change in the internal representation of the picture (in this case, the thousand or so words) indeed result in an equally small change in the presentation, as a computer scientist might expect?

This book aims to answer some of these questions by developing a repertoire of methods for analyzing human-computer interaction based on pictures. Algorithms and tools are demonstrated that allow the machine to construct pictures to satisfy users' requests for information. We present a collection of research results and practical methods for the flexible use of pictures in dialogue systems for such areas of application as engineering, rehabilitation medicine, and the natural sciences.

We also discuss important psychological foundations in the use of pictures for such applications. The kind of processing we describe goes well beyond graphical user interfaces in that we deal with complex pictures containing an abundance of information for the viewer to discover. Further, we demonstrate that much more can be done with pictures than just to scan them and display them on a computer screen. Instead, we show how they can be generated flexibly by the machine and manipulated as well as described systematically by the user to provide the machine with an important source of information. Pictures conveying meaning beyond the sum of their parts can form an important link between computers and users. Our work sheds light on the notion of knowledge-based systems, which we consider to be comprised of the user and the computer *together*.

## 1.1  Pictures and Society

Pictures possess enormous, unfathomable powers, as prehistoric cave-paintings and exhibits of modern art vividly demonstrate.

In the past, when all pictures were created by humans, the number of pictures in existence was limited. Copying was possible only by hand, so that each individual picture was unique and held in high esteem. Indeed, Belting (1991) describes how cults evolved around individual pictures in the middle of the first millennium AD.

Now the situation has changed totally. We are continually bombarded by pictures, and perhaps precisely because of this fact, pictures actually attract a certain amount of general disrespect with regard to their power to convey serious information. Pictures can be created by using a large repertoire of technical tools and some kinds of pictures are created automatically by cameras or computers. This development has led to vast quantities of pictures being transmitted almost instantaneously to all places around the globe. In society in general, pictures are often used for entertainment purposes, as eye-catchers in advertising or as the backdrop for texts. Although most humans are used to pictures, they are still fascinated by them. One reason for the latter is the assumption that pictures do not lie. People believe what they see, because what they have seen cannot be false. This myth is the basis for the manipulation of people with the help of pictures. We will deal with this pheno-menon in the course of this book and will focus a discussion on it in Chapter 19.

In scientific publications pictures and diagrams are typically used as a feature which is merely "nice to have." Usually the point the author is making is fully covered in the run-ning text, while the illustration serves to provide an additional confirmation of the author's argument, not new information. This is aggravated by the practice of many authors of including text within the pictures themselves and even more by authors adding lengthy captions to their figures which spell out for the reader what he or she is to ascer-tain from the illustration. Moreover, proofs in mathematical texts are practically always given in some sort of symbol system, whereas illustrations are used only for specific examples, if at all. The reasoning here is that a text can more easily present an argument for all cases of a particular condition, whereas an illustration can usually only express one of the cases necessary for the argument.

The strict use of a language-like symbol system for proofs may be the method of choice today, but it is not the only way proofs can be conveyed. Tufte (1990) presents as a surprising example the works of Oliver Byrne, who in the late 1800s developed an alternative to the classical ways of writing down proofs in Euclidian geometry. Instead of letter-coding angles, vertices, and triangles, used Byrne the elements themselves with a specific shape, color, and orientation. Tufte characterizes the handling of the classical proof (see Figure 1.2): "Too much time must be spent puzzling over an alphabetic macaroni of 63 encoded lines between diagram and proof." To give an idea of how much more easily Byre's proofs can be understood, the proof of the Pythagorean theorem is shown in Figure 1.3.

Indeed, the lack of a need for pictures often leads to a corresponding lack of care with illustrations on the part of authors. Indeed, illustrations are often really unnecessary from the point of view of getting information across to readers. But even under these circum-stances, pictures can be useful for readers because they increase their ability to memorize the content.

**THEOREM 27.** (Pythagoras' Theorem.)

In any right-angled triangle, the square on the hypotenuse is equal to the sum of the squares on the sides containing the right angle.

*Given* ∠BAC is a right angle.

*To prove* the square on BC = the square on BA + the square on AC.

Let ABHK, ACMN, BCPQ be the squares on AB, AC, BC.

Join CH, AQ. Through A, draw AXY parallel to BQ, cutting BC, QP at X, Y.

Since ∠BAC and ∠BAK are right angles, KA and AC are in the same straight line.

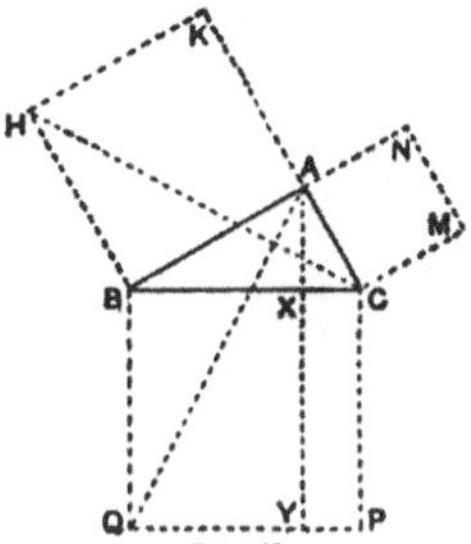

Again ∠HBA = 90° = ∠QBC.

Add to each ∠ABC, ∴ ∠HBC = ∠ABQ.

In the △s HBC, ABQ.

HB = AB, sides of square.

CB = QB, sides of square.

∠HBC = ∠ABQ, proved.

∴ △HBC ≡ △ABQ (2 sides, inc. angle).

Now △HBC and square HA are on the same base HB and between the same parallels HB, KAC ;

∴ △HBC = ½ square HA.

Also △ABQ and rectangle BQYX are on the same base BQ and between the same parallels BQ, AXY.

∴ △ABQ = ½ rect. BQYX.

∴ square HA = rect. BQYX.

Similarly, by joining AP, BM, it can be shown that square MA = rect. CPYX ;

∴ square HA + square MA = rect. BQYX + rect. CPYX
= square BP. Q.E.D.

FIG. 103.

**Figure 1.2:** A classical Pythagorean proof (Tufte 1990)

A high regard for text and low regard for pictures already begins through conditioning in early childhood. Children learn at a very early age to interpret pictures, for example while appreciating their picture books. The facility to understand such pictures is usually not learned by children systematically, but implicitly. By contrast, it soon becomes the goal of every child to learn to read texts: this is then considered to be difficult but worth the challenge. During this learning process, pictures are pushed out of their role as conveyers of information.

This trend is further strengthened through schools. A great deal of time is spent in learning to read and particularly to write texts well. Indeed, to be able to express oneself with a certain degree of sophistication in one's mother tongue is one of the fundamentals goals of primary and secondary education. Even at many universities in North America, freshmen of all subjects are forced to endure a full-year English course, often known under the name "English 100". By contrast, learning to interpret pictures and to draw or paint is relegated to a relatively small number of art lessons in elementary school, which – to make

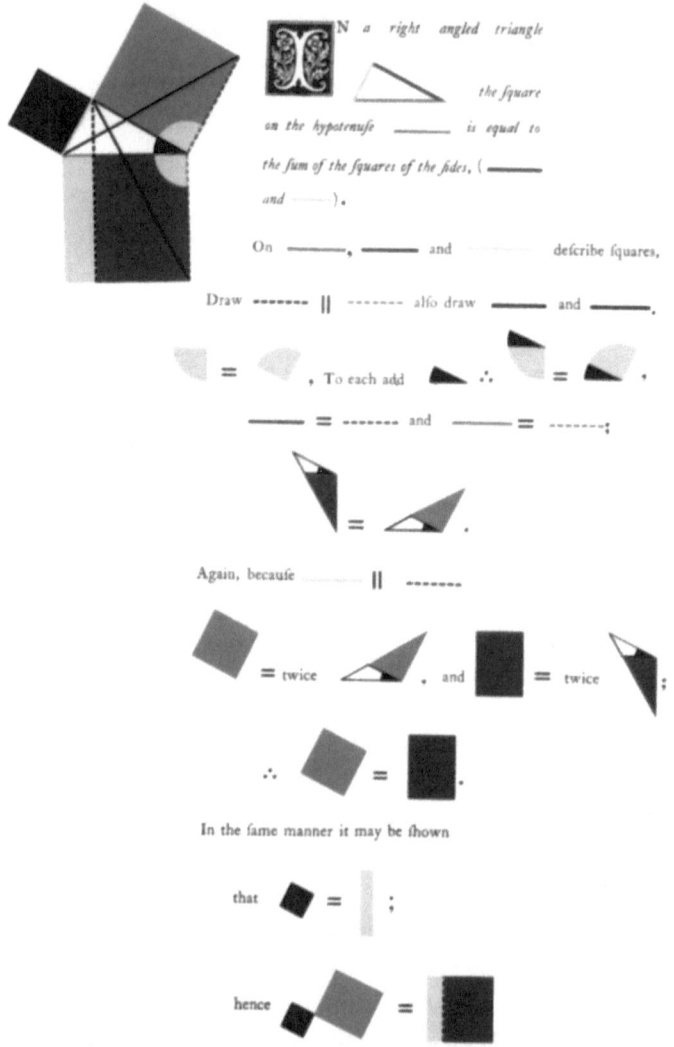

**Figure 1.3:** Pythagorean proof by Oliver Byrne (Tufte 1990)

matters even worse – are typically optional at the secondary-school level. Thus almost all high-school graduates are "visual illiterates", at least compared to their "textual literacy".

The overabundance of pictures available at any given time leads to a further dilution of their effect. In television and in particular in music videos, scenes often change at such a speed that we conjecture that the viewer is entertained no longer by the pictures but by the changes between them. The amount of information obtainable by viewers from any one such picture is relatively small.

Philosophers have warned that the flood of pictures can even have a devastating effect on our ability to perceive reality. An example is the experience during the Gulf War of 1991, where Israeli citizens were so used to Scud missile attacks through the CNN reporting that many went out onto the streets during the attacks so as to get an even better view than was available on television (Baudrillard 1991). Clearly, pictures and reality are beginning to merge in a dangerous way.

When we criticize underrating of pictures, we do not overlook the restricted use of pictures. We are aware of the disadvantages of pictures, like the difficulty of representing abstract terms or expressing different opinions. But there exist a wide variety of situations where pictures are ideal for conveying information, if they are used cleverly. With this book, we hope to contribute towards reaching this goal in human-computer interaction.

## 1.2  Pictures and Language in Computer Science

Both language and pictures have received a great deal of attention in the computer science community. Nonetheless, the goals set and the methods developed to achieve these goals have differed greatly, so that language and pictures have reached different stages in their computational treatment.

Linguistic information processing has been dominated by symbol manipulation languages. In the early days of computer science, LISP became the language of choice; it is still in vogue, particularly in the United States. Since the early 1970s, Prolog has gained steadily in importance, so that today it is the language of choice for symbol manipulation in Europe and Japan. In any case, the availability of such languages makes the study of computational models for language very tempting. Indeed, concepts of natural languages have established themselves as the foundation for knowledge-based systems. Practically all data structures used for knowledge representation are functionally equivalent to Gottlob Frege's notation for logic, which he developed in the 1870s (Frege 1973) and itself has its roots in language. On the basis of this kind of knowledge representation, many algorithms for parsing natural languages have been developed since the early 1960s, as have methods and tools for their generation.

Although formal languages underlie most computing systems, pictorial representations have become commonplace in user interfaces in the 1980s. Graphical user interfaces use pictograms (icons) to make commands or other information visible to the user. However, these pictograms are in almost all cases *static* and correspond to a symbol in the underlying formal language. Indeed, a user should not examine pictograms too carefully, since the details are unimportant and would, in fact, be misleading. Only rarely is a collection of pictograms arranged on the screen by the machine so that the user has to ascertain more than the sum of the meanings of the individual pictograms. Indeed, as will be shown, pictograms are chosen explicitly to reflect single concepts.

More complex forms of graphics, particularly those aiming at photorealism, have been of central interest in computer graphics for two decades. However, whereas in linguistic processing most of the effort has gone into *representational issues* to facilitate problem solving, most of the effort in computer graphics has gone into *presentational issues*, i.e., improving realism. There are two broad reasons for this divergence in the developments within computer science. The first is rather simplistic: It is not difficult to produce a good-looking sentence on the screen, but far more difficult to justify the steps undertaken to get there, starting from a representation of knowledge. By contrast, a huge amount of effort has gone into algorithms for synthetically producing photorealistic images, and while part of the solution is improved geometric modeling, the links to knowledge representation and problem solving are few and far between. The second reason is more fundamental: Language can, at least in principle, be broken down into individual words which can be manipulated (recombined) to form new sentences as the result of a problem-solving process. This process, however, is much more difficult to carry out on pictorial representations.

So there is a great – and often overlooked – need for more flexible processing of pictures by computers. To demonstrate this need, let us look at four examples of pictures that have not been created by algorithms alone, and see what needs to be done before such manipulations can be carried out automatically.

*Example 1: Varying sizes of objects.*
Figure 1.4 (left) shows an anatomical illustration taken from a medical book. The medical image is used to explain certain parts of the foot, and for pedagogical reasons, the image is not drawn to scale. Moreover, the illustrated details were chosen carefully so as to fulfill the communicative intent associated with the surrounding text. By contrast, Figure 1.4 (right) shows the wire-frame representation of a foot (Viewpoint Datalabs 1995). It is not possible today to produce images of the quality of those in medical text-books from computer models.

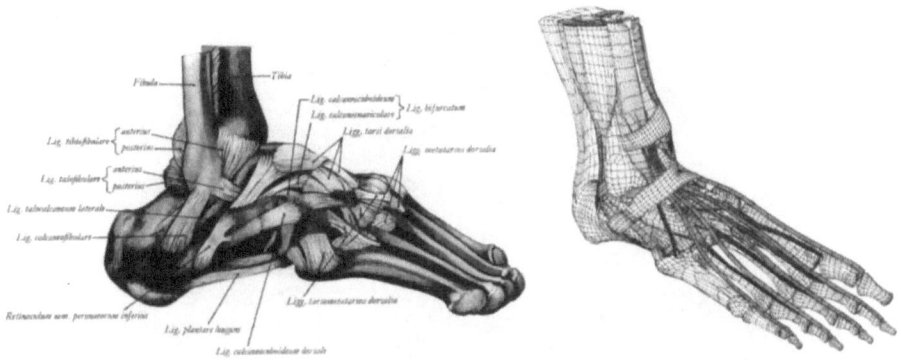

**Figure 1.4:** Drawing of a foot taken from a medical book (left) (Waldeyer and Mayet 1987) and the rendering of a computer model (right) (Viewpoint Datalabs 1995)

*Example 2: Continuously varying scale.*

Maps are often not drawn uniformly to scale. Instead, areas of greater importance are drawn in a larger scale than areas of less importance. This allows the map-maker to put more detail in appropriate places. For example, Lichtner (1983) reports on a study of maps for the city of Hannover, Germany, in which it was found convenient to vary the scale from 1:25,000 to 1:100,000 in a single map! Figure 1.5 shows an example of the variation of two grids used as the basis of such maps.

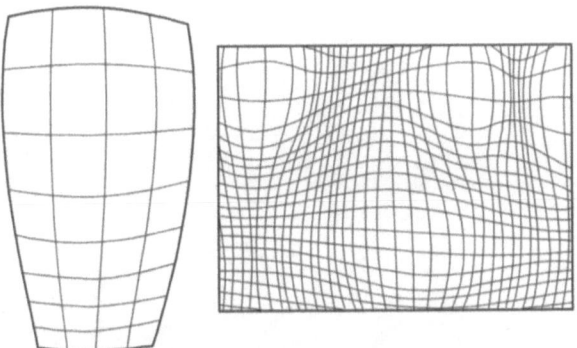

**Figure 1.5:** Varying grids used in map making  (Lichtner 1983)

This technique has actually been known to mankind for many centuries: Figure 1.6 shows an example of a map of the city of Jerusalem in the 6th century AD, where the scale is not correct; moreover, the perspective is mixed, in that the front view of houses is projected onto the top view of the city.

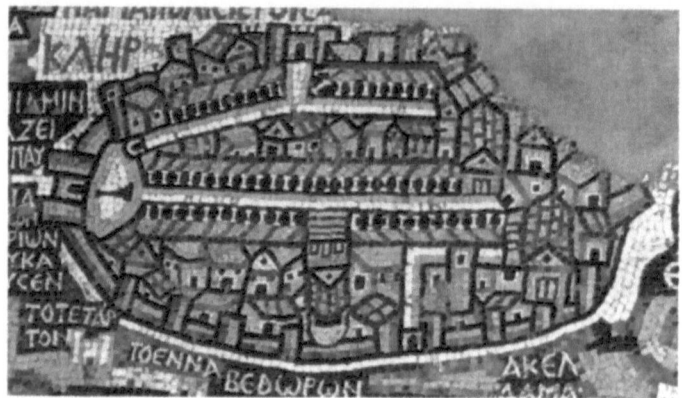

**Figure 1.6:** Mixing perspectives in a map: Jerusalem in the 6th century AD

*Example 3: Varying levels of detail.*

Shadows and shading often provide the viewer of an image with clues as to the three-dimensional shape of the object illustrated. However, as Figure 1.7 illustrates, these shadows and shading need not necessarily result from the placement of light sources, but rather from the designer's communicative intent. And certain details are left out (like some cogs on the outermost gear) to avoid cluttering the image with irrelevant information.

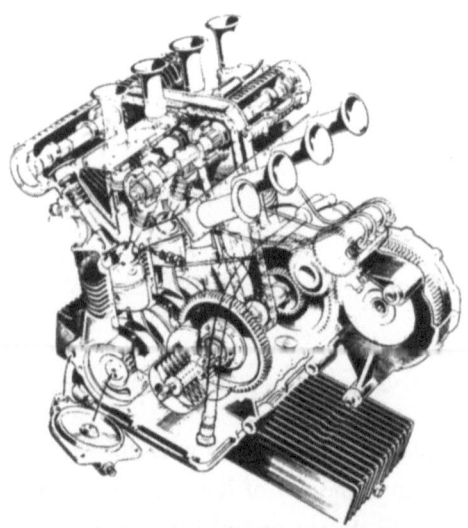

**Figure 1.7:** Shadows drawn to enhance the 3D nature of objects (Klaver 1990)

*Example 4: Lighting effects in photos.*

Not even a photograph is necessarily "objective", as Gombrich (1986) observed. Figure 1.8 shows two prints made from one negative of a picture of the "Wrapped Reichstag" in Berlin in 1995. Notice how each print creates a different mood.

**Figure 1.8:** Two prints from one negative (courtesy of Ralf Wöhling)

From the point of view of computer science, such enhancements to images go against the grain. The goal of practically all work in computer graphics to date has been to model geometric objects as correctly as possible, and subsequently to render images so as to resemble photographs as closely as possible. Indeed this is in keeping with the goals of computer science in general, to model accurately and precisely. It is extremely difficult to calculate appropriate changes in the shape of objects as in Figure 1.4. Even simple-looking changes of scale as in Figure 1.5 are difficult to compute algorithmically; however, they can be decided upon relatively easily by an experienced cartographer. Special shadows and removal of details, as were carried out for Figure 1.7, involve a great deal of artistic skill, while reproducing the effects that an experienced photographer can produce is well beyond the sophistication of current rendering software.

These examples serve to set the stage for dealing with pictures in dialogue systems. We shall not deal directly with enhancements to pictures such as those alluded to above, as the area of picture manipulation is not yet advanced enough, but we will head in this direction and develop background material that we believe will eventually lead to more flexibility in picture manipulation.

## 1.3 Dialogue Systems

When a person shows a photo to a friend, a dialogue about the picture is possible because both can look at the image and study it. The dialogue may pertain to details of the picture, in that one helps the other to interpret the scene, for example with respect to features that are difficult to discern or unusual. The participants may exchange stories about what happened before the photo was taken or afterwards. Or perhaps opinions will be exchanged about objects or processes that are themselves not visible but are logically related to what is portrayed. The participants in the dialogue are able to synchronize their language with the images they see and arrive at a shared understanding of what they have both seen and heard.

When a computer shows a picture to a user, the situation is completely different. A computer cannot simply *look* at an image and *understand* it to the point of leading a dialogue with a viewer. Sometimes the picture is stored in the computer in the form of pixels, in which case the machine – in the absence of highly sophisticated image understanding software – has little or no information at its disposal about what the user might ascertain from it. Examples can be constructed in which the computer has at its disposal at least some information about the picture in addition to the pixels, but this can be used for only specialized situations. In short, when pictures are used, the interaction is strongly biased toward the user, since he or she can study and understand the image to an extent not generally possible by the computer.

Processes by which images are generated by people and by computers have even less in common with one another than the process of their analysis. Most designers and architects, for example, use pencil and paper to sketch and, most importantly, further develop their ideas. People learn about objects by drawing them; an artist will sketch as a way of making and structuring his or her observations of a scene. By contrast, a program that computes a picture from an internal representation, be this of numeric or symbolic form, does so generally without benefiting from the generation process. Images are produced for users to look at, and there are few positive side-effects for the computer from this process.

Even though a user may discover new relationships among the data elements visualized – and indeed in areas like scientific computing, this is precisely the purpose of producing the visualizations in the first place – it is usually not feasible for programs to carry out such a task. In a sense, a picture can be regarded as an alternative representation of data already stored in another format; as opposed to other forms of data representation, this pixel-based alternative can be viewed as being "write only" for the computer and "read only" by users.

Indeed, similar claims can also be made for text generation programs and their output. People read and understand text, whereas this process is still very difficult to reproduce within a computer which cannot simply be programmed to read a text and understand it. Text generation systems also treat the texts they produce as "write only" data structures and generally do not draw on the text they produce to get feedback, whereas people use writing as a vehicle to develop their ideas, not only to formulate on paper preconceived ideas for the benefit of others. Thus natural language systems have some of the same conceptual problems as systems for generating pictures. The distinguishing feature of pictures in this regard, however, is that the information a viewer gets from a picture is usually completely different from that represented within the computer, and it is this difference which gives "food for dialogue".

## 1.4  Pictures as Systems

The unifying theme of this book is that for pictures to be used effectively in human-computer interaction, the computer must have at its disposal various different kinds of information about the picture. For there to be at least a certain degree of parity between the dialogue partners, the computer should have information available to it pertaining to what the human viewer can see and ascertain. Sources for this information are, for example,

- the original representation from which the picture was generated,
- other such data represented in an accessible form related to the elements in the picture (like a knowledge base),
- the generation process which produces the picture, and
- even the users themselves.

A key observation for getting a handle on computational mechanisms for binding pictures into dialogue systems is that pictures and language both represent *systems*, i.e., objects and relationships among them. By this we mean that neither one nor the other are by any means an unbiased mirror of reality, but both are highly selective in what they express. In fact, as we saw in Figure 1.8, not even a photograph is really "objective".

When a picture is generated for presentation to a user starting from an internal representation within the computer (referred to as a model and analogous to the negative in the example of Figure 1.8), there is rarely a one-to-one correspondence between the system represented by the picture and the one represented by the internal representation. Moreover, if the model is to represent a scene in reality, the process of constructing the model, which corresponds with actually shooting the picture in the above example, is a further source of changes in the systems represented by reality. This process is illustrated in Figure 1.9.

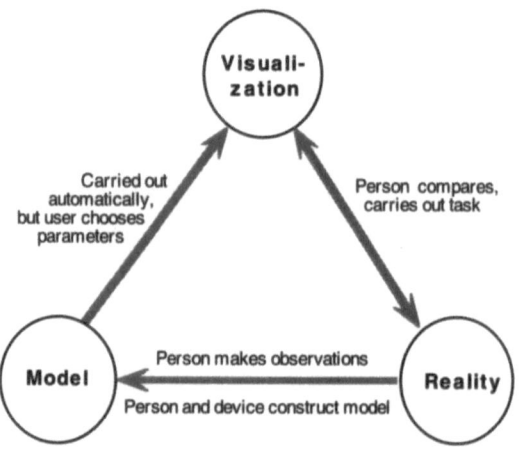

**Figure 1.9:** Reality, model and visualization

To make matters even worse, neither the expression in the formal language nor the pictorial presentation actually *define* a system. Rather, a reader or a viewer *ascertains* a system: Just as the system represented by the computer depends on the machine´s access functions to the data in their specific format, so the process of understanding a picture on the part of the user is very subjective and dependent on many factors relating to the individual viewer.

It may sound like this is a difficult situation to get a grip on algorithmically – indeed it requires considerable care – but it is precisely the individual differences between the systems ascertained by different users which give pictures such enormous potential for eliciting communication between the two. The greater the difference between the system represented within the computer and the one ascertained by the user from the picture, the more information must flow between the computer and the user if a consensus is to be achieved. In fact, we will demonstrate with an example that if the two systems are combined effectively, a powerful synergy results.

The classification scheme around which the book is organized yields the basis for analyzing pictures and their composition with respect to the system they are able to convey. The division between visible objects and relations (presentational pictures) and invisible ones (abstract-graphical pictures) is intimately related to the geometric description of a scene on the one hand and logical description of the underlying process on the other. The bottom line is our contention that human-computer interfaces which leave the user a significant amount of freedom of interpretation – even at the risk of leaving behind false or ambiguous first impressions – are ultimately more rewarding to use. We even discuss one system whose success in fact relies on precisely this ambiguity of pictures (Petjersen and Goodstein 1988). There is evidence to suggest that the more engaged a user is in the process of interpreting output, the deeper his or her understanding of the issues involved. This in turn means that more information can be formulated explicitly and even made available to the machine to support the user in his or her chosen tasks.

## 1.5  Organization of the Book

The book is organized into five parts. After this introductory part, the second part (Chapters 2 to 5) introduces the fundamental concepts related to pictures in general and their use in interactive systems. This part also introduces a classification of pictures used to structure the remainder of the book. The next three parts treat the three kinds of pictures of this classification in turn:
- *abstract-graphical pictures* (Chapters 6 to 9), which enable the presentation of properties and relationships that are invisible to the naked eye,
- *pictograms* (Chapters 10 to 13), which are pictures representing objects and relationships other than those actually depicted, and
- *presentational pictures* (Chapters 14 to 17), which show objects and relationships that are generally visible in reality.

The final part (Chapters 18 and 19) presents concluding remarks. Now we outline the individual chapters in more detail.

Chapter 2 studies pictures in existing computer systems and is intended to draw the reader's attention to the use of pictures and language in various typical areas of application. We survey desktop publishing, drawing programs, hypertext, image processing, 3D computer graphics, and discrete event simulation. We show how typical application programs handle pictures and study the relationship between internal representations and external presentations on the computer screen. We conclude that one of the stumbling blocks for interaction with pictures is the use of direct manipulation in the creation of the underlying models.

A systematic study of pictures in human-computer interaction must contain fundamental definitions, drawing on the work of others. In particular, we need a classification which will enable claims to be made about some pictures, without having to make the same or similar claims about other pictures. Chapter 3 presents such a classification which will be useful from the point of view of our ensuing analysis as regards computer science. The material in this chapter draws on the literature in the area of *semiotics*.

One of the basic assumptions when using computer graphics is that users understand what the pictures are trying to say to them. Chapter 4 thus surveys the psychological literature on the human understanding of pictures. We discuss the cognitive processes involved in detail, thereby shedding light on what the designers of interactive systems must pay attention to when using pictures. In particular, we discuss the notion of *normalization*, which is the process humans use to remove the ambiguity in pictures. Normalization generally leads to some kind of reasoning process, which in turn gives rise to new information being generated on the part of the recipient. We also discuss human memory performance pertaining to pictures.

The flow of information between computers and users is the topic of Chapter 5. We first discuss information theory and demonstrate the need for another model. In particular, we argue for separating the information which is derived by a reasoning process on the part of the recipient of a message, from the actual content of the message. We coin the term *transputed* information for the former and *transmitted* information for the latter. These terms are of fundamental importance and are used throughout the book in the analysis of what is really happening when pictures are used in interactive systems.

We now turn to *abstract-graphical pictures* in Chapter 6. These pictures can be found in a wide variety of forms, hence we begin by discussing their characterization in more detail. In particular, we treat abstract-graphical pictures with respect to their focus on certain aspects of systems: the relationship between elements, the functionality, the behavior, and the properties of elements. Next we discuss the role of abstract-graphical pictures in problem solving.

Chapter 7 turns to the *algorithmic analysis* of abstract-graphical pictures. We demonstrate that such pictures in their printed form represent an enormous reservoir of information, which is basically not accessible to computers because abstract-graphical pictures cannot be analysed automatically with any success. We present a methodology of dealing with this, which relies on user support for algorithms operating on the pictures. The user gives the algorithms hints as to what to analyze and how, whereas the computer responds by using image processing techniques to aid the user. We show how this methodology can be applied to two kinds of abstract-graphical pictures, first those found in dictionaries and encyclopedias, and second business graphics. We study these kinds of graphics in detail and look at prototypical dialogue systems for their analysis. Note that this is the only chapter in which the computer uses image processing techniques to support the user. In all other parts of this book, user support is defined with respect to the logical relationships among elements of the application, rather than geometric relationships.

In Chapter 8 we take the methodology another step forward in that the computer is made to carry out logical inferences for the user based on observations of the graphics presented to him or her. We observe that often users ascertain something quite different from a picture than the symbolic, geometric, or numeric data structures from which the picture was generated. This difference has generally been overlooked in interactive systems, which also means that the information which a user ascertains has remained his or her property and has not been made available to the computer explicitly. We now describe how dialogue systems can be developed that treat the user as a source of information about the presentation the computer has generated. We refer to such information as an *oracle* in cases where it is used by the computer to decide between alternatives which the computer alone would otherwise be unable to differentiate. We apply these concepts to discrete computer simulation systems and demonstrate with an implementation how a new quality of user support can be attained.

These notions are generalized further in Chapter 9. We develop the concept of a *viewpoint description*, which is a detailed description that the user constructs to describe a visualization which he or she is shown on the computer screen. This description contains a documentation portion, which captures the current state of the elements of the presentation, and a criticism portion, which describes the state in which the user considers the elements should be. We again apply this to discrete computer simulation. The result is a dialogue system in which the user and the computer are firmly linked together informationally. The key is that each is able to transpute a great deal of information to the other dialogue partner.

In Chapter 10, the topic of pictograms is taken up. First, we mention the historical roots of present-day pictograms, and then discuss some characteristics of pictograms. Next we turn to a formal notation for describing pictograms, leading to the description of a practical system for combining pictograms to form more complex pictures. In this context, we turn to the design of special kinds of data structures, called *picture frames*. These allow building blocks of pictures to be stored, manipulated, and combined. In particular, we present a systematic way in which such data structures can be used in connection with symbol manipulation programming languages. This in turn makes it possible to combine pictures and language directly in the images being generated. Finally, we discuss the question of whether such complex pictures are themselves pictograms.

From a practical point of view in interactive systems, pictograms can actually be equated with *words*. This is the view taken in Chapter 11. We begin by analyzing methods for choosing and evaluating pictograms to see how closely words and pictograms really are linked in these processes. Next we discuss some drawbacks of pictograms relating to physiological and cognitive stress. One way of alleviating these sources of stress on users is to allow them to speak the names of their commands to activate them as an alternative to clicking on the corresponding pictogram. We report on the design and evaluation of an experimental user interface.

Although pictograms are equated with words in the design stage, they are nonetheless *pictorial* in nature. Chapter 12 thus discusses the design of pictograms from this point of view. We characterize pictograms with respect to the pragmatics of their use. Next we examine the importance of considering the context in which pictograms are used.

Chapter 13 serves to bridge the gap between pictures which are closely related to language (abstract-graphical pictures and pictograms) and presentational pictures. We come to terms with the issue that when we are dealing with graphics generated by machine, the resultant pixel-based data structure is essentially "write only". We discuss how internal representations and presentations can be formalized, and develop the notion of *semi-formal representations*. These have parts which can be manipulated by formal means with respect to their meaning and parts which cannot be manipulated in this manner. We give a number of examples of the use of this term.

Our attention is turned to presentational pictures in Chapter 14, where we treat the problem of *image generation*. This problem arises when the algorithms must design a picture to be presented to a user. Whereas the area of computer graphics deals with the technical details of rendering and how users can construct models, which form the input to such renderers, image generation algorithms assume that a user is no longer available to carry out the design of the communicative techniques. We survey a variety of such techniques, such as how to choose the perspective from which a scene is viewed, how to position light sources, and how to design cutaways for viewing parts of objects which would otherwise be hidden. Finally, we discuss how film-making techniques can be used to help design animations.

In Chapter 15, we begin to search for *alternative forms of graphics*, deviating from photorealistic images. We begin by discussing the merits of standardization and come to the conclusion that it has a certain monotonizing effect. We define as a goal the production of renderings which differ from photorealistic ones and report on the development of a renderer for producing images resembling hand-drawn sketches. We discuss a number of applications of these kinds of images, in particular an application to computer-aided design systems used by architects. We also present the results of an empirical study of the effect of such graphical output. Finally, we discuss alternative rendering in a more general context and relate the cost of modeling to the rendering style used for producing images.

One of the assumptions of computer graphics is that the output of the software being developed will be looked at. However, pictures can also be created in a tactile form, either to be felt by blind people or, in combination with visual graphics, to produce new effects. In Chapter 16, we study this issue and compare tactile images produced by hand for blind children with sketches of the same scenes for sighted adults. From this we derive heuristics for rendering *tactile images*.

In Chapter 17 we are now in a position to study the topic of pictures and their relationship to language in *immersive systems*. First we classify and characterize different kinds of immersive systems and discuss which kinds are suitable for different applications. Our analysis shows that there is a decided lack of language in the interaction, which we argue to be a major deficit. We investigate possible software-based solutions for introducing more language into the interaction.

In Chapter 18 we return to more fundamental issues relating to pictures in interactive systems. We begin with a *comparison of pictures and language* and discuss some of the advantages and disadvantages of each. Of course, an advantage with respect to one particular task can turn out to be a disadvantage with respect to another. We discuss the possible existence of a language of pictures and we come to terms with the fundamental concepts relating to pictures and language discussed in the classic works on this subject.

Finally, Chapter 19 sums up by asking the question, to what extent may we modify images before they are presented to viewers, and when does a *perceptual enhancement* become a *falsification*? We provide a number of recommendations for principles we feel should be followed by design engineers who wish to incorporate pictures into interactive systems.

# Part
# II

# Fundamentals

# Chapter 2

*Man and a snake*
Vitlycke, Sweden

# Pictures in Computer Systems

Pictures appear on today's computer screens in many areas of application. Their use varies from decoration – as they appear in the background of some desktop applications – to records of important information, such as in satellite photos of environmentally sensitive areas.

To what extent can users actually make use of the information encoded in such pictures that commercially available, state-of-the-art applications display on computer screens? How can users access this information? Clearly the answers to these questions determine whether the pictures used in an application can actually help users solve the problems for which the applications are intended, or whether they are just used to make a program more esthetically pleasing (which, admittedly, is also a contribution of sorts).

In this chapter, we will examine six classes of software for which pictures and their processing are the center of interest: desktop publishing, drawing programs, hypertext systems, image processing software, 3D computer graphics systems, and finally, as an example of technical software, animation used in computer simulation. For each of these, we will discuss the issues raised above. This will set the stage for the techniques of binding such pictures more firmly into human-computer dialogues, the goal we pursue in the remainder of the book.

We hypothesize that the key to making effective use of pictures in human-computer interaction is to represent within the computer diverse kinds of information about the pictures over and above basic graphic information. The ability of the computer to communicate with a user about the content, use, and semantics of pictures depends very strongly on the degree to which information about the picture is accessible to the computer.

Although most software using graphics does not have complex and complete information about the picture, it does make use of simple forms of information over and above the basic graphic information. Usually such information is added to the graphic information for better organization and handling of modeling or editing processes of the graphics as well as the basic graphic elements. Already such information enables human-computer dialogues, but at a lower level.

The first and simplest piece of information about a picture as a whole is *naming the picture*, usually realized by finding a fitting file name (Figure 2.1). In most cases, the user is responsible for making appropriate use of this possibility and to express the main information of the picture in the filename; however, some restrictions, like limiting the file-name to 8 plus 3 characters in the operating system MS-DOS, are still inconvenient.

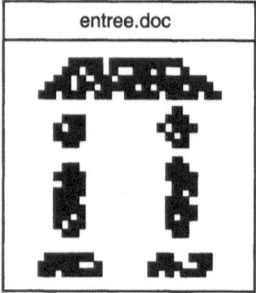

**Figure 2.1:**
Naming the picture

The *identification of basic graphic elements* is necessary for graphics designed as a collection and arrangement of adapted basic graphic elements (Figure 2.2). The basic graphic elements can be pixels in their simplest form or the well-known geometric primitives from drawing programs like circles, rectangles, or lines. A dialogue between the computer and a potential user can be led about the picture as a whole or its basic graphic elements, but only in connection with direct manipulation of the picture.

**Figure 2.2:**
Identification of
basic elements

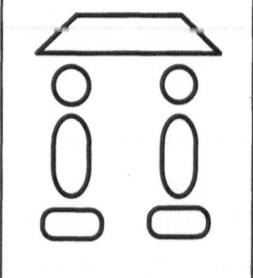

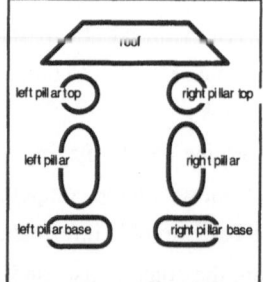

**Figure 2.3:**
Naming of
basic graphic
elements

The possibility of *naming the basic graphic elements* by users improves the possible interaction between human and computer, because users can then interact textually and refer to the names of basic graphic elements (Figure 2.3). If the names are chosen with respect to the meaning of basic graphic elements, a context-sensitive search is possible for the user to get information from the computer about the picture. This feature gets its importance by the fact that usually different users deal with one picture.

*Structuring of basic graphic elements* improves the quality of the designing process of pictures (Figure 2.4). The structuring information is optional and not necessary for displaying the picture on a screen or printing it, but it makes a dialogue possible about the hierarchy or dependencies between basic graphic elements as well as the groups defined.

**Figure 2.4:** Structuring of basic graphic elements  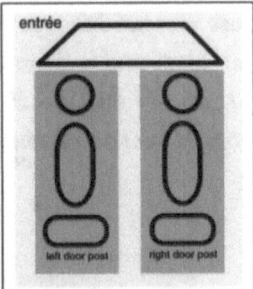 **Figure 2.5:** Naming structured basic graphic elements

*Naming structured basic graphic elements* corresponds to human behavior dealing with the world (Figure 2.5). We have our language as a complex system for describing the world and the elements around us. In most languages, there exist possibilities to express structures and hierarchies. During a human-computer dialogue about the picture this information enables queries about the structure of the picture with respect to the content of different basic graphic elements.

If the computer generates a pictorial presentation from internal data, then the computer can subsequently *access any semantic information* about the picture encoded in the internal data. In this case, the graphical data computed by the machine is only of secondary interest to the computer and has as its only purpose to visualize the internal data to the user. Both kinds of data – graphic and semantic – are available to the computer and the correspondence between these kinds of data is what empowers the computer to lead a dialogue with a user who only has the graphic visualization at his or her disposal. For example, the computer can lead a dialogue about a graph if it was generated from an equation, but not if the user drew the graph with a drawing program (Figure 2.6).

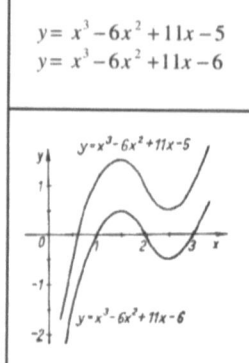

$$y = x^3 - 6x^2 + 11x - 5$$
$$y = x^3 - 6x^2 + 11x - 6$$

**Figure 2.6:**
Equations and their graphs

The following sections present different software dealing with pictures and highlight mechanisms by which users access information encoded in pictures. The classification scheme of Figure 2.7, derived from the above discussion, helps to investigate different computer systems with respect to capabilities of leading a human-computer dialogue about the pictures.

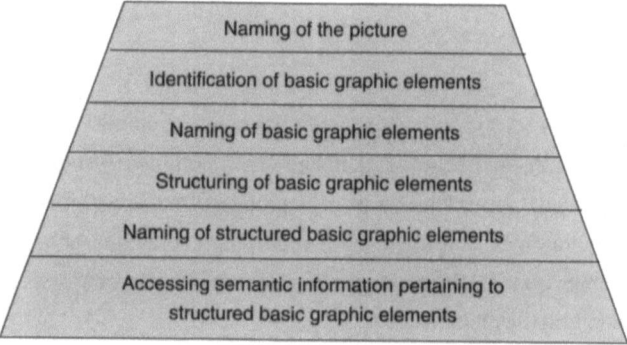

**Figure 2.7:** Kinds of information about the picture

## 2.1 Desktop Publishing

Desktop publishing systems are aimed at enabling end-users, typically non-computer scientists, to produce quality print materials. Products such as QuarkXPress and Ventura Publisher emphasize functionality to arrange the page layout, whereas the texts and pictures are entered with conventional text or graphic editors (see Figure 2.8).

The most important feature of desktop publishing is the so-called WYSIWYG (What You See Is What You Get) principle, in which the layout of the document is visible on

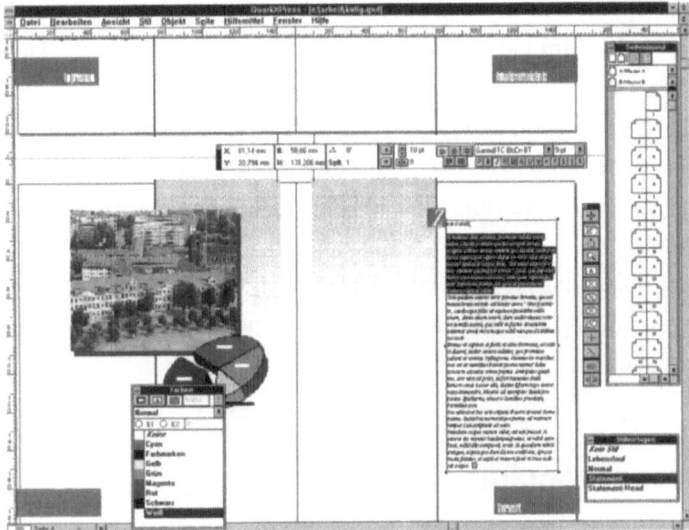

**Figure 2.8:** Designing the page layout with QuarkXPress™
(courtesy of Maren Strümke)

the screen in the way the document will be printed on paper. This fact enables a user to modify the document interactively.[*]

Desktop publishing provides possibilities for professional design of text layouts with different kinds of pictures from different sources. Pictures have to be incorporated in texts and should be arranged esthetically (see Bove, Rhodes, and Thomas 1986). Pictures for documents can be:

a) diagrams produced with a draw program, such as Corel Draw or Designer,

b) illustrations taken from an external source, such as a scanner, and represented in one of a number of file formats, such as TIFF, or

c) diagrams from special application programs which produce different kinds of graphics as output, for example spreadsheet programs, like Excel.

In each case, the information in the pictures of the document – both as it appears on the computer screen and as it appears on paper after being printed out – can only be accessed by a human viewer of the page. It is the responsibility of the author to provide necessary information about the pictures in his or her textual formulations and to guarantee that the picture conveys the information intended.

---

[*] Actually, the WYSIWYG principle is sometimes more of a vision than a reality. Few systems are purely WYSIWYG: for example, the colors seen on the computer screen are rarely those appearing on a printout.

Coming back to the classification of Figure 2.7, none of the kinds of information about the picture is required for pictures to be included into documents in a desktop publishing program. Most of them are optional. If a picture comes from an outside source, the desktop publishing program knows the filename if it was included as a file and not as a clipboard. The other information about identification, naming, and structuring of basic graphic elements can be available if the desktop publishing program has a graphic editor at its disposal.

The current state of the art in desktop publishing system functionality does not include human-computer dialogues about the contents of pictures, nor are users able to search or ask for information encoded in a picture.

## 2.2  Drawing Programs

Diagrams produced with drawing programs contain a rich structure in their internal formats. Besides using graphical primitives such as circles and rectangles, individual items can be grouped hierarchically to any depth. However, this information is generally no longer used once the drawing process is complete, even though it could in some cases shed light on the meaning of the diagram and aid in its interpretation. For example, it is impossible to show the structuring of geometric primitives outside the graphic editor: this information is lost both when printing the picture on paper as well as when the picture is imported into a text in a desktop publishing system (see Figure 2.9).

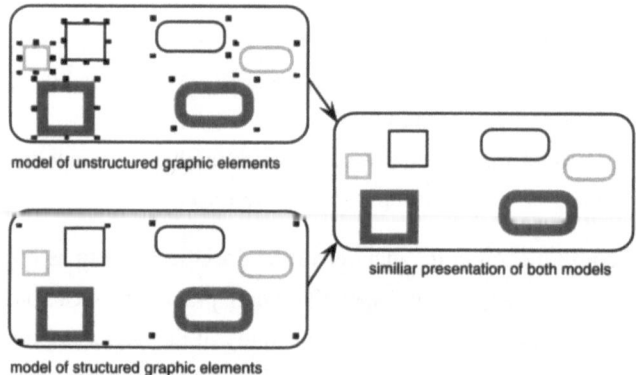

**Figure 2.9:** Losing information by exporting pictures

Only the picture itself and not the internal structure of a picture can be exported and presented to an end-user. However, it must be noted that the structuring functionality of drawing programs is only designed for the drawing process, and not for end-user manipulation, which would be necessary for end-users of desktop publishing systems. Other functionality could be useful to support such interaction, such as naming of structures.

Recent research has aimed at making more of this structural information. In the experimental system of Schleich and Dürst (1994), the user of a drawing program is provided with multiple views of the data (Figure 2.10). In particular, the structural information can be visualized as a hierarchy (View 2 of Figure 2.10).

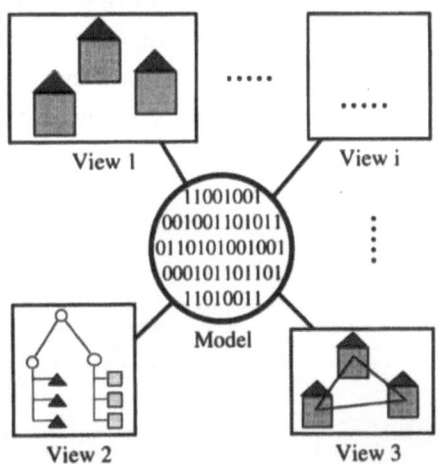

**Figure 2.10:** Multiple views of a model in a drawing program (Schleich and Dürst 1994)

Thus it is possible, for example, to assign attribute-value pairs to members of a group of elements within an editor for the hierarchy as a shorthand notation for manipulating the elements of the picture directly. This improves the efficiency of using drawing programs.

The simplicity of the internal representations of the pictures outside of graphic editors makes it extremely difficult to enable users to search in the pictorial portions of their documents. While for texts elaborate string-searching functions based on regular expressions are available, very few commercially available desktop publishing systems provide users with an appropriate string-searching function to allow users to access texts in pictures created with drawing programs (for research results in this area see Kurlander and Feiner 1992). Indeed, most string-searching functions used in spelling checkers will miss strings encoded in pictures, for example as labels of parts, even though such functionality would not be difficult to build in.

## 2.3  Hypertext Systems

Besides enormous amounts of books, all libraries have many utilities to help find information about a special topic, including, for example, alphabetical catalogues of authors, subject catalogues for semantic search, and bibliographies for special subjects.

One of the predecessors of present cross-references are concordances used in literature. Concordances are "an alphabetical verbal index showing the places in the text of a book or in the works of an author where each principal word may be found often with its immediate context" (Webster 1986). After the first concordances for the Bible (for a modern version, see the Oxford Cyclopedia Concordance), other concordances for masterpieces by Shakespeare, Goethe (see Märkisch 1973) and others followed. Concordances can also be seen as the predecessors of *hypertext systems*.

A hypertext system is "an approach to information management in which data is stored in a network of nodes connected by links. Nodes can contain text, graphics, audio, videos as well as source code or other forms of data" ('Smith and Weiss 1988). The main feature of hypertext systems is the non-linearity of hypertexts which is represented inter-

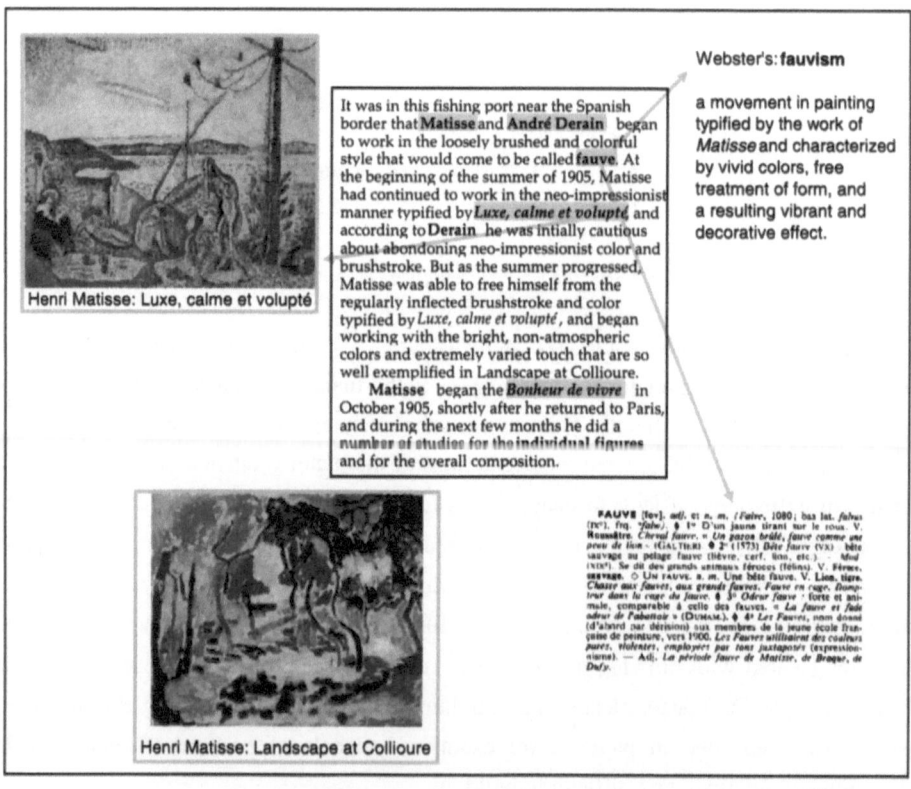

**Figure 2.11:** A hypertext example (Barnes 1993, Webster 1986, and PETIT ROBERT 1985)

**Table 2.1:** Kinds of usage of a hypertext (Kuhlen 1991)

| fish-eye | Exploring the neighborhood of an object while only displaying distant objects vaguely |
|---|---|
| zoom | closer examination of selected localised data |
| guided tour | moving about a pre-defined path |
| browsing and navigating | selectively looking around as desired (beware: "don't get lost in hyperspace") |
| searching for terms | exploring the system on the basis on semantic identifiers |

nally by a collection of nodes, a hierarchical network, or a graph (see Gloor 1990). Users can explore a hypertext by direct manipulation with different techniques (see Table 2.1). A snapshot of a hypertext document about art is shown in Figure 2.11 and demonstrates the combination of different media and the connection between the information chunks.

The World-Wide Web (the Web) has become the most well-known hypertext system. The Web is a collection of hypertexts available all over the world and accessible via the Internet. All information provided for the Web has to be coded in the HyperText Markup Language (HTML) and can be browsed with the help of different Web viewers, like Netscape or Mosaic. Each document can be addressed by its Uniform Resource Locator (URL).

Navigating through the Web is possible in different ways, for example by

- opening new nodes via activating links,
- going back to the previous node,
- jumping to other URLs directly via predefined links (bookmarks in Netscape) or
- opening a new URL.

At present, HTML is not very comfortable, but nonetheless allows including pictures in the documents. Like all other elements, pictures can be linked to other nodes in the Web. What is especially interesting within the context of the book is the possibility of mouse-sensitive pictures which allow defining more than one link for a picture depending on the mouse position on which the user has clicked. This enables designers of Web documents to create the illusion for the user that the machine has some understanding of the picture.

In summary, because pictures can be starting points for connections to other information, semantic information about the picture should be stored in a hypertext document. A user gets the feeling that the computer is able to interpret pictures with the help of other information connected to the picture, even though such information is hard-wired, generally by a person.

## 2.4 Image Processing Software

Image processing is the improvement and analysis of digital images or sequences of digital images. It includes the pre-processing and enhancement of pictures as well as their classification and interpretation. The digitization of a scene can be carried out by different types of sensors, such as cameras or radar devices. The result is an image stored as a two-dimensional array of values (bitmap). Image processing algorithms attempt to extract information encoded in the bitmaps with the goal of representing the contents of the images with respect to the task at hand (Ballard and Brown 1982, Vernon 1991).

In general, images must be pre-processed to minimize the effects caused by errors resulting from sensor characteristics or noise. After pre-processing the image using techniques for image restoration and geometric correction, and enhancing the image by suitable operators, the optical quality is usually improved and relevant information emphasized. Subsequent segmentation subdivides the image into regions or objects with similar characteristics and relevant features which are to be extracted and recognized. The image is then organized in more manageable parts for further analysis. By relating a certain meaning to these parts, they can be classified and interpreted using pattern recognition.

Applications of image processing range from medicine (computer tomography) to industrial production (robot control), and office automation (document analysis) to Earth observation (satellite image interpretation). Perhaps the best-known images provided by satellites are those recorded by geostationary satellites and transmitted to meteorological offices around the world (see Figure 2.12). With the help of satellite images, maps denoting, for example, regions of forest damage can be made. Meanwhile, satellite images are also used for the analysis of the dimension and consequences of natural catastrophes. They are ideal for monitoring changes in our environment.

The number of images and the volume of data available for Earth sciences is growing quickly. In 1972, the Landsat satellite was launched carrying a "multi-spectral scanning system" sensor for measuring electromagnetic radiation in digital form. American archive holdings total almost 1 million scenes of Landsat data, corresponding to 60 terabytes ($6 \cdot 10^{13}$ bytes). Further, the launch of the first of several platforms for the Earth Observing System (EOS) is planned for 1998, and the data acquired from this programme alone is expected to be measured in petabytes ($10^{15}$ bytes) by the year 2015 (Oelson, Doescher, and Holm 1991). The amount of data is thus very high, and most of this will never meet a human eye. There are far too many satellite images around to warrant human inspection, hence suitable access mechanisms for searching in large collections of images are extremely important.

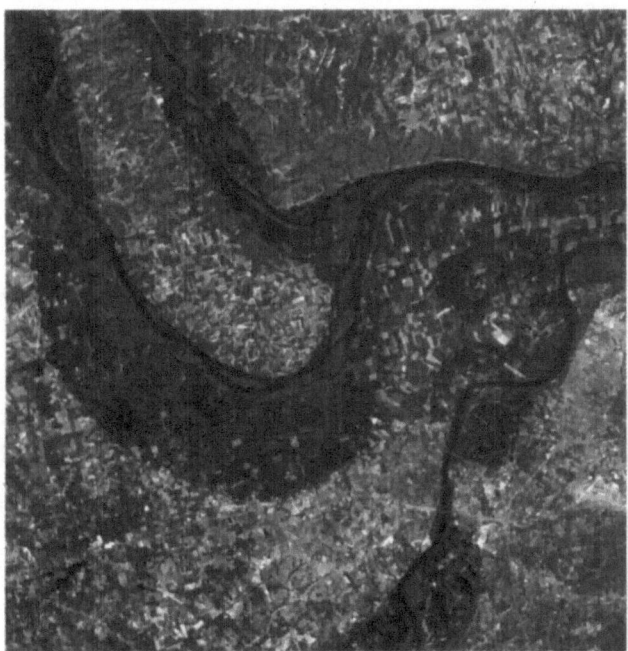

**Figure 2.12:** Example of a satellite image
(product of the European Space Agency's ERS-1 satellite)

An analyzed image and information pertaining to it is represented in one or a combination of several ways, such as lists, graphs, or hierarchical structures. The images themselves are denoted by time and place, giving access to them according to when they were taken and which area is portrayed. The data extracted from satellite images is usually a numeric value of a specific attribute. Such attributes generally have meaningful names, so that a search can be started based on attribute-value pairs.

Most engineering drawings are generated by CAD systems. Hence a search for an image with certain attributes can be carried out on the data from which the image was generated, rather than by an analysis of the image itself. However, there are still many drawings left over from the days when they were done by hand, and their interpretation is an important application for image processing and analysis techniques (Baird, Bunke, and Yamamoto 1992). The objective is to create a higher-level description of the contents of the paper-based document. Therefore, the different parts of the document – text and graphics – are separated and analyzed (see Figure 2.13). This information can then be used to access the pictures by a program or even by a person.

Finally, whole sequences of images play an important role in some applications, like traffic monitoring. The detection of moving objects in the field of view, the extraction of feature positions from real-time scenes and the tracking of these objects throughout the

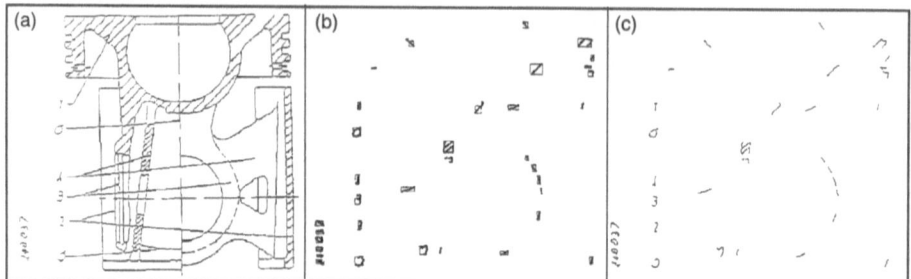

**Figure 2.13:** Example of information extracted from an engineering drawing (Klöditz 1995). The initial scanned image is shown left, candidate regions for text recognition center and a first approximation for text recognition right.

whole image sequence are important characteristics of a vision system. Movement information, stored as vectors pertaining to certain regions of the images, are determined and represented explicitly (Ali and Dagless 1992). This is an attribute that can be used in a search of several images at once.

## 2.5 Three-Dimensional Computer Graphics Systems

The field of computer graphics aims at being able to represent the geometry of objects within the computer and to combine these representations with information about lighting effects to produce images that look like photos taken by a camera (see Bouatouch and Bouville 1992, Burger and Gillies 1989). The internal representation is referred to as a *3D model or a scene description*, the program to compute the graphics a *renderer* and the output a *photorealistic* image (see Foley et al. 1990). An example of a model and an image computed by a renderer is illustrated in Figure 2.14.

There are (at least) four kinds of users involved in computer graphics:

1. *The person developing graphics software.*
   This user works by visually inspecting the rendered images to determine empirically whether the desired effects have been attained.
2. *The person developing models.*
   Complex interactive software tools have been developed to aid users in modeling. These tools tend to be based on geometric primitives which can be combined to yield composite objects of varying complexity. In this case, the user visually inspects the rendered image in order to check that the model corresponds to what he or she wants.
3. *The person who composes the image.*
   This person arranges the light sources, chooses the camera settings, and other parameters of the renderer.

```
Ambient light color: Red=0.196078 Green=0.196078 Blue=0.196078
""

Gradient top color: Red=0 Green=0 Blue=0
Gradient middle color @ 0.74026: Red=0 Green=0 Blue=0
Gradient bottom color: Red=0.094118 Green=0.207843 Blue=0.298039

Named object: "HeadH"
Tri-mesh, Vertices: 1160     Faces: 2320
Mapped
Vertex list:
Vertex 0:    X:-29.999985 Y:1020 Z:200  U:0      V:0
Vertex 1:    X:-27.311272 Y:1020.978577Z:199.839264 U:0.016625    V:0
Vertex 2:    X:-21.728243 Y:1023.01062 Z:199.753876 U:0.051096    V:0
Vertex 3:    X:-14.108171 Y:1025.78418 Z:199.728714 U:0.09814     V:0
Vertex 4:    X:-5.308359  Y:1028.986938Z:199.748871 U:0.152467    V:0
Vertex 5:    X:3.813898   Y:1032.307251Z:199.799088 U:0.208785    V:0

....

Vertex 1158:X:-29.95192  Y:1019.992554Z:89.999969  U:1.361592    V:1.949848
Vertex 1159:X:-29.996811 Y:1019.983826Z:89.999969  U:1.361857    V:1.949848
Face list:
Face 0:     A:0     B:1     C:30    AB:1   BC:1   CA:0
Material:"WOOD MR"
Smoothing:  1, 10
Face 1:     A:0     B:30    C:29    AB:0   BC:1   CA:1
Material:"WOOD MR"
Smoothing:  1, 10
Face 2:     A:1     B:2     C:31    AB:1   BC:1   CA:0
Material:"WOOD MR"
Smoothing:  1, 11

....

Named object: "Camera01"
Camera (41.397041mm)
Position: X:-10 Y:-19.975632 Z:1.39598
Target: X:-10 Y:20 Z:0
Bank angle: 0 degrees
Near 0 Far 1000

Named object: "Light01"
Direct light
Position: X:810 Y:290 Z:960
Spotlight to: X:-40 Y:1040 Z:0
Hotspot size: 44 degrees
Falloff size: 45 degrees
Global Shadow
Light color: Red=1 Green=1 Blue=1
```

**Figure 2.14:** Example of 3D model and the rendered image (courtesy of Axel Hoppe)

Of course, computer graphics are not just made for computer scientists, but are actually intended for others:

4. *The end-user viewing the graphics.*

Computer generated graphics can be viewed on a computer screen, on a video screen, or on paper. In any case, end-users generally have virtually no way of manipulating the image. All a user can do is look, study, and appreciate. However, end-users usually do have the freedom to choose which image or sequence to view next.

The users of categories 1 and 4 normally have no chance to interact with the image. Only the modeler and the composer of images have the model editor at their disposal. In general, interaction with the model is based exclusively on direct manipulation, which has the drawback that although the naming of geometric primitives or structures is possible, it is used very rarely. Indeed, commercially available systems generally do not provide functionality for allowing the user to request more information about a modeled photorealistic image, nor do they provide other search functions like "largest object", "all circles", or "highest point". Nonetheless, recent work has produced tools for graphically searching image databases, even without keywords (Jakobs, Finkelstein, and Salesin 1995).

The reason for the lack of more information about the picture is the assumption that users know everything about the picture, because they can look at it. A developer of a 3D model can explore everything by direct manipulation in the model editor, but he or she can lead a dialogue about the picture only on a very basic level. We will come back to this point later in Section 17.4, where we will examine methods by which renderers can share with end-users some of the information which they gather about the picture, rather than producing only the image and discarding all other information.

Recent developments in graphics standards are improving the lack of facilities for naming objects in a systematic manner (Damnjanovic, Duce, and Robinson 1993). PHIGS offers a set of names which may be associated with an output primitive to determine its properties (e.g., visible, highlighted, or detectable by a particular pick device on a particular workstation). Control over the primitive is exercised by filters associated with each such property. GKS-9x goes a step further by replacing the filters by application-specific searching and selection criteria, rather than forcing them to be taken from a fixed set. This makes it possible to encode names in a model and to search for these with respect to a rendered image. Such features will greatly improve the flexibility with which images can be used in dialogues in conjunction with language.

## 2.6 Computer Simulation

Computer simulation is but one example of many systems used in engineering applications with elaborate pictures as visualizations of complex processes and data structures. These systems are characterized by the graphics often being of secondary interest; of primary interest is the construction or analysis of plans or models, which are based on process descriptions rather than 3D geometry.

The most widely used language for discrete event simulation is GPSS (see Schriber1991 and 1992). Being over 30 years old, the programming style is akin to Fortran and originally there was no built-in animation. But some newer systems have been developed which offer animation facilities for special kinds of simulators. An example is PROOF (see Brunner, Earle, and Henriksen 1991) which was developed to complement any one of a number of simulators, for instance GPSS: The programmer augments his or her GPSS programs to produce a trace file, and writes code in PROOF to define the graphical layout. This enables 2D animations to be produced (see a snapshot in Figure 2.15).

Besides GPSS, there are many other simulation languages, like SIMULA, SLAM (see O´Reilly and Ryan 1992), and SIMAN (see Pedgen, Shannon, and Sadowski 1990), which all have in common that they provide semantics by their language constructs and are restricted to linearity, the common attribute of languages.

In recent years, alternative kinds of simulators have been developed which make stronger use of graphical user interfaces. Such element-oriented simulators, of which Create! (see Hoppe, Kirchner, and Rüger 1990, Rüger and Behlau 1995), Extend (Krahl 1994), AutoMod (Norman 1992) and SIMFACTORY II.5 (Goble 1991) are examples, are designed for ease-of-use by non-specialists. The model is built up using direct manipulation and its layout can be re-used as the layout of the animation.

The purpose of such simulations is to develop the model, so that an existing system (such as a factory) can be improved or a future one can be designed and analyzed (see Carrie 1988, Law and Kelton 1991). Therefore, even more information is stored in the machine than is apparent from the animation. However, only low-level interaction is made possible, such as altering which data is being visualized or the color or speed of the animation. Other kinds of manipulations which, for example, make changes in the computational parameters during the simulation, can be carried out in some simulators (for example GPSS/PC, see Cox 1987). However, such manipulations lead to unreproducible simulation runs and are of questionable value.

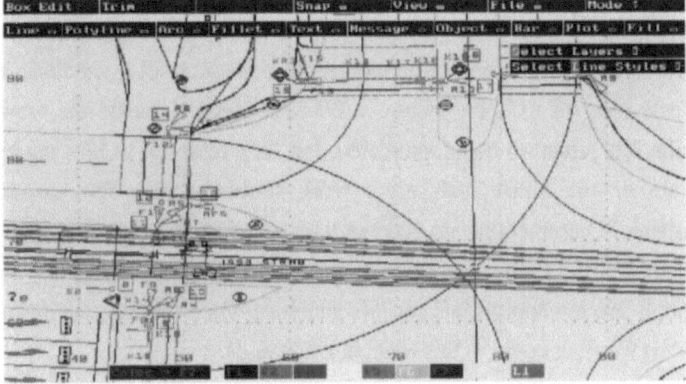

**Figure 2.15:** Snapshot of a PROOF animation stemming from a GPSS simulation of a road crossing (courtesy of Peter Lorenz)

For the visualization of a simulation model it is interesting that there usually exist different classes of simulation elements which can be visualized individually. The background is the high complexity of models which can be reduced by hiding single classes of elements. Figure 2.16 shows the different possibilities of Create! to present the same underlying model differently on the basis of the classification of the elements in control and material flow elements.

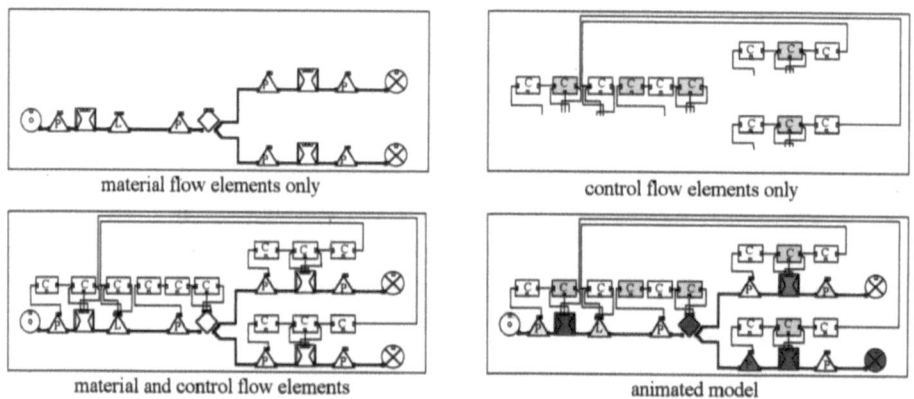

material flow elements only    control flow elements only

material and control flow elements    animated model

**Figure 2.16:** Kinds of model presentation of the element-oriented simulator Create!

The animation of a simulation run is based on simulation results produced by the computer. For this reason, a correspondence exists between the graphic symbols in the animation and the elements of the simulation model. This correspondence is the key for the computer to access the semantic information about the pictures of the animation. Other kinds of information (recall Figure 2.7) depend on the abilities of the editor for the animation, but are mostly available.

In recent years, several 3D animation systems have become available which can be coupled directly with simulators. Because of the need for real-time processing, these animation systems tend to omit time-consuming features like shadows and special lighting effects (see for example Figure 2.17). The images enable the viewer to get a feeling for the real situation being simulated, but they tend not to be used by engineers doing the simulation, since such users work routinely with the abstract-graphical pictures. Instead, 3D animations are necessary on a management level to convince policy makers and investors of the feasibility of the solution being simulated. Pictures with special symbols are not appropriate for this audience when the conventions used are not widely known (we shall come to this topic in Chapter 3).

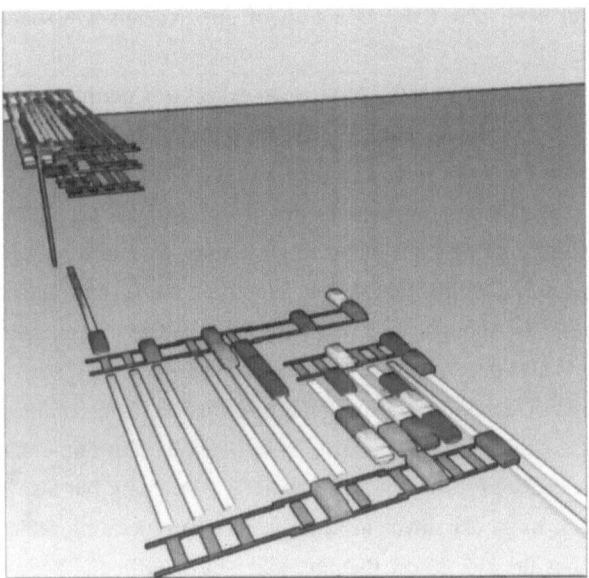

**Figure 2.17:** Snapshot of the 3D real-time animation tool AniPLuS
(courtesy of Ralf Helbing)

## 2.7 Summary

We chose six special application fields to investigate the role of pictures in computer systems. We left out areas like CAD, scientific visualization, and virtual reality. Because there is no real end to this enumeration, we stopped there.

The systems discussed in this chapter characteristically exhibit only marginal abilities to be used in a dialogue. Perhaps the most obvious deficit is that the pictures are relatively static in the sense that the machine is limited in the extent to which it can adjust the picture to suit the apparent needs of the user.

The most powerful mechanism for incorporating pictures in dialogues is found in hypertext systems and in the animation of computer simulation. The basic functionality of hypertext systems is to present more detailed information for each single part of the documents on user request. Even though the author must define a function to be called upon clicking on each active region of the picture, the impression is created to the end-user that the machine has actually interpreted the picture. Animations in computer simulation visualize the results of simulation runs and for this reason they have semantic information about their graphical objects in animation. If the animation system has access to these data, the user can ask for semantic information about the picture by direct manipulation. But even here there is a lack of context-sensitive search functions and semantic requests.

The other kinds of systems exhibit fewer, and in fact less pertinent, internal representations about the pictures. In the case of satellite images, for example, initially only the camera identification and the time and date are associated with a picture: other information may or may not be computed by the image processing algorithms and stored along with the picture. In desktop publishing systems, a picture may be named (if it is taken from a file) or not (if it is just drawn directly in the system); geometric primitives are usually represented though not available to the end-user (i.e., reader of the document). The latter is also generally true for 3D computer graphics systems.

Table 2.2 summarizes the extent to which information about pictures is stored in the various kinds of commercially available systems surveyed in this chapter. It should be noted that in some systems, most notably desktop publishing but also modelers for 3D computer graphics, users use direct manipulation, where pointing rather than naming is employed. This has the side-effect that end-users have difficulty accessing information which the author pointed at, whereas if the author had been forced to name more objects, the end-user could use string matching facilities to search for these objects.

Table 2.2 defines the background for the work reported in this book. It displays clearly the lack of data structures gathered about pictures. Perhaps even more important, the information represented internally is often not made available to the end-users of the pictures.

**Table 2.2:** Summary of the available information about pictures

| | desktop publishing | drawing programs | hyper-text | image processing | 3D-graphics | simula-tion |
|---|---|---|---|---|---|---|
| Naming of the picture[*] | required | required | required | optional | required | required |
| Identification of basic graphic elements | optional | optional | optional | optional | required | required |
| Naming of basic graphic elements | optional | non-existent | optional | non-existent | optional | required |
| Structuring of basic graphic elements | optional | optional | optional | non-existent | required | required |
| Naming of basic graphic elements | non-existent | non-existent | required | non-existent | optional | optional |
| Accessing semantic information pertaining to structured basic graphic elements | non-existent | non-existent | optional | non-existent | non-existent | required |

[*] The "required" entries in this row assume that individual pictures are stored in separate files, each with a meaningful name originally chosen by user.

*Two men with axes fighting on a boat*
Fossum, Sweden

# Classification of Pictures

## 3.1 Classes of Pictures

Pictures were the first form of written communication when human beings wrote their emotions, experiences, memories, and hopes on cave walls thousands of years ago. To remind the reader that cave paintings are the origin of our contemporary pictures, a collection of petroglyphs from all over the world is presented in this book.

If one asks several people what a typical picture looks like, one will get as many answers as people asked. Figure 3.1 shows examples of possible answers. But even in this colorful presentation of different pictures, differences in usage, contents, artistic means, and necessary cognitive perception are observable. For example, it probably would not make any sense to present real-looking 3D pictures of a town instead of a city map to a foreigner who has just arrived, even though such a picture may in fact be esthetically pleasing.

To use the right kinds of pictures for a defined purpose, we need to classify pictures. We will present three different classes of pictures and illustrate them by showing typical examples. The classification scheme has been developed for the special needs of computer scientists but is strongly influenced by semiotics. The kind of visual signs dominating a picture defines the class to which a picture belongs. Therefore we have to explain the term "dominating." The discussion at the end summarizes the classification scheme.

Our classification differentiates with respect to the content of pictures between *presentational* pictures, *abstract-graphical* pictures, and *pictograms*.

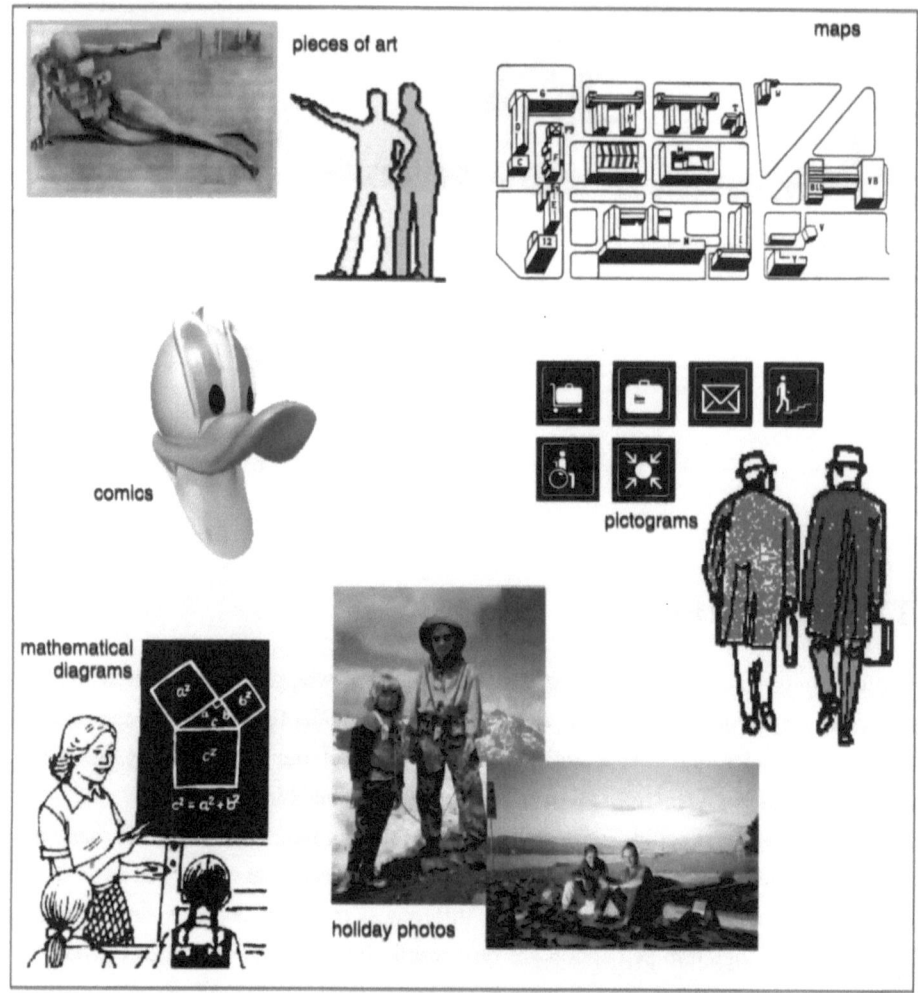

**Figure 3.1:** Examples of "typical" pictures (Schuster 1992, Evans 1987, courtesy of Frank Godenschweger, Stiebner and Urban 1988, Heaton 1986)

### 3.1.1 Presentational Pictures

Presentational pictures present properties and relations in reality (including virtual reality and imagination) which are *visible* to humans. Although parts of reality can be distorted, manipulated, or otherwise misrepresented, geometric and physical aspects of surfaces and the behavior of fluids or real objects are of central interest in presentational pictures. The bandwidth of presentational pictures is very high and includes line drawings as well as photos (see Figure 3.2).

**Figure 3.2:** Presentational pictures of a real object
(middle from Ching 1985, right © Kreuter Foto Kalender)

It is interesting that snapshots of virtual reality systems are classified as presentational pictures. The goal of virtual reality is to create the same feelings and perception as experienced when living in the real world. Photorealistic imagery and motion in real time are therefore the primary goals of virtual reality.

A look at the virtual reality scene of the campus of the University of Magdeburg makes it obvious that virtual reality snapshots can be classified as presentational pictures (see Figure 3.3).

**Figure 3.3:** Virtual reality snapshot (courtesy of Matthias Kunze and Heiko Dorwarth)

### 3.1.2 Abstract-Graphical Pictures

In abstract-graphical pictures, properties of and relations in reality which are *invisible* to humans can be presented in an abstract way. The problem of making invisible properties obvious to the human eye can be solved in two ways:

*Adding graphical symbols* like

- geometric primitives (rectangles, ellipses, cubes, circles, free-hand curves, etc.),
- arrows and lines, and
- text labels (consisting of letters and numbers).

The graphical symbols can be varied by shadows and textures for the geometric primitives, by different thickness and styles of arrows, lines, and text labels. Figure 3.4 shows a choice from the wide variety of graphical symbols for creating abstract-graphical pictures.

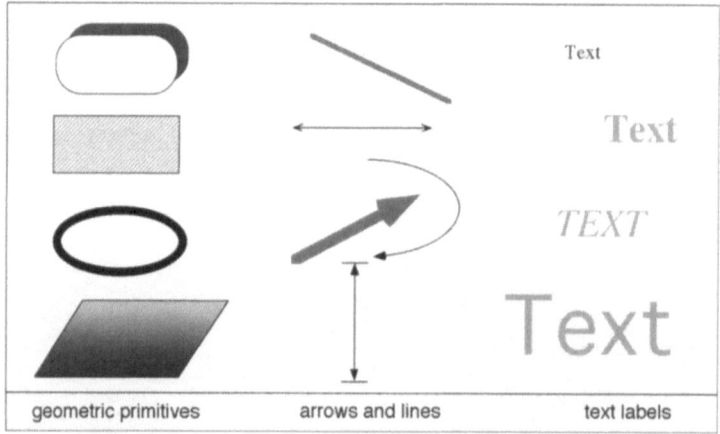

**Figure 3.4:** Graphical symbols

*Mapping invisible properties onto visible attributes*
For displaying invisible parameters, a correspondence to visible attributes like color, position in 2D or 3D, or a pattern can be defined. In 3D visualization, color is widely used for parameters like pressure, temperature, or thermodynamic effects around or in a real object. Figure 3.5 shows an example of the vorticity in the North Atlantic.

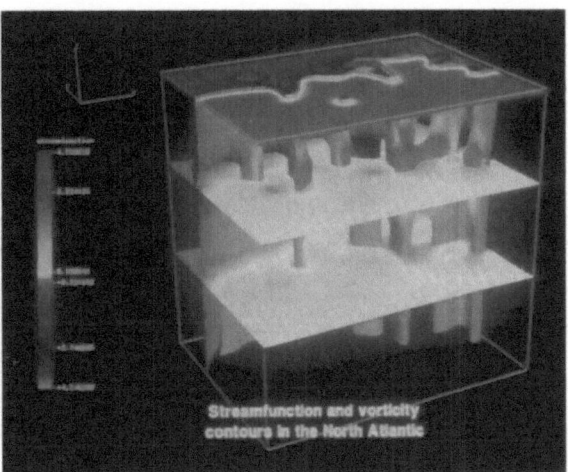

**Figure 3.5:** Vorticity in the North Atlantic
(Earnshaw and Wiseman 1992)

### 3.1.3 Pictograms

Pictograms represent something more abstract than what they actually show. Even if they show only one concrete object (e.g., a horse crossing a road) this serves as a representative for an abstract group of objects (not only this horse, but all horses may cross the road here).

In contrast to the other classes of pictures, pictograms only represent something *en bloc*. Single parts of pictograms do not contribute directly to the interpretation of a pictogram as a whole, even if these single parts can be interpreted separately.

The meaning of a pictogram is either very obvious to almost everybody or has to be learnt. For example, the pictograms used for the different kinds of sports are very obvious, while the correspondence between a traffic sign and what it is intended to express has to be learnt in driving lessons.

In general, pictograms do not have the ambiguity typical of presentational and abstract-graphical pictures. One meaning can be represented by any one of a number of pictograms, as illustrated by the collection of user-icons in Figure 3.6. This collection also demonstrates the use of pictograms within abstract-graphical pictures. All of these user icons were found in abstract-graphical pictures presenting a soft- or hardware architecture.

Another important feature of pictograms is that their meanings are well defined, but context-sensitive, and that they can be replaced by words. The latter is the basis for the language-independence of pictograms and the reason for their special use in international contexts like airports and international sporting events. Even for children or illiterates, pictograms are important for communicating or getting information.

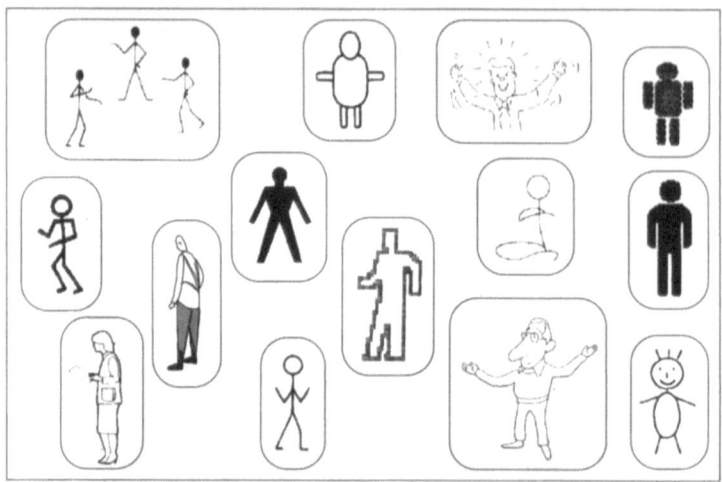

**Figure 3.6:** Different user-icons appearing in the literature[*]

Pictograms are designed with the goal of common understandability, but the first drafts of pictograms are often criticized very harshly because of the differences in individuals' perception of them. One of the biggest problems in designing pictograms is to represent the typical character of the object or the action that has to be represented in the pictogram. Only if a whole group of people associate the same pre-defined meaning with a picture can we classify the picture as a pictogram.

## 3.2  Pictures Made of Visual Signs

Computer scientists are interested either in generating pictures from internal representations or in analyzing pictures to derive conclusions about structural elements in a picture, so it is necessary to deal with the smallest components of a picture – *visual signs*. To clarify the status of the three different classes of pictures and their interrelationships, we shall draw on semiotics, the science of signs. Semiotics might be far away from computer scientists' knowledge and experience, but it gives necessary and constructive input to questions pertaining to a classification of pictures. When we have a better grasp of the nature of visual signs, we will return to the classes presented above in order to define them somewhat more precisely. Even the sceptical reader will hopefully get interesting insights into the nature of pictures.

---

[*]Taken from Pfleeger (1989), Redmiles (1992), Fehrle (1993), Fehrle, Strothotte and Szardenings (1990), Buhr (1990), Herczeg (1986), Krömker (1992), Hübner (1990), von der Herberg (1988), Thimbleby (1990), Buhr (1984), Robertson, Card and Mackinlay (1993), Kugas (1993), and courtesy of Frank Godenschweger.

Semiotics gives us the theoretical background to discuss differences between the classes of pictures in much more detail and to present the whole classification scheme including discussions of each class of pictures.

The current situation in semiotics is characterized by many theories explaining different classifications of signs or single phenomena, sometimes contradicting each other. Up to now there is no generally accepted complete theory, but a lot of interesting investigations and theoretical ideas on how pictures are made up of visual signs. Because of the vagueness of this topic, it seems to be necessary to refer to the history of some of the theories to explain the context in which they have been developed. The main motivation for this chapter is to find an answer to the question of which visual signs constitute the characteristics of the members of each of the classes of pictures.

Semiotics investigates all cultural processes as communicative processes and therefore analyzes the smallest unit used for communication. Looking ahead a little, we will observe that the relationship between a visual sign and its interpretation is influenced by visual codes which are defined by conventions. A main goal of semiotic work is to decode visual codes controlling visual perception.

Which kinds of signs are we dealing with in visual communication?

### 3.2.1 Natural and Non-Natural Signs

A very old differentiation of visual signs which has been used since ancient times is the one into *natural signs* (like silhouettes, frost patterns on a cold window, and mirages) and *non-natural signs* (like drawings and paintings). A natural sign does not have to be a natural object. The reflection in a man-made mirror (which is definitely not a natural object) is a natural sign as well as the reflection in a lake, because what we see in a mirror has a natural relation to the environment that we and the mirror are in due to physical laws. Scholz (1991) proposes distinguishing for both kinds of signs between whether or not the relation of the sign to what it signifies is a natural one.

To further understand the character of natural signs, we shall study a few more of their properties. The relations between a natural sign and what it signifies exist independently of actions, intentions, or conventions of humans. Every natural sign signifies a specific, single event. There are no natural signs that indicate nothing; a natural sign always indicates something. Natural signs like shadows, mirages, or marks are pictures of something that really exists.

The other class of pictures – non-natural signs – are strongly influenced by human intervention. They are made and used for communication. This leads to the conclusion that the pictures we are dealing with are usually, and in the context of computer science always, non-natural signs. This is an important restriction which makes the term *picture* more manageable for the purposes of this book. This restriction allows us to eliminate from further consideration such nasty examples of pictures as patterns in sand or in snowflakes – since these are natural signs, they are beyond the scope of the book.

### 3.2.2  Other Classes of Signs

De Saussure (1967) distinguishes between *motivated* and *arbitrary* signs. Motivated signs are defined by the correspondence between an object and its sign, while arbitrary signs get their interpretation via agreements between users of these signs. This classification implies that only interpreting arbitrary signs requires knowledge about conventions, while dealing with motivated signs is based on analogies obvious to the members of the population using the sign. Therefore arbitrary signs are sometimes called *conventional signs* and, analogously, motivated signs are sometimes called *non-conventional signs*.

Peirce (1935) followed up on the idea of non-conventional signs, but proposed three kinds of signs with respect to the related object: *indices, symbols,* and *icons*.

An *index* draws the viewer's attention to the object being alluded to through an unconscious impulse (Eco 1972). Indices denote functional relationships (like tracks of deers as indices for the presence of deers, raindrops as indices for rain, etc.). But the interpretation of an index also depends on knowing certain conventions and on experience, otherwise an index is not recognised as one, but as an event selected by chance. Marcus (1992) suggests as an example that a trail of muddy footsteps in a front hallway that the children have just entered is an index.

A *symbol* stands for a thing, a concept, or a feeling and may be completely arbitrary in appearance. Symbols are not motivated; the association between the sign and its meaning is thus not intuitively understandable, but has to be learnt. Symbols are governed by iconographic conventions which define the code for a symbol system, like musical notations or the flags of the states of the world. The relationship between the sign (see Figure 3.7) and what it stands for, its interpretation (the country of Canada), is determined by social conventions.

It is more or less generally accepted that both kinds of signs, symbols and indices, are conventional signs and their comprehension depends on the knowledge and experience of the viewer. Peirce (1935) postulated that the situation is completely different in the case of icons. We will discuss this more deeply in the next section.

**Figure 3.7:**
Flag of Canada

Peirce (1935) defined an *icon* as a sign that resembles what it stands for and that has properties which resemble those of what it stands for. The observation of an icon initiates a perception process which *resembles* the perception carried out when viewing the real object being portrayed. In the same way, Morris (1946) defined an iconic sign as one that has properties which *resemble* those of the depicted object (the so-called resemblance theory).

This definition of an icon, focusing especially on the *resemblance* between sign and reality, was quite popular for a long time around the middle of this century. Since then, there has been quite substantial criticism of the term icon and its definition.

### 3.2.3  Are There Visual Signs Independent of Conventions?

To answer this question, we draw on theories of Umberto Eco (1972), Nelson Goodman (1968), and Oliver Scholz (1991), who uncovered a variety of problems related to iconic signs.

The basic idea that an icon may resemble what it signifies appears relatively obvious, but appearances are deceptive. To analyze resemblance theory, we have to study the relation between resemblance and depiction, and clarify whether resemblance constitutes depiction.

First, the relation of resemblance is a symmetric one, but the relation of depiction is not. For example, if object A resembles object B, then object B resembles object A. By contrast, if C is a picture of D, it is definitely *not* true that D is a picture of C. Second, resemblance is a reflexive relation, whereas depiction is not reflexive. What would it mean for a picture to be a picture of itself? Third, resemblance is comparative and often gradual with respect to the amount and intensity of correspondence (think about pictures where you have to find all the differences). Being a picture or not is a binary choice – there is no grading. All these arguments refute the idea that resemblance is sufficient for depiction and question the notion of resemblance as a basis for defining the term icon.

We can see this with an example: An image of one of the authors (Figure 3.8) does not have the same properties as the author herself has. In the photo, we can recognize the form of the eyes, eyebrows, nose, etc., but only because we can bridge the gap between the real person and the photo with the help of recognition codes and graphical conventions. The nose, for example, is only two-dimensional in the portrait, but nonetheless we recognize it as nose.

Eco (1972) takes this idea to the extreme and says the first conclusion has to be that a portrait of a person is not completely iconic, but only to a certain extent, because the material on which a portrait or photo is made (canvas or paper) does not have the same structure as skin, and the portrait cannot speak or move like the depicted person. If we assume a resemblance between sign and object, the term iconic sign does not mean

**Figure 3.8:**
An image of a person does not have the same properties as the person herself

anything, because the only real and complete iconic sign of a person would be the person himself or herself. Thus Eco cuts away the basis for the resemblance theory.

We will cut short this discussion and refer only to Goodman (1968) and Scholz (1991) for more on this topic. We turn instead to the implications of defining iconic signs via resemblance.

A well-known assumption is that for understanding pictures nothing has to be learnt. Edna Daitz (1953) wrote: "To understand a statement we must first have learnt the language in which it is made – but in the sense in which there are foreign languages there are no foreign pictures." The question "Are there no foreign pictures?" became a matter of dispute. Copi (1958) answered: "Do we comprehend any picture on seeing it for the first time? ... There may be some pictures whose content or subject matter is immediately evident to anyone who looks at them. But many pictures require much learning for their interpretation. These include maps, diagrams, political cartoons, cubist paintings; and in religious symbolism; all unintelligible to the uninitiated."

Scholz (1991) points out that this reaction is not clear enough. Not only is learning necessary for understanding *special* kinds of pictures, but *all* pictures have to be "read" and the capabilities for this process have to be learnt. For example, humans have to learn how to differentiate between foreground and background to perceive depth in a picture. More obvious are the different methods for projecting three dimensions onto a two-dimensional medium (for example orthographic, oblique, or isometric projections, and one-point or two-point perspective projections). These graphical conventions influence our perception of pictures and have to be learnt.

The conclusion, which Eco and Scholz justify in much more detail, is that so-called iconic signs are conventional signs in the same way as symbolic signs. "The iconic signs reproduce some of the conditions of perception of an object, but only after they have been selected and explained on the basis of graphical conventions" (Eco 1972, translated by the author).

The logical consequence of this insight is that neither the difference between iconic and symbolic signs (Peirce 1935) nor the differentiation between motivated and arbitrary signs (de Saussure 1967) can be sustained. Where does this lead us?

### 3.2.4 Arbitrariness of Conventional Signs

We have to find a new criterion for differentiating between icons and symbols, which are both conventional signs, because the counter-arguments against the resemblance theory cannot be ignored.

Scholz (1991) discusses at length the term *arbitrariness*. While being conventional is a binary choice (a sign is either conventional or is not), arbitrariness is a gradual property of a sign. Conventional signs can have different levels of arbitrariness. In Webster (1990) there are two definitions of the term *arbitrary* which are appropriate in our context:

- based on or determined by individual preference or convenience rather than by necessity or the intrinsic nature of something,
- existing or coming about seemingly at random or by chance or as a capricious and unreasonable act of will.

The significant aspect here is that arbitrariness is not a binary property but has various degrees. We use the term *arbitrary sign* for the situation that the relation between sign and what it signifies is arbitrary. Arbitrariness does not mean that the sign can be chosen arbitrarily by a person, but that the relation is unmotivated and there does not exist a natural relation between the sign and what it signifies.

Back to symbols and icons – the two non-natural kinds of signs. We can summarize their relation to arbitrariness by saying that a symbol shows a high degree of arbitrariness whereas an icon has a low degree of arbitrariness.

### 3.2.5 Summary of the Semiotic Excurse

The differentiation between indices on the one hand and symbols/icons on the other hand is undisputed and corresponds to the classification into natural and non-natural signs. The main question is what distinguishes iconic signs from symbols because, as we have shown above, there is substantial criticism of two issues:

- *The theory of resemblance.* Proponents draw on the resemblance between signs and what they signify: icons would resemble what they signify, symbols would not. Counter-arguments are the difference between the resemblance and depiction relations and the inability to define precisely the term *resemblance* (see Section 3.2.3).

- *The concept of conventionality.* Advocates want to differentiate as follows: symbols are seen as conventional signs, while icons are not, because they are viewed as being intuitively understandable. As we have discussed above, producing pictures is always subject to conventions which have to be known to the viewers of pictures. Otherwise, viewers will interpret the pictures differently from how producers intended. The conventions may differ in their degree of universality and the size of the population using them, but conventions are always involved in the production and reception of pictures.

## 3.3  Classification Scheme for Pictures

The classical question for analyzing pictures is "What is a picture?". Scholz (1993) argues in the tradition of Goodman that already the formulation of the question is misleading, because it implies that something always and under all circumstances is or is not a picture. It has to be noticed that an object's property of being a picture is context-sensitive with respect to

- the situation it is used in, and
- the group of people who are dealing with the object as a picture.

This gives us the opportunity to explain the term *dominance* in more detail than at the beginning of this chapter, where we said the kind of visual signs dominating a picture defines to what class a picture belongs. We use the term "dominating" not in a quantitative way, but in the sense that signs which are essential for the viewer's tasks dominate a picture. Dominating a picture is therefore context-sensitive and we are not using any commonly applicable criterion, like size of signs or the surface area used. We leave the decision whether a group of signs dominate a picture or not to the viewer.

   To solve the problem with the initial question, we will follow Scholz's proposal and ask under what circumstances an object functions as a picture – *when is an object a picture?* Because we are dealing with pictures in computer science, communication via pictures is always intended to perform a specific task. So our classification, which we will discuss next, always depends on the task the viewer has at hand.

### 3.3.1  Characteristics of the Classes of Pictures

We now return to the terms introduced for the classes of pictures in Section 3.1 (presentational pictures, abstract-graphical pictures, and pictograms). We are now in a position to use the concepts of semiotics to discuss their significance.

*Presentational Pictures*

Because presentational pictures present properties of and relations in reality which are *visible* to humans (recall Section 3.1.1), presentational pictures are dominated by iconic signs. This dominance of iconic signs, in the sense of dominance we have discussed above, implies a low degree of arbitrariness. Nonetheless, the elements of presentational pictures can be chosen from a wide variety of possibilities to depict real objects. Present a real object to a group of people and ask them to make a picture of it, and you will get as many pictures as you have people in your group.

But still, presentational pictures must obey certain conventions pertaining to how objects and phenomena of the real world are presented. For example, curved surfaces may be illustrated by line drawings in one of a number of ways that viewers are still able to interpret. The long history of developing techniques for presenting depth in a picture demonstrates that producing and therefore viewing pictures is influenced by conventions, although we are normally unconscious of them.

The conventions used in presentational pictures are often generally applicable, which can leave the impression (and often did so) that presentational pictures are "intuitive" or "easily understood." But this is not the case, since the conventions must be learnt (perhaps at an early age in childhood). One effect of the general applicability of the conventions used in presentational pictures is that they normally do not need a legend for explaining special signs. We will come back to this point later.

The fact that presentational pictures are considered to be conventional should not lead to the conclusion that they are unambiguous.

*Abstract-Graphical Pictures*

In abstract-graphical pictures, properties of and relations in reality which are invisible to humans can be presented in an abstract way (recall Section 3.1.2). According to the context in which a picture is used, an abstract-graphical picture is dominated by symbolic signs. These symbolic signs can be either the graphical symbols we presented in Section 3.1.2 (see Figure 3.4) or areas with specific visible attributes (like color, texture, or brightness, which are substitutes for normally invisible properties).

The symbolic signs are largely arbitrary and are defined by conventions. The fact that many of these conventions are specialized for particular purposes explains why abstract-graphical pictures always need a legend to explain the meaning of the symbolic signs used in the picture. Exceptions are made in cases where the producers assume that all intended viewers are familiar with the symbolic signs and their interpretation. But let us not forget that even weather charts reaching the same audience through newspapers on a regular basis are accompanied by the same legend day after day!

*Pictograms*

For all these reasons we consider pictograms to be pictures. Here we differ from other authors, for example Horton (1994). Pictograms can be defined by the context and the motivation of their use and not by dominant usage of one of the sign categories (in contrast to presentational and abstract-graphical pictures). It should be clear at this point that pictograms consist of conventional signs (either symbols or icons).

Pictograms contain much less information than we normally expect from a picture (see also Chapters 5 and 10). Thus their meaning is easy to remember, and indeed this is the real reason for the fact that pictograms seem to be intuitively understandable. It is a fallacy that pictograms do not have to be learnt. Because of the conventionality of the signs used, a viewer has to decode these signs with the help of conventions. Because many of these conventions are learnt at an early age, we are very familiar with them and do not recognize them as conventions. The fact remains that conventions are involved in decoding pictograms.

Pictograms should not say a thousand words – they should say ONE word (a small number of signs). Usually designers of pictograms avoid the ambiguity that is the main feature of presentational and abstract-graphical pictures. A pictogram should denote one meaning for all who deal with it. We will study this assertion in more detail in Chapter 10. Pictograms often contain more than one sign, but in general significantly fewer signs than abstract-graphical and presentational pictures.

If we compare this semiotic analysis with the use of so-called *icons* in direct manipulation interfaces (see for example Shneiderman 1992), we come to the conclusion that the latter are indeed a mixture of icons, indices, and symbols (Marcus 1992). In the early days of direct manipulation (in the era of Xerox's Star and Apple's Lisa), the general term *icon* was established, even though it is incorrect from the semiotic point of view. In fact, all three kinds of signs can be found in computer interfaces; to avoid confusion we will call them all *pictograms*.

Since the three kinds of pictures are not completely disjoint, the relationship between them is non-trivial. The key is that not only the picture itself determines which class it falls into, but the use to which it is put; remember the question "When is an object a picture?". The way we have split up the set of all pictures is summarized in Figure 3.9; the overlap between abstract-graphical and presentational pictures represents pictures that can be either or, depending on the viewer. Pictograms can be in either class.

Although classifying a picture is context-sensitive and not objective, this classification is useful in the context of human-computer interaction, because the different kinds of pictures have different areas of usage and need different kinds of handling.

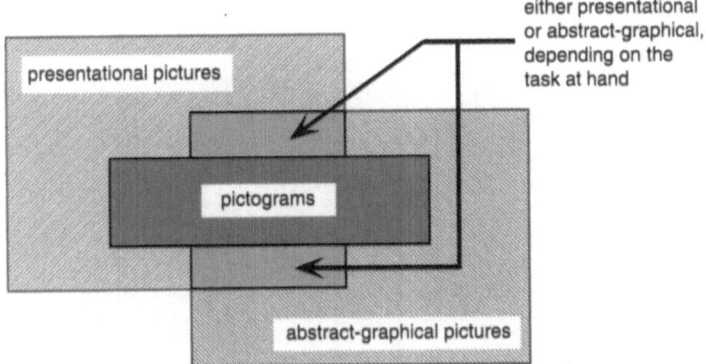

**Figure 3.9:** Classification scheme for pictures

## 3.3.2 Contours of the Terms of the Classification Scheme

We can now address special problems of differentiation within the classification scheme. First, when is a picture presentational and when abstract-graphical?

The distinction between the two kinds of pictures is very subtle, particularly when a presentational picture is overlaid by graphical symbols that may constitute an abstract-graphical picture in their own right (recall Section 3.1.2). What about Figure 3.10, where most parts are typical for presentational pictures, but the graphical symbols together form an abstract-graphical picture? In such cases, our approach puts the picture in one of the two classes depending on the *viewer's task at hand*. This may be an answer to "When is an object a picture?". An image can be classified as being presentational in one context, abstract-graphical in another.

It is a surprising observation that the existence of only a small number of graphical symbols can dominate the presentational nature of a picture and therefore cause it to be classified by an observer as an abstract-graphical picture. One explanation of this phenomenon is that graphical symbols draw attention to themselves, because they often have to be interpreted via specialized conventions, while understanding the iconic signs that build the presentational character of a picture is often automatic or unconscious. We will return to this phenomenon when we discuss the psychological processes involved in understanding pictures (see Chapter 4).

One efficient method of differentiating between presentational and abstract-graphical pictures is based on the question: *Does the picture still make the intended sense without the graphical symbols?* If not, the picture is an abstract-graphical one because the graphical symbols are the important conveyors of information. Let us recall that the answer to this question strongly depends on the purpose of the picture and the field of application, i.e., the context in which the picture is used. Some examples will illustrate the distinction.

*Example 1: Weather charts*

**Figure 3.10:** Presentational or abstract-graphical? Weather chart for July 12th, 1995
(© Deutscher Wetterdienst 1995)

The weather chart in Figure 3.10 would not make sense without the symbols representing areas of high and low pressure and cold and warm fronts. Also, the existence of the legend explaining the graphical symbols makes it obvious that the intended purpose of this picture is to inform about the weather. Even though the geography of Europe would be visible in a weather chart without graphical symbols, the main information intended about the weather in Europe would not. Therefore, weather charts can be normally classified as abstract-graphical pictures.

*Example 2: Movement in Comics*

**Figure 3.11:** Cartoons and their graphical symbols (Heaton 1990).
On the left, the falling of the hats is emphasized by little arcs, but the movement is still recognizable in the right where they are deleted.

Especially in cartoons, graphical symbols are used to represent movement (Figure 3.11). However, these graphical symbols represent only the temporal aspect of the scenes, and removing them does not generally change the meaning of the cartoon. Since a comic is still funny and entertaining without graphical symbols, we can, in general, classify them as presentational pictures.

*Example 3: Screen Dumps*

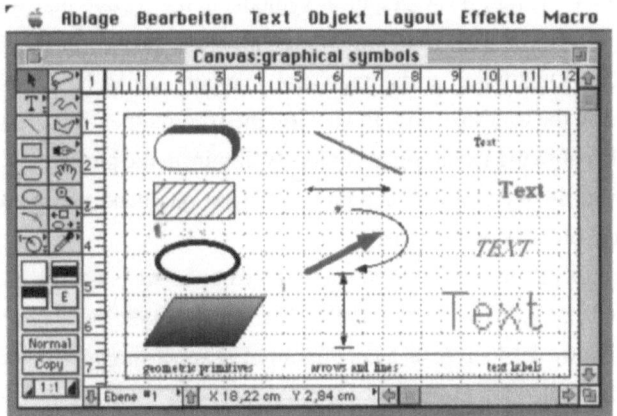

**Figure 3.12:** Screen dump corresponding to Figure 3.4

Because a screen dump (see Figure 3.12) should show exactly what a computer user can see on the screen, it is a presentational picture. This is also true if the picture presented on the screen itself is an abstract-graphical one like Figure 3.4.

*Example 4: Computer-Aided Design (CAD)*

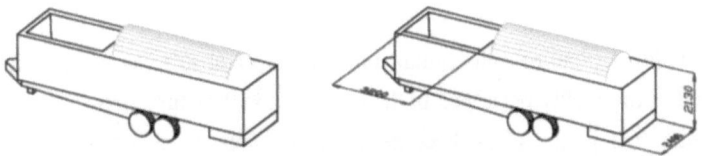

**Figure 3.13:** An example of CAD drawings (courtesy of Uwe Kircheis)

CAD is used for constructing objects in detail and the result is normally a technical drawing with labels showing the dimensions, as in Figure 3.13. All the dimension labels are graphical symbols, while the other signs presenting the object are iconic ones. It is interesting to notice that CAD drawings with dimension labels usually do not have a legend although the intended purpose is to convey information about exact dimensions.

The reason is that all users are assumed to be familiar with the meanings of different types of lines, arrows, etc. Whether such a CAD drawing is an abstract-graphical or a presentational picture, depends on the purpose of the drawing. If the appearance of the drawn object is important and the dimension labels are of little interest, then it can be classified as presentational, otherwise it would have to be abstract-graphical.

In all the above examples, it is evident that for pictures containing iconic signs as well as graphical symbols, what makes the picture either abstract-graphical or presentational is the use to which it is put. If the graphical symbols in the picture play an essential part in allowing the viewer *to carry out his or her task*, the picture is classified as being abstract-graphical. Otherwise, if the graphical symbols could be eliminated without adversely affecting the user's purpose in viewing the picture, then it is classified as being presentational, because the iconic signs obviously dominate the picture.

We now turn to the relation between pictograms on one hand and presentational and abstract-graphical pictures on the other.

For the design of pictograms, both iconic and symbolic signs can be used. The preference for symbols or icons in pictograms decides their nature as abstract-graphical or presentational. Figure 3.14 suggests a continuum of abstract-graphical and presentational pictograms via the following examples:

- for customs made of iconic signs (left),
- for an elevator made of iconic and symbolic signs (middle), and
- for a meeting point made of symbolic signs only (right)*.

The relations between the three kinds of pictures are numerous and can be as follows:

- pictograms can be either of presentational or of abstract-graphical character (recall Figure 3.14),
- pictograms can be part of an abstract-graphical picture (recall user icons in Figure 3.6),
- presentational pictures can contain pictograms or abstract-graphical pictures, if they are part of the reality portrayed in the presentational picture, and
- presentational pictures can become abstract-graphical pictures by adding graphical symbols, if the specific context needs this addition.

---

* While we consider the rightmost pictogram of Figure 3.14 to be made of symbolic signs (arrows and a circle) only, there is another interpretation: The circle can be interpreted as a head, while the upwards pointed arrow can be interpreted as a body with arms. Indeed, this interpretation holds for each arrow.

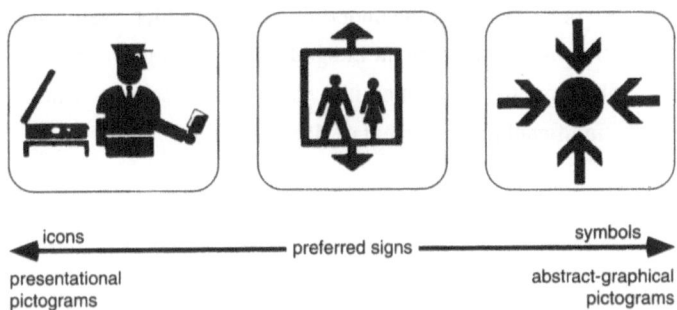

icons — preferred signs — symbols

presentational pictograms | abstract-graphical pictograms

**Figure 3.14:** Continuum between abstract-graphical and presentational pictograms

## 3.4 Discussion

The classification scheme has been developed for the specific purpose of analyzing pictures used in interactive systems. Such uses include:

- generation of complete pictures from verbal descriptions of data,
- generation of combined text-picture presentations,
- addition of pictorial elements or texts to existing pictures,
- handling semantic information about pictures (generating, providing access to, searching in, etc.), and
- user interaction with pictures via verbal input or gestures.

We will show in the remainder of the book that each class of pictures needs a specific kind of storage, semantic representation, user interaction functionality, etc. The key point of the classification is to be able to discuss the issues such as:

- what a picture is made of,
- which kind of signs are used, and
- how many signs are used,

because these criteria define how the pictures can be handled within interactive systems. While our classification scheme for pictures has been developed specifically for their use in interactive systems, other classification schemes assume the pictures are embedded in surrounding text (see the pioneering work of Knowlton 1966, as well as Alesandrini 1987). In previous classifications, the use of pictures in an analogical sense is important, whereas in our case pictures reflect the underlying data to which users refer in the course of a dialogue. Pictograms today play an integral role in interactive systems and must be paid a corresponding amount of attention in a classification scheme, whereas pictograms are not generally significant in the context of illustrated texts.

*Deer Hunt*
Valltorta Gorge (Spain)

# Chapter
# 4

# Picture Processing by Humans

Picture processing depends on a variety of conditions. Two of these are the environment and context of the picture and the knowledge of the observer. Let us have a look at van Gogh's "Crows over the corn field" in Figure 4.1.

A possible reaction could be to recognize the cornfield and the black birds and to imagine the day van Gogh observed this landscape. This reaction is probably completely different if the observer is told that this painting is one of van Gogh's last before his suicide. Suddenly, the black birds, for example, are interpreted differently. By the same token, pictures used in human-computer interaction are also subjective and depend on the setting. In this chapter, we come to terms with the fact that we must study psychological issues relating to human understanding of pictures as a prerequisite for the effective use of pictures in human-computer interaction.

Traditionally, pictures have been made by humans for humans. In modern times, various different techniques have come into use for producing and analyzing pictures, for instance using computers to generate pictures (the field of computer graphics) or image processing to analyze images produced by special cameras. These techniques are clearly understood, even though the use of these methods has, in practice, not reached the level of perfection that would be desirable.

In the field of human cognitive processes for producing and comprehending pictures, there is a wide gap between the different particular theories and practical experience. A method frequently used to try to refute theories is to find examples from everyday life.

**Figure 4.1:** Vincent van Gogh: Crows over the corn field,
painted July 7th – 10th, 1890 (Erpel 1989)

Our goal here is to survey some of the important issues rather than to provide a thorough treatment of the subject. The chapter does not contain an analysis of the various cognitive theories, nor does it attempt to settle the difference between the representatives of different sub-disciplines. Instead, we present some interesting and in part surprising results of psychological experiments concerning the comprehension of pictures to clarify those characteristics of pictures pertaining to human-computer interaction.

## 4.1 Pictures and the Iconic Code

Although everybody is used to looking at pictures, and a lot of people are able to produce such pictures themselves, there is no general answer to the question of what a picture is, either in the sciences or stemming from everyday experience. Most investigations in this area refer only to pictures drawn by artists reflecting reality, i.e., presentational pictures in our classification scheme. We begin our discussion of the problem of defining the main features of pictures by citing Weidenmann (1988), who has carried out extensive investigations into the comprehension of graphics. He refers to the following characteristics of pictures as being widely used for presentational pictures, but which he considers to be insufficient for a definition:

- Pictures are perceived visually.
- Pictures are similar to the objects being represented.
- Pictures can be perceived at a glance.
- Pictures are made by humans.
- Pictures are independent of particular (natural) languages.

No single characteristic is enough to define pictures or to differentiate them from sculptures, traffic lights, etc., and together they are not sufficient to characterize, for instance, a piece of abstract art. The second characteristic apparently refers only to presentational pictures. Modern technology allows the automatic production of pictures so that even the fourth claim is often not true. Therefore, these characteristics cannot constitute a definition of the term *picture*. It seems to be an unsolved problem to define the term *picture* in its generality, although much research has been done in this area (see for example Boehm 1994 and Sachs-Hombach 1995). The problem is getting worse as techniques are developed for generating, processing, and presenting pictures by machines instead of humans.

One central aspect of pictures is the *iconic code*. A code defines in general the syntactic and semantic rules for building correct symbol combinations. Some symbol combinations produce a meaning and are relevant for communication. The iconic code is a so-called weak code as opposed to a strong code like the Morse alphabet. The reason is the absence of well-defined syntactic and semantic rules for the iconic code. The symbol repertoire consists of a number of circle-like regions, line-like objects, and contiguous regions of a common pattern. Variations of these elements include color, position, pattern, and other attributes. But there are no rules for combining them to express a specific meaning. Eco (1972) captures the essence of this argument when he says that in a human face, a little circle and a semi-circle mean the eye and the eye-lid, while the same little circle and semi-circle in another context mean a banana and a grape. Figure 4.2 shows various meanings of black circles and dots in different contexts.

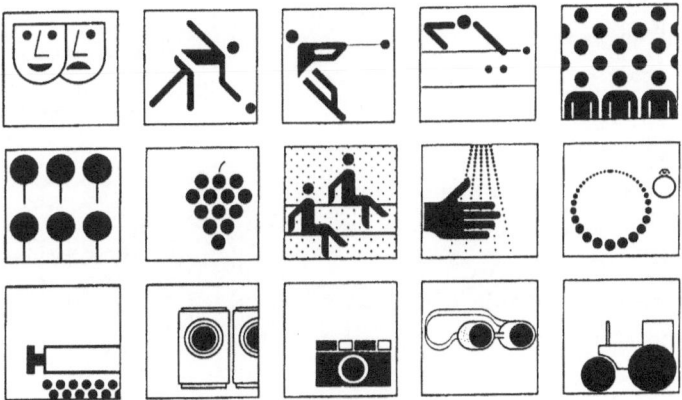

**Figure 4.2:** Black dots in different contexts (Braun 1993)

The attribute *weak* for the iconic code is not merely a disadvantage with respect to language and its formalization; on the contrary, it is also an advantage for all picture producers as code users, because they have at their disposal a multitude of design possibilities. Pictures represent the private code of their producers, and the production process is only restricted by the pragmatic criterion that the picture is important for the observer. It is interesting in the context of the iconic code that despite the weakness of the code, pictures have a high communicative capability.

It is confusing that researchers who have investigated the iconic code have referred to presentational pictures, in particular works of art. In our case, the iconic code tends indeed to be weak for presentational pictures. By contrast, abstract-graphical pictures often use symbols, each of which has a meaning that is generally agreed upon, which actually suggests a strong iconic code. An example of an abstract-graphical picture which has a strong code is the German definition of the Nassi-Shneiderman flowchart symbols (DIN 66261), which defines the use and the meaning of each symbol very precisely (see Figure 4.3). However, while the meaning of each individual symbol is often formalizable, there may be no algorithm to determine the meaning of an entire picture composed of such symbols. This is particularly the case when symbols are placed over a presentational picture, yielding an abstract-graphical one (recall Figure 3.10). Thus the iconic code for abstract-graphical pictures may be stronger than for presentational pictures, but it is still weak and thus leaves room for interpretation.

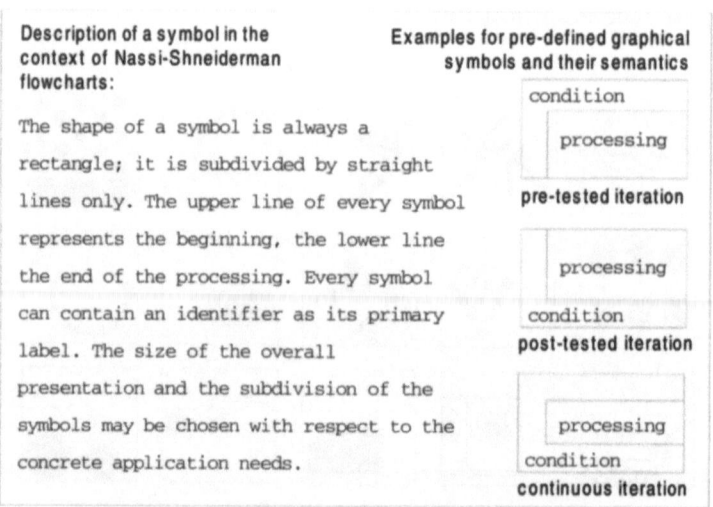

**Figure 4.3:** Excerpt from the German DIN Standard 66261
for Nassi-Shneiderman flowchart symbols

## 4.2 Perception, Learning and Cognition

Human understanding of pictures is only a small part of research into human understanding processes in general. There is still no generally accepted theory of human understanding and thinking. However, in many fields, such as neural psychology, perception-psychology, cognitive psychology, and communication theory, these processes are observed, analyzed, and measured so as to be integrated into existing theories.

In the literature there is not even consensus in the first and most fundamental question, how pictures are perceived by humans. Gibson (1971) assumes that perception is stimulus driven, meaning that information is picked up directly from the optic array. On the other hand, Gombrich (1969) emphasizes the role of the viewer, in that they assume that viewers construct their own interpretation based on conventions and expectations. Indeed, this approach allows Gombrich (1986) to introduce the notion of *projection* of the experience and expectations of the viewer onto the phenomena seen. However, this requires firstly empty or vague places in a picture which can act as a "projection screen", and secondly hints to direct the viewer as to how these gaps can be filled. (We will come back to this point in Section 15.7 when we compare the effect of shaded images with the effect of sketches).

Yet another position is taken by Arnheim (1974), who contends that picture perception is the viewer's response to the basic forms and forces present in the picture. To him, the Gestalt laws of organization are the primary conveyors of meaning.

In any case, it has been shown that the time viewers need to decipher a picture can be surprisingly small (see Willows and Houghton 1987, Houghton and Willows 1987). Indeed, the gist of a picture can often be ascertained within 300 milliseconds. However, it is also rather dependent upon the fixation point of the viewer. For example, Figure 4.4 shows the so-called duckrabbit, an image of a rabbit, assuming the viewer fixes on point A, while the same picture is usually interpreted as being a duck if the viewer fixes on point B (Tsal and Kolbet 1985; see also Jastrow 1900)[*].

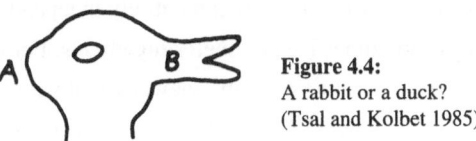

Figure 4.4:
A rabbit or a duck?
(Tsal and Kolbet 1985)

---

[*] See also http://lainet3.lainet.com/~ausbourn/illus-10.htm

However controversial are questions surrounding the issue of perception of pictures, it is undisputed in the scientific literature that pictures can be used for teaching facts, concepts, and procedures. Yet many different kinds of pictures are possible of one and the same object, and learning performance depends heavily on the specific kind of picture in relationship to the viewer's task.

Initially subjects' learning performance can be studied without regard for how this learning takes place. Studies show that a number of factors influence the effectiveness of pictures. Among these are (Peeck 1987):

- *the esthetic, artistic, and technical quality,*
  such as balance in composition and the use of color,
- *the authenticity and validity,*
  i.e., the extent to which viewers believe what they are shown, and
- *the density of the information,*
  referring to both the number of picture elements and the degree of detail to which each element is depicted.

The extent to which learning can take place is affected by a variety of factors. Also referring to Peeck (1987), important groups of these are:

- *affective factors,*
  describing for example whether a picture appears interesting or imaginative,
- *motivational factors,*
  describing how willing and eager the viewer is to study the picture to ascertain its "message", and how the picture itself affects this willingness. For example, an esthetically pleasing, credible-looking picture may motivate the viewer more than a diagram with obvious errors. Finally, there are
- *cognitive factors,*
  which determine the extent to which the viewer is able to decipher the nature of the objects or concepts depicted.

These three groups of factors are not entirely independent of one another, and their interrelationships sometimes lead to interesting effects. For example, an image that is difficult to decipher may serve to raise the viewer's motivation to a higher level than an image that is easy to decipher (Klix 1992). Another example is contained in an observation by Dwyer (1972) who noted that "aesthetically pleasing visuals may be deceptive in their instructional value".

Considerable attention has been paid in the literature to types of picture and their effectiveness. The discussion in the literature was initiated by Dale (1946), who suggested that the higher the level of realism, the greater the probability that it may facilitate learning. This suggestion may have been motivated by the fact that photos were still rare in instructional materials of the time. Certainly such reasons have driven the quest for photorealism in computer graphics over the past decades.

Dale's thesis has been repeatedly challenged in the last half-century. Travers (1964, p. 380), for example, went so far as to call it "worship of the false God". Only recently has such criticism had an effect within the computer graphics community; we shall return to such non-photorealistic renderings in Chapter 15.

Investigations by Dwyer (1972) suggest that the effectiveness of realism is very dependent on the time and effort the reader is willing and able to invest studying the picture. Figure 4.5 shows examples of Dwyer's pictures of the human heart used for instructional purposes. If viewing time is limited, simple line drawings tend to be most effective. Given more time, there is a better chance that viewers will take advantage of the additional information provided by the details. However, such details may also "detract from relevant and important learning cues" (Dwyer 1972, p. 91).

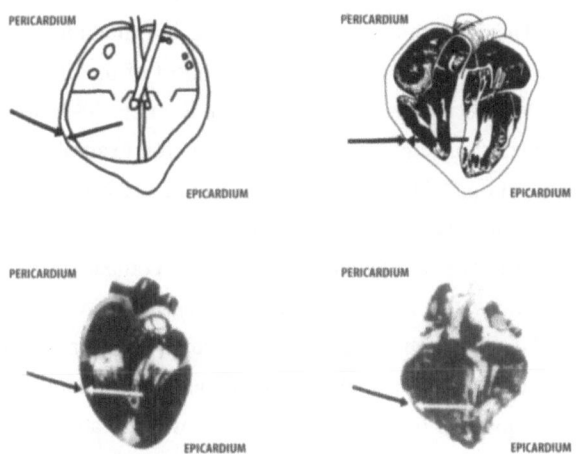

**Figure 4.5:** Pictures of a heart used by Dwyer (1972)

# 4.3  Cognitive Theories

For our purpose, it is convenient that the visual sense is more popular in research than the other senses. Experiments show that the understanding process is divided into more than one level. These encompass actions from the first glance at a picture to detailed ideas about it. In the first phase, neural processes receive light as visual impulses. In the eye's receptors, the optical energy is transformed into electrical energy which is transmitted via nerve fibers into different parts of the visual cortex, a special area of the brain. The brain, including its nerve fibers, contains millions of neurons. But the information that reaches the brain is not a copy of the outside world, because the electrical signals are sifted and altered on the way to the brain. This pre-processing contains the first filter mechanisms of the human neural system. The fact that input information is distributed among different parts of the visual cortex makes parallel visual analyses possible. These analyses are based on the chaotic and collective activities of millions of neurons.

The next step contains operations like the recognition of color and size, the location of objects, and the interpretation of the outside world with the information encoded in the neural structures. The cognitive processes of humans have to be analyzed to give answers to questions such as:

- How do humans recognize information?
- How do humans associate situations already recognized or pictures with their past experience?

Now it is necessary to point out different approaches to explain cognition: cognitivism and connectionism. The basis for cognitivism is the information-processing paradigm which is still dominant in research and literature. In most of the literature, this approach is assumed without any discussion (see for example Staufer 1987, Spada 1990). At the other end of the scale, connectionism is represented for example by the research of Peschl (1990), Winograd and Flores (1992), and Varela (1990), the last of whom very severely criticizes the information processing approach.

The main idea of cognitivism is to define cognition as computing with symbolic representations. Hence it follows that intelligent behavior has as a prerequisite the ability to represent the world. The term "representation" is a central one for this approach. In this context we must recall the popular slogan "No computation without representation" (see Varela 1990). For the question of how to represent knowledge about the world, Minsky's model of knowledge processing is used (we will come to this in Section 10.3). Newell and Simon (1972) postulated five components for such an information processing system:

- a set of simple symbols (alphabet of the system),
- a set of rules for generating complex symbols and symbolic structures (the grammar of the system),
- memory, from which simple and complex symbols as well as more complex symbolic structures can be retrieved,
- a set of operations and processes which operate on the set of symbols and symbolic structures and can, for instance, change, add, or delete them, and
- processors that control the behavior of the system.

For discussions on how the complicated human cognitive processes can be explained on this basis, we refer to Anderson (1989) and Klix (1980). Here we point out that the basic structures, Minsky's frames, are highly aggregated constructs with information about stereotyped situations. They are not comparable to neurons.

The last statement illustrates the differences between the two approaches. Connectionism postulates the existence of a network consisting of many simple and non-intelligent components which are massively connected and similar to neurons. Peschl (1990) calls these components *units* which work in parallel and locally without superior control. The combination of such units shows interesting qualities which embody the sought-after cognitive performance (see Varela 1990). The principle of such networks is the development of appropriate connections between units with the help of a rule for changing the connection. The best-known rule for this learning is the Hebbian rule (Hebb 1949) based on the correlated activities of neurons.

At this point we leave aside psychological approaches to explain some different theories concerning cognitive processes. We refrain from judging these approaches and theories because we find ourselves in a dilemma. Computer scientists think naturally in terms of the information processing approach, and indeed many of the results of Artificial Intelligence are very interesting (see Winston 1992). But the wide gap between highly qualified systems such as those for medical diagnosis (for instance MYCIN, INTERNIST; see Jackson 1990 as well as Miller and Masarie 1990) on the one hand, and the inability of Artificial Intelligence to imitate the faculties and abilities of four-year-old children on the other, shows us the need for new approaches.

Regarding pictures, we find that most research experiments in cognitive and perceptual psychology about the understanding of pictures are based on cognitivism. Many studies are based on the dual coding theory of Pavio (1971), who tried to explain the differences between remembering pictures and words. He postulated a distinct cognitive processing system for each symbolic system. Pictures activate the visual system while linguistic information activates the verbal system. The special feature of pictures is their double coding, which means that pictures activate a verbal connotation, too. This theory seems logical, but is not generally accepted, which shows that we still have a long way to go in the area of picture understanding.

All these investigations demonstrate the aptness of Weidenmann's summary: "As to the central question, how information is extracted from pictures, and how the recognition of pictures is bound to the knowledge base of the viewer, there exist neither sound empirical nor theoretical bases" (Weidenmann 1988).

## 4.4 Understanding of Pictures: The Communicative Theory Point of View

In spite of the above sceptical statement, Weidenmann tries to analyze and describe the understanding of pictures in a communicative-theoretic framework, independent of cognitive psychological questions, stressing the representation of pictorial information. He developed a scheme of phases of picture understanding (see Weidenmann 1988 and Figure 4.6).

In this context, pictures have to be considered to be *informative products*. This leads to two conclusions. First, pictures are treated by the observer as a product, and the situation of looking at a picture is a communicative one. Second, the picture is considered to be the result of a decision making process by the producer relative to the *subject* and the *gestalt* (content and form).

The cognitive-psychological basis for Weidenmann's investigations are so-called *mental models*. Mental models are the particular representation of the context for every person (see Norman 1983). Humans develop mental models about their environment, so that cognitive processes influence existing mental models or extend them. The conclusion is that the mental models of novices and experts of the same event, for instance, are very different from one another. Mental models influence the production and reception process of pictures, because the producer of a picture projects his or her mental model into the picture and the recipient constructs a mental model on the basis of his or her perception of the picture. A central point of mental models is their pictorial nature, since the main source for mental models is visual perception. This has links to "imagery" research, in which *mental pictures* are investigated (see Kosslyn 1980 and Sachs-Hombach 1995b).

To describe Weidenmann's different phases of understanding pictures (Figure 4.6), we need to explain some special terms:

*Ecological schemes* are special mental models which develop as a result of human perception and action. These are the results of frequent and direct experience and relations in the real world. These schemes are very salient and easy to use, and allow a first understanding of pictures very quickly. Automatic understanding uses these special schemes, which are very efficient. Other schemes involve symbolic knowledge representation, i.e., codified information.

*Normalization* is a human process for removing the ambiguity in pictures. Normalization is applied when the information to be processed cannot be related to an existing scheme. Ecological schemes are used first to remove ambiguity during the normalization process. If this proves impossible, then additional searching or extracting operations in existing knowledge or operations are implemented to develop new schemes.

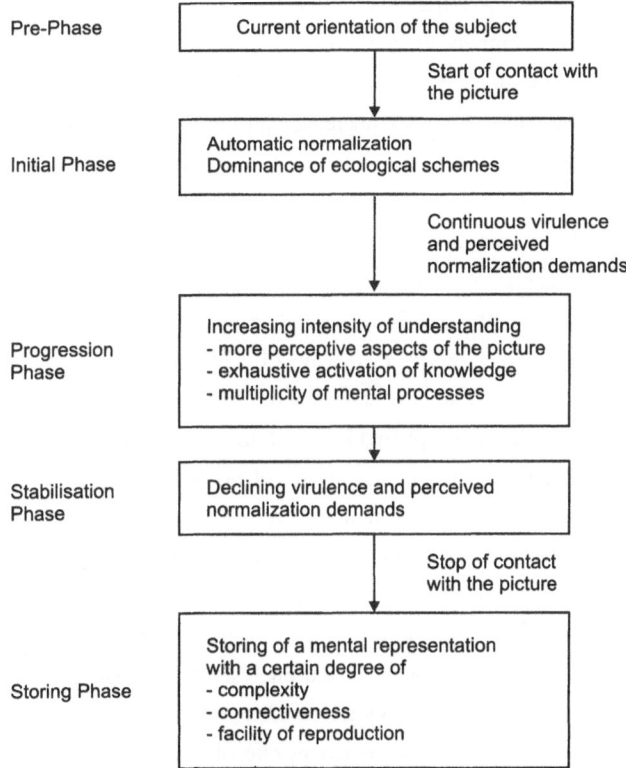

**Figure 4.6:** Phases of picture understanding (Weidenmann 1988)

The perceived *normalization demands* influence the intensity of understanding. They stem from the relations of the characteristics of the picture to the characteristics of the observer, and can be influenced by special tasks given to the observer. The subjective perception of how interesting a picture is can be a measurement for the perceived normalization demands. This means "normal" pictures have low normalization demands, while pictures with very innovative designs often elicit higher normalization demands.

*Virulence* is an attribute of schemes, scripts, or frames which are especially closely connected with one another. The number of other frames activated increases with the virulence of an activated scheme.

To summarize the communicative aspects of picture understanding, we will discuss the different phases of Figure 4.6. In the *pre-phase*, a subject in a particular situation (with respect to emotions, orientation, current ideas, etc.) first looks at a picture. Instructions, motivation, the context, or other factors influence the special situation. In the *initial phase,* the observer tries to understand the picture with the help of automatic normalizations. If no virulent concepts are activated, the observer perceives no normalization demands. In this case, the viewing of the picture stops. In the other case, the *progression phase* is commenced, the observer perceives more picture elements, and many complex psychological operations are carried out. During the *stabilization phase,* the perceived normalization demands decrease and the virulence stabilizes. The result is that the viewing of the picture stops. In the *storing phase*, the information generated during the progression and stabilization phases are stored in frames and schemes.

An essential factor in this theoretical framework is that high perceived normalization demands lead to an intensive examination and processing of the picture by the viewer. For the design of human-computer interfaces, it can thus be very useful to provoke high normalization demands on the user. Two ways of achieving this goal are possible. First, the picture itself may be made to appear very interesting to the user for some reason, and second, the picture may be accompanied by a task the user has to carry out with it.

Two interrelated variables of a picture, its level of interest and its ambiguity, directly influence the perceived normalization demands of the user. This is not the right place to give instructions on how to make pictures interesting and ambiguous, but several techniques for producing ambiguity in pictures have provided the basis for cognitive research. One example is the experiment of Kunen, Green, and Waterman (1979) showing that memory performance depends on the intensity of the analysis while looking at a picture. They presented outline drawings of different objects to their subjects. The outlines differed – they were drawn with solid lines or were dotted in one of several ways (dense, medium, or sparse). The results with dotted outlines were the best. Their explanation, that the dotted outlines required more cognitive processing, can be seen as a parallel to high perceived normalization demands because of the ambiguity of the dotted outlines. To appreciate this, see Figure 4.7. To us, this picture seems much more interesting than a similar picture with a clearly drawn Dalmatian in it.

**Figure 4.7:**
An intriguing
dotted drawing
(Anderson 1980)

**Figure 4.8:** A page from "Where's Waldo?" (Handford 1987)

If a picture is accompanied by a task for the observer, he or she has to extract information from the picture. If the user does not know the picture very well, he or she perceives normalization demands to carry out the task. The best example to show this effect is the well-known picture book series "Where's Waldo?" (see Handford 1987) which is very popular among children, not only in North America. The pictures in these books are crowded with more or less similar-looking people doing strange things (see Figure 4.8).

There are too many details there to be a coherent story for children to follow, but the idea that makes these books best-sellers is their title, "Where's Waldo", which is the general question to be answered with respect to each picture. Waldo (see Figure 4.9) can be found in each of the pictures because he always wears a shirt with red and white stripes and a woolly hat and has a camera with him. (Finding Waldo in Figure 4.8 is left as an exercise for the reader!)

This example shows how directly the perceived normalization demands and the associated time and intensity of the normalization process depend on the task to be carried out by studying a picture.

**Figure 4.9:**
Waldo (Handford 1987)

These examples show how the theoretical scheme of the human understanding of pictures provide a suitable framework for categorizing existing interfaces and designing new ones. In later chapters, this framework will be put into practice and discussed.

## 4.5  Human Memory Performance

The discussion of human memory performance depends on theoretical models of the memory structure and the kinds of information being stored and accessed in the memory. The field of memory research is like other psychological research fields in that there is more than one theory. We will present two (taken from Spada 1990), discuss the interesting results, and then show that these theories are not contradictory. Their common elements provide the basis for a discussion and for the experiments presented below.

The *multi-storage model* of Atkinson and Shiffrin (1968) differentiates memory into three separate stores. *Sensory registers* at the beginning of the information process receive external impulses and store them for a very short time period of only some hundred milliseconds. But the capacity of these sensory stores is very high. For the different senses, different kinds of specific registers have been designated, for instance an iconic memory or an echoic storage. A short-term store gets its information from the sensory registers and from a *long-term store*. The short-term store is a central unit where information is stored for only some minutes. Another term for it is *working memory*, because all the information that has to be processed consciously is there. Its capacity is very small: Miller (1956) describes the limit as being five to nine semantic units. The *long-term store* has a seemingly unlimited capacity and is permanent, where the entire knowledge of a human is stored. Besides the memory structure, the multi-store model also contains *control processes*. These are controlled by the human and relate to strategies like searching in the long-term store, rehearsal, or information transmission between the different stores.

The *one-storage model* of Shiffrin (1977) is a refinement of the multi-storage model. The most important change is the hypothesis of only one big storage unit, the long-term store. The other stores discussed above (sensory registers and short-term store) are only parts of this long-term store. All the steps for inputing information work on this store. The term "working memory" is used for activated semantic units in the long-term store and so it is not a separate store. But only the information units activated at any one time can be processed.

At this point it is not important which model is the right one, because we can make a number of summary statements which are true for both models. These are:

- A large amount of sensory input can only be stored for some milliseconds.
- Interesting input is stored in the working storage for a short time.
- Information processing is only possible with information from the working store.
- The long-term store has unlimited capacity.
- Information processing is controlled by control processes.

This outline sketch suffices for our purposes. We now briefly present some practical results from psychological experiments related to the human ability to recall pictures.

Weidenmann (1986) describes the performance of memory with pictures as "phenomenal." He refers to experiments by Stading, Conezio, and Haber (1970) who showed subjects 2,560 slides in a short time. After some days they were shown item-pairs which contained a known and a new slide. The memory performance was higher than 90%.

An interesting question is which factors influence memory performance positively. The following experiments investigated several possibilities.

- That memory performance depends on the *meaning quality of the picture* was the result of investigations of Bower, Karlin, and Dueck (1975). They show that the memory performance is significantly better when the subjects knew the meaning of the pictures.
- Mandler and Ritchey (1977) observed that *relevant changes to the meaning of a picture* were identified with a much higher probability than those with irrelevant changes.
- Friedman (1979) postulated the frame-stereotyped storing of elements of a picture. In her experiment, subjects saw a picture from the cognitive frame "kitchen." In the memory test, the toaster on the kitchen table was changed to a radio. This change was rarely noticed, while a change into an untypical kitchen object was quickly noticed.

Summarizing memory performance pertaining to pictures alone, it can by said that picture memory performance is in general extremely high, and this is the reason for the immense significance of pictures in communicative processes.

**Figure 4.10:** Images used to measure memory performance
(Nelson, Metzler, and Reed 1974)

A considerably body of knowledge has been amassed on memory performance as a function of the way information has been presented. For example, Neslon, Metzler, and Reed (1974; see also Staufer 1987) compared memory performance when trying to remember pictures in each of a variety of styles, then compared the results to memory performance when trying to remember a phrase describing the picture. Figure 4.10 shows three pictures used in the experiment: a photo, a line-drawing showing the context, and a line-drawing showing only the objects (persons) in focus in the photo. In addition, the phrase "A laughing old man holding a child" was used as a fourth message.

Figure 4.11 shows the results. The memory performance for the pictures varied insignificantly, whereas the performance pertaining to the sentence was significantly worse.

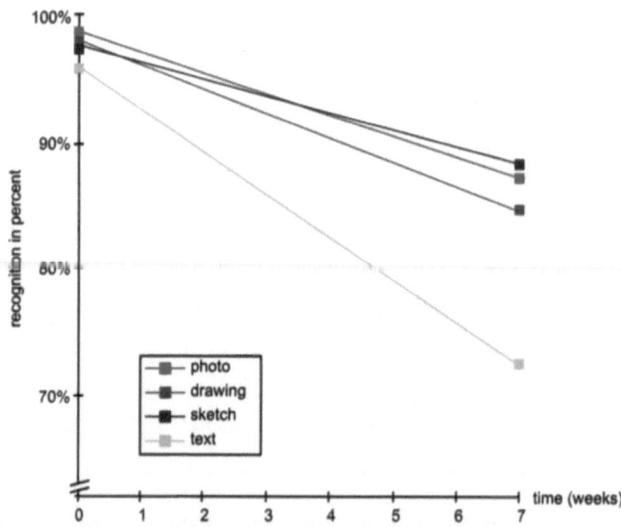

**Figure 4.11:** Memory performance for the four media (see Nelson, Metzler, and Reed 1974)

Another kind of experiment involves comparisons between memory performance of pictures and words. Especially in education, the effect of words and pictures or combinations of them have been discussed. The different results (see Weidenmann 1986) were explained according to the dual coding theory of Paivio. Experiments by Haber (1970) justify the thesis that pictures are not coded verbally, because of the difficulty of describing a picture verbally. These results show the disagreement between researchers in the field on representing pictorial information.

It is indisputable that students prefer to have pictures in teaching material, especially colored pictures. Another indisputable fact is that pictures can positively or negatively influence the reading of texts. A curious episode in this context was the discussion in the last century about large pictures on posters in schools, because of the fear that children could get confused by the abundance of information in these pictures (see Bernhauser 1979).

*Wondjina Figure of the Australian Aborigines (humanoid without ears and mouth causing rainfall)*

# Chapter

# 5

# Information Flow During Human-Computer Interaction *

Whenever a user operates a computer, information flows across the interface between the two. But what is the nature of this information? How does it flow, how can this flow be quantified? How does the context affect the flow of information? To what extent does the flow depend on the user's competence before beginning the session on the computer? In this chapter, we will address these and related questions. The goal will be to devise a framework for designing and analyzing human-computer dialogues.

## 5.1 Information Theory

The term *information* is used in many different ways throughout the scientific and philosophic literature. It is sometimes used argumentatively in informal ways, other times it is measured with precision. Despite the lack of agreement on usage of the term, everyone has an intuitive understanding òf its meaning. This is reflected in the definition in Webster's Ninth Collegiate Dictionary (Figure 5.1).

* Pete Wright of the University of York contributed significantly to this chapter within the EU-funded project "Interactively Rich Systems."

**in·for·ma·tion** \,in-fər-'mā-shən\ *n* (14c)  **1** : the communication or reception of knowledge or intelligence  **2 a** (1) : knowledge obtained from investigation, study, or instruction  (2) : INTELLIGENCE, NEWS  (3) : FACTS, DATA  **b** : the attribute inherent in and communicated by one of two or more alternative sequences or arrangements of something (as nucleotides in DNA or binary digits in a computer program) that produce specific effects  **c** (1) : a signal or character (as in a communication system or computer) representing data  (2) : something (as a message, experimental data, or a picture) which justifies change in a construct (as a plan or theory) that represents physical or mental experience or another construct  **d** : a quantitative measure of the content of information; *specif* : a numerical quantity that measures the uncertainty in the outcome of an experiment to be performed  **3** : the act of informing against a person  **4** : a formal accusation of a crime made by a prosecuting officer as distinguished from an indictment presented by a grand jury — **in·for·ma·tion·al** \-shnəl, -shən-ᵊl\ *adj* — **in·for·ma·tion·less** \-shən-ləs\ *adj*

**Figure 5.1:** Information (Webster 1990)

According to Strombach (1992; see also Sperber and Wilson 1986), information is considered to have a *source,* such as a person, a book, or the television; a *destination,* such as a person or a computer; a *channel,* consisting of physical states or processes, such as tones, electrical impulses, waving a hand, or winking an eye; and a signal. A message must be encoded by the sender and decoded by the receiver (Figure 5.2).

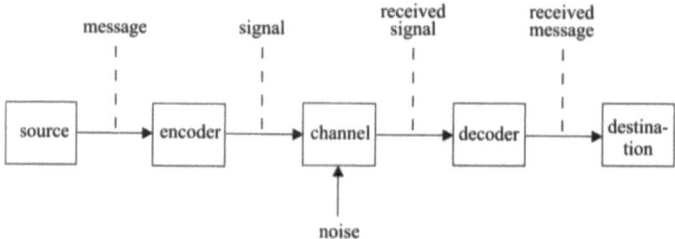

**Figure 5.2:** Sending a message across a channel (Sperber and Wilson 1986; see also Shannon and Weaver 1969)

Applied to human interaction, Figure 5.2 can be made more specific to account for speech (Figure 5.3).

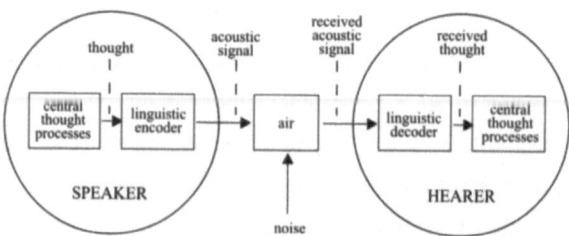

**Figure 5.3:** Speech communication (Sperber and Wilson 1986; see also Shannon and Weaver 1969)

Shannon and Weaver (1969; see also, e.g., Gunzenhäuser 1962) suggested measuring the content with respect to the probabilities of individual symbols in the alphabet of a language. Given a set of $n$ symbols $x_1$, $x_2$, ..., $x_n$, where the symbol $x_i$ appears with probability $p(x_i)$, the amount of information $I$ in a message of length $m$ is

$$I = \sum_{i=1}^{m} p(x_i) \ln p(x_i) \quad \text{bits.}$$

While Shannon's view of information formed the basis for a great deal of scientific literature in the 1960s, most of the literature since then discards this view for two reasons (Strombach 1992). First, in the context of computer science, a more pragmatic view of information is required to complement the more engineering approach to such topics as programming and user interface design, rather than following a strictly mathematical tradition. Second, and perhaps more important, is that as soon as people are involved in a communication process, the meaning of a message is what is of interest, rather than the probabilities of the symbols used. The meaning of a message depends not only on the syntax of the message but also its semantics and pragmatics (Brown and Yule 1983). Under this latter view, the potential information of a message is much more complex. It depends not only on the transmitted content of the message but also on semantic and inferential processes used by the recipient in interpreting the content of the message. What makes matters difficult is that representing semantics within the machine is still an open problem and models for the representation of semantics are not yet properly understood.

The literature in information theory tends to concentrate on the transmission of signals and symbols. A somewhat different situation arises when pictures are what is being transmitted. When these pictures are conveyed to users, to count the number of bits in a picture in the Shannonian sense yields a measure for the information flow which is difficult to use. It is interesting to recall again the old proverb "A picture says more than a thousand words." In part it asserts that a picture says words. Perhaps these could be measured in some way, but how? It also asserts that many words are "spoken" by a picture. Presumably the set of words is different for each viewer of the picture. But if a picture says words, how can these be dependent on the recipient? After all, a lecturer gives the same speech to all those present.

Indeed, the context of a picture accounts for its usefulness to a large degree. In human-computer interaction, this is rather complicated, however, as the communication often involves a melange of pictures and language (or symbols).

## 5.2 Information Transfer Between Humans

To try to understand better the mechanisms underlying human-computer interaction, we shall first take a step back and examine certain aspects of human communication as they have been studied by sociologists and psychologists. Human beings communicate in a language enriched by such parameters as speed, tone, and intonation, and accompanied by gestures and other body language. This situation can be compared to human-computer interaction involving some symbols (words), plus pictures from the computer and gestures from the user. In both human-human communication and human-computer interaction we thus have a part that is more readily formalized (language) and a part that is less readily formalized (pictures, gestures).

The sociologist Goffman (1959) analyzed human communication and developed the following definitions for information produced by a person in order to convey information to another person. He proposed

*information given*, composed of word symbols or their substitutes which the producer uses exclusively for the purpose of communicating information that the producer and recipient associate with these word symbols.

This is thus the part of the communication which can be formalized in a relatively straightforward manner. Goffman went one step further to define

*information given off*, pertaining to further information conveyed by the producer which can be used by the recipient to draw conclusions about the producer, provided this information was conveyed by the producer for reasons other than the transmission of information.

Goffman underlines the importance of *reasoning* on the part of the recipient. It is only on the basis of this process that the information given off by the producer can be obtained by the recipient. Indeed, if the recipient cannot infer anything from the message because no appropriate reasoning mechanism is available, no information is considered to have been given off. Thus not only must the form of the information given be amenable to a reasoning process on the part of the recipient, but the success of this aspect of the communication depends on the abilities of the semantic and inferential abilities of the recipient (see again Brown and Yule 1983).

The linguistic perspective of Sperber and Wilson (1986) distinguishes between coding models and inferential models of communication to make a similar distinction to that of Goffman. Sperber and Wilson argue that most human communication depends on the ability of a recipient to decode the "semantic representation" or "thin" linguistic meaning of a message. This process they see as analogous to a Shannon-and-Weaver type of coding mechanism. The thin meaning they equate to the common core of meaning associated with a sentence which can be understood without any knowledge of the context in which the sentence is used.

Sperber and Wilson argue further that the interpretation of an utterance depends on an additional inferential mechanism that cannot be modeled by the type of coding mechanism postulated by Shannon and Weaver. This inferential mechanism is used by the recipient to interpret utterances, and the interpretation assigned to the utterances will depend on the recipient's background knowledge and inferential abilities. Thus the interpretation assigned to a message is an interaction between the thin meaning of the message and the recipient's cognitive processes. It is not coded into the message and the sender has no guarantee that intended inferences will be drawn by the sender. Sperber and Wilson make this clear when they say, "The semantic representation of a sentence deals with a sort of common core meaning shared by every utterance of it. However, different utterances of a sentence may differ in their interpretation; and indeed they usually do" (Sperber and Wilson 1986, p. 9).

## 5.3  Transmitted and Transputed Information in Human-Computer Interaction

The definitions of Goffman and the communication model of Sperber and Wilson were developed primarily to deal with intentional communication. That is to say, a receiver often uses the message received to infer something about the sender's goals, needs, or wants. Indeed a sender can use this fact to deceive, mislead, or in other ways adversely affect the actions of the receiver.

In the case of human-computer interaction, it is harder to see the role of intentional communication unless we consider interaction as communication between a designer and a user. Yet it is often the case that during interaction, both the user and the computer can be described as drawing inferences based on the information they receive in a way analogous to that described by Goffman, and Sperber and Wilson. We now wish to capture this analogy in a way that gives us some leverage on the problem of engineering interfaces which support the recipient of information in his or her process of inference. We will not concern ourselves with postulating a model of reasoning, but simply assume such a model and then make explicit the difference between information contained in a message (the thin meaning) and information derived from it by a process of inference. The former we shall refer to as *transmitted* information and the latter as *transputed* information. The terms are apt in view of their Greek origin:

> **trans**: over a distance
> **mittere**:    to send
> **putare**:    to consider or determine (requires thought)

In this sense, the transmitted information (*trans + mittere*) is the part of the information flow that is sent from a producer to a recipient over a distance, while transputed information (*trans + putare*) has to be determined by the receiver on the basis of the transmitted information and the receiver's knowledge. The addition *requires thought* in the definition of *putare* refers to the reasoning process that must be supplied by the recipient. The use of the term *transputed* information corresponds with the basic principle of transputers, i.e., the distribution of a computation among several processors.

Using these notions, our view of the process of information transfer in human-computer interaction can be described by the following four steps:

1. We begin by observing that a sender wishes to send data to a receiver via a channel (Figure 5.4).

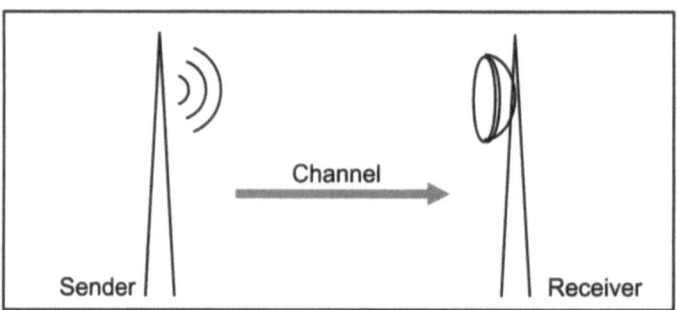

**Figure 5.4:** A so-called *channel* connects the sender with the receiver

2. The sender now sends data ⟫ to the receiver across the communication channel (Figure 5.5).

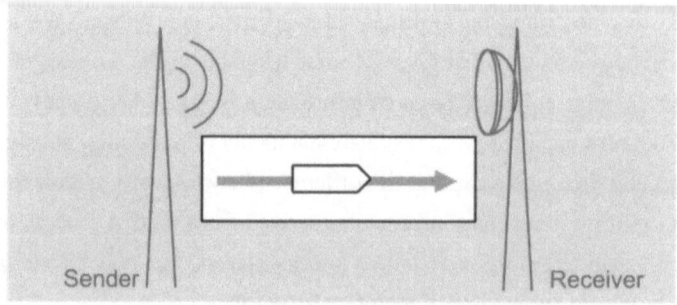

**Figure 5.5:** Data ⟫ being sent across the channel

actually denotes the thin meaning, or in our terminology, the *information transmitted* across the channel.

3. We now observe that the receiver possesses information ⟨⟩ after the message has been sent that was not possessed before receiving the message (Figure 5.6).

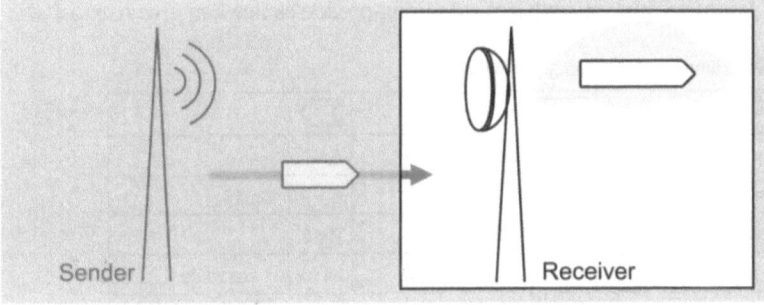

**Figure 5.6:** Receiver possesses more information ⟨⟩ after the communication

4. We are now interested in the difference between the information transmitted and the information possessed by the receiver after the message was sent. Assume for the time being that ⟨⟩ ⊇ ⟨⟩, i.e., that all information sent across the channel is actually possessed by the recipient after the communicative act (This restriction is in fact unimportant for what follows; we make it only for ease of understanding). Therefore we can re-draw ⟨⟩ as ⟨⟨⟩. Observe that ⟩ is the difference between the additional information which the receiver has and that which was sent to him, i.e.,

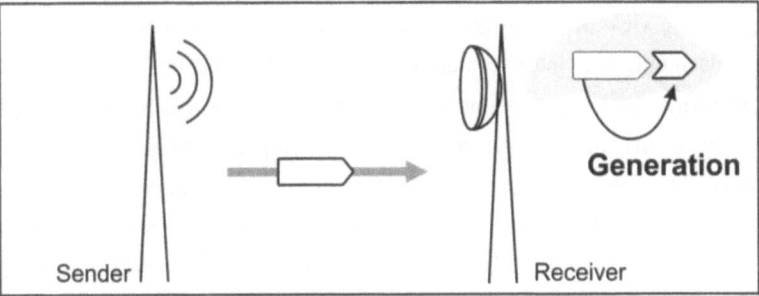

**Figure 5.7:** Did the receiver generate the extra information?

To understand the course of events in these four steps we must ask where this difference $\sum$ comes from. This difference has been observed by others, for example Kuhlen (1990), who refers to it as the "pragmatic added-value". From a cognitive viewpoint, one can say that the receiver *generated* the information by application of inferential rules (Figure 5.7).

Table 5.1 shows some examples of reasoning processes that can give rise to $\sum$.

**Table 5.1:** Examples of reasoning processes

| type of reasoning | $\sqsupset$ | $\sum$ |
|---|---|---|
| deduction | A>B & B>C | A>C |
| extrapolation | 2, 4, 6, 8, X | X = 10, 12, 14, |
| interpolation | 1, 3, y, 7, 9 | y = 5 |
| generalization | these swans are white | all swans are white |

From an engineering viewpoint, we find it more useful to think of the *sender* as *transputing* the information $\sum$ to the receiver, which can be envisioned as shown in Figure 5.8.

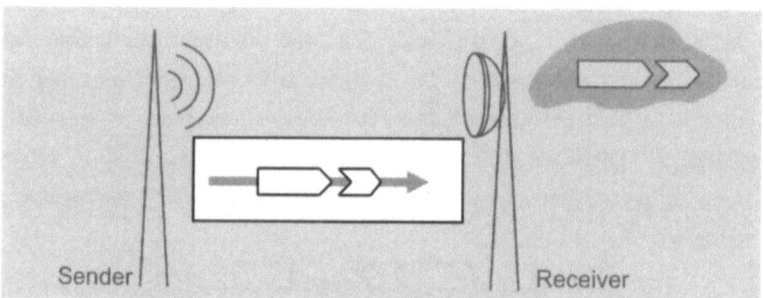

**Figure 5.8:** Was the extra information sent across the channel after all?

This engineering view of the process is unconventional but valuable for several reasons. Engineers designing user interfaces are ultimately responsible not only for choosing the *content* (information to be transmitted) presented to a user and for providing the user with facilities to transmit information back to the computer, but also for the *form* of the information. This, in turn, has a marked effect on what additional information the receiver can generate. Hence for engineers it is of paramount importance to think about how to design visualizations to elicit such generation on the part of users. By the same token, engineers must think about providing users with the ability to have the computer generate such additional information based on their input.

An analogy from the area of data structures is appropriate, where techniques have been developed for organizing data in a variety of ways. Data structures for implementing a given data type usually differ in the computational complexity of the operations that can be carried out on them. The data structure ultimately chosen for an application enables important (i.e., frequently performed) operations to be executed efficiently. In the same manner, an engineer must devise a visualization in such a way that the user can generate, and in fact generate *easily*, the additional information needed for his or her task. In fact, the user may not even be able to generate the information if the visualization does not lead him or her in the direction of an interpretation.

To summarize,

> *transmitted information* is composed of word symbols or their substitutes which the producer uses exclusively for the purpose of communicating information that the producer and recipient associate with these word symbols.

In addition,

> *transputed information* pertains to information over and above the transmitted information and which is computed by the recipient, typically on the basis of a reasoning process.

We say that a sender both *transmits* and *transputes* information to a recipient.

### 5.3.1 Information Transmitted and Transputed by a Computer

In many user interfaces for office or other clerical applications, users enter data and receive answers which they put to use but otherwise do not really think about much. For example, if a traveller asks for information about train connections, the person behind the information wicket at the railway station will type in the appropriate queries and convey the results to the traveller, often without questioning their correctness. This is an example of the computer transmitting information to the user, who simply passes it on.

In a variety of other situations, however, the output from a computer or another electronic device is more subtle, and an interpretation on the part of the viewer is intended by the designing engineer. Here the engineer must think carefully about how the user can be brought to the right conclusions. We shall discuss three examples.

*Example 1: A gas gauge*
Consider the gas gauge in Figure 5.9a. Without any specific markings on the scale, the interpretation is left largely to the viewer. The viewer must use his or her judgement to decide how to react. The gauge shown in Figure 5.9b is somewhat more explicit. By convention, if the needle moves into the red range, corrective action – such as gassing up – is recommended explicitly to the viewer. The fact that corrective action is necessary is *transmitted* in the latter case to the viewer; by contrast, in the former case, it is *trans-*

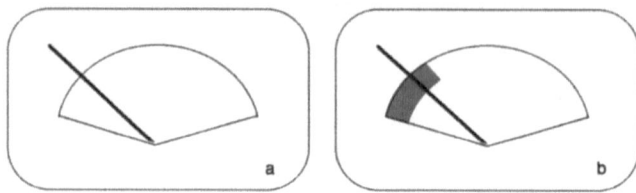

**Figure 5.9:** Two gas gauges

*puted* to the viewer – if it is conveyed at all. This is an example of where an extra graphical feature contributes to transmitting information to the viewer which would otherwise be transputed.

*Example 2: Extrapolation of numerical values*
Figure 5.10 shows a graph of numerical values. What is *transmitted* to the user are the actual data points. An attentive viewer is able to predict the *y*-values for *x*-values lying off the end of the horizontal scale. This additional information is *transputed* to the viewer.

If, by contrast, the user is shown an ordered table, he or she may still be able to predict the same values as from the graph, even though it may be more difficult to do so. It is even more difficult to predict the same information from the unordered table, which is not sorted by *x*-values. This illustrates the point made earlier that the designer of a presentation must be aware of what kinds of information should be transputed by a presentation. Just as a programmer must program a data structure so that the desired operations can be carried out efficiently, the designing engineer must choose a visualization to enable information to be transputed. Even though the prediction is computed by the viewer with a reasoning process, the graph supports this process by a presentation which is conducive to the reasoning process, whereas in the case of the unsorted table, it is not strongly supported. This, in turn, was our original reason for attributing the results of such a reasoning process to the sender of the message.

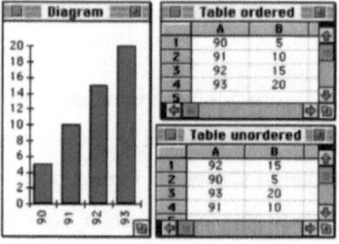

**Figure 5.10:**
Three presentations
of the same numerical data

*Example 3: Ultrasonic images*

In the previous examples, the designer could influence rather easily which information was to be conveyed to the user. To illustrate that this is not always the case, Figure 5.11 shows the ultrasonic image of an unborn child. The trained eye of a doctor quickly recognizes important elements, whereas an untrained eye sees only simple features. Indeed, doctors spend years of their life learning to interpret such pictures. "To interpret" here means to produce a verbalization that reflects the state of the organs visualized in the image. Such an interpretation is an example of information transputed to the viewer via the image.

Note that if the viewer is not able to interpret an image, the computer may be able to support him or her in this process. If the information to be transputed is accessible to the computer, then the information can be extracted by the computer and transmitted to the viewer, for example by pointing out features in the image and naming them explicitly. (In the case of pictures as in Figure 5.11, image processing algorithms often cannot carry out an analysis automatically, but in other cases, like in simple robot navigation, such an analysis can in fact be carried out.) In cases where the information to be transputed to the viewer is not accessible to the computer, an experienced person must enter this data explicitly so that it can be transmitted to the viewer. We shall develop such a methodology, in which expert users construct so-called viewpoint descriptions, in Chapter 8.

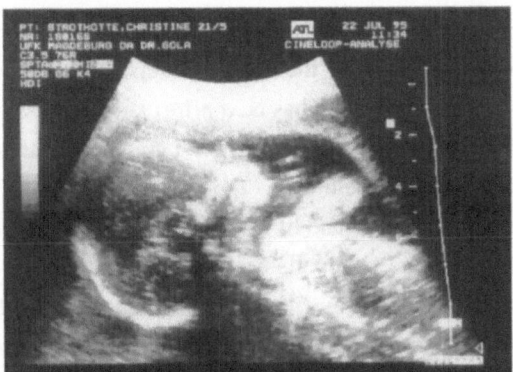

**Figure 5.11**: Example of an ultrasonic image of an unborn child

### 5.3.2 Information Transmitted and Transputed by Users

Information transputed by a user is significantly more subtle. Recall that what information is transputed by the user is calculated by the recipient (here the computer) and not the sender (here the user). Thus we are dealing with information which the user may not even possess, even though it can be determined uniquely and may even be implied by the user, perhaps without his or her knowledge. Again we provide three examples.

*Example 1: A beautifier for diagrams*

Pen computers have the obvious drawback that graphics drawn with the pen do not look as neat as those drawn with graphical primitives. Even with primitives for drawing straight lines, an image can conceivably look sloppily drawn (Figure 5.12a). Pavlidis and Van Wyk (1985) and more recently Kurlander and Feiner (1992) have developed a system for automatically replacing the input by graphics with straight lines, corners that meet, etc. (Figure 5.12b). Here the original input is what the user transmits to the computer; what he or she transputes is what the computer makes of his input, i.e., the neat diagram.

a                                                                                         b

**Figure 5.12:** A beautifier for diagrams (Kurlander and Feiner 1992)

*Example 2: Placing duplicated objects in a graphical*

Graphical editors provide users with the ability to duplicate objects that they have already drawn. However, the application has no *a priori* knowledge of where the duplicate is to be placed in the drawing. The approach of most graphical editors is to place the new object somewhat to the right and below the original and treat it as the selected object for further manipulation (Figures 5.13a and b).

The graphical editor Canvas™ supports users in placing objects that have been duplicated. If a user moves the duplicate to a particular position (Figure 5.13c) and then issues the duplicate command again, the editor will place this third object in the same position relative to the second as the second is relative to the first (Figure 5.13d). The editor assumes that the user is in the process of constructing a sequence. From the point of view of the editor, without any knowledge about the user's intentions, the position of the duplicate is arbitrary, and Canvas' positioning of the second duplicate can be seen as an educated guess. By issuing the duplicate command a second time right after positioning the first duplicate, the user has transputed to the system where he or she wishes the new one to be placed, even though the user may not even be aware of this fact.

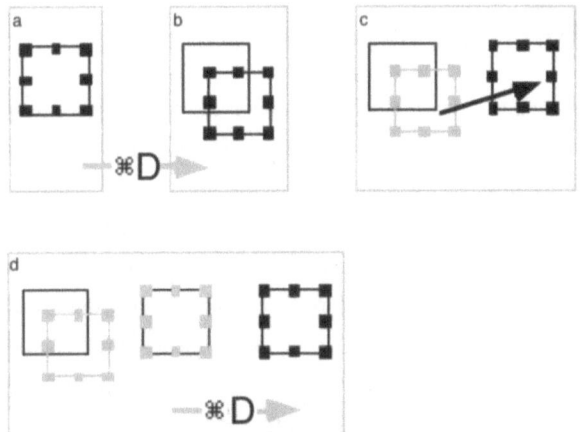

**Figure 5.13:** Duplication of an object in a graphical editor. The user selects
a graphical object (a), duplicates it (b), and places it in the desired position (c).
If the second object is now duplicated, the third object will be placed in the same
position relative to the second one as this one is relative to the first (d).

*Example 3: Active help*

Consider the case of a text editor which is able to provide users with help (Fischer,
Lemke and Schwab 1985). If a user makes inefficient use of the available function keys,
an active help system will interrupt him or her from time to time to draw certain pieces of
information to his or her attention. Thus for example if the text editor has a function key
for "move-to-beginning-of-next-word", but the user repeatedly uses the space bar to
move the cursor forward, the machine recognizes this inefficient use of the space bar and
points out the shorthand notation for the task to the user. Here the computer carries out a
reasoning process, analyzing the user's input to determine what he or she is *actually*
doing when pressing the space bar repeatedly.

The fundamental assumption of the active help system is that the user is in fact
unaware of the shorthand notation. In other words, because the user has made inefficient
use of the available function keys, the help system considers the user to have *transputed*
to it the fact that he or she does not know how to use the shorthand notation. This is an
example where the user may or may not be aware that he or she is transputing information (depending on whether the user knows that the actions are being monitored by an
active help system or not); however, he or she has no idea what information is being
transputed until the computer's reaction is received.

## 5.4 Methods of Transputing Information

The perhaps counterintuitive aspect of the concept of information transputed by the user in the context of human-computer interaction is that we regard the result of the computer's reasoning process as being part of the user's input. This departure from the traditional separation of input and output, which has its historic roots in a hardware-oriented point of view of human-computer interaction, is precisely what opens up new possibilities. For if the machine can derive reliable information from user input, this additional information can well be regarded as being an integral additive part of the input. It only becomes machine output when the computer communicates its conclusions back to the user. This distinction is subtle but important.

The key to the successful transputing of information, both for users and for the computer, is that the terminology of the information transmitted can be analyzed appropriately by the recipient. In particular, this means that the sender's encoding of a message must be matched by the receiver's decoding. Indeed, we implicitly require a "high-level" language to be used for the communication, since otherwise the symbols of the message cannot be connected simply with those of the knowledge representation of the recipient. Alternatively, when word substitutes like graphics are used, it is essential that the recipient (in this case the user) can interpret the graphics using word symbols which themselves are part of his or her knowledge representation.

The reliability of the assessments as to what information was transputed by a producer is vital. Goffman (1959) acknowledges reliability in interaction between humans as an important issue; in his case, the information given off can either be hidden or falsified. However, since in human-computer interaction the goal of both the computer and the user is to make the communication succeed, only misinterpretations need be considered. Since error recovery is a problem which is very difficult to automate, it must be left up to users to monitor the information transputed and to convince themselves of its correctness.

Even more subtle is the question of whether, given the design choice, the machine should transmit or transpute a piece of information. To try to transpute the information, of course, relies on the user's reasoning ability, hence there is more risk that it will not be communicated. On the other hand, users may well have more confidence in information transputed to them, since they arrived at it by drawing their own conclusions. To transpute information also makes the recipient keenly aware of the reasoning process involved in arriving at the conclusion, which could lead to a sharpening of user's cognitive skills. If instead the result is simply transmitted, these steps in the reasoning process may not become known to the user.

However, there is a cognitive overhead associated both with receiving information that is transmitted as well as information that is transputed. Presumably the overhead associated with transputed information is higher, since the recipient must actually generate it. In any case, care must be taken not to overload the recipient, particularly in safety-critical situations. This question is beyond of the scope of this book and requires further study.

## 5.5  Analysis of Some Dialogue Systems

To illustrate the concepts we have developed, we will now discuss a number of examples of human-computer interaction.

*1. Database queries*
A user working with a database system by formulating individual queries which are treated in isolation by the machine transputes little information to the computer. Although a translation of the query into operations on tables is carried out, this does not involve a reasoning process but a straightforward calculation. The computer transputes no information, assuming the user simply passes on the answers to a third party (recall the example in the first paragraph of Section 5.3.1). However, as soon as the user begins to draw conclusions about which queries to formulate next as a result of the computer's responses, these queries then constitute information transputed by the computer.

*2. User's mental models*
A user's mental model helps him or her to learn and remember the operation of an application program (Sowa 1984). If the computer gives the user explicit hints as to which mental model to build up, for example through the choice of pictograms and screen layout (which may even be explained in a handbook, as with the desktop metaphor), this information is transmitted by the computer. As soon as the user transfers information from one context to another, for example by knowing how to delete a file when he or she sees the icon representing a trash can (Figure 5.14), this new information is what is transputed to the viewer.

This example also serves to illustrate how misinformation can be transputed to a user, independent of whether this was intended or not. If the user realizes that a file can be deleted by moving its icon onto that of the trash can, he or she might conclude that a diskette can be erased by dragging its icon onto the trash can in the same manner. However, this action actually ejects the diskette.

**Figure 5.14:**
Putting a file
into the paper basket

### 3. User modeling

A user model is a typical example of an explicit representation of information transputed by a user with respect to the use of the application. For example, the active help of Fischer, Lemke, and Schwab (1986) for a text editor mentioned above ascertains what the user knows about how to use the editor by observing which commands he or she uses in what situations. Here the information transmitted by the user encompasses the editing commands; the information transputed is that pertaining to his or her competence in using the editor and is recorded in the user model.

### 4. Scientific visualization

Systems for scientific visualization are designed to give users access to pictorial representations of numeric data. The basic idea is that the user can discover more information from such representations than from numeric data in which an algorithm searches for regularities or anomalies. Thus the goal is to allow the user to reason about the computer's output; hence the computer transputes a great deal of information. However, user input in such systems is usually very primitive: users typically work directly on parameters of equations, leaving the machine little or no room for reasoning on its own. Hence users have practically no chance to transpute information in such systems. Indeed, it is an open question requiring further research to determine what kinds of information a user would even want to transpute in this context.

### 5. Expert systems

The goal of expert systems is to enable non-expert users to achieve a level of performance in an area of application which is similar to that of human experts (Jackson 1990). Since the emphasis of such systems is on reasoning on the part of the computer, the user transputes a great deal of information. However, since non-experts are the typical users and they simply enter data to obtain results which they themselves do not think about much, the machine typically transputes very little information.

# 5.6 Discussion

In this chapter we have developed a model for analyzing the flow of information between users and computers. We have shown in particular how the recipient's processing can account for information conveyed from the producer to the recipient. Our definition of information transmitted on the one hand and transputed on the other hand depends heavily on symbolic knowledge representation on the part of the recipient. However, this points to a weakness in the much sought-after user interfaces based on pointing at rather than naming objects (Norman 1984). Practically all current systems that offer search facilities do so on the basis of names of objects; this is particularly true for temporally separated objects. If the user interacts primarily by pointing to objects rather than naming them, a common vocabulary between the computer and the user which could be used for searching and reasoning based on symbols is missing.

User interfaces that rely on direct manipulation but also facilitate the user's association of graphic symbols with words with which he or she is familiar are referred to as having a *low distance* (Hutchins, Hollan, and Norman 1986). While information can still be transmitted under these circumstances, in practice the second-order effect of information being transputed is severely restricted. It is quite noticeable that in systems that require no common vocabulary between the user and the computer, neither generally carries out any reasoning. So-called "intelligent" systems, such as medical diagnosis systems, tend to have user interfaces which are language-oriented for this reason. By the same token, systems that build up user models and make use of them usually do so in terms of symbols which are then used in the interaction with the user.

Another important aspect of the ability of users and the computer to transpute information is the *language level* used in the communication. Hutchins, Hollan, and Norman (1986) differentiate between high-level and low-level languages: A high-level language is one that "expresses frequently encountered structures of problem decomposition." By this they mean that a task can be described in the same language as is used within the task domain itself, rather than having to be decomposed into low-level operations. A high-level language aids the recipient in the reasoning process by making it more efficient (fewer inferences), and so leaving less room for errors in the reasoning process.

The use of *metaphors* (Carroll and Mack 1985) is an excellent way to aid users in the reasoning process of learning how to use an application. The user recognizes certain objects which he or she can name, thereby determining the context alluded to by the metaphor. An active reasoning process, which can usually be verbalized by the user, subsequently leads to the user possessing more information about the application than was transmitted to him or her by the machine. Once a user has learned the concepts, the use of a metaphor helps him or her remember what was already learned. Helping the user retain or re-establish the conceptual link to what was learned earlier can also be regarded as transputed information.

# Abstract-Graphical Pictures

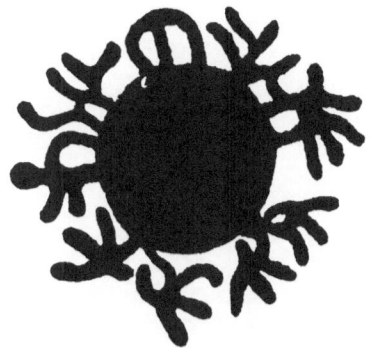

*Symbol of the sun*
Fossum, Sweden

# Abstract-Graphical Pictures and Some Applications

## 6.1 Characterization

In Section 3.3.1 we defined an abstract-graphical picture as a presentation of properties of reality and relations in reality that are *invisible* to humans. This includes pictures of the non-visible interna of real systems (see Figure 6.1) as well as non-real objects which only exist in a person's imagination.

In order to appreciate the role that abstract-graphical pictures play, we draw on the fundamentals of *system theory* (see Bertalanffy 1969 and Leeson 1981). A system is defined as a number of elements that are related to one another. The elements as well as the relationships among them, including their identifiers, are all part of a system.

The act of creating a picture is a process of selecting and presenting a segment of reality (or even a person's imagined reality). The selection process, in turn, is nothing but the definition of a system and its visualization. Because of the complexity of most systems, it makes sense that abstract-graphical pictures focus on selected aspects of a system. Besides the fact that a system consists of related elements, there are more interesting aspects, like:

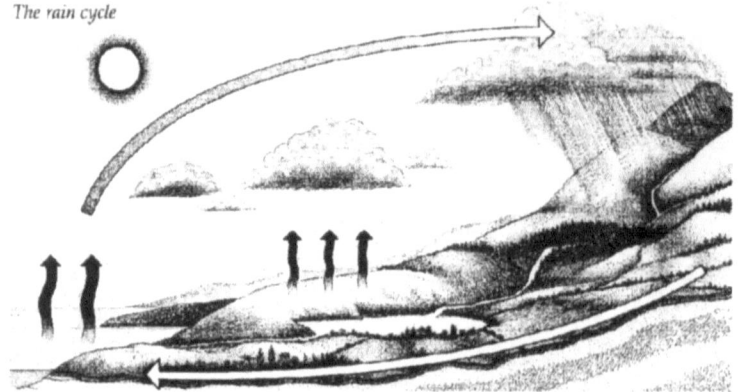

*The rain cycle*

**Figure 6.1:** An abstract-graphical picture for demonstrating the rain cycle (Heaton 1986)

- Every system has a structure which is the sum of all relations between the elements of the system.
- Every system shows its specific behavior which is usually time-dependent.
- Every system serves with its general functionality a special purpose or goal.

An important observation is that graphical symbols (recall Figure 3.11) are used to emphasize the special aspect of the system represented in the abstract-graphical picture.

Because abstract-graphical pictures are as varied as reality and human imagination, we are not able to present a complete classification with disjunctive classes for abstract-graphical pictures. It is nonetheless instructive to investigate common kinds of pictures with respect to which aspect of a system they focus on. To demonstrate the character of the different classes, we will give some examples of each type. We shall draw most of the examples from the field of software engineering, since this area is also of fundamental importance to the topic of this book. But to demonstrate the generality of this theoretical framework for abstract-graphical pictures, we have also chosen to include examples from other fields of endeavor.

## 6.2 Focus on Relations Between Elements

If abstract-graphical pictures focus on relations, they normally use graphical symbols (in particular lines and arrows) to represent the relations. The style of the lines and arrows often reflects a special kind of relation between the elements. Typical examples of this kind of picture are:

*Architectural Pictures*

These are pictures where different elements of a system are represented by ellipses and rectangles (often with labels) connected by lines or arrows, to describe the co-operation in elements of a system (see for example Figure 6.2). In computer science, these picture are often used to depict the architecture of a software or hardware system, where the graphical symbols (lines and arrows) represent data exchange between elements.

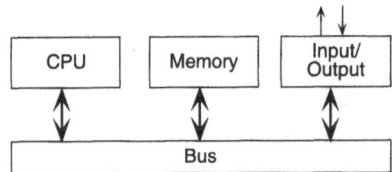

**Figure 6.2:** Computer architecture

*Pictures of Data Structures*

The abstract character of data structures can be made easier to understand by visualizing them. Indeed, books on data structures are full of such pictures (see for example Sedgewick 1988). Which units of the data structure are seen as elements of the system depends on the necessary level of detail. For example, Figure 6.3 shows the visualization of a special kind of tree, a minmax heap, in which parent-child pairs are joined by lines and the ordering relation among the elements is denoted by an arrow and its direction (Atkinson et al. 1986). As the name indicates, minmax heaps were developed in order to find maximum and minimum elements of a data collection quickly.

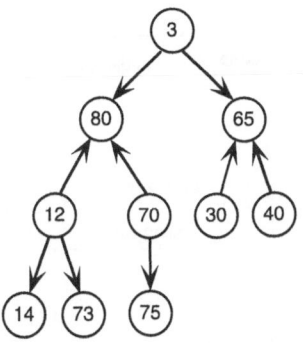

**Figure 6.3:** A minmax heap

*Plane Geometry*

This area of endeavor focuses on vertices, arcs, and angles between arcs. An example is the well-known theorem of Pythagoras (see Figure 6.4). While there exist many assertions about triangles, a symbol system is generally used to augment the geometric entities or properties (recall Chapter 1). The result of the theorem is then stated in the symbol system (e.g., $c^2 = a^2 + b^2$). In Figure 6.4, the North American symbol for the right angle is augmented to express the relation between the vertices $a$ and $b$. The German symbol for the right angle is a curve and a dot, as in Figure 6.5.

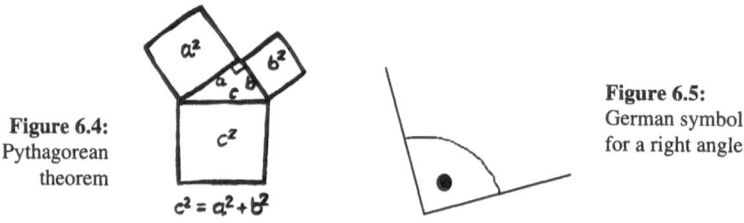

**Figure 6.4:**
Pythagorean
theorem

**Figure 6.5:**
German symbol
for a right angle

## 6.3  Focus on Functionality

A function is an "action for which a person or a thing is specially fitted or used or for which a thing exists" or "any of a group of related actions contributing to a larger action" (Webster 1990, p. 498). Having a special functionality is the ability of a system to realize a special function. Some pictures, such as bubble charts, are designed to present the functionality of systems.

*Bubble Charts*

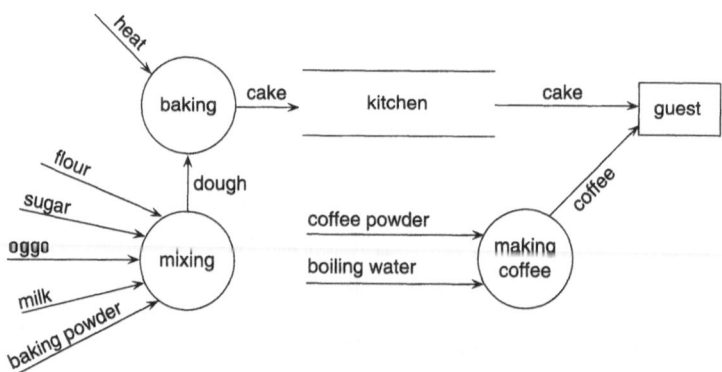

**Figure 6.6:** Life cycle of a cake

Bubble charts are used as tools for modeling when the functions of a system are much more important and more complex than the data. They consist of four typical components: process, flow, storage, and terminator (see Yourdon 1989). A *process* realizes a conversion of input to output data, or the other way around. The graphic presentation of a process can be a circle, an ellipse, or a rectangle, complemented by a text label briefly describing the activity of the process. The *flow* is visualized as an arrow and represents the movement of data or physical objects. These arrows are labeled to define the meaning of data which flow. *Storage* represents a group of non-moving data and is often represented graphically by two parallel lines. The *terminator* represents an external object communicating with the system. It is often drawn as a rectangle. Figure 6.6 shows a bubble chart for the life cycle of a cake.

## 6.4  Focus on Behavior

If an abstract-graphical picture focuses on the behavior of a system, it has to describe what happens in the system over a period of time. If the time aspect is explicitly represented in pictures, the graphical symbols are used to represent the progression of time, whereas if the time aspect is more implicit, the graphical symbols represent the change in states of elements in a system.

*Time-Dependent Graphs*
In various different areas, like the sciences or business, diagrams can be found in which a time scale is used to represent the development of a system or single aspects of a system. Usually the first quadrant of the co-ordinate system is used with the $x$-axis as the time scale. The $y$-axis represents the aspects of the system whose behavior is interesting. The dependency between the time values and the $y$-values can be presented by points, lines, bars, rectangles, or other geometric forms. Figure 6.7 shows a line graph of the development of the number of students in Germany as an example of time-graphs.

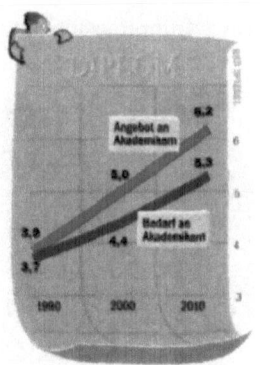

**Figure 6.7:**
Development of students in Germany (DER SPIEGEL, December 13th, 1993)

*Evolutionary Pictures*

In the sciences, it is often important to demonstrate with the help of pictures the evolution of systems over a period of time. Examples can be found in biology, where the spread of decay in a tooth is shown (see Figure 6.8); in astronomy, where the evolution of stars is demonstrated; and chemistry, where different states of chemicals are portrayed. Typical of these kind of pictures is the presentation of different stages of development of systems and their connection by means of arrows standing for the time between the stages.

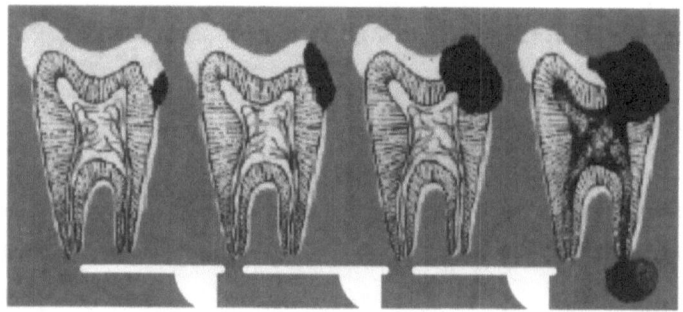

**Figure 6.8:** Caries in different stages (Baer 1981)

*Petri Nets*

Petri nets are used especially for modeling computer-based systems in a graphical manner with an underlying formalism to allow a mathematical analysis of the system designed. The graphic presentation of Petri nets is described as "intuitively understandable" (see Reisig 1985), despite the strong semantic definition of the graphical symbols used. The reader is invited to verify this statement by interpreting Figure 6.9. A Petri net consists of places (represented by circles), transitions (represented by rectangles), arrows from places to transitions, arrows from transitions to places, a given capacity for each place, and an initial marking.

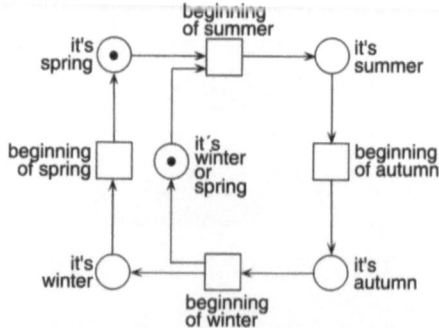

**Figure 6.9:** Four seasons and their transitions (Reisig 1985)

## 6.5   Focus on Properties of Elements

A very common purpose of abstract-graphical pictures is to draw the reader's attention to the properties of single elements in a system. Often such graphics accompany text or are otherwise embedded in a larger context; rarely are they used as "stand-alone" presentations. Examples are:

*Contour Graphics*
By superimposing colors or textures onto images of objects, abstract-graphical pictures map values onto the corresponding positions in two dimensions. A common application is to denote the elevation of mountains on a map; Figure 6.10 shows an example where pressure is mapped onto the color of a 2D image (model of space shuttle during atmospheric re-entry).

**Figure 6.10:** Pressure mapped onto a 2D image
(courtesy of Eva Pärt-Enander and Anders R. (Knutby) Karlsson)

The latter example lies on the boundary between a presentational picture and an abstract-graphical one: We can treat figure 6.10 as a presentational picture if the surface is indeed colored the way it appears; however, if the object is not visible the way drawn, then it is an abstract-graphical picture.

*Business Graphics*
Such graphics typically map numerical values of data to distances on two-dimensional surfaces (paper or a computer screen). This allows a viewer to get a feeling for the numerical values, to compare them qualitatively and also to ascertain trends. Figure 6.11 shows an example.

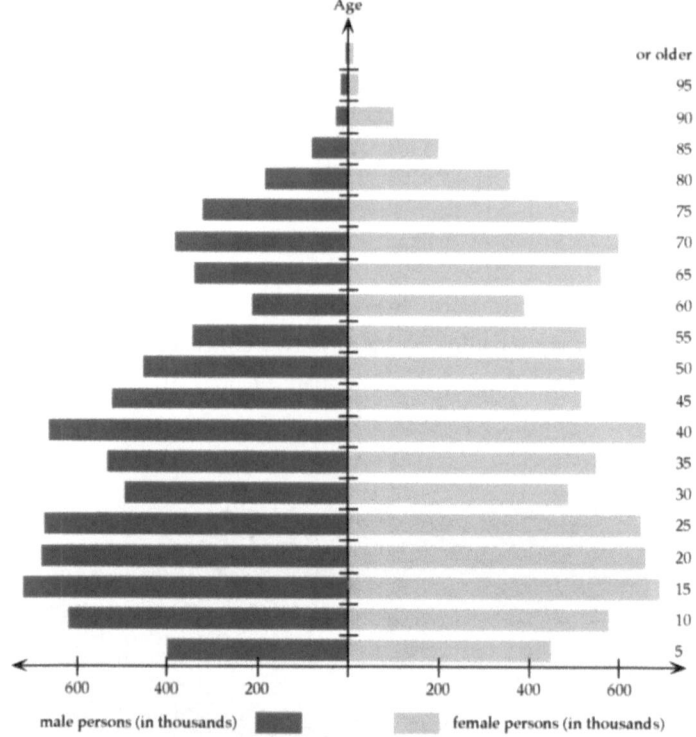

**Figure 6.11:** Age structure of the population in 1974 of the former GDR

*Symbolic Structures*

In Artificial Intelligence applications, programming systems are commonly used for keeping track of symbolic structures, in particular with respect to objects and their properties. For example, the programming language LISP has a `property list` explicitly associated with every object. They are generally visualized in a 2D manner, as shown in Figure 6.12.

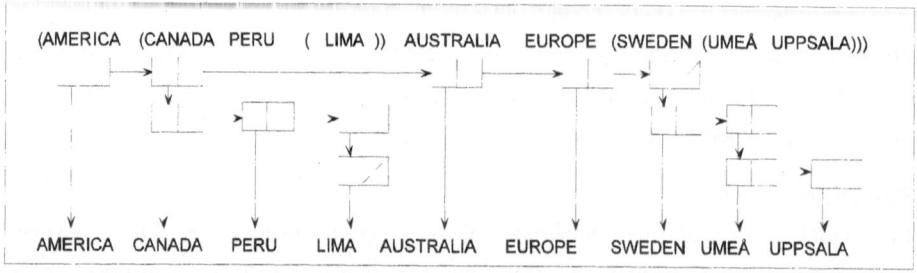

**Figure 6.12:** A LISP example

## 6.6   Abstract-Graphical Pictures for Cognitive Processing

We are concerned not only with encoding information explicitly in an abstract-graphical picture and transmitting it to the user, but also with the ease with which information can be transputed, as explained in Chapter 5. This means that we must pay attention to the psychological complexity of problem solving using abstract-graphical pictures as a starting point. We shall discuss some of the issues briefly, without attempting a full treatment. The interested reader is referred to the literature for a more complete account.

Larkin and Simon (1987) discuss at length the difference between a kind of abstract-graphical pictures (referred to them as diagrammatic representations) and linguistic statements of problems (which they refer to as sentential representations). The following text explains a sample problem:

We have three pulleys, two weights, and some ropes, arranged as follows:

1. The first weight is suspended from the left end of a rope over Pulley A. The right end of this rope is attached to, and partially supports, the second weight.
2. Pulley A is suspended from the left end of a rope that runs over Pulley B, and under Pulley C. Pulley B is suspended from the ceiling. The right end of the rope that runs under Pulley C is attached to the ceiling.
3. Pulley C is attached to the second weight, supporting it jointly with the right end of the first rope.

The pulleys and ropes are weightless; the pulleys are frictionless; and the rope segments are all vertical, except where they run over or under the pulley wheels. Find the ratio of the second to the first weight, if the system is in equilibrium.

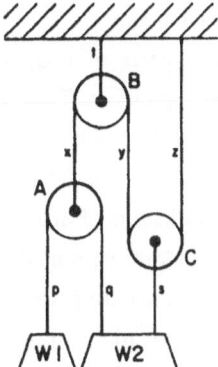

**Figure 6.13:**
A representation for the pulley problem (Larkin and Simon 1987)

Figure 6.13 shows the corresponding abstract-graphical picture. The fundamental difference between the text and the picture according to the authors is that the picture explicitly presents information about the topological and geometric relations among the components of the problem, whereas the linguistic statement does not. An expression in a formal language may, of course, preserve other kinds of relation, for example temporal or logical sequence. Nonetheless, the authors consider two such representations to be "informationally equivalent".

Simon and Larkin work out reasons why and under what circumstances abstract-graphical pictures are superior to statements in a formal language from the point of view of problem solving in many circumstances. They identify three operations that determine the efficiency of problem solving by the viewer of a representation:

- *search*: how quickly and with which resources (e.g., amount of short-term or long-term memory) can certain pieces of information be derived,
- *recognition*: how well can features be identified and associated with prior knowledge of the person trying to solve a problem, and
- *inference*: how well can conclusions be drawn about what is perceived.

The results of the cognitive activity studied by Simon and Larkin are actually transputed information in the theoretical framework of Chapter 5. In our terminology, they propose measures for analyzing the psychological complexity of transmitting and transputing information to a user.

Simon and Larkin suggest three aspects of the success of abstract-graphical pictures for human problem solving:

- *Localization.* For many kinds of problem statements, objects that must be grouped together when carrying out individual steps of a problem solution can actually be drawn physically close to one another in an abstract-graphical picture. This is often not the case for linguistic problem statements.
- *Minimal labeling.* Labeling of objects of relations in a system leads naturally to frequent searches while solving a problem. This is time-consuming, as there is often no convenient way of organizing the labels so that they can be located effectively. Abstract-graphical pictures tend to need less labeling to represent a problem statement, as the picture yields its own identification of many objects and relations.
- *Use of perceptual enhancement.* Abstract-graphical pictures can often be drawn in such a way that the important features are perceived more easily than less important ones by use of appropriate techniques to direct the viewer's attention. For many kinds of problem statements, such perceptual enhancement of the representation is not as readily achieved in a linguistic statement.

While these are certainly generalizations with exceptions, they identify features of abstract-graphical pictures that are important in enabling them to be processed successfully by users.

## 6.7 Discussion

The characterization of abstract-graphical pictures, and the different foci we have presented, are not intended to be exhaustive. Indeed, our purpose has been to give an idea of different kinds and uses of abstract-graphical pictures. The examples chosen show how difficult it is to find a general classification for such pictures. A classification implies underlying assumptions about the intent of the viewer and his or her tasks.

The key to the successful use of abstract-graphical pictures is the realization that they depict *systems* and visualize certain aspects to which the attention of the viewer is to be drawn. In this sense, abstract-graphical pictures play a role like that of natural language. Both imply and present an artificial partitioning of reality – in the one case graphical, in the other case verbal. In abstract-graphical pictures, designing an image means finding a mapping onto a 2D medium so that the viewer can ascertain the objects and relationships that are important for the task at hand. We will come back to this point in Chapters 8 and 9, where we investigate what information users can see (or learn to see) in an abstract-graphical picture. This is useful because the computer which produces the picture only has data structures representing what is being presented to the user, but is lacking information in what he or she actually sees.

The example of LISP structures visualized as abstract-graphical pictures (recall Figure 6.12) illustrates most clearly the close relationship between abstract-graphical pictures and language. The language LISP has been used extensively for natural language processing. Indeed, LISP structures are often so like natural language that simple generators can be written relatively easily, though the issue of knowledge representation, which must be addressed to progress from restricted domains to larger ones, remains unresolved. Nonetheless, for all LISP structures, abstract-graphical pictures can be generated (even pretty-printed) to denote their semantics. By the same token, it is possible to convert many abstract-graphical pictures into LISP code, which we just claimed is very language-like. However, the relationship between most abstract-graphical pictures and language is not so close that such code would in fact be meaningful. The problems associated herewith will occupy our attention in the next chapters.

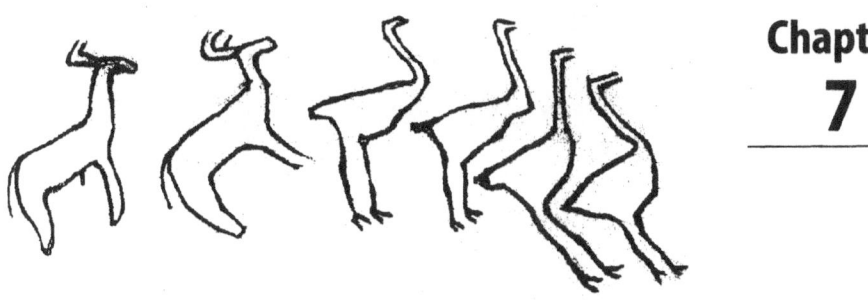

*Antelopes and Ostriches*
Taghtania-South, Sahara Desert, Africa

# Analysis of Abstract-Graphical Pictures

We now turn to the more practical issue of making the information encoded in abstract-graphical pictures available to interactive systems. The problem is that while such pictures usually present information in a well-structured manner amenable to processing by machine, the vast majority of pictorial materials are stored only on paper, or, if within a computer, then in a data format (like bitmaps) that is difficult to access directly. This access is difficult because the structure must first be derived. While this is often trivial for a human reader, it can be hard to do with an algorithm. In this chapter, we develop a user-supported methodology to carry out this task.

A great many abstract-graphical pictures are designed for educational purposes or as explanations. They commonly consist of a presentational part, which reflects reality or imagination, complemented by graphical symbols (see Figure 7.1).

It can be observed that in these pictures the graphical symbols attract the viewer's attention and the presentational part is relegated to the background. We see two reasons for this phenomenon:

1. A substantial portion of the "message" of the picture is encoded in the graphical symbols, because they convey the explanation or instruction which the picture has to give.

2. The graphical symbols initiate high normalization demands (recall Chapter 4) because they require a particular interpretation in the concrete context of the presentational part of the picture. The presentational part itself is often more or less well-known and easily recognizable, and therefore of lesser interest.

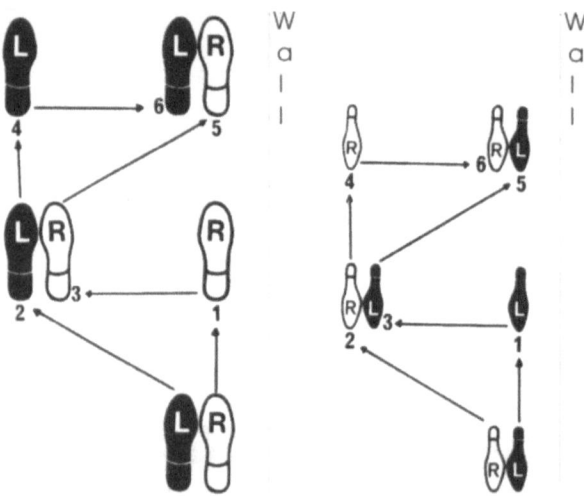

**Figure 7.1:** Instructional pictures for dancing the slow waltz (Hädrich 1994)

Graphical symbols have an abstract character in the sense that their meaning cannot be derived intuitively. They are well-defined by convention and are often rather arbitrary (recall Chapter 2). If viewers have learnt the meaning, recognition is immediate, otherwise the viewer is left guessing, although this works surprisingly well most of the time. The interpretation of graphical symbols has to be learned for different contexts, though it is possible to deduce the meaning of symbols in one context on the basis of their meaning in another.

## 7.1 Requirements

Computer-based instruction or explanation should be able to adapt to the concrete situation and the information needs of a user, because this ability is the most important advantage of using a computer in comparison to written material like books. It makes sense for an instructional system or other system working with pictures to have a repertoire of presentational pictures, a collection of graphical symbols, and information about how to combine them in an abstract-graphical picture for the specific purpose of instructing or explaining. Figure 7.2 shows two abstract-graphical pictures that differ only in their graphical symbols, but convey different information to the viewer with respect to the instructional task.

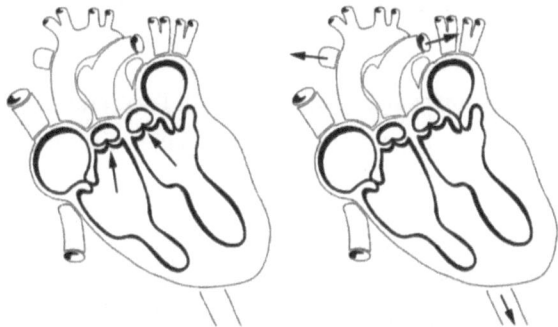

**Figure 7.2:** Functions of the heart (Baer 1981)

If we want to use pictures for instructional purposes, we can draw on many pictures created by the designers of educational material. In school books, manuals, or operating instructions, we find a wide variety of good examples of abstract-graphical pictures and these pictures are often much better than those most computer scientists could program computers to produce. It is therefore worth developing an acquisition component to analyze the graphical symbols in abstract-graphical pictures that carry a meaning when associated with the presentational part of the picture.

Furthermore, we would like to be able to use such pictures in dialogue systems: when the user views an abstract-graphical picture, he or she should be able to ask questions about the picture and receive reasonable answers. For this purpose, the machine must have information about the pictures so as to be able to interpret user input (both pointing and naming), as well as to have access to further information.

When using abstract-graphical pictures for instructional purposes, systems are therefore necessary which

- are able to acquire pictures from written documents by extracting the graphical symbols from the presentational part of the picture, and
- are able to compose an instructional picture by adding graphical symbols to the presentational part.

In the following, we shall study the first of these points; the second will be dealt with later on, in Chapters 10 and 14.

## 7.2 Methodology

Abstract-graphical pictures are able to convey a considerable amount of information to the viewer. This can be transmitted (for example raw numeric data), or transputed (for example a trend or a prediction to which the viewer is led).

The vast majority of abstract-graphical pictures available today are either

- in printed form on paper,
- stored as graphical primitives such as a collection of lines, arrows or text, or
- stored as bit matrices, which themselves form the output of scanning software.

While we do not expect an algorithm to be able to analyze presentational parts of such pictures and "understand" them, it is much more realistic to analyze the graphical symbols with the goal of extracting a small amount of information about the picture. This information can then serve as the basis for the re-use of the pictures, as suggested above. The analysis of these graphical symbols is particularly important, since they often convey the primary message of the entire picture.

Kugas (1993; see also Böcke and Strothotte 1988; Kurze, Strothotte, and Kugas 1994) developed a methodology for analyzing abstract-graphical pictures in the above sense. The key to the approach, however, is that a user is required to aid the algorithm in its analysis. The method is as follows:

1. The picture is analyzed using both standard image processing software to compute a vectorization of the graphical portions and OCR software to convert the text (insofar as characters appear in the picture) into ASCII format.
2. The vectorization is analyzed to structure the information encoded in the graphical symbols. Of particular interest are arrows: arrow heads are identified and heuristics applied to link them with lines or curves to which they are likely to belong. Next, heuristics are used to associate any text appearing in the pictures with graphical symbols. The heuristics are simple and relate to the geometric layout; text is generally associated with the closest geometric object in its neighborhood or the bounding volume enclosing it, while the objects at either end of an arrow are associated with it.
3. The results are shown to the user, who is given the opportunity to edit the machine's interpretation. Colors are used to associate related objects with one another. By clicking on individual objects and combining them, the user corrects any errors made by the algorithms.

A simple example is shown in Figure 7.3. In this first step, a vectorization of the graphics and recognition of the characters is performed. The second step associates the textual label "transformation" with the arrow, while the texts "Rudolf Scharping" and "Oskar Lafontaine" are associated with the ends of the line. Finally the label is used as the name of a relation joining the labels of the two figures, resulting in the predicate "transformation (Rudolf Scharping, Oskar Lafontaine)".

Rudolf Scharping ——————— *transformation* ——————▶ Oskar Lafontaine

**Figure 7.3:** Example of an abstract-graphical picture.
The information extracted by the analysis algorithm is the predicate
`"transformation (Rudolf Scharping, Oskar Lafontaine)"`.

It is important to note that our emphasis lies in building upon existing algorithms for image analysis, rather than developing new algorithms. The algorithmic level has been studied in detail over many years (see for example, Pavlidis 1982, Ballard and Brown 1982, Haberäcker 1991, Rosenfeld and Kak 1982, Jaroslavski 1990, Sack and Touissant 1987) and has produced many results applicable to the practical issues at hand. Many of these algorithms are available in general-purpose software, for example AdOculos™ (DBS GmbH), IDL™ (Research Systems, Inc.), UTOPIA™ (CWA mbH) and Optimas™ (Stemmer PC-Systeme GmbH).

We contend that the key to constructing good algorithms is that the applications must draw on the visual perception capabilities of its users; they are the specialists in the application domain and they know their own goals. Often situations will arise in which all general heuristics will fail to solve a problem whose solution is immediately obvious to the user. Hence the major challenge is to provide users with means to express themselves, so as to bridge the gap between the requirements of the application and the algorithmic techniques available in off-the-shelf software.

## 7.3  An Application to Pictures in Dictionaries

Interesting abstract-graphical pictures can be found in encyclopedias and some dictionaries. The purpose of such illustrations is generally to enable the reader to use language correctly, rather than to have to resort to words like "thing" or "gadget". They make sure that objects are denoted by the correct word. Conversely, they enable a reader to see what an object with a given name looks like, often to make sure that he or she has chosen the right word (PONS 1992).

Hupka (1983) carried out a study of the use of illustrations in French language dictionaries. Table 7.1 shows the categories in which the pictures fall for two of these dictionaries (NDFCI 1980, Petit Larousse 1971) for all entries beginning with the letter "A".

**Table 7.1:** Classification of pictures in some dictionaries (Hupka 1983)
(for entries beginning with the letter "A")

| Dictionary | Total | Plants | Animals | Techno-logy | Medi-cine | History | Archi-tecture | Mathe-matics | Others |
|---|---|---|---|---|---|---|---|---|---|
| NDFCI | 86 | 24 | 22 | 6 | 7 | 5 | 3 | 4 | 15 |
| PL71 | 140 | 29 | 27 | 20 | 6 | 8 | 14 | 7 | 29 |
| Webster | 38 | 0 | 17 | 4 | 0 | 5 | 4 | 4 | 4 |

We have augmented the data by investigating the Ninth New Collegiate Dictionary (Webster 1990), which is not particularly rich in illustrations, in the same manner. The results show that it is largely real objects which are portrayed, many of which have names that are not in common usage.

Further, Hupka (1983) undertook a general classification of such illustrations. The text in the dictionary normally explains the functionality of objects, while the illustrations tend to concentrate on their appearance or the naming of subparts. The following classification resulted from his study:

1. A single object is illustrated
   with a high degree of iconicity (recall Chapter 4). This class of illustrations can be found more often than all other classes together. For an example see Figure 7.4a.
2. *Several representations of a class of objects are shown,*
   because their appearance is very different (see Figure 7.4b). The reason for showing more than one example is in many cases not very obvious, because the collection is never complete and can demonstrate only a part of the range. The intention of these illustrations is to visualize a class of objects.
3. *An object is shown in its context,*
   so that its structural relationship to others is accentuated. Figure 7.4c shows how important the environment can be.
4. *The inner structure of an object is highlighted*
   even if it is normally not visible (see Figure 7.4d). These illustrations are used to demonstrate the functional principles or the internal structure of an object.

Finally, two more specialized types complete the spectrum:

5. *The illustration does not accompany a text,*
   but is designed to be studied alone and in its own right. Examples are the OXFORD/DUDEN (1989) Picture Dictionary (see Figure 7.5) and the PONS (1992) Picture Dictionary (see Figure 7.6). The emphasis here is not only on the visualization

but also on conveying the names of objects to users. Furthermore, objects tend to be illustrated in their usual context, which aids the viewer in developing associations between objects.

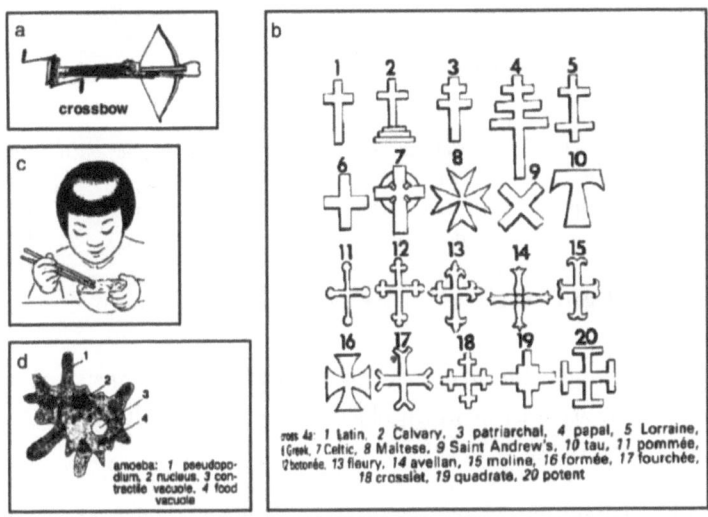

**Figure 7.4:** Examples of different classes of pictures in dictionaries (Webster 1990)

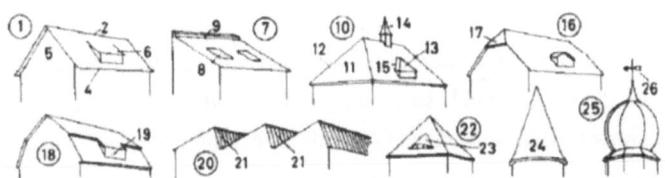

**Legend:**

| | | | |
|---|---|---|---|
| 1 gable (saddle) roof | 8 skylight | 15 (roof) valley | 22 broach roof |
| 2 ridge | 9 fire gable | 16 hipped-gable roof | 23 eyebrow |
| 3 verge | 10 hip (hipped) roof | 17 partial-hip end | 24 conical broach roof |
| 4 eaves | 11 hip end | 18 mansard roof | 25 imperial dome |
| 5 gable | 12 hip (arris) | 19 mansard dormer window | 26 weather vane |
| 6 dormer window | 13 hip dormer window | 20 sawtooth roof | |
| 7 pent (shed) roof | 14 ridge turret | 21 north light | |

**Figure 7.5:** Example of the page under the keyword "roof" in the Duden/Oxford Picture Dictionary

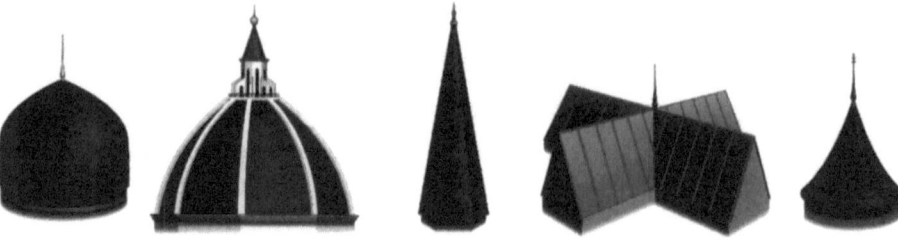

**Legend:**

| Glockendach | Kuppeldach | Helmdach | eingeschnittenes Satteldach | Kegeldach |
|---|---|---|---|---|
| bell roof | dome roof | helm roof | hip-and-valley roof | conical broach roof |
| toit en coupole | toit en døme | toit en flèche | toit à quatre versants | toit en poivrière |
| de cúpula | cúpula | de aguja | de cuatro aguas con canalera | cónico |

**Figure 7.6:** Example in the PONS (1992) Picture Dictionary

6. *The choice of the illustration to accompany a text appears arbitrary.*

In general, the decision as to which objects are illustrated often appears rather unsystematic (Hupka 1983).

A question which editors of such materials must deal with is whether a photo of an object should be used to demonstrate its real appearance, or whether a drawing should be used. This is a practical application of the theoretical discussion in Chapter 5: Barthes (1964) considered photos "messages sans code" (messages without a code), while he considered diagrams to be "messages codés" (coded message). Indeed, he considered that a photograph is not a "transformation" of reality, only a recording. He used this to explain why photos are easier to understand, since they are without code and therefore more "immediate". But now this view seems antiquated: for example the choice of camera position and lighting have a marked influence on the way a scene is perceived. Barthes may have been right if only transmitted information were to be considered, but it is precisely the differences due to the settings of the camera and the environment that are responsible for information being transputed.

Returning to interactive systems, a great deal of work has been done to develop computer-based dictionaries (for example by the University of Waterloo for the Oxford English Dictionary), but little has been done to integrate illustrations into such materials. In some systems, pictures are stored in a bitmap format; in hypertext systems, certain regions of pictures are made sensitive, and certain functions are activated by clicking on the regions (recall Chapter 3).

Kugas (1993) applied the methodology outlined in Section 7.2 to the OXFORD/DUDEN Picture Dictionary. The aim is to make the representational parts of the pictures available for re-use in dialogue systems and to provide access to the picture via string-searching on

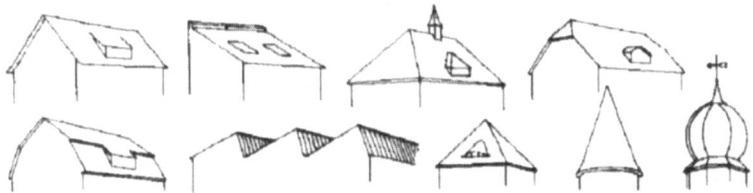

**Figure 7.7:** The result of applying the methodology to Figure 7.5

the basis of keywords. Note that in these pictures there is no single "message" which could be formulated as the "meaning". The graphical symbols tend to be less significant than the pictorial aspect.

In these systems, image processing and OCR software identifies the textual labels in the picture and the (many) vectors of the presentational parts. In the second step, the heuristics begin by searching in the neighborhood of the recognized characters for the endpoint of a line or a circle. If an endpoint can be found, the position of the other endpoint is associated with the label. At this time, the user is shown the association and can make corrections. Finally, these graphical symbols are removed, leaving the presentational part. The result of this procedure as applied to Figure 7.5 is shown in Figure 7.7, where only the presentational pictures are visible, while the extracted relations and groups are not shown.

While it would be desirable to endow the computer with more information about the pictures, we feel that with today's technology it is unreasonable to expect an algorithm to analyze the presentational part of a picture with the goal of extracting information. For the time being, we will have to be content with the computer having at its disposal only information pertaining to the graphical symbols. However, we shall often observe in this book that such information is already an important step in the direction of enabling user interaction with pictures.

## 7.4  An Application to Business Graphics

As a more specialized example of the workings of the method introduced in Section 7.2, we shall treat its application to business graphics. Such graphics today routinely appear in many kinds of printed materials; however, OCR software fails dismally in their interpretation. Pictures are almost always ignored by OCR software, and indeed it is difficult to conceive of a foolproof algorithm for their interpretation.

The key to interactive interpretation of business graphics is the utilization – alluded to earlier in this chapter – of the fact that in such graphics, numeric values underlying the

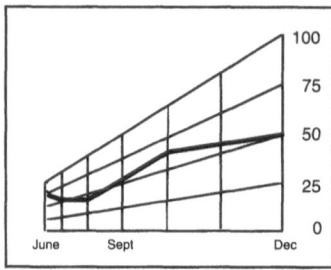 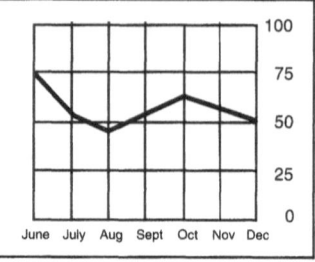

**Figure 7.8:** Example of a misleading business graph (left) of data (right)

pictures are almost always proportional to a length or an angle. Thus, a viewer can get a feeling for the orders of magnitude of the data as well as carry out direct comparisons by simple visual inspection.

Software tools for constructing business graphics make it easy to distort images, so that this principle does not always hold. For example, Figure 7.8 shows two examples of business graphics of the same data; the difference speaks for itself. Such graphics can be used to deliberately mislead the viewer (Zelazny 1985).

While programs like EXCEL produce well-behaved, correct-looking business graphics, much material is professionally designed and looks somewhat more interesting. To illustrate the amount of creativity that goes into the designs, Figure 7.9a–i shows all nine business graphics contained in a recent issue of a popular (but serious) weekly news magazine (DER SPIEGEL). A careful analysis of this set reveals the astonishing fact that two of the graphics are plainly misleading! Figure 7.9a and Figure 7.9b show numerical values, but in Figure 7.9a the difference in values is not proportional to the distance, while in Figure 7.9b the percentage is not expressed as an angular fraction of the circle. This is a flagrant example of the misleading nature of such graphics in practice.

It is interesting to observe that almost all these graphics contain a presentational part, even though these would be practically meaningless without the accompanying numerical data. The presentational part serves to make the picture more appealing. It sets the stage and conveys the nature of the data in an optically more pleasing manner than a caption. It is interesting that the presentational parts of the picture are related to the information which is to be *transputed* by the picture. Thus for example Figure 7.9f clearly indicates that the automobile industry is "going downhill"; this message is in fact more important for understanding the point of the article in which it appears than the raw data itself. However, it is primarily the information to be *transmitted* to the reader that can be captured by an algorithm. The information which is to be transputed is often encoded in the presentational part and is not accessible to the computer.

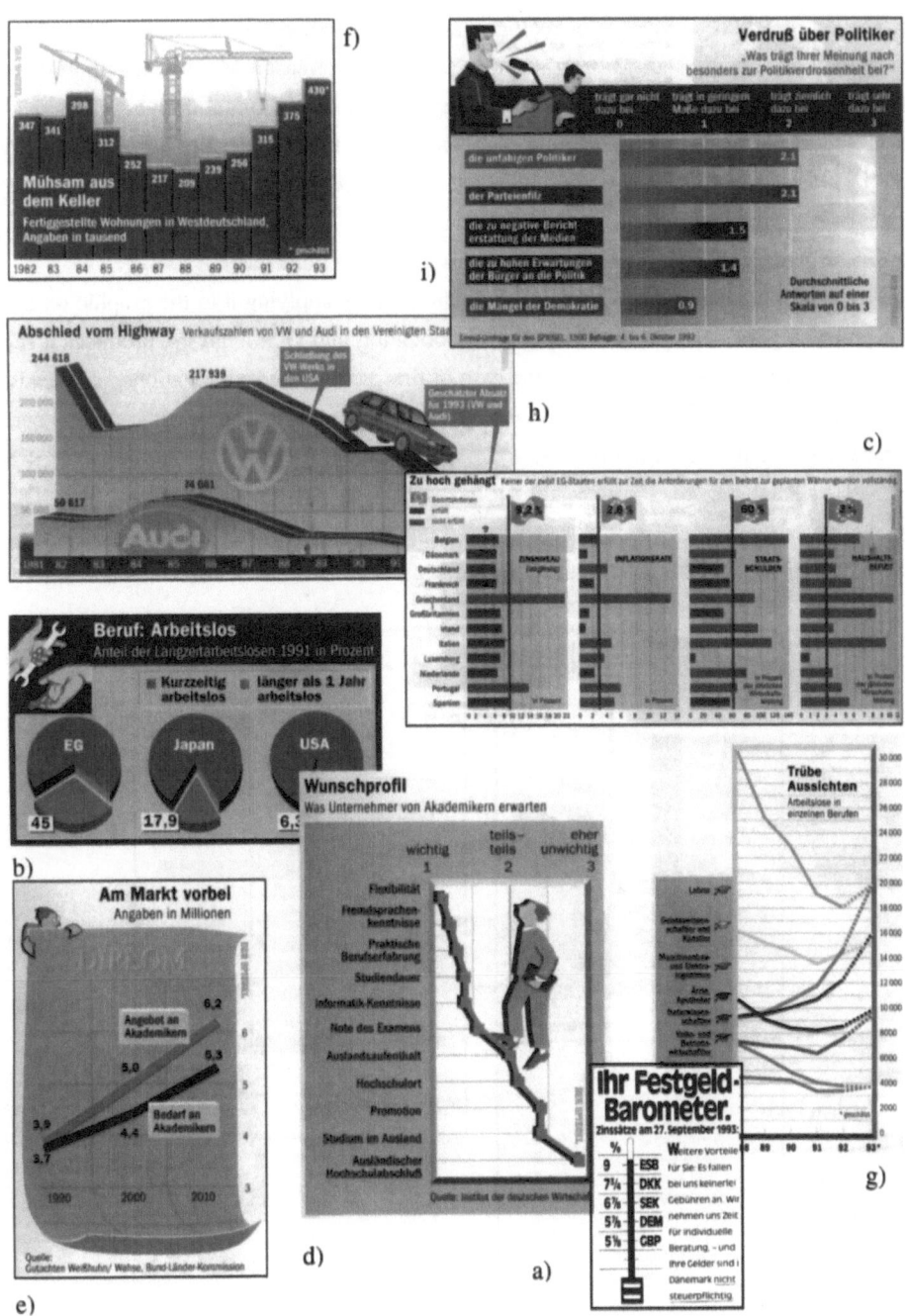

**Figure 7.9:** Examples of business graphics. The complete set of business graphics from one issue of the weekly news magazine DER SPIEGEL (October 18th, 1993)

Kurze et al. (1995) developed a dialogue system for converting the numerical values contained in a business graphics into an EXCEL table. The reason why this is important is that today even though most business graphics are produced from underlying numerical data, the reader of the document who may want to use the data usually has no access to the raw data. Even so, he or she may want or need to use it, either to perform some calculations on it or perhaps to present it in a new way. One application is to convert a business graph into a tactile and acoustic form for use by blind users.

We shall illustrate the methodology of Section 7.2 by applying it to the graphic on the far left of Figure 7.9. The first step, the vectorization and OCR analysis, produces a sequence of vectors and characters. In the case of this picture, the vectorization was already too complicated for the heuristics to be able to associate any features with one another, hence step 2 yields no further results.

The resultant picture, which is shown to the user, is illustrated in Figure 7.10a. The user is given two scales, one for distances and one for angles. Either of these can be rotated in three dimensions and placed over the picture. Each axis can be calibrated by

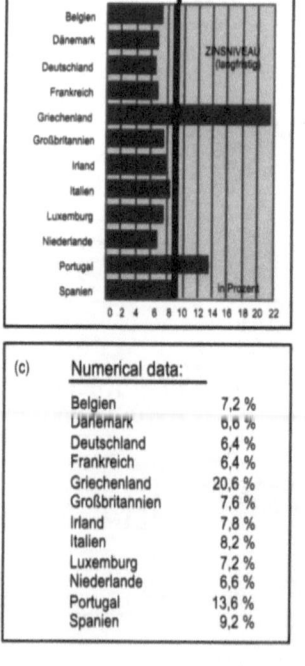

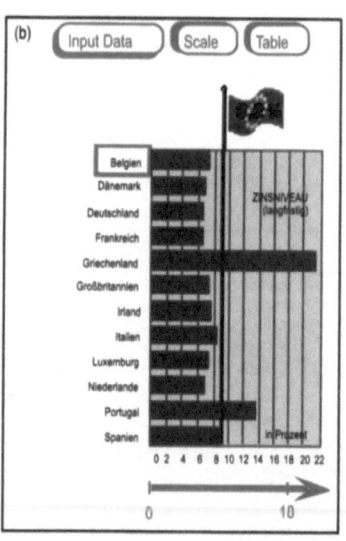

**Figure 7.10:** Example of the interaction to capture the numeric data
(a) The user begins the editing process
(b) The user adds a scale by which other features can be measured
(c) An EXCEL table results from the interaction.

clicking on the corresponding textual labels. Data points can then be identified by clicking on the underlying picture. The user now places scales, either a straight line for linear measures or a circular one for angles, over the part of the picture to be measured. He or she clicks on any of the numerical values (shown in red in Figure 7.10b) to calibrate the scale of the horizontal axis (in the example, the user chooses the 0 and the 22). Finally, the user moves to a data collection mode and clicks on attribute-value pairs (for example, Belgium and the line at the right end of the bar). This serves to identify the data to be extracted from the picture. The resultant EXCEL table is shown in Figure 7.10c.

The data is now in a form where it can be used further, referred to by the user, or easily searched in using string-searching or value-searching functions. And, the attractive picture can still be used in a presentation of the data.

## 7.5 Discussion

Our emphasis in this chapter has been on an analysis of abstract-graphical pictures. However, rather than taking the classical approach of a purely *algorithmic* analysis, we have developed a methodology which incorporates an analysis on the part of a *user*. It is no secret that image processing algorithms today still have difficulty in recognizing features the trained human eye has no problems with (the converse is of course also true, but is not the point here). In fact there is no need for algorithms to labor at such problems with little hope of success (or, more aptly put, for image processing specialists to labor at solving problems that for all intents and purposes are unsolvable in the sought-after generality). This is when the user comes in to link up and bind together the requirements of the application and the facilities offered by general-purpose software.

*Flute player (Kokopelli)*
North American Indian Symbol

# Users' Analysis and Criticism of Abstract-Graphical Pictures

The stage has now been set for a study of ways in which end-users of interactive systems can work with abstract-graphical pictures. Having shed light on how users understand pictures (Chapter 4) and mechanisms for using pictures to convey information (Chapter 5), we now want the user and the computer to join forces via the pictures presented. In order for abstract-graphical pictures to link up the user and the computer effectively, we need convincing ways in which the user can close the circuit by giving his or her input a new quality with respect to the pictures.

The fundamental challenge is to find ways to empower a user to initiate and lead a dialogue with the computer *about* the picture. The goal is to broaden the computer's source of data which the picture reflects, as well as to develop the user's feeling for this data. The requirement is that users be able to make full use of their intuitive reasoning power, conveying their observations to the computer in an understandable manner without necessarily having to justify them in a formal way. In other words, the user is to give some of the information which is transputed to him or her back to the computer. However, the user need not provide details of his or her own reasoning process. Achieving this goal will enable the development of a stronger role for pictures in interactive systems.

In this capter, we will develop a methodology for closing the circuit between users and the computer in this sense. The basis will be that a user is able to *criticize* a picture presented by the machine, to initiate a reasoning process on the part of the computer. This results in changes in the machine's representation of the underlying data, which in turn results in a new abstract-graphical picture, completing the circuit. For systems that exhibit this behavior, we coin the term *oracle systems*.

Our approach in this chapter will be to develop our techniques using a specific example of a particular kind of abstract-graphical picture. We have material flow simulation as our application and concentrate on the kinds of animation produced by major simulators. This will allow us to demonstrate oracle systems *in action* in a real application to complement the theoretical approach. The idea of oracle systems is complex and influences the architecture of interactive systems; for this reason, their benefits cannot be demonstrated clearly with the help of a small clear example. It is therefore necessary for the reader to understand computer simulation and its methodology. Thus the reader will be led through some detailed descriptions, which will set the stage for the presentation of oracle systems.

The chapter is organized as follows. In Section 8.1 we discuss the role of animation, a special kind of abstract-graphical picture, in simulation, and we show the general drawbacks in making effective use of the information conveyed by animation. Section 8.2 discusses users' observations during animations and develops the architecture of oracle systems. Section 8.3 gives a detailed analysis and concretization of the different parts of an oracle system for simulation. The prototypical implementation of an element-oriented simulator in Section 8.4 shows how a user can solve typical simulation problems in the oracle system. The scenario described demonstrates clearly the effects and benefits of the approach.

## 8.1 The Role of Animation During Simulation

Besides statistical data on the flow of materials through a model, most simulators offer an animation module which shows users how the objects move about. Figure 8.1 shows a snapshot of the popular animation system PROOF. Animation in the context of computer simulation is an integrated part of the presentation techniques for the simulation results the user has to interpret. Some important features define the contours of this kind of animation:

1. The animation always has an obvious raison d'être, since it has to give the user a feeling for what is going on in his or her model during the simulated time and to uncover the problems of the dynamic behavior of the model.
2. The data has a unique origin. Animation is based on the simulated numerical results and has to display them. Additional graphical data are necessary to describe how to express the different kinds of simulation results. For example, the appearance of a

fork-lift truck is defined by the additional graphical data, but the information pertaining to when the truck has to move and from where to where will be part of the
simulation results. The graphical data is responsible for the appearance and the simulation results for the content of the animation; they do not overlap one another. The
simulation results form the basis of the animation and are the driving force.

3. The quality of the graphics of the animation is significantly lower than what is
normally expected of 3D photorealistic renderers (recall Chapter 3) due to real-time
processing. In simulation, mostly 2D or so-called $2^1/_2$D presentations are used. The
graphical capabilities of animation software is sometimes still quite poor, so the
examples of products like PROOF (Figure 8.1) are highlights on the scene.

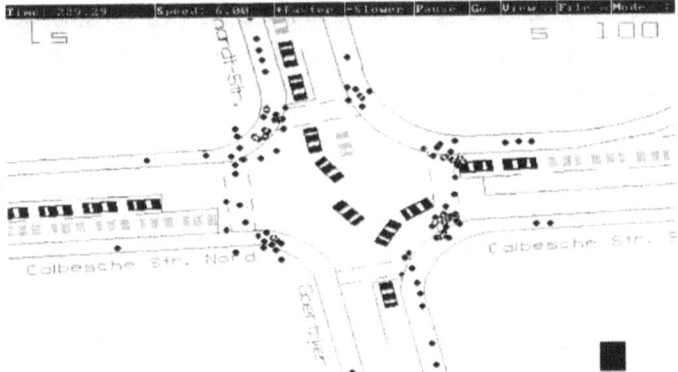

**Figure 8.1:** Example of a PROOF animation (courtesy of Peter Lorenz)

### 8.1.1 Simulation Methodology

In general, simulation is the process of representing a dynamic process in a system with
the help of a model, which can be used for experimentation to derive information that
can be applied to reality (VDI 1992). This definition of simulation shows the diversity of
skills and abilities required of a user during the simulation process. To understand the
potential problems encountered by users, we have to study in detail the process of simulation from the user's point of view. One commonly used methodology for simulation is
shown in Figure 8.2 (see Law and Kelton 1991).

The *systems analysis* has as its goal to define the problem, to analyze the application
area and to collect necessary input data from different sources. During the phase of
*modeling*, the user has to represent the important features of the real system in a model

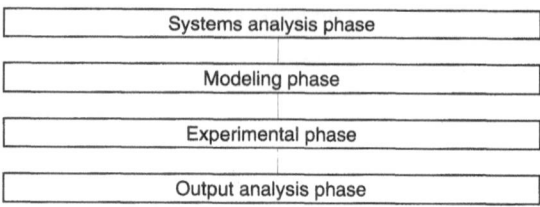

**Figure 8.2:** A coarse methodology of simulation

and to validate this model with respect to the real systems and the simulation goals. For the *experimental phase*, an experiment plan has to be developed to make it possible to derive conclusions about the real system. Because of the large amount of data that result from the different experiments, an *output analysis* is necessary. In this phase, the user has to apply different statistical methods to determine the significance of different values. This can be the end of a simulation study if the user assesses the results as being complete and correct, otherwise he has to restart the process or – more likely – to rethink some phases of the methodology.

Animation is always used when it can present the current dynamic behavior of the model to a user better than tables or statistical or graphical presentations of numbers, like charts or diagrams. This is the case in the modeling and experimental phases, where the results of simulation runs have to be assessed by the user. A user can only extract trends, assessments, and problematic zones in a model from an animation alone. Concrete values or statistical results require numerical data.

The question why modeling is one of the biggest problems for users will be dealt with in the next subsection. First we need to define the kind of simulation we are dealing with, because the process of modeling depends very largely on the kind of simulation and the chosen class of simulation instruments. For the following, we will limit our application field to material flow systems, because the animation in this area is very close to the simulated system and exhibits a dynamic behavior like reality.

### 8.1.2  Model Validation and User Support

The modeling process of a real system is carried out in a cyclic fashion: the user creates a model, and the computer simulates it and produces results, which are then presented to the user. After the user has analyzed the results, interpreted them, and decided if the model is valid, the cycle can begin once more. This process can be divided into three parts (Figure 8.3).

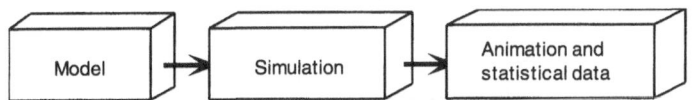

**Figure 8.3:** The three parts of simulation

In the context of this book, it is important to look at what information is transmitted and what is transputed to the user by the animation (recall Chapter 5). We do so by analyzing the possible user reactions to the three components of Figure 8.3, with the animation as the starting point and the support available from the computer.

*1. The user modifies the animation or graphics of statistical results.*

The user can interact directly with the animation by changing some of its parameters so as to alter its format. Examples of this include the speed of the animation, the colors used, or the position of the virtual camera in case of a 3D animation. By changing such parameters, he or she may be able to gain new insights into the animation, though the user can change neither the simulation nor the model.

*2. The user modifies the simulation.*

The user can change input parameters of the simulation, like time intervals between collecting statistical values or the simulation time. This leads to a change in the animation, which promotes in the user a feeling for the model and the simulation. Some simulators with an on-line animation feature allow changes of values of the internal state of some variables during the simulation, so that after the modifications the model exhibits a different behavior. A problem with this is that the computer's behavior is not easily reproducible, since no changes have been made to the model.

*3. The user modifies the model.*

By manipulating the animation, users should have access to the model, but this is not possible in any of today's major simulators. Instead, users modify the model directly, usually with special editors. Users are not given any help to debug the model but are forced to work intuitively and – most important – alone.

To appreciate the difficulties a user faces during this procedure, see Figure 8.4 and the following explanation.

The user first studies the animation more or less intensively to observe aspects that may be relevant; the goal here is that the computer transputes to the user information about the model. After figuring out which parts of the model may be responsible for the symptoms he or she observed in the animation, the user then makes appropriate changes to the animation. After the system has re-computed the simulation and presented the new animation, the user can then verify the correctness of his or her changes or continue to investigate in the same manner.

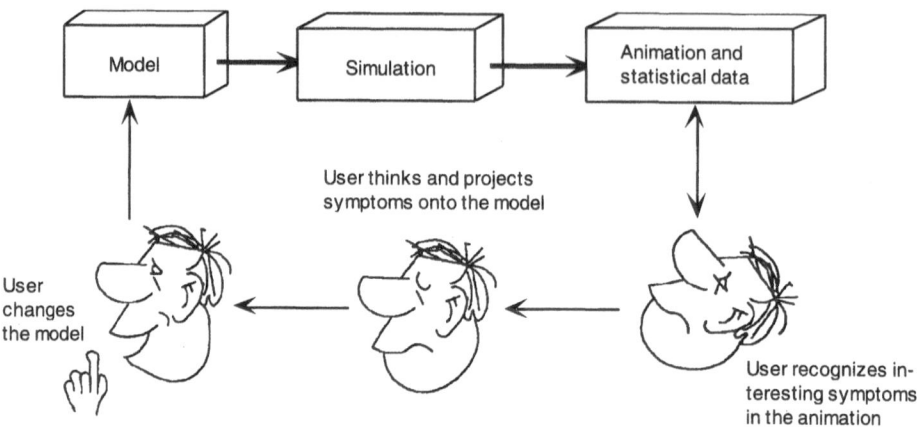

**Figure 8.4:** User changes of the model without the support of the computer

The analysis of the user support mentioned above is based on experience with different simulation instruments such as GPSS/PC, DOSIMIS-3, SIMAN/CINEMA, and SIMPLE++. In general, during the modeling process, which itself is quite complex, the user only gets help from the computer on a very low level. So the computer can aid the description and formulation of a model by using editors of varying sophistication. But the computer does not give substantial help for modeling according to the real system or the simulation goals, and it cannot support the user while validating his or her model.

No doubt simulation is an efficient tool for the design and planning of future systems and for improving efficiency and reorganizing existing installations (Jünemann 1989), but there exists a reluctance to accept simulation among planners and technologists. A current study of Hollocks (1992) in the UK showed that only 9 % of companies that are potential users of simulation actually use it. The general direction of all proposals for making simulation more acceptable among end-users is the enrichment of computer support offered to the user. Examples of proposals are the common availability of animation and visualizing systems (Lorenz 1991, Zell and Scheer 1991) and the further development of element oriented simulation concepts (Noche and Wenzel 1991, Kreutzer 1986).

### 8.1.3 Underestimation of Animation

There is a trend in the simulation community to visualize all the information from a simulation study and to assess the quality of a simulation instrument only with respect to its visualizing components, the quality of the animation, and the effort necessary to create it. However, the question that really should be asked is: What can a user see in an animation and what information can he or she extract?

It is interesting that a gestalt psychologist, Rudolf Arnheim (1972), asked a similar question more than 20 years ago: "How much do we know about what exactly children and other learners see when they look at a textbook illustration, a film, or a television program?" The simulation community has no general answer to this question up to now. However, the question is still very topical. Arnheim himself considers that "the answer [to this question] is crucial because if the student does not see what he [or she] is assumed to see, the very basis for learning is lacking."

Although animation is held in high esteem, we have to ask if the role of animation specifically as a presentation technique is underestimated. A common situation is that the computer produces the animation, but all the information which the user extracts from the animation, i.e., transmitted but in particular also transputed information, is the *exclusive property* of the user. The computer has no access to this data: it has no more information after producing the animation than before. Presentations of simulation results are convenient and helpful to the user but are of no value to the computer. We claim that this is one of the reasons for the lack of user support by the computer during in today's simulators.

To solve this problem, the two extreme possibilities are:

1. The computer needs its own vision system (recall Chapter 3) to extract data from its own presentations.
2. The user who extracts a lot of information from the presentation provides the computer with this data, i.e., the user gives the information transputed to him or her back to the computer. The assumption is that the data is not known *a priori* to the computer.

The first of these options appears unrealistic considering the present state of vision systems (see Vernon 1991 and Groß 1994 for example). We develop the idea for the second case in the following subsections. Fruitful co-operation between the user and the computer, based on the animation as the starting point of the human-computer interaction, will now be discussed further.

## 8.2  Information Sources for the Computer

### 8.2.1  User Observations

During an animation, the user may observe errors or the critical behavior in a model that does not correspond to the simulation goals. This is possible due to the excellent cognitive abilities of humans (recall Chapter 4), with their fast and efficient perception.

For the problem of model validation, the computer needs information about the animation, i.e., the dynamic behavior of the model. The source of this information should be the user, who has knowledge about simulation as well as about the application field of the particular simulation study, and who can analyze the animation and the other simulation results. User input criticizing an animation on the basis of the user's knowledge, and containing more information than the computer could derive from the animation itself, will be referred to as an *oracle*. Detailed information about the origin and the meaning of the word oracle will be delayed until the next section.

A user's oracle is a suitable starting point for the computer to find out the corresponding reasons in the model. In this way the user can initiate necessary model modifications during model validation. In this sense, the computer can provide substantial help for the user because it can draw on the topological data of the model and the statistical data of the simulation run. The computer just needs rules to describe how the criticisms observed during the animation can be projected back onto the model.

The high-level structure of oracle systems is shown in three parts in Figure 8.5. Important points of this structure are:

- the oracle of the user plays an important role because it is based on the relevant world knowledge of the user and his or her subjective assessments of the animation, and
- the knowledge-based component is connected to the other components but is not part of the simulation application.

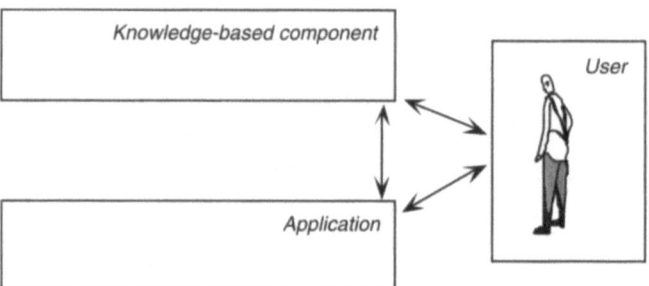

**Figure 8.5:** Coarse architecture of oracle systems

## 8.2.2  Oracles Yesterday and Today

The word *oracle*, which is derived from the Latin noun *oraculum*, appeared in the English language in the 16th century. Oracles were already very important in the Greco-Roman era, but began losing their importance after about the fourth century AD. Until then, the following meaning of the word had evolved: initially it referred to a place at which the Gods gave prophecies, later it denoted the prophecies themselves.

The shift of the definition of the word oracle through the centuries is evident from the diverse definitions in various dictionaries. Basically three different definitions are used:

1. Oracle as a place

   This is the oldest use of the word, derived from the definition of the Latin noun *oraculum,* which means place of speech.

2. Oracle as a spoken word

   Later, the word oracle began to be used as an utterance itself: "divine communication delivered in response to a petitioner's request" (New Encyclopaedia Britannica 1991).

3. Oracle as a person

   In the modern French language an oracle is defined as being "a person who speaks with great authority or competence" (Petit Robert 1985).

In modern times, the word oracle has begun to be used in various branches of science and technology. In complexity theory, for example, *oracle Turing machines* consist of a normal Turing machine plus an extra oracle tape and a question state. The oracle itself is used to refer to a language of the Turing machine. The transition from a current state of the tapes to the next depends on the answer of the oracle (Reischuk 1990). The oracle is used in this context in situations in which the next state cannot otherwise be determined. Another example of the use of oracles is in medical diagnosis. INTERNIST-1 is an expert system that requires the relevant symptom and patient data observed by the doctor to compute a solution to a diagnostic problem the doctor alone could not solve (Jackson 1990). Miller and Masarie (1990) criticize the system because of its supposed super-human problem-solving capabilities, which are incomprehensible to the user, and thus refer to it as the *Greek oracle.* After the input of patient's data, the user plays only the role of a passive observer. His or her actions are merely yes-no answers to questions.

The new kind of oracle which we now define is based on the premise that an oracle is an utterance. However, initially it remains an open question as to who should play the role of the oracle. Unlike researchers in expert systems, who have the machine play the role of the oracle, we decided to give the user a higher priority, because on the basis of his or her complex information processing and problem-solving capabilities, the user decides between alternatives that are undecidable for the machine. It is the user who has the knowledge of the context of the application.

We therefore define an *oracle* as being

> *information input by the user that results in a reasoning process in which both the user and the machine are involved in turn, and that results in a change in the machine's representation of data.*

By virtue of the reasoning process on the part of both the user and the computer, the two are firmly bound together, with information being transputed in both directions. In the reasoning process, the user contributes his or her world knowledge and grasp of the situation, so that the machine can choose between otherwise undecidable alternatives. This definition is comparable to the use of the word oracle in complexity theory, in that every time the machine cannot make a decision because the basis for it is not represented, the oracle is asked to make the choice.

The definition highlights the criticism of the "Greek oracle model" previously pursued in expert systems. Our definition implicitly contains the assumption that the user is a decisive source of knowledge. Further, the definition implies that even if the user had adequate input mechanisms at his or her disposal to input all necessary information, the machine could not carry out appropriate diagnoses independently. Indeed, this definition of an oracle supports the desires of the critics of the Greek oracle model, namely to construct systems where "a mixed initiative system is ... mandatory" (Miller and Masarie 1990). Oracles can be viewed as a possibility for users to make their knowledge available to the machine at exactly the time when the machine needs the data. The result is that user input is made more effective.

### 8.2.3 Architecture of an Oracle-Based Model Modification

On the basis of the user's oracle, the phase of model validation described in Section 8.2.1 is expanded to include new user support possibilities for making the necessary changes to a model. To achieve this goal, an architecture for oracle-based model modification will be developed below.

One prerequisite for oracle-based model modification is the computer's access to the model and the simulation results. Because these data are the basis for the reasoning process of the computer, it is necessary to collect them as facts in a knowledge base. The second part of the knowledge base is composed of rules for model modifications. With an oracle as an initial input and a knowledge base as described, the reasoning component can find possible reasons for the criticized behavior of the model.

From these requirements, a detailed architecture for oracle-based model modification can be derived (Figure 8.6).

The general scenario for the functionality of an oracle system is as follows: The model is used as a basis for the simulation, which produces simulation results in the form of animation and statistical data. This produces data that refers to parts of the model on the one hand and direct results of the simulation on the other. This data is placed in a knowledge base, since it includes facts the computer will need at a later point for projecting the behavior of the animation onto the model. The user assesses the quality of the model by analyzing the animation. This task can *only* be carried out by the user, since

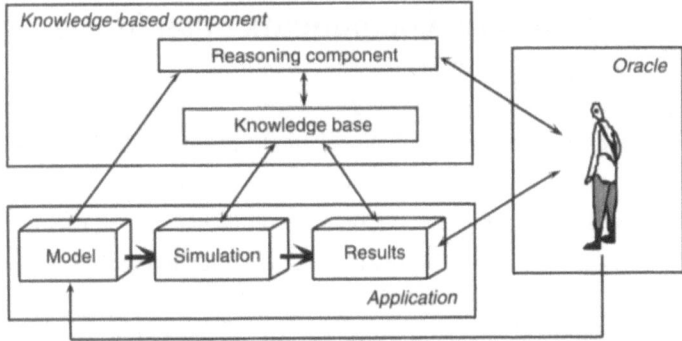

**Figure 8.6:** Architecture of oracle systems

only he or she is acutely aware of the goals of the simulation, which can often not be formalized without an unreasonable amount of work. The user is aware of the simulation goals, but only in an informal manner. He or she can recognize the problematic parts of the animation and input this information as an *oracle* to the reasoning component.

Now the machine uses the oracle as well as by-products of the simulation stored in the knowledge base. It may well be that the reasoning process needs still further information, upon which the machine asks for another oracle. This is the reason for the arrows in *both* directions between the animation and the reasoning component in Figure 8.6. Suggestions for changes in the model are then passed on to the user for his or her comments. The combination of the application, the user, and the knowledge base in the system is necessary for three reasons:

1. Clarity of the implementation

   Involving the user makes it possible to construct a reasoning component with a relatively small number of rules. This is because no attempt is made to model in any complete sense the knowledge of the application area. The user's oracle initiates and directs the reasoning process in a useful manner, so that the system has an appropriate starting point for its investigations using facts and rules.

2. Limitation of the knowledge processing

   The knowledge base of the system is only used when reasoning is necessary, but not for the computation or other numerical algorithms needed in that context.

3. Machine search in the representation

   Users are not left alone in their validation of the representation, nor in its analysis. It becomes the machine's task to search in the representation for data that will not be visualized in the presentation, rather than leaving this task to the user (recall Figure 8.4). This is an appropriate use of the machine's strength, searching in a complex representation based on formal criteria.

## 8.3    Requirements and Components of an Oracle System for Simulation

The basis for the idea of oracle-based model modification is the well-known maxim "editing is easier than creating". According to this, it is easier to correct an existing text than to write down the first sentence on a blank sheet of paper. One reason is described by Fischer (1986), when he writes "In reality, it is often relatively easy to determine the negative aspects of a goal state or a system."

It is easy to see that the principle of a step-by-step removal of the critical behavior of the model will not lead to an optimal model in a mathematical sense, but very likely to a satisfactory model. This result satisfies the demands of the user in most situations; this is particularly true for the field of material flow simulation, where there are no established general optimization methods.

To build an oracle system, it is necessary to add a knowledge-based component and to define the kinds of oracles that can be understood by the reasoning component. Although every simulation instrument has its own particular requirements, there are general principles to be followed when designing such systems.

### 8.3.1  Typical Oracles in Simulation

The oracles formulated by the user refer to the simulation results presented in the animation. The criticism of the user can only refer to information that is visible in the animation. Included here are:

- the states of static and dynamic elements,
- the behavior of movable elements, and
- statistical results.

Oracles can be associated with one of these kinds of information. Because the oracle should be interpretable by the reasoning component, primitives to express them have to be pre-defined by the developer of the oracle system. Table 8.1 shows some possible oracles.

This overview has to be adapted to particular simulators when their animation systems present new aspects of models. In most cases, the localization of a critical symptom in the animation is enough as the starting point for the reasoning component, because the type of symptom can be derived from statistical results. If this is not the case, the computer can always ask the user for the type of symptom.

**Table 8.1:** Possible oracles

| Objects of criticism | Aspects of the criticism | Examples |
|---|---|---|
| States<br>• blocked<br>• waiting<br>• passive<br>• in use | Criticism pertaining to time<br>• "too often"<br>• "too seldom"<br>• "too long"<br>• "too short" | Element "Gas station" is too often blocked. |
| movable elements<br>• vehicles<br>• palettes | Criticism pertaining to speed<br>• "too fast"<br>• "too slow"<br>• "colliding" | "Vehicle 2" is moving too slowly. |
| statistical data<br>• throughput<br>• blockage<br>• load | Criticism pertaining to values<br>• "too high"<br>• "too low" | Throughput of the "Gas station" is too low. |

### 8.3.2 Knowledge Base

Irrespective of which knowledge representation is chosen, facts and rules for the reasoning process are necessary. Facts are information from the model and the simulation run. Information pertaining to the model consists of

- topological facts like predecessor and successor relations, dynamic links for movable objects, types of the model elements, and
- parameters of the elements, if they exist.

Which of the simulation results are necessary depends largely on which information is needed by the rules. Certainly the following kinds of results should be included in the knowledge base:

- throughput,
- load, and
- blockage time.

Because the knowledge base depends on the simulation run, it must adapt dynamically. Therefore, all facts are extracted automatically from the model and the simulation run with the help of different generators (see Figure 8.7).

The rules describe the search strategy through the model. They start with the elements described in the oracle and determine the direction and the criteria for further investigation, which depends on the problematic state of the element currently being investigated. That is the reason why investigating the current element with respect to problematic

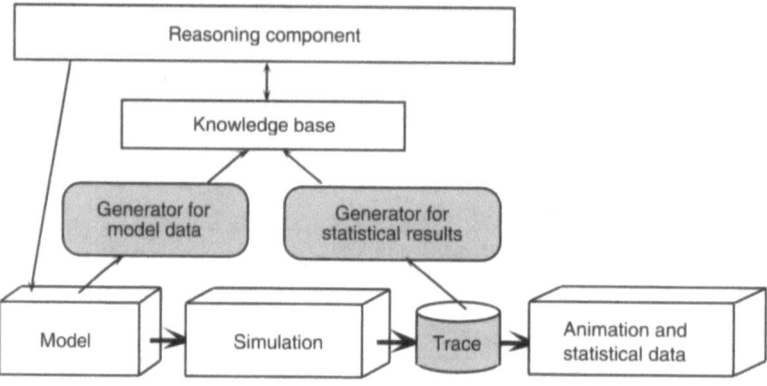

**Figure 8.7:** Generation of facts for the knowledge base

states is the first step of the reasoning component. Typical problematic states of model elements are:

- overloaded,
- breakdown,
- underloaded,
- blocked, and
- waiting.

The specific state of the elements has to be derived according to the statistical results. There therefore exist both general and element-specific rules, because different elements produce different kinds of statistical results.

The states "overloaded" and "breakdown" of an element imply that the element currently being investigated is, in fact, the reason for the symptom observed by the user. By contrast, the states "underloaded" and "blocked" point out that the investigation should continue onto other predecessors or successors. The rules consist of two parts, a condition and an action. The condition is the concrete state of the element and the action describes the search strategy through the model to find out possible reasons for the symptoms described in the oracle.

Because the details of the rules depend on the particular simulator, no concrete examples will be given at this point, but in the next section we introduce an implementation of an oracle system.   .

### 8.3.3  Results of the Reasoning Component

Obviously, an oracle system cannot solve all the problems a user may face. The reasoning component cannot give correct and complete answers to all possible criticisms the user can formulate. It can provide help for special situations and can suggest solutions for special kinds of problems. We shall now discuss what kinds of solutions it should be able to produce.

The first result the reasoning process should produce is the reason for the criticism for the oracle. The description of the reason should name the element as well as the state responsible for the problematic condition recognized by the user. Possible problematic states of elements that can be isolated by oracle systems as possible reasons are, for example, that

- an element is overloaded,
- incorrect strategies or distributing elements were used, or
- sources and sinks behave incorrectly.

A suggestion for modifying the model to eliminate the reasons for the oracle should be the machine's second step. Changes in a model can take two forms, parameter variations and structure variations. All the problematic states described above can be corrected by a parameter variation of the model element. For more complex changes of the model structure, an expert system would be necessary.

In summary, at this stage the computer is able to find out the reasons for the oracle problem and to suggest parameter variations as changes to the model.

## 8.4  A Prototypical Implementation

### 8.4.1  Environment for the Implementation

To test the ideas about oracle systems, a prototype oracle system was built. As the simulation instrument, the simulator Create! was chosen, because of its graphical user interface, the element-oriented concepts, and the implementation language Smalltalk. Create! was developed at the Fraunhofer Institute of Material Flow and Logistics in Dortmund (see Hoppe, Kirchner and Rüger 1990; Schürholz 1991; Nyhuis 1994; and Rüger and Behlau 1995). It consists of a simulation kernel and different sets of simulation elements for special application fields. The capabilities for creating new and editing existing elements allow the simulator to adapt very well to meet the requirements of end-users. Because of its element-oriented concept, users of Create! model by arranging and connecting elements in a graphical editor. This allows them to design the layout of their model to match to the real layout of the simulated system. Create! produces an abstract animation where the states of the elements are shown by color changes. It therefore uses information written in a trace file during the simulation.

For the reasoning component, it was decided very pragmatically to use a Prolog-like interpreter which was implemented in Smalltalk by Raab (1992) and provides common Prolog predicates. One particular addition was necessary because of the communication between the Smalltalk system and the interpreter. A special Prolog predicate "st80call" was implemented which enables a Smalltalk call and value exchange.

For the development of the knowledge base, two generators were built, one for the model data and one for the trace file information. The resulting data is transformed into Prolog-like syntax and asserted in the knowledge base. The rules of the knowledge base can be divided into five categories, each of which contains general and element-type-specific rules. The latter complete the former, but do not correct them. The categories are:

1. *Initial and cycle rules*

   The reasoning process is started by an initiation rule. The general initial rule names only the problematic element, while the specific initial rule names, in addition, the kind of the problematic state. These rules use different rules for the search strategy.

2. *Rules for the search strategy and the model*

   The search strategy can be derived from the state of the current element. In the case of a blockage in the current element, the system will investigate the successor elements with higher priority and the predecessor with lower priority. For the next element, an investigation criterion will be defined that specifies which element should be investigated.

3. *Rules for the investigation criterion*

   If an element fulfils the criterion, it will be investigated with the help of the different pre-defined states of the element. This element then becomes the next current one and the investigation cycle repeats itself.

4. *Rules for pre-defined states of elements*

   Different possible states are pre-defined with the help of statistical data and are sometimes very element-specific.

5. *Rules for termination*

   Special states of elements can be recognized as possible reasons for the oracle (recall Section 8.3.3) and terminate or interrupt the reasoning process.

These categories of rules are able to realize a complex reasoning process about the reasons for the oracle. The general process is as follows. According to the initial rules, the first element which should be investigated is named. Using the rules for determining the pre-defined states, the state of the current element is determined. From this, the state of the next element to be examined is determined as well as the investigation criterion. If the investigation criterion is fulfilled and there is no termination condition, the investigation will continue with the next element.

## 8.4.2  Scenario

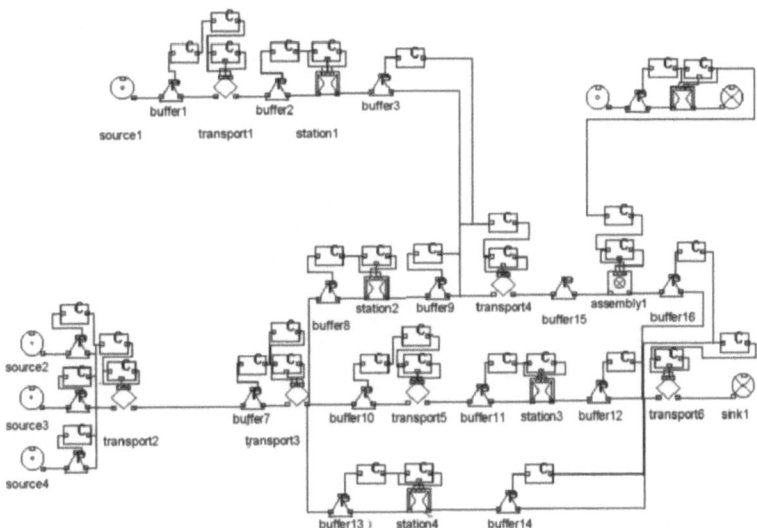

**Figure 8.8:** Topology of the reference model

The basic functionality of this implementation will be demonstrated on a reference model which was considered optimal as far as the load of machines and throughput of the objects flowing are concerned. Figure 8.8 shows the topology of the reference model.

From this reference model, different variations were derived by making changes in the parameters. These were then the problematic models that were investigated by the oracle system. Table 8.2 lists the variations of the problematic models.

**Table 8.2:** Problem models of the reference model

| problem model | variations |
|---|---|
| problem model 1 | lower acceptance time of sink |
| problem model 2 | lower delivery time of the source 1 |
| problem model 3 | lower delivery time of the sources 2, 3 and 4 |
| problem model 4 | longer processing time of assembly 1 |
| problem model 5 | longer processing time of station 4 |
| problem model 6 | longer processing time of station 3 and 4 |

The oracle-based model modification was applied to the problematic models when the user selected an element as not being satisfactory. At this stage, the user can also name the problematic state, as Figure 8.9 shows.

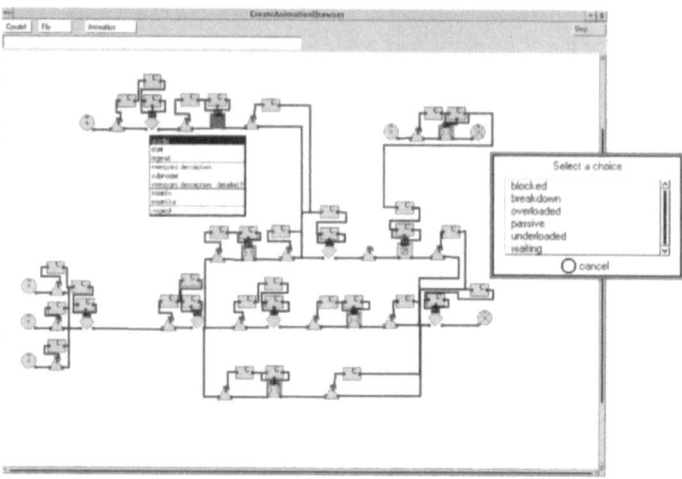

**Figure 8.9:** Formulation of an oracle with direct manipulation

After this, the Prolog interpreter can carry out reasoning with the help of all the facts from the model and the rules about the problem. A possible reason will be conveyed to the user, who decides whether he or she is satisfied or wants to know other possible reasons. For all problematic models listed in Table 8.2, each of the errors "implanted" were found by the oracle system. For a more detailed analysis of the reasoning process, the problematic model number 6 has been selected because it contains two errors. Figure 8.10 shows the oracle browser for the oracle that named station 1. The oracle browser presents all the current computed reasons and the searching direction for these as an explanation for the solution.

In the problematic model 6, the parameters of the processing time of the stations 3 and 4 were changed. The effect of these changes are that the transport 3 is blocked because both branches of stations 3 and 4 are not processing enough elements per unit time. Thus the branch with station 2 now has only a low throughput, resulting in transport 4 delivering only parts of the upper branch (with station 1) into buffer 14 in front of the assembly.

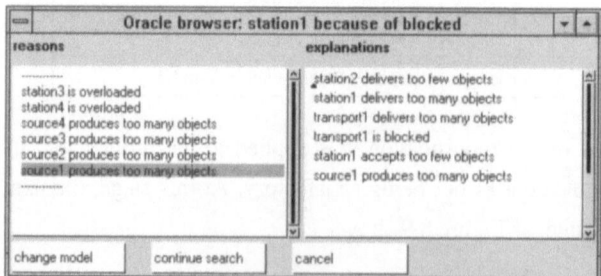

**Figure 8.10:** Presentation of possible reasons

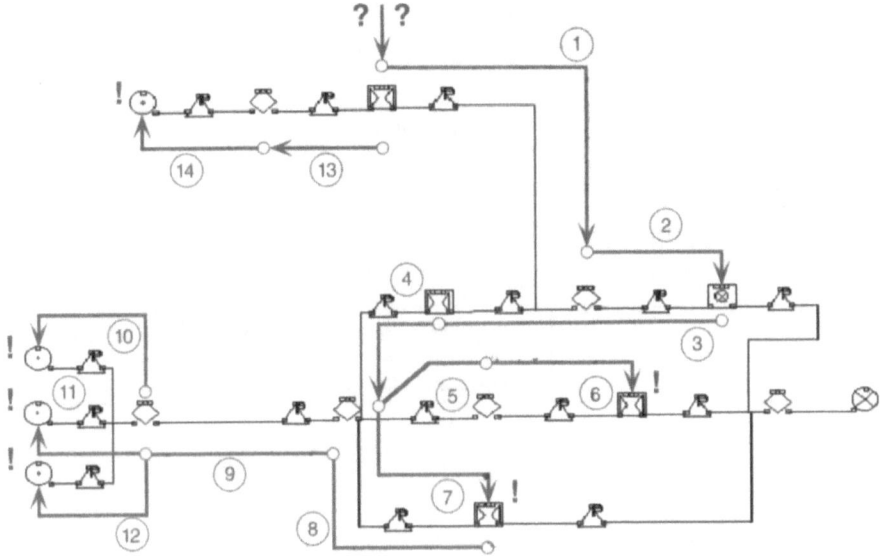

**Figure 8.11:** Search path of the reasoning component for oracle "station 1"

The shortage of elements from station 2 results in a continuous wait in assembly 1, which in turn means that no elements can be removed from buffer 14, and transport 4 is blocked. This also has an effect on the upper branch with station 1 which is subsequently blocked. With the help of Figure 8.11, the searching path through the model 6 can be observed.

Usually there is more than one reason for an oracle, because

- the model contains more than one error,
- rules with higher and lower priority for the same cases exist, and
- wrong behavior of sources and sinks is always possible.

The possible reasons found by the oracle system are shown in Table 8.3.

The statement that the oracle system was able to find all the reasons for the oracle "station 1" ends the detailed description of the functionality of the oracle system for the simulator Create!. This short description shows only a small part of the implementation, but serves to demonstrate the underlying principles. For more experiments and detailed information, see Helms (1994) and Naß (1993).

**Table 8.3:** Reasons for oracle "station 1" in problem model 6

| reason | explanation of the searching path |
|---|---|
| overloading of station 3 | After investigating station 4, since it is the successor of transport 3, the middle branch containing station 3 is investigated because it is accepting too few objects. |
| source 2 produces too many objects | Should there no further successors at a distribution element |
| source 3 produces too many objects | despite a blockage there, the predecessors are examined, too |
| source 4 produces too many objects | see if they are producing too many objects. |
| source 1 produces too many objects | Since there are no further possible reasons at station 1 for the blockage, the reasoning component uses a rule with a low priority which states that a blockage can also be the result of a predecessor producing too many objects. |

## 8.5 Discussion

In this chapter we have introduced the notion of oracle systems. We chose material flow simulation as a testbed, since toy examples are not able to demonstrate the real nature of the interaction. Due to the difficulty of using simulators for material flow systems and their overall complexity, this is an important application area.

Oracle systems are able to bind the user and the computer together firmly. Both participants in the dialogue carry out a reasoning process, meaning that each has a very substantial service of the other to draw upon. Assessments and criticisms of the visualizations presented are formalized by the user to make an interpretation by the computer possible. The computer then searches in the underlying data structures, applying rules to a large amount of data. The user input reduces the computer's search space to a manageable size.

*Vultures and headless human-like figures*
Çatal Hüyük, Anatolia, Turkey

**Chapter**

**9**

# Viewpoint Descriptions

Arnheim's question pertaining to what we really know about what learners see when examining pictures (recall Section 8.1.3) cannot be answered with the technique of oracles alone, since only certain aspects of that what a user sees are relevant. Indeed, oracles can be viewed as a very narrow answer to the question of what a user actually sees. A more complete answer can be developed with *viewpoint descriptions*, in which a user describes more fully what he or she sees in an animation.

Information a user extracts by observing an animation – observation of the statistical results of a simulation – has up to now been the exclusive property of the user. There has been no way for him or her to make this information explicitly available to the machine. The idea of using this information within the machine opens up new possibilities for supporting users in their work with simulation systems. Indeed, up to now it has also been an open question as to whether a user is even able to correctly interpret an animation. It has always been assumed that this is so, with the conclusion that therefore the animation must be useful for the user. However, the prerequisite is that the user has *learned to see*, i.e., that he or she is able to extract relevant information from the animation. This aspect of learning to see plays an important role in the motivation of viewpoint descriptions.

## 9.1  Viewpoint Descriptions in Simulation

In designing a formalism for viewpoint descriptions for computer simulation, we must first examine the goals, advantages, and applications of visualizations in general, as these shed light on the intention and purpose of visualizations.

The purpose of visualizations is to raise the user's confidence in a simulation, in particular in the relationship between the model and the situation to be simulated, as well as in the correctness of the model. Further, visualizations are important for the user to ascertain unexpected or previously unknown relationships between individual objects. Kreutzer (1992) considers an advantage of animations to be that visualized dynamic processes are easier to follow than textual representations, that intuition and the understanding of dynamic processes are more easily achieved and that the user can recognize and focus on anomalies and bottlenecks more readily.

These high hopes placed in visualizations have hardly been tested experimentally. Indeed, there are no reports in the literature known to the authors about what a user can actually expect from a presentation. The idea behind viewpoint descriptions is to assure that information transferred to the user in the form of a visualization can then also be made available to the machine. All the goals, advantages, and applications of animations and presentations mentioned above referred only to the user, whereas the machine has simply played the role of producing these visualizations, without any information about the semantic content. Furthermore, the possibility of describing what they see and leading a dialogue about this can be an important motivational factor for users.

Viewpoint descriptions require that users are actually able to communicate about what they see. People who enjoy communicating in general will presumably use viewpoint descriptions and oracles in their investigations of the simulation models. It is not wise to force a user to formulate a description of what he or she has seen, but the machine's results will be less focused without this kind of information.

Finally, in any formalism for viewpoint descriptions, everything a user can see or should also be able to see should be able to be described. We therefore need to analyze animations and the information they contain as well as how users deal with animations.

## 9.2  Information Conveyed by Animations

From an analysis of different animation systems like Proof Animation™ (Brunner, Earle, and Henriksen 1991; Earle and Henriksen 1995), Arena™ (Drevna and Kasales 1994), and AniPLuS (Helbing and Lorenz 1995, Kirchner and Helbing 1995), and animation

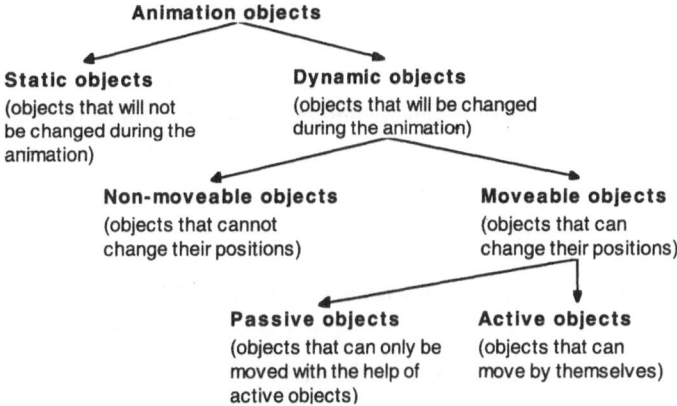

**Figure 9.1:** Categorization of animation objects

components integrated in simulation systems like DOSIMIS-3 (Schmidt 1992) and GPSS/
PC (Cox 1987), we derived the categorization of animation objects in Figure 9.1.

Every animated system contains arbitrary combinations of animation objects. Every
category of animation objects conveys different kinds of information which should influence the development of the formalism of the viewpoint description.

All animation objects deliver information about
- the embodied real objects,
- the relations to other objects,
- the containment in object hierarchies, and
- the geometric position in the graphical presentation.

The dynamic objects deliver additional information about
- the current state,
- the current values of variables, and
- the statistic values.

The moveable objects deliver information about
- the state of movement,
- the state of waiting, and
- the dynamic positioning,

whereas passive objects deliver, over and above this, information about the active objects
transporting them. All these pieces of information form only the basis for the formalism
for viewpoint descriptions.

## 9.3 Formalism of Viewpoint Descriptions

The kind of information we expect to be able to extract from a viewpoint description given by a user includes his or her general impression after viewing a presentation, his or her implicit goals in using the application program, and his or her subjective assessment of the correctness of the representation and the results of the machine's computation. We will use the term viewpoint description as follows:

> A *viewpoint description* of a simulation run contains observations and assessments of a user in a formal notation, which describes and evaluates the current state and the behavior of the model with respect to the simulation goals.

Two different types of information must be communicable in a viewpoint description (see Figure 9.2). The first is the current state of the model, i.e., what is really happening during the simulation; this is called the *documentation*. Here the user describes what he or she was able to ascertain from the animation, how he or she interpreted the result, what he or she understood, and what relationships he or she sees between the results and the goals of the simulation. This assessment and description can be subjective; it is not necessarily objective.

Secondly, the user must be allowed to describe what he or she thinks he or she *should have seen*, in that the user can formulate goals for the presentation, requirements that should have been met, questions, results, and an estimation of the relevance of each part of the model. We refer to this information as the *criticism* of the model; this is to serve as a basis for the machine's modification of the model.

**Figure 9.2:** High-level structure of viewpoint description

It is important to note the difference between the two aspects of viewpoint descriptions, documentation and criticism. They were chosen explicitly with the goals of the underlying simulation study in mind. In the documentation it is not the overriding concern to deal with the goals of the simulation study, either implicitly or explicitly, since the documentation *describes* the current state of the animation. However, the second part, the criticism, typically contains numerous references to the way the animation *should be* in the eyes of the user, and this is dependent on the goals of the simulation study. In the documentation part, application goals are only present insofar as they determine the choice of the observations of a particular part of the presentation, i.e., the focus of what is being described. Even in the criticism portion, the simulation goals cannot be formulated explicitly, but appear implicitly in how the criticism is expressed.

### 9.3.1 Documentation

The description of the current state of a simulated process is to answer the question posed to the user, "What do you see?". From general experience with animations, the documentation must thus contain the system description of a model, assessments of the quality of parts of the model, and a statement of the causal dependencies within the model (see Figure 9.3).

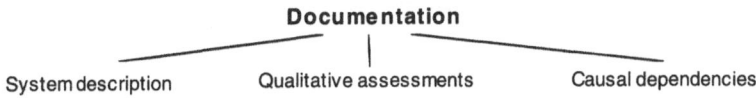

**Figure 9.3:** Structure of the documentation of viewpoint descriptions

These three kinds of documentation can be classified with respect to their degree of difficulty, the time when they were formulated, and the time to which they refer. The *system description* of the model is time independent after modeling, as there are no changes in the model due to successive simulation runs. Furthermore, its formulation is not particularly intellectually challenging, since only static information must be considered. The assessment of the current *quality* of a part model, however, is entirely time-dependent, so that in principle it can be entered at any time. Further, the description of the quality requires analyzing dynamic processes over a period of time, though only for one part model which is constrained in space. The most challenging aspect, the statement of *causal dependencies*, is a formulation of quality dependencies, since dynamic information from several submodels is necessary and as well as a reasoning process on the part of the user, since he or she must ensure that the analysis of the various parts of the model are compatible with one another.

### System Description

We cite the definition of Kreutzer (1986): "A system is defined as a collection of objects, their relationships and behavior relevant to a set of purposes, characterizing some relevant part of reality." It corresponds in content to other definitions for the term system, like those of Law and Kelton (1991) and Klinger (1991) (see Figure 9.4).

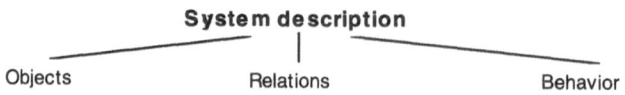

**Figure 9.4:** System description

Objects contain elements, macros, or (recursively) other parts of models. This organization allows users to describe submodels without having to identify the individual elements to which they refer. Furthermore, such a system description of the model contributes to its understanding. In addition to the topological grouping of submodels, system objects make it possible for the user to describe object relations of a physical kind (material flow) like "isAcceptingFrom" or a logical kind (information flow) like "isControl For". To describe the behavior of objects it is necessary to refer to their technological type (e.g., "transport", "station", or "conveyer").

**Examples of objects, relations, and behavior:**

```
SubModel[1]  =      element[5], element[1], element[3].
SubModel[3]  =      element[2], element[6], SubModel[1].

SubModel[3]         isAcceptingFrom SubModel [1].
element[21]         isControlFor SubModel[4].

SubModel[3]         is an assemblyStation.
```

*Qualitative Assessments*

In the qualitative assessment part, submodels can be assessed with regard to their dynamic behavior. The following characteristics are used:

- possible states of animation objects (i.e., "beingBlocked", "outOfOrder", "working", "beingPassive"),
- special states of moveable objects (i.e., "moving", "waiting"),
- special state of temporal objects (i.e., "appearing", "disappearing"),
- relevant statistical values (i.e., "load", "throughput", "contents").

The choice of possible characteristics depends on the existing animation objects and their statistical values traced in the particular simulation system. The existence of temporal or moveable objects is not a general feature of simulators.

The characteristics mentioned above have to be complemented with the concrete values of different attributes. Attributes refer to amount (relative and absolute), time, time span, speed, direction of movement, connection paths, movement, events, location, and kind of movement. The association of the characteristics, the attributes, and their values depends very strongly on the simulator. One possible association is shown in Figure 9.5.

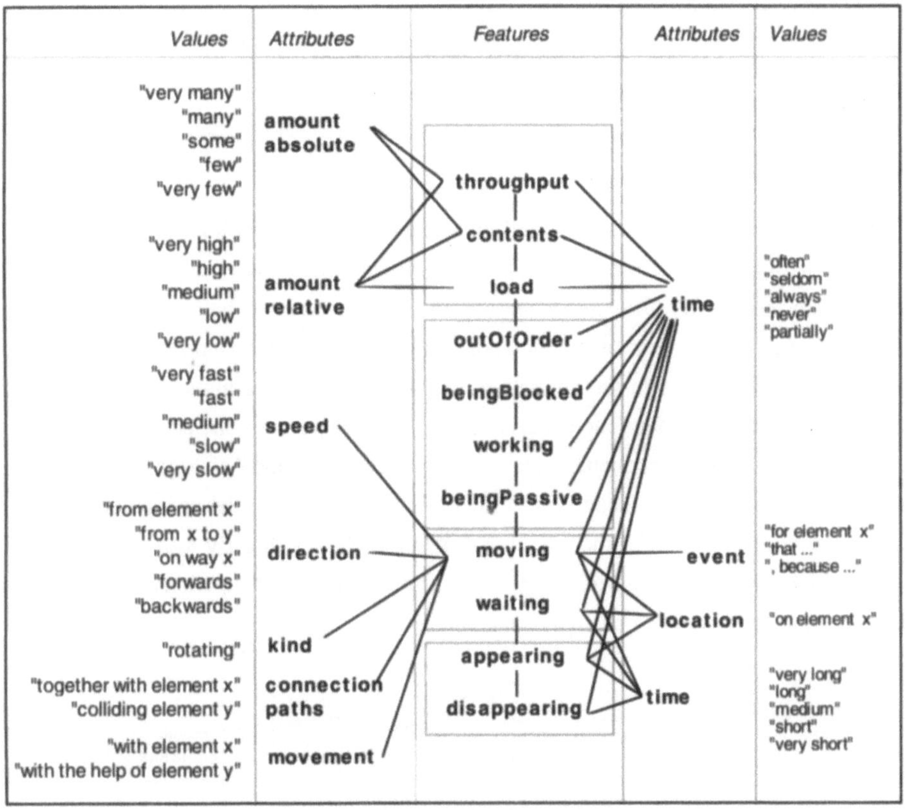

| Values | Attributes | Features | Attributes | Values |
|---|---|---|---|---|
| "very many"<br>"many"<br>"some"<br>"few"<br>"very few" | amount<br>absolute | throughput<br><br>contents<br><br>load | time | "often"<br>"seldom"<br>"always"<br>"never"<br>"partially" |
| "very high"<br>"high"<br>"medium"<br>"low"<br>"very low" | amount<br>relative | outOfOrder<br><br>beingBlocked<br><br>working | | |
| "very fast"<br>"fast"<br>"medium"<br>"slow"<br>"very slow" | speed | beingPassive | | |
| "from element x"<br>"from x to y"<br>"on way x"<br>"forwards"<br>"backwards" | direction | moving<br><br>waiting | event | "for element x"<br>"that ..."<br>", because ..." |
| "rotating" | kind | appearing | location | "on element x" |
| "together with element x"<br>"colliding element y" | connection<br>paths | disappearing | time | "very long"<br>"long"<br>"medium"<br>"short"<br>"very short" |
| "with element x"<br>"with the help of element y" | movement | | | |

**Figure 9.5:** Possible qualitative assessments

To guarantee a temporal differentiation, it is necessary to develop constructs describing the temporally valid range of the assessments. Section 9.3.4 deals with extension of the qualitative assessments for the simulation time.

**Examples of quality assessments:**

```
SubModel[1]  is often beingBlocked.
SubModel[4]  load high.
SubModel[8]  is always outOfOrder.
```

### Causal Dependencies

To allow the user to input information about the context of the simulation model, causal relationships between the states of the objects can be described. In particular, the qualitative assessment of part of a model can be set in relation to other parts of models in a "cause-and-effect" manner.

**Example of a causal dependency:**

SubModel[3] is often beingBlocked, because SubModel[1] load low.

## 9.3.2 Criticism

The criticism of a presentation (as opposed to the documentation) implicitly contains the goals of the application, in that the *estimation* of the model, *the relevance* of different parts of the model, the *problems* to be solved, and the *tasks* to be carried out become known. Therefore, this part of the viewpoint description contains attributes that refer to weak spots and changes in the animation, either ones that have already taken place or ones that should take place. The subdivision of the criticism into one part referring to an estimation, one to relevance, one to statements of problems, and one to tasks (see Figure 9.6) is motivated by the intended use of this information. While the estimation provides facts for the investigation of the model and therefore serves directly as a basis for decision making, the statements of the problem initiate such investigations and the tasks directly name the necessary changes in the model.

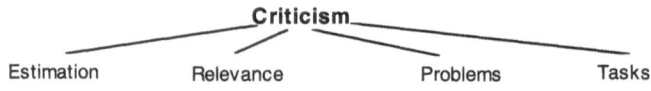

**Figure 9.6:** Organization of the criticism

To understand the background here, we should compare the terms "problem" and "task". In cognitive psychology, tasks and problems are differentiated very carefully. Brander, Kompa, and Peltzer (1989) postulate that both can be projected into the scheme "transformation of an initial state into a final state with the help of a solution". A problem is characterized by a given initial state, while for tasks the final state is additionally given. By contrast, Edelmann (1986) assumes the existence of algorithms that guarantee a solution as the criterion for differentiating problems and tasks. Both theories can be interpreted in the context of oracle-based model modification and viewpoint description. For the solution of problems, the computer requires a reasoning process for deriving model modification, whereas tasks name directly the necessary changes in the model and the computer has algorithms at its disposal for carrying these out.

### *Estimation*

The criticism of a viewpoint description contains user estimations that serve as a basis for the oracular modification of the model, in addition to the documentation. An estimation is an expression referring to an object and its assessment like "okay" or "sufficient" or a value on a scale of "very good" to "very bad"; however, it does not indicate a problematic state (see the paragraph about problems).

**Examples of estimation:**

```
SubModel[6] okay.
SubModel[9] sufficient.
```

## *Relevance*

An important point in the criticism is that the relevance of parts of the model or of information observed by a user is also assessed by the user with respect to the application goals. In particular, attributes are used which underline the low relevance of a part of a model ("notRelevant") as well as attributes which make clear that certain goals must absolutely be attained within part of a model ("load necessary $x$", "contents necessary $y$"). Examples are:

**Examples of relevance:**

```
SubModel[2] notRelevant.
SubModel[5] load necessary 75.
```

## *Problems*

Within the problem statements of the criticism portion, criticisms are specified which refer to changes that should be made in the presentation. In particular, those portions of the model are assessed which motivate the oracular modification of the model. In general, problems are specified because of severe errors the user observed in the animation. The user need not necessarily have noticed a particular symptom of the error, but even a vague specification of which part of the model is affected ("is problematic") can suffice as the starting point for the oracular modification of the model, so long as the machine has enough data to locate the error in the underlying representation.

**Examples of problems:**

```
SubModel[1]  is problematic.
SubModel[4]  throughput too low.
```

The naming of error symptoms refers to one of the characteristics of the qualitative assessments and has to be complemented with an evaluating attribute. Appropriate evaluating attributes have to be found for the different characteristics; a possible combination is shown in Figure 9.7.

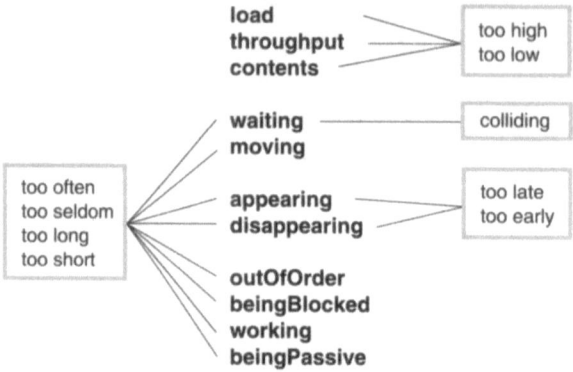

**Figure 9.7:** Possible combination of characteristics and evaluated attributes

## Tasks

Tasks name the necessary changes of parameters of the model and have to contain the description of the parameter and its new value(s). The formulation of a task initiates a model modification, but not an oracle-based one, because the computer does not need a reasoning process to carry it out.

**Examples of tasks:**

> SubModel[3] change parameter "capacity" to 150.

### 9.3.3  The Complete Formalism

The developed content of a viewpoint description up to now is structured like a tree (see Figure 9.8), in which each leaf represents a special type of expression of a viewpoint description. The term *group of expressions* will be used for them. All internal nodes are just for organizing expressions.

If we examine the relationship between oracles and viewpoint descriptions, it is evident that the latter offer a formalism in which oracles can be described. Indeed, oracles are a well-defined part of viewpoint descriptions: As statements in the "criticism-problem" portion of the viewpoint descriptions, they initiate a reasoning process, to find out the reasons why the user criticizes the animation. Viewpoint descriptions are much more powerful, because they not only initiate a reasoning process but support it by providing dedicated information, such as quality assessments, relevance, and estimations. Therefore, viewpoint descriptions can provide an answer to Arnheim's question applied to visualizations.

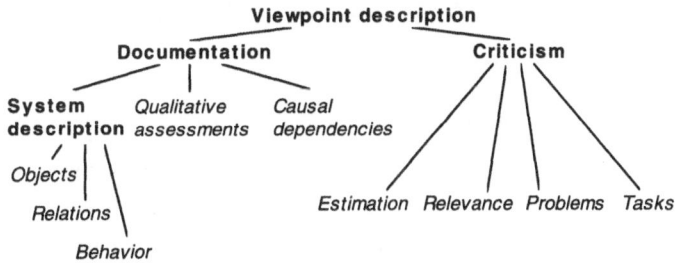

**Figure 9.8:** Tree-structure of the formalism of the viewpoint description
*(the italic terms are groups of expressions)*

### 9.3.4  Temporal Aspects and Verbal Descriptions as General Additions

A necessary extension of viewpoint descriptions pertains to their temporal aspects, since many constructs are dependent on time and thus must be associated with points in time or spans of time. For this purpose, the viewpoint description formalism can be expanded by keywords or constructs for specifying points in time, a span of time, and combinations of these. However, such expansions imply that the rules in the reasoning component must also be expanded appropriately. Possible extensions include binding time-dependent assessments to numeric output data, which are usually also time-dependent themselves.

**Examples for temporal additions:**

```
SubModel[1] has low load, up to now.
SubModel[1] has low load, since beginning.
SubModel[1] has low load, every 5th time slot.
```

Because the formalism of the viewpoint description is very strong, verbal descriptions have to be added to each node of the tree in Figure 9.8 and not only to the groups of expressions. These verbal descriptions can be used for informal evaluations observed by the user. They are not interpretable by the computer because of their lack of formalization. The computer only has to manage this information and to make it available to the user when he or she needs it. The result is that the verbal description serves not for communication between user and computer but only human-human communication, like written documentation.

## 9.4    Implementation of the Viewpoint Description for the Simulator Create!

The simulator Create! described in Chapter 8 was chosen for an implementation of the viewpoint description. The first step was adapting the formalism to the special needs of Create!.

Model elements suggested to the user for building a model, and macros and submodels as combinations of the model elements, are the *objects* of the *system description* portion of the viewpoint description. As *relations*, the following exist: "isDeliveryFor", "isAcceptingFor", "isControlFor", and "isMaterialFlowFor". The technological types of the model elements pre-defined in Create!, like "transport", "station", "assemblyStation", "conveyer", or "warehouse", are the allowed attributes for the *behavior* of objects. The characteristics for the *qualitative assessments* were derived from the possible states of the model elements in Create!, like "beingBlocked", "outOfOrder", "beingPassive", "wor king", and the relevant statistical data like "throughput", "contents", and "load". The full set of characteristics, attributes, and values is shown in Figure 9.9. The expressions of the *relevance* part refer to the relevant statistical data "throughput", "content", and "load". The *problems* of an animation refer in the same manner to the state of the model elements and the relevant statistical values, e.g., the qualitative assessments. These have to be complemented not with a descriptive, but with an evaluative attribute. If these attributes complement a statistical value, the evaluating attribute describes it as "too low" or "too high", or names a value which should be met. If the state of a model element has to be complemented, the evaluating attribute refers to the time span or frequency, like "too often", "too seldom", "too short", or "too long". If the user cannot name a detailed problem, he or she can refer to an object simply as "problematic". The variety of possible expressions in a viewpoint description for a Create! model is shown in Figure 9.9.

### 9.4.1   How to Use the Viewpoint Description

It is easy to see that an actual viewpoint description is quite complex, so it is essential for potential users that an effective user interface be available. The viewpoint description requires the following features:

- projecting the tree structure of the viewpoint description onto a menu hierarchy,
- preparation and selection of the large number of alternative choices (attributes),
- incorporation of the model layout or the animation model for direct manipulation, and
- presentation of abstract data.

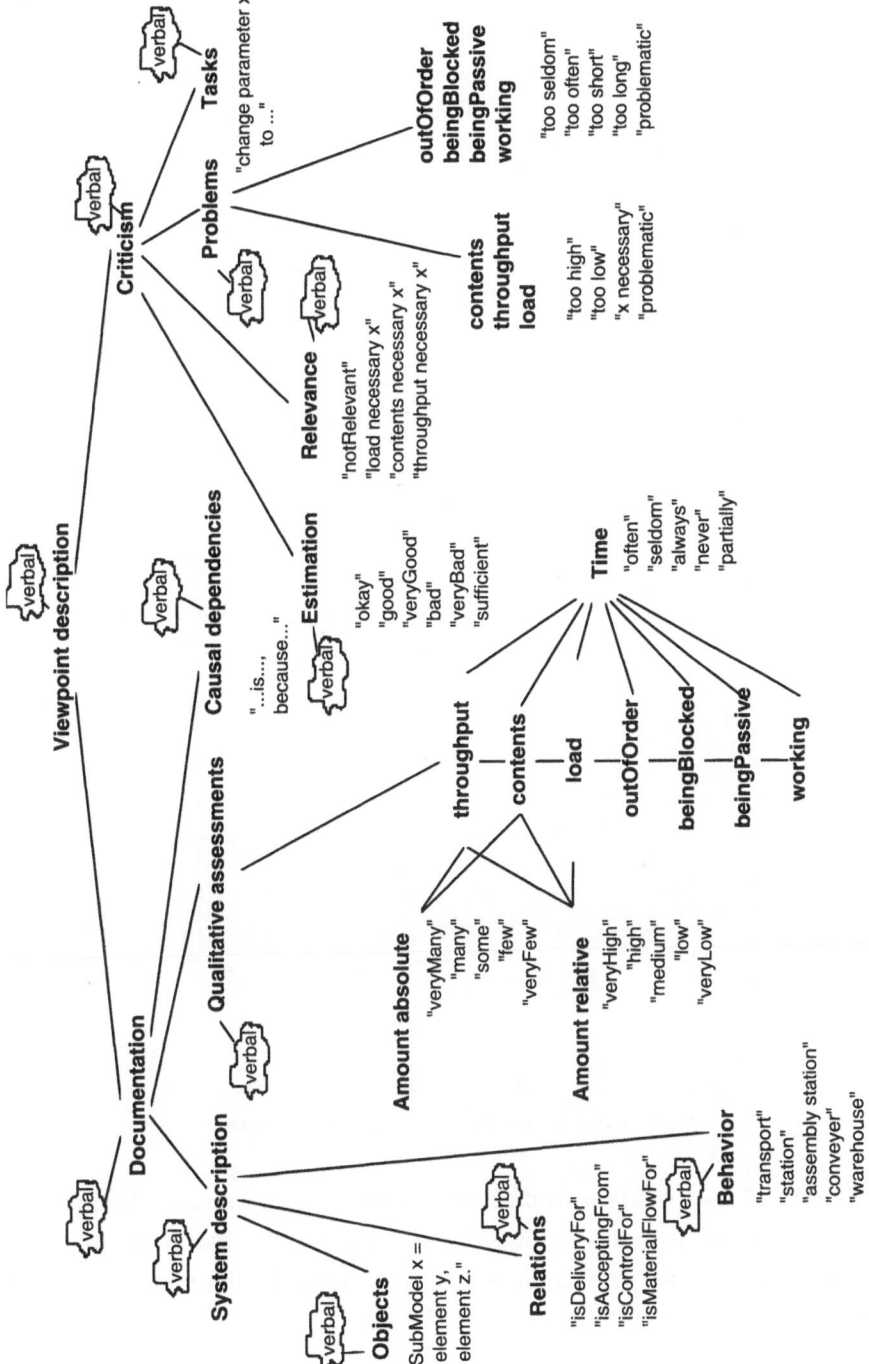

**Figure 9.9:** Summary of a viewpoint description

The viewpoint description should be the result of observations made during an animation of a simulation model. Therefore, input of the viewpoint description should be integrated with the presentation of the animation. The implementation uses the existing animation and user interface features of Create! already described in Chapter 8.

A user has two modes at his or her disposal to input a viewpoint description. First, the user can describe it as text restricted by the syntax definition. This option is important for expert users who are very familiar with viewpoint descriptions. Figure 9.10 shows the text editor with a viewpoint description already typed in by a user. The viewpoint description compiler will save the text and check it for syntactic correctness.

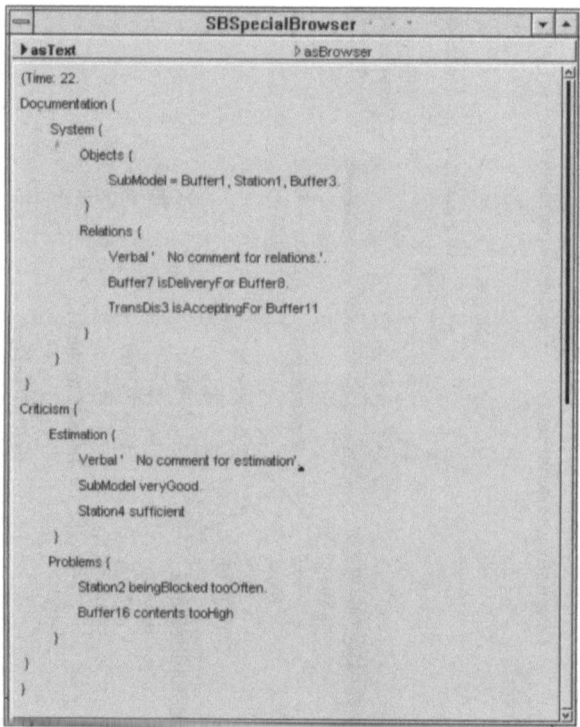

**Figure 9.10:** The text editor for viewpoint descriptions

The second and most widely used mode is a combination of selecting objects in the model and selections in menus and lists. Except for the verbal description (where the keyboard is required), the user can input a complete viewpoint description with direct manipulation by carrying out the following four steps:

*Step 1*

The user points to the object in the model that he or she wants to evaluate with the next expression. This is possible because the model is displayed graphically and Create! allows the selection of one or more model elements.

*Step 2*

An element-oriented action menu is linked to each model element and contains the necessary functionality. Examples are the actions for the graphical editor ("zoomIn", "zoomOut"), actions for the animation ("start", "legend"), and actions for using viewpoint descriptions like "subModel", "viewpoint description", and "viewpoint descrip tion detailed" (see Figure 9.11). To input expressions directly into one of the groups of expressions, the user chooses the last menu item "viewpoint description detailed", and then goes on to step 4.

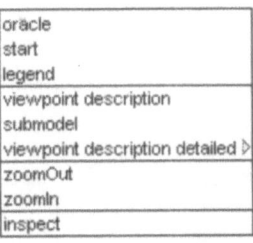

**Figure 9.11:**

The menu structure in the animation browser

*Step 3*

By activating "viewpoint description" the user gets the browser for the complete viewpoint description shown in Figure 9.12. A complex menu structure is presented to the user, who selects a group of expressions.

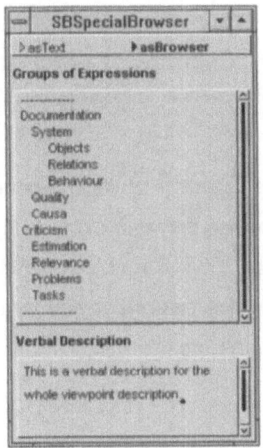

**Figure 9.12:**

The browser for one complete viewpoint description

*Step 4*

The kind of browser presented to the user depends on the group of expressions he or she has previously chosen. These browsers are different, but they all contain a set of dependable lists. Each list represents a different part of an expression. If one item from each list is chosen, a complete expression is defined and can be added to the viewpoint description. To support the user, a list of expressions already defined is also part of the browser. Figure 9.13 shows as an example the group of expression "Problems". In the middle part of the browser are the lists for choosing the appropriate object, attribute, and value. The upper third of the browser contains the list of already defined expressions. By activating "addStatement" an expression is constructed out of the selections of the lists in the middle part of the browser and added to the lists of expressions. The "Verbal Description" part serves as a text input.

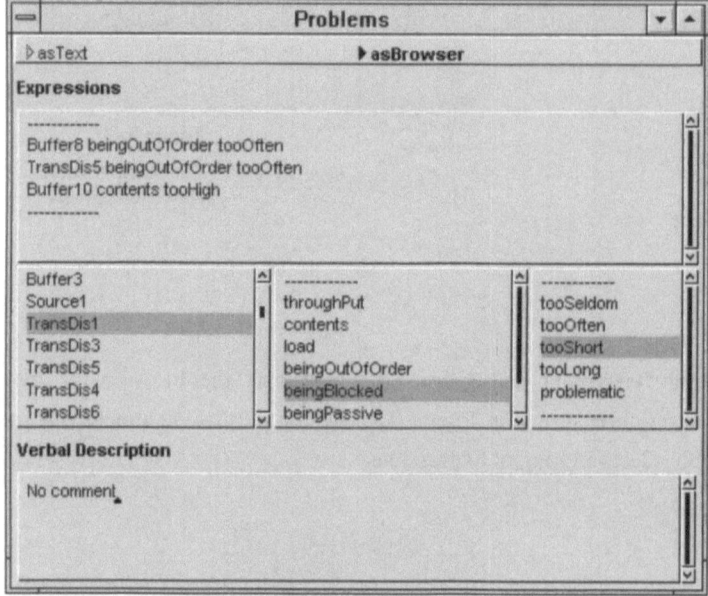

**Figure 9.13:** A browser to input "problem" expressions

The menu structure presented in Figure 9.12 was influenced by the ergonomic aspects of user interfaces and is a compromise between excessively long menus and menu hierarchies that are too deep (see Rohr 1988, Thimbleby 1990). The quality of the implemented user interface for viewpoint descriptions is scheduled to be evaluated by the users who work with it at a later point in time.

### 9.4.2  Example of a Viewpoint Description

To illustrate the previous sections on the structure of viewpoint descriptions, we give an example relating to the reference model in Section 8.4.2 (see Figure 9.14, recall also Figure 9.7).

```
time: 1801.
Documentation {
System {
 Objects
    { SubModel Upper = Source1, Buffer1, Transport1, Buffer2,
          Station1, Buffer3.
      SubModel Trans = Transport2, Buffer7, Transport3.
      SubModel Montage = Transport4, Buffer15, Montage1
    }
 Relations
   { Upper isDeliveryFor Montage.
     Montage isAcceptingFrom Trans
   }
 Behaviour
   { Upper is station.
     Trans is transport}
 }
 Quality
 { Montage is often beingBlocked.
   Trans load low.
   Upper throughput low
 }
 Causal Dependencies
 { Montage is often beingBlocked, because Upper throughput low.
   Trans load low, because Montage is often beingBlocked
   }
}

Criticism {
Estimation
 { Station3 good.
   Upper veryBad
 }
Relevance
 { Station4 notRelevant.
   Montage load necessary 80
 }
Problems
 { Montage throughput too low}
Tasks
 { Source1 change parameter "generation" to 5}
}
```

**Figure 9.14:** Example of a viewpoint description

# 9.5 Applications

### 9.5.1   Addition to the Knowledge Base for Oracle-Based Model Modification

Viewpoint descriptions contain information about the behavior of the model that can be computed from the model data and the statistical results. So far oracle-based model modification operates only with the latter to analyze the reasons for the problem named in the oracle. It is consistent to involve other parts of the viewpoint description in the search for the model's problematic behavior.

An analysis of the different kinds of information has shown which groups of expressions are suitable. Which groups these are and how the knowledge base needs to be extended is explained in the following:

*Qualitative Assessments*
If an expression contains the message that a state of an object is really significant, like "object 5 is often beingBlocked", then this will be added as a fact to the knowledge base. This fact will influence the reasoning process in such a way that to evaluate the state of this specific element, the fact will be used and not the rules for the investigation criteria that describe how to find out the state of the element with the help of statistical data from the simulation run.

This procedure has the advantage that the user evaluation has a higher priority than the computer assessment on the basis of statistical results, which are not sensitive to the context of the simulated system and the simulation goals.

*Causal Dependencies*
An expression in the "Causal Dependencies" portion contains a cause-and-effect relationship. This information will be added to the knowledge base as a fact and can be used for the reasoning process right at the beginning. If the effect of the cause-and-effect relationship is named as a problem, the computer can present the cause as a solution. If a user inputs the expression "trans is often beingBlocked, because buffer load high" and trans is named as a problem, the computer promptly suggests the overloading of buffer as a reason. The backtracking mechanism of the reasoning process makes it possible to find other reasons besides this initial one.

*Relevance "not Relevant"*
If objects are evaluated as "notRelevant", they should usually not be starting points for oracle-based model modification. For each of these kinds of expressions, one fact will be added to the knowledge base. A user who names such an object as a problem will

be asked if he or she really wants to investigate it, given that is was earlier determined as not quite as relevant.

*Relevance "statistical value necessary x"*
Usually there is a pre-defined threshold for accessing an object as problematic .or not. This information will be used by the rules for the investigation criteria. Because the threshold is not adaptive, the relevance evaluation "station5 load necessary 80", will mean that when the load of station5 is 86%, the response will be "station5 (okay)". The rules for the investigation criteria have to change to consider these kinds of facts and not to examine them according to their thresholds.

*Estimation*
From the estimation "trans okay", the conclusion can be derived that trans works satisfactorily and cannot be in a problematic state that needs investigating. A fact "trans (okay)" will be added to the knowledge base and trans will be skipped in the reasoning process.

The use of these kinds of information requires extending the architecture of the oracle-based model modification, because the knowledge base no longer contains only model data and statistical results, but also the data from the viewpoint description (see Figure 9.15).

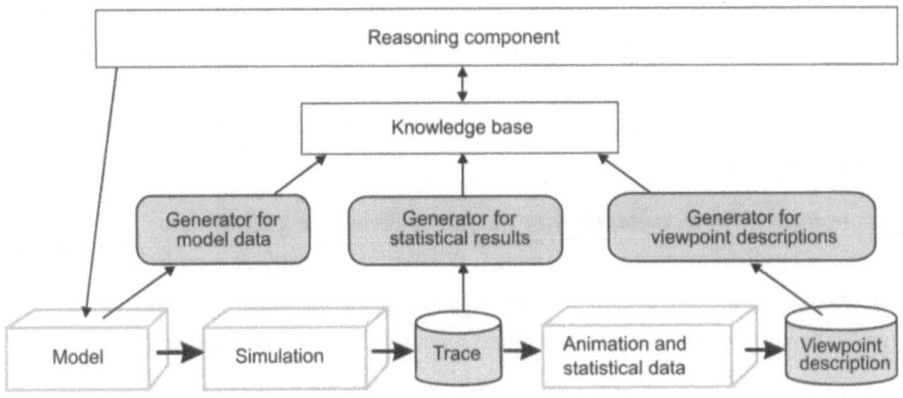

**Figure 9.15:** Using the viewpoint description for complementing the knowledge base

It could be that these suggestions for using viewpoint descriptions do not seem very useful, because the computer presents the results of its reasoning process using the viewpoint description, which the user already knows. However, this is only valid under the assumption that the person who formulates the viewpoint description is the same person who uses the oracle-based model modification. It is imaginable that a modeler compiles viewpoint descriptions and provides them for another user, who may know little about the model and want to experiment with it.

Involving the viewpoint description in the reasoning process has the important advantage that the user's subjective assessment is held in higher esteem than the computer's solution. The evaluation of an object leaves behind a quantum of uncertainty, because it is context-sensitive and has no correspondence with the existing rules of the knowledge base. The oracle-based model modification can be influenced immensely by a viewpoint description, which is why the user has a serious responsibility. Wrongly observed or interpreted assessments in a viewpoint description can massively falsify the results of oracle-based model modification. The most important effect of involving viewpoint descriptions in oracle-based model modification is the possibility that different users with different knowledge about simulation and different skills get individual results.

### 9.5.2  Model Documentation with Viewpoint Descriptions

If the formalism of the viewpoint description can be used for describing all the observations and information extracted by the user, it is consistent to deploy this formalism for documenting a model and its behavior. In this subsection we develop techniques to augment existing schemes for *model documentation*. The goal is to provide effective tools to the user for the automated generation of particular parts of the documentation. A complete documentation cannot be expected, but the available information can be structured and provided as a document with blanks for the user to fill in. This topic was developed in co-operation with Mirko Wittek and is described extensively in Wittek (1993) and Helms (1994).

### *Organization of Documentation with Respect to Viewpoint Descriptions*
Although the documentation of software, or more specifically of simulation models, is still unpopular, the importance of documentation for providing information is indisputable. Gass (1984) suggests a division of model documentation into the three parts:

- model environment,
- model description, and
- model history.

The *model environment* contains all the information about the model, like constraints and prerequisites, with the model itself as a black box. The *model description* documents the model structure and behavior. The *model history* describes the process of developing it.

Parts of the model description in particular can be derived automatically by the computer, because the internal model representation is available. The transformation of the internal model representation into an adequate part of the documentation depends very largely on the kind of simulation system. Using a simulation language like GPSS to describe a model makes the documentation process similar to documenting a Pascal program. The modeler can add comments to the source code, and if this is done well then other users can more or less understand the principles and functionality of the model by reading the documented source code (see Figure 9.16).

```
BARBER SHOP MODEL
    GENERATE  20,5        ARRIVALS EVERY 20 ± 5 MINUTES
    ADVANCE   1           HANG UP COAT
    SEIZE     MARC        CAPTURE THE BARBER "MARC"
    ADVANCE   17,8        HAIRCUT TAKES 17 ± 3 MINUTES
    RELEASE   MARC        FREE THE BARBER "MARC"
    TERMINATE 1           EXIT THE BARBER SHOP
```

**Figure 9.16:** Example of a documented GPSS model

For element-oriented simulators, the problem of describing a model cannot be solved so easily because of the lack of sequence. The model is usually designed by arranging and connecting elements in a 2D model editor and defining the concrete parameters of the elements. To assist in documenting the model, different simulators provide the option of printing the model layout as a picture and printing the model parameters as a textual list on paper. In general, therefore, the documents are augmented by handwritten texts from the modeler about the dynamic behavior and the results achieved by the model. Statistical results and verbal descriptions of parts of the model should be included in the context of the whole simulation study.

If a modeler has used viewpoint descriptions, then the necessary information for documenting over and above the pure facts of the model already exists in the viewpoint description. The observations of a user during the animation of the model are in fact very useful to another user who wants to understand the model and its behavior. Because the interface for inputting a viewpoint description is very model-oriented, the creator of the documentation can describe the model directly. In particular the possibility of supplementing every expression group in a viewpoint description with a verbal description enables a user to describe the model completely.

A model description as part of the model documentation consists of three parts: the model layout, the parameterization of the model, and a viewpoint description (see Figure 9.17).

Even the viewpoint description cannot solve the problem of documenting a model, but it is a contribution toward reusing the information and knowledge the user has input already as a viewpoint description. The usefulness of this kind of documentation depends

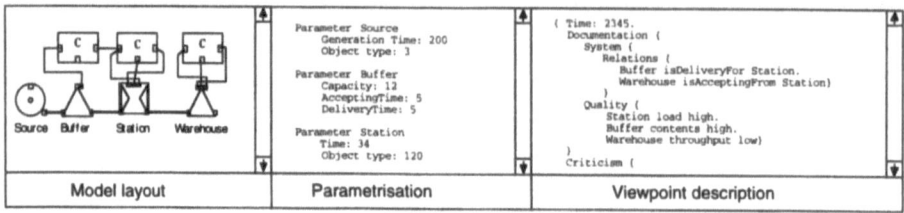

| Model layout | Parametrisation | Viewpoint description |

**Figure 9.17:** Elements of a documentation

on the user taking responsibility for the universality and correctness of his or her viewpoint description as the source of the model documentation.

### *Generation of Model Documentation*

The question of how to generate and structure the documentation must now be addressed. It should be easy for a user to fill in the blanks and integrate the documentation derived from the viewpoint description into other kinds of documents. Figure 9.18 shows one way of creating a model documentation from the computer's data, independent of the model life cycle.

The verbal descriptions for all the expression groups of the viewpoint description and the extensions of the automatically generated model documentation offer creative opportunities for the user responsible for the documentation.

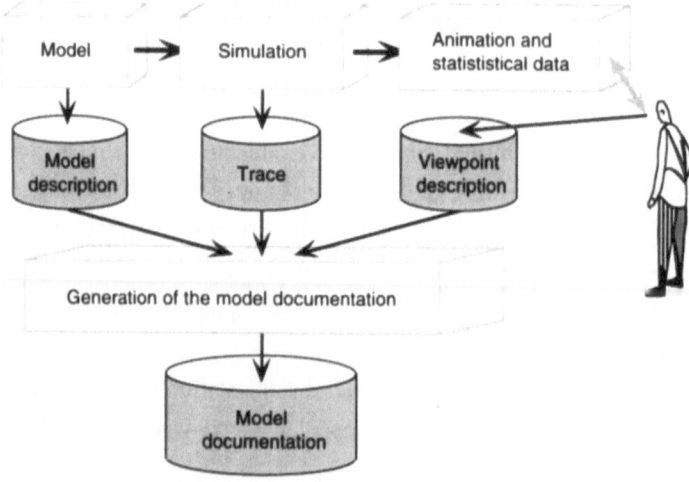

**Figure 9.18:** Generation of a complex model documentation

## *Implementation and Example of a Viewpoint Description*

The structure of a viewpoint description (recall Figure 9.8) has to be very obvious in the text presentation. The format of the text which is generated should

- be portable,
- allow very good structuring of the text, and
- support the presentation of enumerations and tables.

There are a wide variety of such text formats, but the most widely used one is the L^TEX format. The most important argument for L^TEX is its availability on almost every hardware platform.

In our implementation, the viewpoint description can be output as a L^TEX document, or as a L^TEX fragment which can be included in an existing L^TEX document. To present the tree structure of the viewpoint description, the L^TEX environment description was chosen and applied hierarchically. This makes it possible to present the viewpoint description as a hierarchical list where the single items are indented. The expressions of each expression group are realized as an itemize environment. A short example of a L^TEX -structured viewpoint description is shown in Figure 9.19.

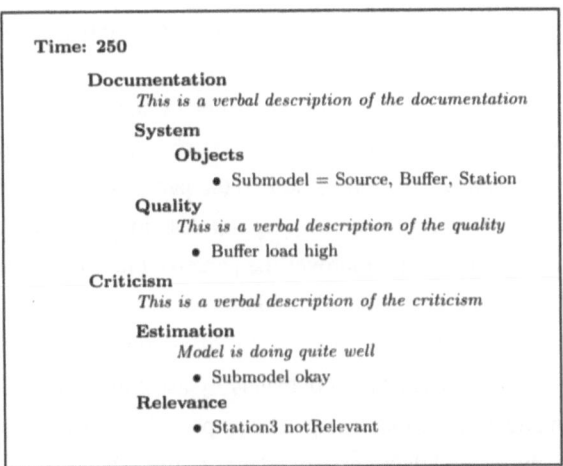

**Figure 9.19:** Example of a printed viewpoint description in L^TEX format

## 9.6  Discussion

This chapter, as an extension of Chapter 8, has offered a solution to the problem that the computer does not benefit from visualizing its data to the user. In general, the user looks at an animation with greater or lesser interest and then follows the prescribed methodology. Experience with animation as a presentation technique for simulation results invites parallels with current discussions about the value of modern media and their influence on society, and especially on children.

One argument discussed very often is that the large amount of visual impressions does not allow detailed perception of what is observed. The French philosopher Jean Baudrillard drives home this point when he says: "The abundance of pictures destroys all imagination. One cannot get a feeling for them, cannot interpret them. Not enough time is available" (Baudrillard 1991, translated).

Of course it would be unfair to apply this view of society in general to computer simulation or any other specific area of application of computer graphics. Nonetheless, we must ask to what extent the widespread use of animation systems since the end of the 1960s has really led to a more thorough treatment on the part of users of the dynamic processes being visualized. Or is the animation simply a marketing gimmick, which merely improves the esthetic value of a presentation? If so, we must conclude that animation is not esteemed as highly as it could be.

The concept of a viewpoint description does not by any means solve all problems associated with the use of visualizations, but it has changed the role of animation in a way that a detailed analysis and interpretation on the part of the user is expected. Recalling Chapter 4, the request to formulate a viewpoint description is a task for the observer of pictures and therefore it usually improves the perceived normalization demands of the user. Like the question "Where's Waldo?" in Martin Handford's books (recall Chapter 4), it leads to the task of describing the user's view of an animation in detail. One prerequisite for improving the normalization demands by assigning a task can be cited here, too. A user must be able to see that he or she is expected to know about the meaning of individual graphic objects and their correspondence to formulate a viewpoint description. At this point we can close the loop to the beginning of this chapter, where we postulated that *learning to see* in an animation is one of the really important skills of every simulation user.

**Part**
# IV

# Pictograms

*"Sorcier" (Magician)*
Trois Frères, Ariège, Southern France

# The Nature of Pictograms and Their Use

We have illustrated the wide variety of pictures with 127 examples so far. Chapter 3 presented a classification scheme for pictograms, abstract-graphical pictures, and presentational pictures, but the description of pictograms remained rather vague. We now investigate pictograms in somewhat more detail with respect to what information can be transmitted or transputed with them and their ability to provoke normalization demands.

The systematic use of pictograms for communication is a 20th-century innovation. The beginnings can be traced to the post World War I period in Vienna, where Otto Neurath designed expositions for the new *Museum für Wohnbau und Stadtplanung* Krampen (1986). It was his goal to inform the populace of social and economic problems and the political changes associated with these. Mostly numeric data was presented in the museum, systematically encoded through pictograms. The system was referred to as the *Wiener Bildstatistik* (Viennese Picture-Statistics); it forms the basis of modern pictograms as well as some kinds of business graphics.

Of interest in the present context is the relationship between pictograms and internal representations of their meaning. We first study *typicality* of pictograms as well as normalization demands placed on viewers. Then we examine methods of describing pictures within computers, paying particular attention to the description of pictograms. Finally, we shall present and discuss a practical example of the use of pictograms in a dialogue system.

## 10.1 Typicality of Pictograms

There is no clear separation between abstract-graphical and presentational pictures on the one hand and pictograms on the other, but the following properties of pictograms can help to distinguish between them:

- pictograms represent general, not special, properties, feelings, or situations,
- pictograms need to be simple,
- pictograms should be drawn with large objects, bold lines, and simple areas (see Marcus 1992), and
- pictograms follow one design style with respect to attributes like size, the grid for single objects, and line quality.

The first property of pictograms – that they offer general and not specific information – says why it is so important for pictograms to be typical. The basic principle of *typicality* is the paradox that although a pictogram can show only a single representative of a class of objects, most observers would estimate this pictogram as being typical for the whole class of objects, concepts, or actions. Staufer (1987) describes the properties of pictograms with a high typicality as follows:

They should
- exhibit enough relevant details,
- be used not infrequently, and
- represent a quite sizeable class of objects.

High typicality of pictograms results in their easy comprehension and a high probability of remembering their intended meaning. However, a pictogram with a high typicality does not have to look exactly like any one member of the class it represents. Staufer (1987) demonstrates this effect in the case of a mailbox pictogram that Xerox Star had to choose from among the five very different versions shown in Figure 10.1 (Bewley et al. 1983).

The chosen version (far right) is more or less abstract and does not really resemble a real mailbox, but is typical of mailboxes in general. This typical form is often the result of a combination of features of different members of the class, so that it does not look like any one of the real objects. A prototype of a real object with a high typicality is very often more or less abstract. To create these prototypes is one of the most difficult problems in designing pictograms.

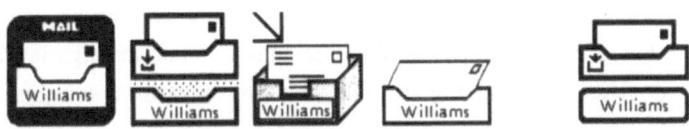

**Figure 10.1:** Different versions of a mailbox pictogram (Bewley et al. 1983, Staufer 1987)

A more detailed analysis of the steps involved in this process would go beyond the scope of this book; the interested reader is referred to the literature (e.g., Staufer 1987, Rohr 1988, Chang 1986, and Shu 1988).

## 10.2 Pictograms and Their Normalization Demands

Recall from the communication theory of Chapter 4 that the process of understanding pictures is strongly influenced by normalization demands as perceived by the observer. For pictograms that should be immediately identifiable and comprehensible without complex reasoning, the normalization demands should be very low. The normalization demands depend on the experience and knowledge of the potential observer pertaining to the conventions for decoding them (recall Chapter 2). These conventions should therefore be the basis for the design of pictograms.

If pictograms are made for specialists, they can refer to specialized conventions known only to the small number of people for whom they are intended; they do not have to be comprehensible to everyone else. Figure 10.2 shows pictograms which are very common in meteorology, but very cryptic to the authors of this book.

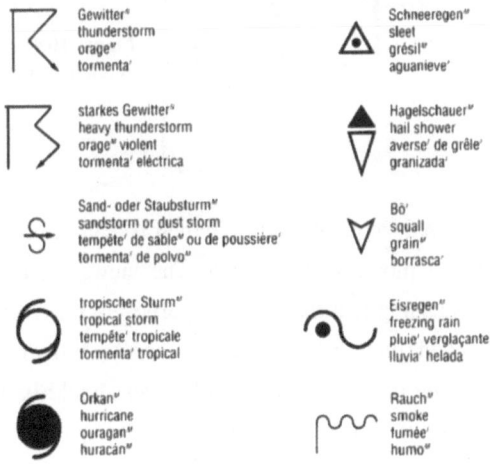

**Figure 10.2:** Pictograms that are difficult to understand except by meteorologists

As an example of a pictogram with high normalization demands for most viewers, which is usually not the goal of pictogram design, the authors found the sign in Figure 10.3. The reader is invited to study it before reading the footnote for an explanation.

**Figure 10.3:** Pictogram with high normalization demands[*]

This example shows another feature of pictograms. If a good pictogram is seen and interpreted once, its meaning will rarely be forgotten again. This makes pictograms important even if they are not intuitively comprehensible, as they can often be remembered with a very high probability.

The rule that pictograms should initiate only low normalization demands is not true in every case. Exceptions are pictograms for extraordinary situations, where the observer is surprised or shocked and gets an additional impulse to be careful or attentive. A good example of this phenomenon is the pictogram shown in Figure 10.4, demonstrating very dramatically the effect of not being careful enough

**Figure 10.4:**
A dramatic pictogram

We are now in a position to analyze pictograms and their role in information flow in user interfaces on the basis of the model in Chapter 5. The viewer of a pictogram should immediately recognize its meaning and therefore its purpose – this is information which is transmitted. Well designed pictograms should transpute little or no information, because normally no reasoning on the part of the observer should be necessary, particularly since they are often viewed only briefly and perhaps through the viewer's

---

[*] A verbal description of the pictogram is: No lifeguard on duty

peripheral vision, as in the case of road signs. There is a clear difference to abstract-graphical or presentational pictures, whose richness of possible transputed information makes them so valuable for communication. But which part of the information do pictograms lose in comparison to presentational pictures? Because this question is very important for understanding pictograms, we shall now analyze in detail the question of how pictures in general and pictograms in particular can be described in a formal manner.

## 10.3  Methods for Describing Pictures

At this point we have to widen the scope of the discussion and to analyze the formalization of pictures in general. This is especially difficult because of their ambiguity.

The ambiguity of pictures requires us to focus on how we might encode the description of pictures. How much information need be encoded in addition to the bitmap representation of the picture? Clearly image processing algorithms are of little help here (recall Section 2.4). How can the description of the picture be represented? To answer these questions, we must recall the fact that pictures represent reality or artificial reality imagined in the mind of the designer of the pictures.

It has long been the dream of philosophers, mathematicians, and many others to have a notation describing thought and, more generally, reality. This is clearly a utopian goal, since no consensus exists on how humans think, nor is such a consensus within reach. A more concrete goal is a notation for the logical analysis of human expressions to describe the world around them. This isolates the problem of analyzing and understanding the human cognitive processes involved in arriving at linguistic formulations. In this search we deal strictly with representations on external media – the written or spoken word. This reduction of the problem is already controversial (Varela 1990).

What makes it particularly difficult to devise a formal description of pictures is the fact that they exhibit a weak iconic code (recall Chapter 4). The fact that the elements of the iconic code are not defined semantically makes pictures very interesting and can give them an element of surprise, but this does not solve our problem. We need a classification of the contents of pictures, since we want to work with them in the context described above. The symbol system of the description mechanism must exhibit a strong code.

Many attempts have been made to devise formal notations for describing the world and what is going on in it. Before the era of computers, such work concentrated on taking what computer scientists today call *natural languages* and showing how to reduce utterances to a clear, concise, and unambiguous notation. The underlying hypothesis was that only such principles of the world can be formalized as can be formulated in language.

Perhaps the most influential of all researchers in this area was Gottlob Frege. In his fundamental work, carried out in the 1870s and 1880s at the University of Jena (Patzig 1981; for a recent edition of this work see Frege 1986), Frege showed that it is possible to construct a logical language in which all the syllogistic forms of natural language reasoning in Indo-Germanic languages can be expressed uniquely. This step became particularly important with time because it enabled a unification of several other approaches to logic which had previously been developed. Indeed, he was able to show that these approaches complemented one another instead of competing with one another.

In modern times, attention has shifted to the representation of *knowledge* rather than *linguistic utterances*. The term "knowledge" is somewhat confusing, since it implies more than just, say, information; indeed, it even implies some kind of relationship to human memory, since humans are said to "have knowledge". Stripped of its seductive terminology and examined more closely, however, most knowledge representation schemes developed by computer scientists can be reduced to – are indeed functionally equivalent to – the notation developed by Gottlob Frege (see Barr and Feigenbaum 1981). Representational forms such as semantic nets, state space diagrams, and Prolog-like forms are therefore equivalent to one another in the sense that they can all be reduced to a semantically equivalent expression in the notation of Frege. The difference between these modern forms is primarily one of the complexity of the algorithms used. In an implementation using semantic nets, related nodes can often be accessed simply by following a pointer, whereas in a Prolog-like notation, accessing such nodes means searching in a database of facts.

### 10.3.1 Frege's Notation

Frege showed that very few primitive symbols suffice to express all logical forms. He restricted himself to three symbols:

a) a symbol for the negation of an expression $p$,

b) a symbol for the "if-then" relationship between two expressions $p$ and $q$, and

c) a symbol for the general applicability of an expression of the form "$x$ is an $F$", where $x$
   is a variable for an object and $F$ is a predicate.

For example, if we replace $F$ by the predicate "human", the expression "$x$ is an $F$" combined with the symbol for general applicability has the meaning, "Every object is a human", which is clearly false. The negation then yields "Not every object is a human", which is obviously true (as well it ought to be, because the negation of a false logical expression must be true). If we first apply the negation symbol and then that for general applicability, we arrive at "For all objects it holds that they are not an $F$", or "There exist no humans". By the same token, the standard expression of Aristotle "All humans are living" is expressed by the (admittedly awkward) expression "For every object it holds that if $x$ is a human then $x$ is also living".

The expression "$p$ and $q$" is equivalent to the – again somewhat awkward – expression "It does not hold that if $p$ holds, then $q$ does not hold", and "$p$ or $q$" is expressed as "if $p$ does not hold, then $q$ holds".

As an aside, it is interesting to look at the notation used by Frege. He used

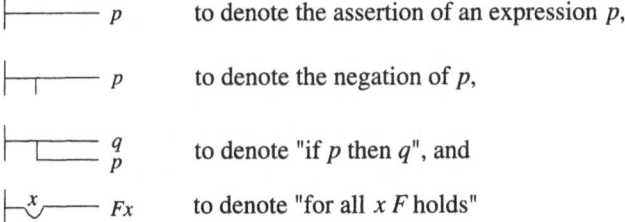

This notation can be taken further to express

to denote "for all $x$ not $F$ holds",

to denote that "not all $x$ are not $F$", ie. "there exist $F$'s"

Further,

means "all $F$'s are also $G$'s"

This means that the single expression "$p$ and $q$" is written as

and "$p$ or $q$" is written as

A complex example is "if this ostrich is a bird and cannot fly, then there exist birds that cannot fly" can be formulated by letting $a$ be the ostrich, $Fx$ that $x$ is a bird and $Gx$ that $x$ cannot fly. In the notation of Frege, this example is written as:

## 10.3.2 Pictureless Knowledge Processing

Knowledge representation schemes today do not include pictures, but they have not been forgotten. In fact, they are generally considered to be unnecessary. As a case in point, let us look at the development of Marvin Minsky's ideas on knowledge representation from this point of view.

In the mid-1970s, Minsky proposed a framework for knowledge processing that brought together and integrated various ideas of the time. While he drew heavily on research by past masters, such as Otto Selz and F. C. Bartlett, Minsky's fundamental paper, with its informal style, has worked like a catalyst for future generations of researchers. We shall briefly review Minsky's work; the interested reader is referred to Minsky himself for more details (Minsky 1975). We shall discuss his work for more historical reasons, to discover the roots of today's pictureless knowledge representation.

Minsky proposed that knowledge is represented in data structures called *frames*, each of which represents a stereotypical situation. When a new situation is encountered, a frame is selected from memory that closely matches the situation and can be adapted to fit the details at hand. A frame contains information on how to use it, what one can expect to have happen next, and what to do when these expectations are not confirmed.

Collections of related frames are linked together into *frame systems*, which are networks of nodes and relations. The effects of important actions are mirrored by transformations between the frames of a system, where such frames typically share certain parts, thus making it economical to co-ordinate information gathered from different viewpoints. Of interest to us is Minsky's distinction between visual and non-visual kinds of frames. For non-visual frames, such as ones dealing with the notion of *trading*, the social contexts and the linguistic symbols used in these contexts determine which frames are present and what information they contain. A "complete" system of non-visual frames would probably cover all language available to humans in those contexts.

For visual frames, a single frame may, for example, represent a set of vantage points; other frames in a system then represent other fundamental sets of vantage points. An example using a cube is shown in Figure 10.5: each frame represents a "canonical" view of the object without regard for the details of the exact angle of view.

It is important that even for Minsky's so-called *visual* kinds of frames, images themselves play no role. Indeed, the frames of a system are chosen so as to make the image superfluous. The number of different frames is kept low by choosing only those with fundamentally different views.

Even for non-visual frames, Minsky subscribes to the thesis of Bartlett (1932) that "thinking ... is biologically subsequent to the image formation process". He contends that

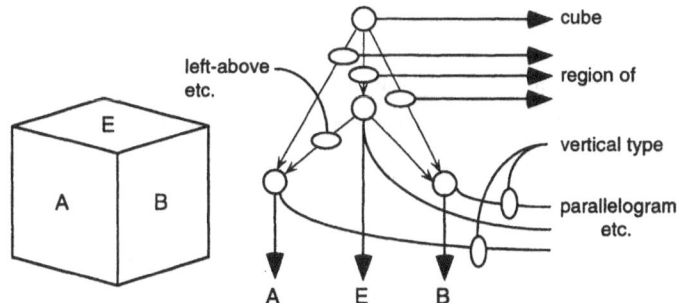

**Figure 10.5:** Organization of a visual frame representing the different canonical views
(see Minsky 1975)

humans condense and conventionalize complex situations and sequences into compact *words* and *symbols*. Pictures are thus not represented *per se* in Minsky's model of knowledge processing.

Minsky's model was so influential that most researchers in this area to date have adopted this premise that images need not play a role in knowledge processing in machines. Indeed, popular programming languages for implementing knowledge-based systems, such as LISP (which tends still to be favored in the United States) and Prolog (which tends to be more widely used in Europe), provide programs with facilities to implement systems along these lines. Perhaps this is primarily a *marriage of convenience*: programs need to be written and no programming languages or systems for working with images as the basis for knowledge representation have come into use outside specialized laboratories.

We shall not go into the details of the various representational forms here because their differences are unimportant for the purposes of this book. Instead the interested reader is referred to the literature (for example Barr and Feigenbaum 1981). Following Barr and Feigenbaum, we define any such representation form which is equivalent to Frege's notation as *Fregean structures*. But not all modern forms of knowledge representation are Fregean structures. In particular, analogical representations have received some limited attention (see the seminal work in this area by Funt 1980). However, these have had little or no effect on human-computer interaction and are thus of little consequence in the present context.

Returning now to pictograms, we see that these play no role in theories of knowledge representation. Instead, they are external presentations (i.e., on paper or a computer screen) of concepts or things, whose meaning can be described by Fregean structures. As we will see in the next section, this can lead to a basis for a special kind of dialogue system.

## 10.4  Picture Frames

To bring pictures into the representation of knowledge, Strothotte (1989) designed data structures called *picture frames*, which are extensions of Minsky's frames. The extensions deal with pictures and techniques for modifying them to represent flexibly the solutions to problems.

### 10.4.1  Constituent Parts of Picture Frames

The central part of a picture frame is a picture of a typical scene in the domain of the application. The picture contains the objects in the configuration normally found when working in the domain. Besides the usual slots and methods of Minsky's frames, a picture frame has *graphical slots* for making additions or changes to the picture. The parts of a picture frame can be summarized as follows:

*A basic picture and its name*
A (black and white) picture is represented by a bitmap or a collection of graphical primitives from which a bitmap can be computed directly. The basic picture may either be a presentational picture or an abstract-graphical one. It can also be a pictogram.

*Slots for manipulations of the picture*
In these *picture-manipulation slots*, minor modifications of the basic picture are recorded. A slot is associated with each part of the picture that could conceivably be changed (rotated, translated, etc.). Placing a value into such a slot results in the corresponding procedure being invoked, making the corresponding change in the picture.

*Slots for graphical symbols*
These *graphical-symbol slots* serve to add symbols to the basic picture. For example, an object in the picture may have associated with it a graphical-symbol slot called a *label*. When this slot is filled by a value (for example a character string), a line pointing at the object is automatically drawn in the picture from the object to some free space at the side of the picture. The character string is then written into the picture in the free space at the end of the line. To a human viewer of the picture, this has the effect of naming (i.e., annotating) the object.

Changing the image in this manner yields a new picture which is very likely to be an abstract-graphical picture, irrespective of whether the basic picture was presentational or abstract-graphical. The reason is that these extra symbols are considered important enough to be included in the picture and hence are very likely to influence its meaning strongly. In the context of the use of such presentations, the abstract-graphical parts of the resultant picture are likely to preoccupy the viewer.

*Slots to define hierarchies*

These *hierarchy slots* are used to record names of other picture frames that represent more detailed views of parts of the current picture.

*Further slots and methods*

Further knowledge pertaining to the scene of the picture frame is stored in the usual frame-based manner.

The parts of a picture frame are summarized in Figure 10.6. The sample picture, adapted from one in the German Duden *Bildwörterbuch* (Duden 1977), shows a typical office scene. Modifications and additions to such a basic picture can be used to produce explanations for users. In this case, the basic picture is a presentational picture, which does not qualify as a pictogram because of its complexity.

**Name:** *Office*

**Slots for graphic symbols:** *for adding texts, lines, arrows, etc., to the picture*

**Slots for manipulations of the picture:** *for recording and making changes (translation, rotation, etc.) in the basic picture*

**Slots to define hierarchies:** *pointers to other picture frame structures that model common or specific scenes*

**Further slots and methods:** *Fregean structures for problem solving according to Minsky*

**Figure 10.6**: Composition of a picture frame (Strothotte and Böcke 1989)

### 10.4.2 Interactive Problem Solving with Picture Frames

Picture frames are used for problem-solving in a way that extends beyond that of normal frames. Given a problem, the system searches in its knowledge base of picture frames for the one that corresponds most closely to the problem. The facts from the input are recorded directly in appropriate slots; others are computed with the help of certain methods and then recorded in the remaining slots, thereby "solving" the problem. If this process can be carried out successfully, the picture of the picture frame is finally produced as the solution to the problem. Otherwise, the search for a more appropriate picture frame continues and the procedure is repeated.

The important aspect of the use of picture frames is the mechanism to make changes to the basic picture. In normal frames, information is simply recorded in slots; in picture frames, a graphical representation of this information is recorded in the picture in a way that can be understood by an external (i.e., human) observer. Thus the solution is obtained incrementally through a series of manipulations of the basic picture and is available as soon as the problem solving process is complete. This procedure circumvents the process of generation (of natural language or pictures) from an internal form of the solution into an external form, which can be understood by humans.

The graphical symbols added to the basic pictures have the effect of guiding the user through the picture. They highlight features considered to be important for understanding the solution to the problem. They add *language* to the pictorial presentation, since they can include text. This helps users to verbalize the solutions for themselves.

### 10.4.3  An Application in Computer Aided Instruction of Chemistry

The concept of picture frames can be illustrated by a prototype system for the computer assisted instruction (CAI) of chemistry at high-school level.

Chemistry is a subject in which abstract-graphical pictures play an important role in conveying information. Textbooks typically explain experiments with the help of abstract-graphical pictures showing flasks, test tubes, Bunsen burners, etc., using special graphical symbols like arrows and textual labels to denote actions. To a student, such pictures of the experimental set-up are essential, because chemical formulas only say what happens in a reaction at the molecular level, not how to produce the reaction. For example, information such as the physical state of the chemicals, whether heat must be added, and in what order chemicals must be added to one another, is not contained in the equation of a reaction.

### *The Picture Frames*
In high-school chemistry textbooks, there are a small number of basic experimental techniques that can be combined to carry out arbitrarily complex experiments. In each of these techniques, the apparatus changes only slightly from one experiment to the next. The fundamental aspect that changes is which chemicals are used and in what order the basic experimental techniques are applied. Thus picture frames for these basic operations

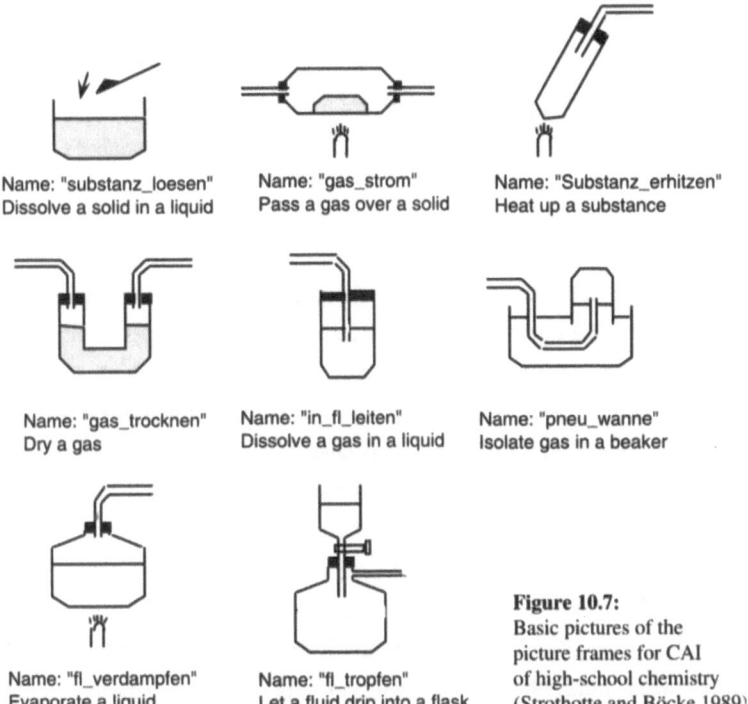

Name: "substanz_loesen"
Dissolve a solid in a liquid

Name: "gas_strom"
Pass a gas over a solid

Name: "Substanz_erhitzen"
Heat up a substance

Name: "gas_trocknen"
Dry a gas

Name: "in_fl_leiten"
Dissolve a gas in a liquid

Name: "pneu_wanne"
Isolate gas in a beaker

Name: "fl_verdampfen"
Evaporate a liquid

Name: "fl_tropfen"
Let a fluid drip into a flask

**Figure 10.7:**
Basic pictures of the
picture frames for CAI
of high-school chemistry
(Strothotte and Böcke 1989)

were designed (see Figure 10.7). Graphical symbol slots are attached to each picture frame to represent the chemicals placed into the various containers.

In this example, the basic pictures have a presentational character. The way the pictures are used qualifies them as pictograms that may be combined to portray larger experiments.

### Sample Dialogue

The system has a set of rules representing chemical reactions and the experimental techniques necessary to carry them out. A user can ask the system questions by calling up an appropriate Prolog predicate. The system determines which reactions are necessary and produces a picture by augmenting the appropriate picture frames. For example, with the following command, the user asks "How is hydrogen ($H_2$) produced?" The variable B is equivalent to the augmented picture: ?- produce ('H2' , B).

Figure 10.8 shows the value of the variable B that represents the solution to the problem the user posed. The system has determined that $H_2$ can be produced by dissolving Zn in HCl (a liquid). Thus the picture frame "substanz_loesen" ("dissolve a substance") (see again Figure 10.6) is selected and appropriately augmented with labels for the chemicals.

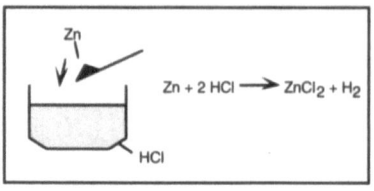

**Figure 10.8:**
Answer to the question:
"How is $H_2$ produced?"
(Strothotte and Böcke 1989)

A more complex example is the question "How is nitrogen ($N_2$) produced?" Here a sequence of reactions must be carried out. The system builds up the experiment one step at a time, showing what chemicals are involved. In these examples, a simple, short text appears in the picture, giving a verbal explanation of the key point, while the details remain encoded in the picture. The system's response is illustrated in Figures 10.9. In the first step (Figure 10.9a), $NH_3$ in fluid form is heated up, producing this same chemical as a gas. Next, the $NH_3$ is dried with the help of calcium chloride, $CaCl_2$ (Figure 10.9b). In the third step (Figure 10.9c), CuO is heated and the $NH_3$ passed over it, yielding $N_2$. Finally, $N_2$ is isolated in an inverted beaker (Figure 10.9d).

As a final example, we show how one picture can be augmented by different graphical symbol slots to answer two very different questions. The left part of Figure 10.10 shows and describes a reaction, whereas the right part explains the apparatus required to produce that reaction. The basic picture is the same, but it is augmented in different ways. Both can be generated, if the picture frames have different sets of slots for graphical symbols.

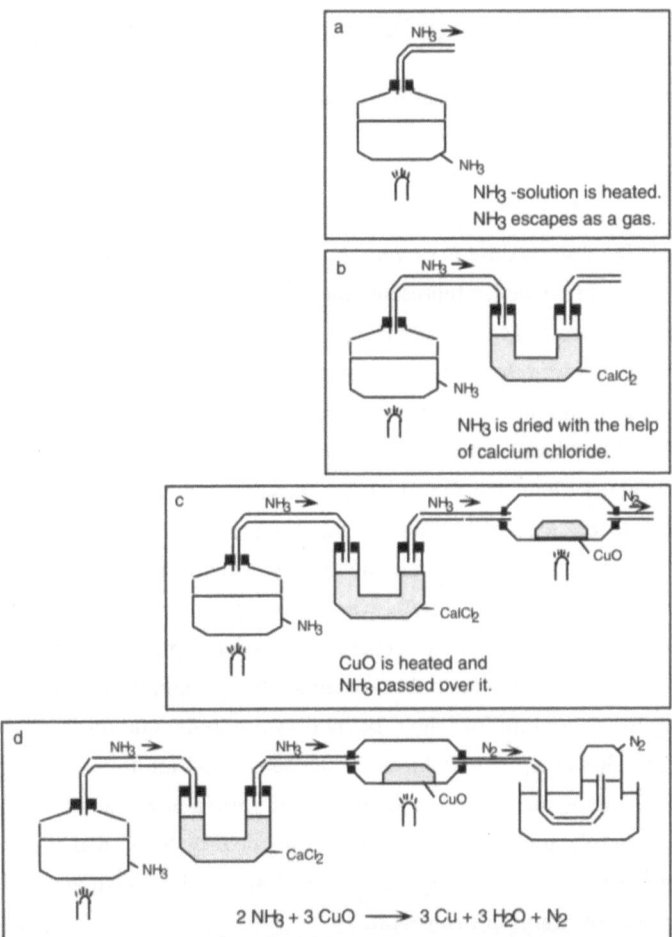

**Figure 10.9:** Producing $N_2$ (Strothotte and Böcke 1989)

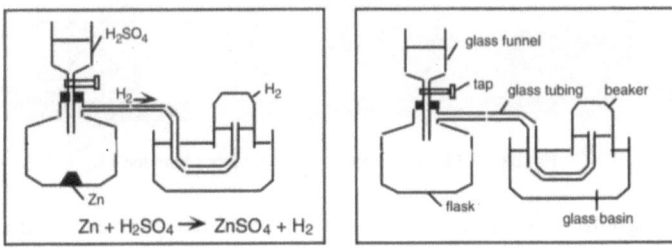

**Figure 10.10:** Example of a picture augmented in different ways (Strothotte and Böcke 1989)

## 10.5 Are Combinations of Pictograms Still Pictograms?

In this chapter we have systematically built up a conceptual basis for pictograms. First, we showed that they must be *typical* of a class of objects or concepts, even though the pictogram must not necessarily be an image of one of the members of the class. Second, they should elicit only *low normalization demands* on the part of their viewers. Third, pictograms can be described by *Fregean structures*, even though pictures are not used in common theories of knowledge representation. Finally, pictograms can be integrated into knowledge based systems as external presentations of solutions to problems solved using data structures which we refer to as *picture frames*.

In the example of the use of picture frames, the basic pictures are all pictograms and are combined with one another during the stage of problem solving. The combination is carried out by the system, but the procedure raises a fundamental issue that we must examine more closely: Can pictograms be combined with one another in general, and is the result of combining two or more pictograms also a pictogram?

The inventor of pictograms, Neurath, was the first to answer this question in the mid-1930s (see Krampen 1986). Neurath generally considered pictograms to be combinable with one another to a certain extent. For example, the pictogram for a shoe factory could be built up by the pictogram for "shoe" being drawn into the one for "factory" to form a new pictogram. However, if two objects of the same kind are to be differentiated from one another, the pictograms ought not be merged to form a new one, but still to be drawn together. For example, to differentiate "transporting coal by lorry" and "transporting coal by train" from one another, a pictogram for "coal" should be drawn and then either one for "lorry" or one for "train" drawn near it.

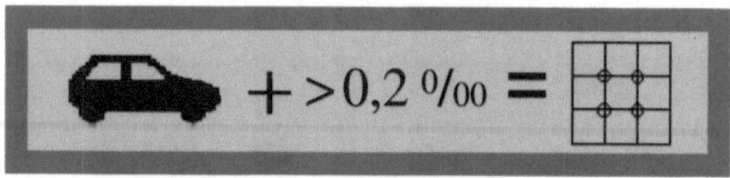

**Figure 10.11:** A complex pictogram from Sweden

Complex pictograms do appear in practice, in particular in places where potential viewers have more than a few seconds to look at an image. Such "pictogram stories" can convey more meaning than can be packed into a single word or short phrase. They are often used to warn people by showing cause-and-effect relationships in recurring dangerous situations. The problem of drinking and driving seems to us a very popular example of this. Examples may be found in Sweden (Figure 10.11) and Canada (Figure 10.12) –

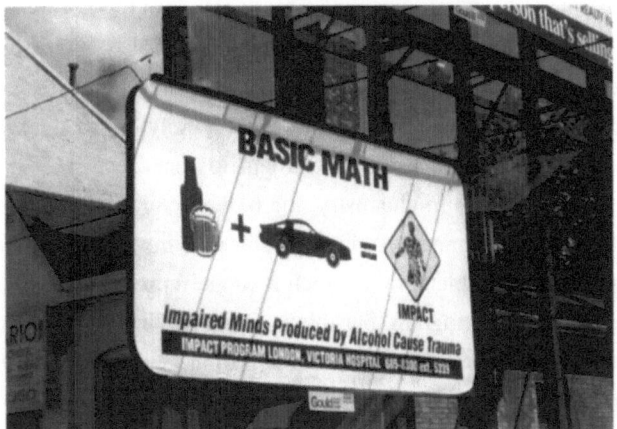

**Figure 10.12:** A complex pictogram from Canada

both describe the effect of drunken driving very dramatically. Of interest was the location: neither of them appeared near a road, but both were in full view of car drivers. The Canadian one is in downtown London (Ontario) on a parking lot and the Swedish one at the customs checkpoint for people coming into Sweden by car off a ferry. They were made to prompt the viewers to think about a certain topic, and the time necessary for viewing and reflection was available in both locations.

Drivers on the Alaska Highway also have a great deal of time – sometimes even too much time – to think about things other than steering their cars. Figure 10.13 shows a pictogram presented to them.

**Figure 10.13:** Pictogram on the Alaska Highway

All of these examples show "before and after" situations, and use graphical symbols for dramatically demonstrating effects. These pictograms are also interesting examples of pictures, as the message cannot really be reduced to a small number of words without losing its effect. Harnessing this power of pictures is surely one of the major challenges in the computational study of pictures, especially pictograms.

Going back to our example in chemistry, the basic pictures of the picture frames are clearly presentational pictograms. Adding graphical symbols and annotations makes them into abstract-graphical pictograms. Such a single representation (like Figure 10.8) could still be treated as a pictogram, but this is unlikely, since it contains quite a lot of detail and evokes somewhat too high normalization demands. The more complex example of Figure 10.9d is also an abstract-graphical picture, but certainly no longer a pictogram. Korfhage and Korfhage (1986) would refer to Figure 10.9d as an "iconic sentence" (they use the word "icon" in a sense similar to which we use "pictogram" in this book), which can form part of an "iconic language". We shall not make such claims about language here, as we are unable to treat the subject with sufficient generality. Suffice it to say that the result of combining two or more pictograms is generally an abstract-graphical (or, less likely, presentational) picture.

*Cloud, clan symbol*
Willow Springs, Arizona

# Pictograms as Words

Having studied pictograms from the point of view of their pragmatics, we are now in a position to take the next step and learn more about the relationship between pictograms and language.

At the level of the implementation of interactive systems, a programmer works with pictograms as simple word substitutes. This is illustrated in Figure 11.1, where the name of a pictogram is being typed in. All algorithmic features of the pictogram are associated with this word. Whenever the end-user carries out any kind of manipulation with the pictogram, the name is accessed and appropriate actions taken.

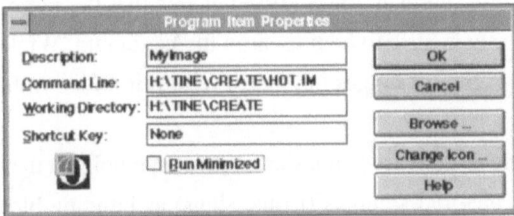

**Figure 11.1:** A programmer's view of a pictogram as a word

In this chapter, we will study the background of this link between pictograms and words. Our approach will be to go to the root of pictograms and examine recommendations in the literature on how pictograms should be chosen for a particular application. We will discover that words are at the heart of practically all procedures for choosing pictograms. Implicit in the procedures is the assumption that the viewer will equate a pictogram he or she sees with a single word; the goal is to make sure it is the "right" one. This is also the underlying principle in procedures to assess the effectiveness of pictograms.

In the final part of the chapter, we discuss some of the drawbacks of pictograms that can result from their visual nature, and show how the closeness of pictograms to language can be exploited to improve user interfaces.

## 11.1  Choice of Pictograms

It is striking that in practically all applications of pictograms, and practically all methods of choosing them, the goal is to find the pictograms most closely represented by a given word or, in some rare cases, by a short description of the abstract concepts they represent. Staufer (1987) goes so far as to say that a verbal statement of the communicative intent of a pictogram is a prerequisite for its design.

Many methods of varying precision have been developed to choose pictograms for a particular application. We shall study in detail the method originally proposed by Rohr (1984). It is one of the more complex procedures for this task, but other procedures tend to be simple derivations of Rohr's method. Furthermore, it very clearly highlights the underlying principles and assumptions concerning the relationship between pictograms and language.

Rohr assumes that the viewer of a pictogram will recognize its "conceptual meaning" on the basis of visual feature elements or feature element combinations; this is in accordance with the recommendations of Hemenway (1982). Rohr's "conceptual meaning" in the context of this book is equivalent to a node in a Fregean structure. She bases her design on work of Howell and Fuchs (1968), who determined that the more abstract such a concept, the more abstract symbols such as slashes, asterisks, arrows, etc., have to be added to a basic picture. Further, Jones (1983) claims that the more abstract a concept, the more pictorial symbols have to be present in the pictogram. While seemingly contradictory, these studies agree in suggesting that several primitive symbols must be present in a single pictogram.

Rohr suggests using a small set of relevant abstract symbols (in the terms of Chapter 3, symbolic signs) and pictorial symbols (iconic signs) as building blocks for pictograms. Constructing and testing all possible pictograms consisting of these primitive ones is precluded by the combinatorial explosion; however, an incomplete but representative set of pictograms can be constructed by varying the number of feature elements and how they combine (abstract symbols only, pictorial symbols only, and a mixture of both).

We shall look at an approach for the design of pictograms for a text editor. Rohr carried out experiments with 18 symbol elements, from which she constructed 72 representative pictograms; some of them are illustrated in Figure 11.2. To determine the

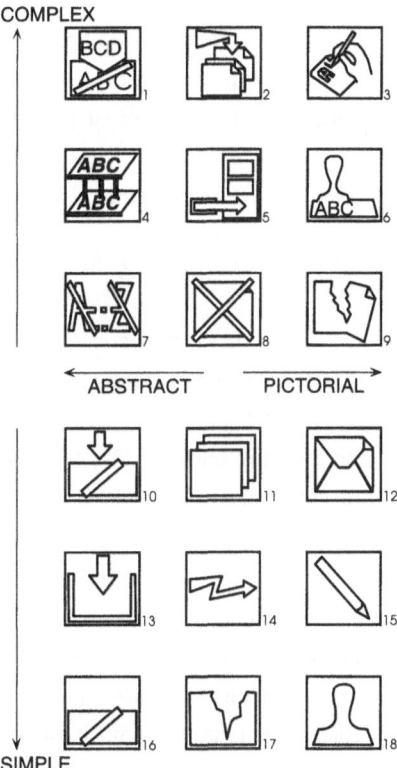

**Figure 11.2:** Examples of pictograms tested by Rohr (1984) © IEEE 1984 (redrawn)

"best" pictograms for each of the user functions available in the application, she had subjects rate each pictogram with respect to its appropriateness for each of the available features of the text editor.

Already here the important effect of language in the design of pictograms can be felt. The reference set of user functions is described linguistically to subjects; examples used by Rohr are "print a file" and "delete a string". Thus the design of pictograms is actually a search for the pictogram that most closely matches a linguistic description, not forgetting that the members of a given set of pictograms must be sufficiently different from one another. This explains why some of the pictograms contain several primitive symbols.

The computation to determine the most appropriate match between user functions and pictograms is conceptually simple. Given $f$ features and $p$ pictograms, an $f \times p$ matrix $P$ characterizes the set of test pictograms: $P_{i,j} = 0$ if pictogram $i$ does not contain feature $j$, but $P_{i,j} = 1/k$ if it does and the feature appears in $k$ of the pictograms (clearly $k \le p$). The test results are represented by a $c \times p$ matrix $T$ for $c$ commands of the application (in the present case, the text editor). $T_{i,j}$ is the average score that the subjects of Rohr's experiment assigned to pictogram $j$ for command $i$. Now a simple matrix multiplication $R = P \times T$ yields an $f \times c$ matrix with a value distribution of the single feature elements for each command, high values indicating the most relevant features. To avoid particularly relevant features appearing in a large number of pictograms, we then compute a new matrix $R^*$ in which we reduce every entry in $R$ using the feature $i$ by the average score of all the other commands using the same feature element, i.e.,

$$R^*_{i,j} = R_{i,j} - \left(\frac{1}{c-1}\right) \sum_{k \neq j} R_{j,k}$$

which guarantees that a high value in $R^*_{f,c}$ indicates that the feature $f$ is particularly distinctive for the command $c$. These features are now included in the final pictogram if the entry lies above some appropriate threshold.

Rohr's procedure can be interpreted in terms of Fregean structures. On the one hand, the procedure for designing a pictogram can clearly be equated to the search for the picture that viewers associate most accurately with a node in a Fregean structure. In this sense, a pictogram equates as closely as possible to a word. This interpretation remains consistent when we consider Rohr's underlying assumption that the primitive parts of pictograms can be mixed and matched to obtain the "best fit". This procedure works because every node in the Fregean structure of a large knowledge base is related to many others and can generally be broken down into a composition of others.

## 11.2 Evaluation of Pictograms

The "communicative power" of a pictogram is the basis for practically all the evaluations discussed in the literature on the subject. The communicative power of a pictogram is defined as "the ability of a pictogram to represent its verbal name" (Staufer 1987). Most methods for evaluating pictograms are based on showing pictograms to potential viewers and asking them to choose the word that each most appropriately describes.

Perhaps the most direct exploitation of the term "communicative power" is in the multiple-choice matching method of evaluating pictograms. Here subjects are asked to choose the best name for each of a series of pictograms from a list of possibilities. A somewhat less restrictive variation of this method is to have subjects write short verbal descriptions of the perceived meaning of a pictogram. These descriptions are then evaluated with respect to a classification scheme (see for example Easterby and Zwaga 1976). Such methods are relatively easy and quick to carry out, but they are rather coarse in the resulting assessments. They yield only a binary value for each pictogram (recognized or not) and comparisons between pictograms for a given viewer cannot be derived.

A further discriminating factor to assess the quality of pictograms is the time required to arrive at correct recognition. To evaluate the original pictograms for the Xerox Star, Bewley et al. (1983) used the "choice-response" time measurement. Various pictograms are placed on the screen in a random arrangement. As soon as the name of a pictogram is spoken aloud, the subject points to the pictogram he thinks it refers to. The details of the results go beyond the scope of this book (they can be found in Bewley et al. 1983 or Staufer 1987).

While such tests can demonstrate the communicative power of a pictogram, they cannot be used to demonstrate their supposed superiority over words or how well they fare in the actual working situation. Claims about such aspects require extensive tests with at least a prototype of the software in which the pictograms are to be used. The tests are both expensive and time-consuming, which explains why they are almost never carried out.

Rohr (1984, 1986) is one of the few authors who went to the trouble of evaluating pictograms in a working implementation of the intended application. Initially she designed two kinds of pictograms, functional and non-functional, to give users access to the operations of a text processor, following the method described in detail in Section 11.1 (recall examples in Figure 11.2). She then gave editing tasks to three groups of subjects, one working with the functional pictograms in the user interface, one with the non-functional pictograms, and the third with command words (see Figure 11.3). She measured the time users took to complete the tasks as well as the time spent asking for help. Her results showed that significantly more help requests were made by users in the "words" group during their initial work, while later on the amount of help required decreased. Furthermore, on the time-per-operation scale, words achieved a position between functional and non-functional pictograms in the first part of the experiment, while in the second part, functional pictograms had improved enough to become superior to the others.

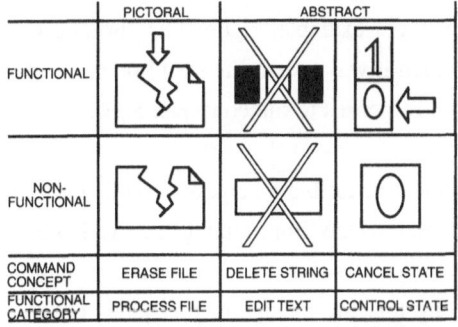

**Figure 11.3:** Comparison of functional and non-functional
pictograms and words (Rohr 1984) © IEEE 1984

The results of our discussions about the procedures for choosing pictograms on the one hand and evaluating them on the other are consistent. The fundamental role of language is evident from the overriding concern with establishing the relationship between pictograms and words or descriptions. The conclusion to be drawn is that pictograms are indeed "word substitutes" (recall Chapter 5).

The main contrast to words is that it is difficult to combine pictograms to yield sentences. However, in interactive systems they are used in situations where they are members of lists, usually in no particular order (see for example Figure 11.4).

**Figure 11.4:** Example of a linear list of Microsoft Word 5.1 pictograms

## 11.3  Ambiguity of Pictograms

The methods of choosing and evaluating pictograms discussed thus far are based on the underlying assumption that they should ideally be unambiguous. This is why, for example, Rohr eliminates features common to many commands.

The requirement that pictograms ought to be unambiguous is lifted in a very clever way by Pejtersen and Goodstein (1988) in a pictorial interface for the on-line catalogue in a public library. They used the truth behind the cliché "A picture says more than a thousand words" and associated a selection of words with each of a small number of pictograms. They designed pictograms to be presented in an interactive system to library visitors who are looking for books on particular subjects. Since it is not feasible to design a single pictogram for each entry in a library's classification scheme, the pictograms were deliberately chosen to be ambiguous, and tests were performed to see which different concepts they represented. For example, Figure 11.5 shows a pictogram along with five possible concepts for which it was tested. Figure 11.6 shows the percentage of subjects tested who gave positive responses to the concepts. Separate tests were made for children, women, and men.

To use this pictorial interface to find a book on a particular topic in the fiction section of a public library, the user selects from among the available pictograms one or more expressing the concept she or he seeks. This means a reasoning process must be carried out by the user, implying that the pictogram transputes certain meanings to the user.

1: Grandparents

2: Homosexuality

3: Celebrities

4: Music

5: None

**Figure 11.5:** A pictogram and five concepts it might represent (Pejtersen and Goodstein 1988)

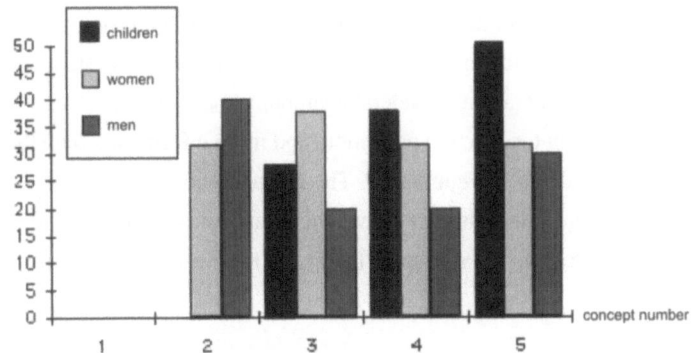

**Figure 11.6:** Test results for children, women, and men of the pictogram in Figure 11.5 (Pejtersen and Goodstein 1988)

Once the number of books satisfying the user query is small, the system switches over to a textual mode, giving the name, author, and call number of the books that qualify.

What has happened in terms of Fregean structures is that the designers of the system have chosen pictograms to denote a set of otherwise unrelated concepts and transputed these to the user via the pictogram. The system is one of the very few constructive uses of the ambiguity of pictograms and the power of computers to transpute information to the user via pictograms.

## 11.4  Some Drawbacks of Pictograms in User Interfaces

Pictograms are two-dimensional by nature and take up space on a computer screen. Although they are essentially word substitutes – as we have just seen – they are generally not used as words in the sense of being accessed via the keyboard. An often cited advantage of such user interfaces is the similarity of the operators available to the user (Hutchins, Hollan, and Norman 1986), who carries out virtually all operations by moving the mouse and clicking its buttons, and always gets visual feedback.

However, there are two fundamental drawbacks in the visualization and direct manipulation of objects both in the application and in the menus for command selection: they are a source of physiological stress and a source of cognitive stress (see Kunkel and Strothotte 1990). We treat each of these in turn.

### 11.4.1 Physiological Stress

To activate a pictogram, the user must first direct his or her line of vision to the pictogram and monitor the movement of the mouse cursor to its position. After clicking on the pictogram, the user must scan the screen for the place where work on the application is to continue and again monitor the movement of the mouse cursor. These steps cause considerable strain on the eyes, and take a considerable amount of time to carry out. The problem is aggravated by the current tendency to pack more and more information onto the screen.

The process is visualized in Figure 11.7. The left part shows a diagram as drawn using a simple draw program. The right part shows the mouse movements used to construct the diagram. This indicates the very chaotic nature of mouse and – more important – eye movements.

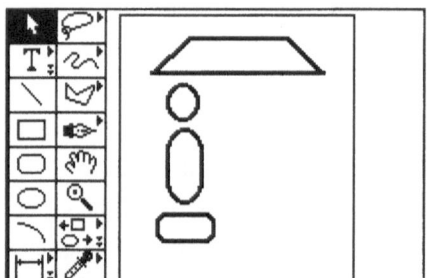
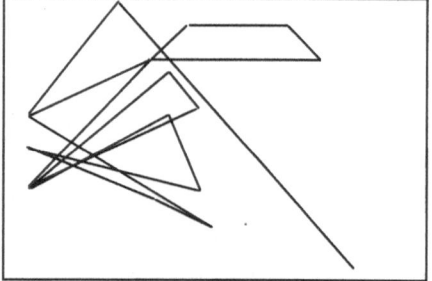

**Figure 11.7:** Example of a drawing (left) and mouse/eye movements necessary to construct it (right)

### 11.4.2 Cognitive Stress

The user's work on his or her primary task, manipulating objects in the application, is often interrupted. He or she is forced to shift attention away from the application to the pictogram for command selection and then back again. This constant shifting between the primary task and the operation of the program results in a significant load on his or her cognitive capabilities.

Kunkel and Strothotte (1990) conjecture that these drawbacks are a consequence of the overuse of visualizations and direct manipulation in user interfaces. While selecting and activating commands is necessary, this should not interfere with the cognitive processing capabilities available for the user's primary task. They also conjecture that the negative effects on the user can be reduced by introducing multiple modes of I/O. Under such circumstances, the user can work with each aspect of the program in a different way. While bi- or even multimodal user interfaces may increase the overall cognitive workload, in the bimodal case, the user employs cognitive resources that are left unused in the unimodal case. They conjecture that for bimodal interaction, there will be more cognitive capacity remaining for the primary task than with unimodal interaction.

## 11.5   Speech to Augment Pictograms in User Interfaces

We now turn to the design of user interfaces in which visualizations of commands (pictograms) and speech input augment one another. The idea is to exploit the fact that pictograms are actually word substitutes. Hence the user should be able to substitute words for the usual mouse clicks.

### 11.5.1   Speech in User Interfaces

In the past, speech recognition devices were used in man-machine interfaces primarily to augment or replace the keyboard. Several studies have been carried out in which speech was used in text and program editors, primarily to enter commands, but the results were not overwhelming. For example, Leggett and Williams (1984) found that speech took about 25 % longer than the keyboard entry of programs, although the error rate was lower with speech. In a similar study, Morrison et al. (1984) found no significant difference in the time taken or the error rates for entering the commands of a text editor with speech compared to the keyboard. Considerable progress has been made recently, however, on using speech for disabled persons wishing to work on computers (see for example Mehnert, Fellbaum, and Hoffmann 1993; Placencia Porrero and Puig de la Bellacasa 1995).

One of the problems with these approaches is that while the hands are freed by the use of speech, the cognitive capacity freed is not used in any useful way. It is thus reasonable to look for ways of combining speech input with direct manipulation techniques. Initial experience with a Pascal program editor indicated that this combination is most useful when both modes are used most of the time and when there is a certain balance between the amount of time the user works with speech and the amount of time he or she works with the mouse (see Pflieger 1987).

### 11.5.2 An Experimental Interface

We now report on a study carried out by Kunkel and Strothotte (1990) that exploits the linguistic nature of pictograms. The purpose of their study was to compare the quality of two prototypical user interfaces for the same application. In the first interface the user enters information unimodally (strictly via direct manipulation) while in the second interface he or she works bimodally (with direct manipulation and speech input). To assess the quality of the interfaces, parameters such as the amount of time taken by subjects to successfully complete given tasks, their cognitive workload, and their preferences when given a degree of freedom were studied. To gain further insight into the user's mental workload, these parameters were also studied when the subjects were working under time pressure.

As a prototypical application for the study, a graphics editor was chosen. Since commercial products (such as Corel Draw) are implemented as "black boxes" into which speech input cannot readily be integrated, and because they offer a repertoire of commands too diverse to be controlled in an experiment, a "stripped down" version of a drawing program was implemented for the study. The user can draw rectangles, circles, and lines, can enter text, and can move around or erase existing objects. The commands for drawing an object such as a rectangle can either be specified by "clicking" the appropriate field with the mouse or by speaking aloud the name of the command. In either case, the portion of the menu corresponding to the activated command is converted to reverse-video, thus giving the user visual feedback. The user then draws the object by moving the mouse cursor to one corner and pressing a button while moving the cursor to the opposite corner.

The following hypotheses were made:

*H1:* The cognitive workload is higher when working with the bimodal user interface than when working with the unimodal interface.

*H2:* The time users require to complete a drawing with the bimodal user interface is less than the time users require with the unimodal interface.

To compare the two different interfaces, a repeated measure design was used. The subjects were trained in the use of both interfaces in highly standardized single sessions by drawing several diagrams from a prepared set (see Figure 11.8 for an example). Subjects were presented with a diagram on the left half of the screen ("Vorlage") and were to reproduce it on the right half. To minimize experimenter influences, the training instructions were given in writing. The experimenter intervened solely when occasional hardware or software problems occurred. To avoid carry-over and order-of-learning effects,

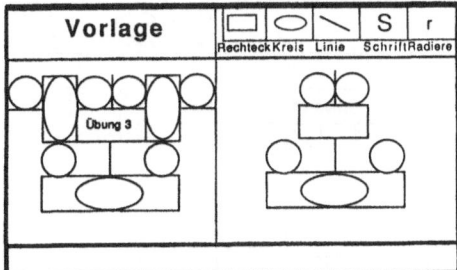

**Figure 11.8:** Sample diagrams used in the study
(Kunkel and Strothotte 1990)

the interface to be learned first – unimodal or bimodal – was selected randomly. After the training, subjects ($n = 72$) were randomly assigned to the three test conditions:

(A) direct manipulation only,
(B) direct manipulation with speech input,
(C) free choice of input mode (command selection).

Subsequent inspection of the data showed that the subjects' occupation, age, sex, and computer experience were evenly distributed in these test conditions. During the test, subjects drew three pictures twice each, once under time pressure and once without time pressure.

To measure the cognitive workload, users were occupied with secondary tasks at irregular intervals (every 10 to 20 seconds). The purpose of the dual task method is to produce measurable performance, where users are performing tasks with a relatively high cognitive component that require few overt responses and produce low error rates. The rationale underlying this method is that human processing resources are limited, therefore if an additional task can be made to compete for those limited resources, there will be a measurable deterioration in performance (Brown 1978). The tasks consisted of simple shape-recognition and arithmetic exercises (see Figure 11.9). The users had to press a mouse button (one not used for drawing) once if the answer was correct and twice if it was incorrect. The exercise disappeared one second after the users' response, or five seconds after being posed, whichever happened first.

Finally, subjects completed a short questionnaire at the end of the session. They were asked about the learnability and ease of use of the interfaces, which interface they would prefer if they had to decide on one of them, their knowledge of programming languages, and some sociodemographic items.

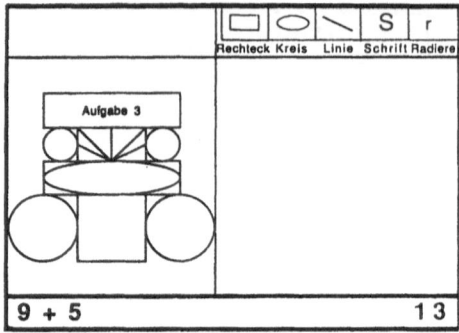

**Figure 11.9:** Secondary tasks
(Kunkel and Strothotte 1990)

The two-factor repeated measure ANOVA run with the data led to the result that the hypothesis *H1* could not be validated. The cognitive workload, as measured in responses to secondary tasks, did not differ, either between the samples or within the samples (either when under time pressure or not). Only if the variable 'time needed to complete the drawings' is included in the analysis as a constant covariate was there a slight tendency ($p = 0.079$) reflecting a higher cognitive workload when working with the bimodal interface under both conditions.

The analysis did supply evidence for hypothesis *H2*. Subjects working with the bimodal interface needed about 15% less time on average to complete the drawings. Whereas subjects from Sample A were not able to enhance the speed with which they worked in the test conditions, related to a baseline measurement, subjects from Sample B increased their speed from the baseline measurement to the condition 'no time pressure', and again from the one test condition to the other.

Subjects' responses to the questionnaire indicate a pronounced but not significant preference for one of the two interfaces. Sixty-two percent of the entire sample preferred the unimodal interface. No significant deviations between the samples A, B, and C occurred.

## 11.6 Discussion

In this chapter we have studied pictograms and their relationship to words. Since pictograms are clearly picture-like in their appearance, the predominant approach in scientific literature has been to treat them as pictures from the point of view of human perception, understanding, and visual recall. However, a careful analysis of the methods used to design and evaluate pictograms reveals an extremely strong link between pictograms and words, or, more generally, Fregean structures. Indeed, the pictograms in a pictogram set are typically composed of simpler elements combined in some formal way, i.e., they reflect some Fregean structure, with the name of the pictogram being the symbol associated with the root of this hierarchical structure.

In terms of our theory of information flow, pictograms are clearly very good for transmitting information from the computer to the user due to their close relationship to words. Their picture-like nature makes them easy to recognize, even using only peripheral vision.

The process of discovering what an unknown pictogram may mean can be construed as one in which information is transputed to the viewer. We may suppose that after discovering and identifying the constituent parts of a pictogram, the viewer carries out a reasoning process to arrive at its meaning. These constituent parts may be those Rohr used in her algorithm for choosing pictograms; the process of pictogram recognition becomes one of searching/backtracking in Fregean structures until the right name has been found. But, once the user has learned to recognize the pictogram, it becomes useful only for transmitting information. This is a clear example of the transition between transmitting and transputing of information via one and the same symbol, depending on the recipient's learning state.

*Giraffe*
Fezzan, Central Sahara Desert, Africa

# Chapter
# 12

# Pictograms as Pictures

We now turn to a discussion of pictograms from the point of view of their being pictures. This extends the idea in Chapter 11 that pictograms are in most cases only a pictorial presentation of words. Our current topic can be seen as a study of the ramifications of the etymology of the word *pictogram,* which is composed of the Latin *pictus* (picture) and the Greek *graphein* (to write), with the consequence that etymologically the word pictogram means 'written picture'. What kinds of pictures are pictograms? What restrictions must be imposed on presentational pictures or on abstract-graphical ones so that the results qualify as pictograms? We will try to find satisfactory answers to these questions using a variety of examples.

We will discuss a classification of pictograms which is oriented toward their use for communicating information to viewers.

## 12.1 Design of Pictograms as Pictures

Seminal work on the design of pictograms was done in the first half of this century and is attributed to Bartlett (1932). He reported that subjects shown many pictograms tried to classify them so as to be able to remember them. In particular, they tried to identify the important features of the pictograms, and grouped them into classes on the basis of formal and spatial similarities or differences between them. Arnheim (1966, 1972, 1978) suggested that everything visible is identified by a viewer with respect to some ordered reference system. Hemenway (1982) determined that this can be achieved successfully if a pictogram set contains only a small number of common graphical elements. Although this can lead to false recognition, Hemenway contends that it has the advantage over words that

- users must learn less,
- it is easier for them to recognize the objects in a pictogram and thus the commands associated with it, and
- it is easier for them to remember the pictograms and their elements.

Smith (1977) goes even further by suggesting that the contents of pictograms can be hierarchically structured, so that a pictogram can be identified by a code indicating its position in the hierarchy.

The qualities of a pictogram can be measured using a variety of dimensions. These include color, size, depth, brightness, form, and the frequency at which items may be blinking.

These dimensions interact with one another; the combination is referred to as the *internal structure* of the pictogram (Staufer 1987). Gombrich (1967) claims that this internal structure of a pictogram cannot be quantified or, in the terminology introduced in Section 10.3, cannot be represented by a Fregean structure. We shall come back to this claim at the end of this section.

As we have already seen in Chapter 3, pictograms can be classified according to their style. They can be anywhere on the continuum from presentational to abstract-graphical. A study by Arend, Muthig, and Wandmacher (1986) suggests in fact that abstract designs are better for pictograms than photo-like designs. In their experiments, abstract pictograms were recognized more quickly by subjects than more photo-like ones and words. Their results further suggest that in designing a pictogram set for an application, the decision for or against photo-like pictograms or ones based on an ordering relation (and if so, which one) must be made in advance of the graphic design.

Finally, the literature indicates that over and above these guidelines, the principles of Gestalt theory should be followed. Since this topic has already been discussed by many authors, we simply refer the interested reader to other sources (Staufer 1987, Koffka 1935, Wertheimer 1923, Metzger 1953).

To highlight the pictorial contents of pictograms, we shall first classify pictograms with respect to their pragmatics and their context. Our approach is pointedly not driven by technology. We step back from today's uses of pictograms in human-computer interaction and focus on pictograms in general as a source of information. Pictograms in human-computer interaction have been well described but represent only a few classes of the variety of pictograms occurring in everyday life. Looking around and analyzing pictograms in general will inspire thoughts about new kinds of pictograms in human-computer interaction.

Besides giving us extra insight into pictograms, drawing inspiration from pictograms in general is important for the design of artificial or virtual worlds (so-called immersive systems, which will occupy us in Chapter 17). This is because in this area everyday situations are simulated under user control. Depending on the application, the artificial world need not necessarily correspond directly to our real world, which means we must address design issues, including ones relevant for pictograms.

## 12.2  Pragmatics of Pictograms

We contend that every pictogram is used primarily to catch the attention of potential viewers and to communicate information to them as they decode its message. We are interested in analyzing the impact on an observer of viewing a pictogram. We postulate that four categories of pictograms can be differentiated with respect to the pragmatics of pictograms. We take as our classification parameter the extent to which this message is really necessary for the user to plan his or her next action. We distinguish four categories of messages from the point of view of the observer. These pertain to the next actions the viewer carries out after receiving the message. We differentiate between pictograms with messages that

- dictate the next action,
- determine which action shall not be carried out next,
- determine the parameters of the next action, or
- draw the observer's attention to possible next actions.

To provide a basis for our discussion, we need to gain some fundamental insights. There are many situations where people have to accept rules defined by others to organize the complex systems we live in or with. Some of the rules are instructions for how people are to behave. Individuals in today's world are not able to act in complex situations without being given rules and selected information about the current state of a system, because many of the rules are counter-intuitive. Pictograms are a very effective method of conveying this necessary information, but different kinds of information need different kinds of pictograms:

1. *Pictograms that dictate the next action*
   This category is very common in everyday life. Examples can be found in traffic where detour signs dictate where to drive (see the North American version in Figure

12.1). Another example of this kind is the pictogram saying to add oil to the car immediately. We need this kind of pictogram because, like the authors of this book, most people are not able to grasp the complete technical system of a car.

**Figure 12.1:** Pictograms that dictate the next action

In interactive systems this kind of message is quite rare. The reason is that through the visualization of several pictograms at once, the user generally has a choice to make, since he or she has the initiative in the dialogue. An exception is an error situation, in which the computer temporarily takes charge of the dialogue to rectify a situation. But in most cases, the computer conveys this very important information textually to the user, for example the question whether a user really wants to remove all files. A more positive example is the warning pictogram (see Figure 12.2), but even this is usually accompanied by an explanatory sentence.

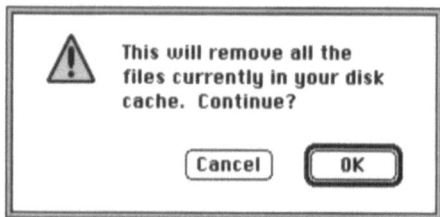

**Figure 12.2:** A warning pictogram

2. *Pictograms that determine which action shall not be carried out next*

These are also common in society in general; obvious examples are signs expressing meanings like "no passing", "no U-turn", or "no entry" (see Figure 12.3). Indeed, many pictograms from category (1) can be negated by placing a red circle with a red line through it on top.

**Figure 12.3:** "Do not" signs

In interactive systems, the negation of a command is generally indicated by using a different line quality or a different font. Thus for example, Figure 12.4 shows the pictograms used in the Fax Manager of PSI Integration, Inc., in different modes. The left part (a) with light gray lines indicates no fax file has yet been selected, while on the right side (b), the fax service is ready for action.

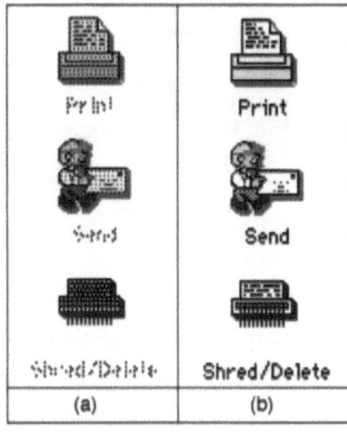

**Figure 12.4:**
Printing in the fax manager is only possible by selecting a fax file

3. *Pictograms to determine the parameters of the next action*

Such pictograms do not dictate *which* action ought to be carried out by the viewer, but leave this decision open and instead tell him or her *how* to carry out the chosen action. Examples are speed limit signs or ones to beware of pickpockets (see Figure 12.5).

In human-computer interaction, this kind of pictogram is rare. The reason is that even though there are often various ways of carrying out a task, the basis for recommending action on the part of the machine is missing.

**Figure 12.5:**
Example of a "how to" sign

4. *Pictograms to present possible next actions*

While pictograms of category (3) *have* to be seen by the intended observer, those of category (4) only *offer* information to an observer in case he or she should be interested. Examples in everyday life are advertising and signs like the one denoting the currency exchange office at an airport (see Figure 12.6).

**Figure 12.6:**
A pictogram of interest to someone looking for a currency exchange office

Because these kinds of pictogram assume the observer is interested in the information presented, most pictograms used in human-computer interaction fall into this category. One reason is that a user of today's graphical interfaces usually has the initiative and can freely choose the next action. Examples are abundant in the desktop metaphor.

This summary of categories of pictograms occurring both in general social life and in human-computer interaction leads to the following conclusions:

- In situations where the success of precise aspects of the communication is essential, language is often the chosen method. Examples are prompts asking the user if he or she is sure that a file is to be deleted.
- Pictograms for determining the parameters of the next action are not actually used in computer applications outside of immersive systems. It is an open problem to find situations in which these concepts could be of benefit.

So far we have only discussed pictograms *per se*, irrespective of the larger context in which they are used. We shall now turn to this topic.

## 12.3  Pictograms and Their Context

Pictograms are designed to convey information to a certain category of viewers. Usually the designer of a pictogram has a certain segment of the population in mind. It is important to realize, however, that viewers in different times or places may not all understand or appreciate the pictograms in the same way.

We shall first examine some of the cultural differences that make the design of pictograms to be used internationally difficult. In a recent article, Russo and Boor (1993) pointed out that trash cans do not look the same all over the world (see Figure 12.7). British users at first glance associate the Apple symbol (Figure 12.7 right) with a letter box (mail box). The Sun Viewer symbol for a mail box, by contrast, may not be understood at all by Europeans, were it not for the textual label (Figure 12.8).

**Figure 12.7:**
Examples of trash
cans (Russo and
Boor 1993)

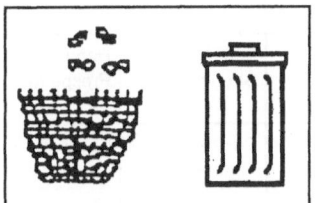

**Figure 12.8:**
Mail box
pictogram used by
SunView (Russo
and Boor 1993)

While images may be recognized, they must also be socially acceptable. Russop and Boor (1993) report the case of a picture developed by Americans for an Egyptian hygiene program (see Figure 12.9 left). When Egyptian women were shown this picture of a woman being fitted with a contraceptive diaphragm, they found it unacceptable; they commented that they themselves do not look like Western women and questioned why the woman's legs were so visible. A series of modifications to the image led to Figure 12.9 (right), which was found to be more socially acceptable.

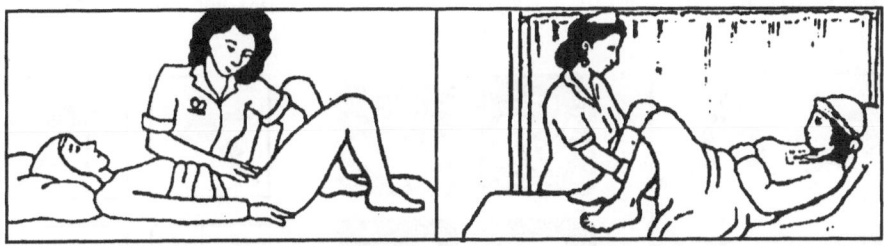

**Figure 12.9:** Pictures used in a hygiene program. The picture shown left was considered socially unacceptable by woman in Egypt; an improved picture is shown on the right (Russo and Boor 1993)

Even simple symbols can have different meanings in different countries. For example, a check mark (✓) is used in many countries to indicate approval, while the same symbol is used to show disapproval in Sweden. Using ✓ to indicate that an answer to a question is right can unnecessarily send a cold shiver down the spine of a Swedish pupil!

Colors are often used in interactive systems, since color monitors have become relatively inexpensive. While in Western societies, for example, red is used for important or dangerous situations, the same color has different meanings in different countries.

Table 12.1 taken from Russo and Boor (1993) gives a summary of color associations in various countries.

**Table 12.1:** Cultural associations of color

|  | Red | Blue | Green | Yellow | White |
|---|---|---|---|---|---|
| **United States** | Danger | Masculinity | Safety | Cowardice | Purity |
| **France** | Aristocracy | Freedom Peace | Criminality | Temporary | Neutrality |
| **Egypt** | Death | Virtue Faith Truth | Fertility Strength | Happiness Prosperity | Joy |
| **India** | Life Creativity |  | Prosperity Fertility | Success | Death Purity |
| **Japan** | Anger Danger | Villainy | Future Youth Energy | Grace Nobility | Death |
| **China** | Happiness | Heavens Clouds | Ming Dynasty Heavens Clouds | Birth Wealth Power | Death Purity |

The dependence of pictograms on the fashion of the day can be seen very clearly by considering the different pictogram systems from the Olympic Games over the last few decades. Every organizing country developed a new system, not because a new system was really necessary, but because they wanted it to be original and attractive. Figure 12.10 shows examples from Tokyo (1964), Mexico (1968), and Munich (1972).

**Figure 12.10:** Examples of the pictogram systems used for the Olympics in Tokyo, Mexico, and Munich

The 1994 Winter Olympics were an occasion to break the trend and come up with a completely new design. The new ones were based on the cave drawing of a skier dating back 4,500 years. The resulting esthetically highly pleasing pictograms from Lillehammer are shown in Figure 12.11.

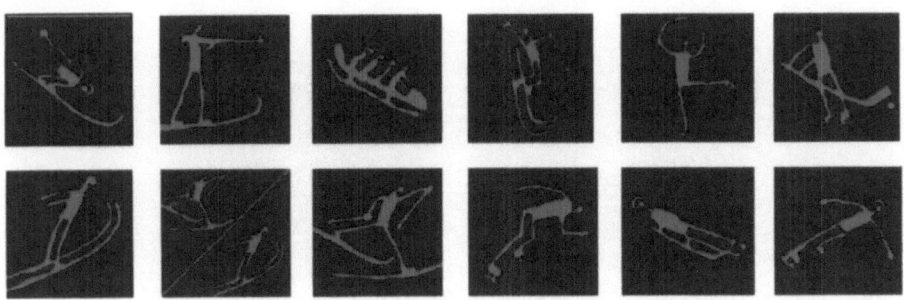

**Figure 12.11:** The pictograms from the 1994 Winter Olympics

*Cave painting*
Gutu district, South Zimbabwe, Africa

# Formal Representations and Informal Presentations

We now turn to the transition from pictures composed of and including graphical symbols to more complex pictorial presentations, whose meaning can no longer be captured easily by Fregean structures. This immediately raises the issue of formalization: To what extent can or even should information encoded in pictures be represented formally, and how can the informal context, which traditionally has been handled *implicitly* in human-computer interaction, be treated algorithmically and conveyed to users?

This chapter comes to terms with the issue in a particular way. First, we examine pictures as data structures and how they are processed. Next, we analyze the nature of formalizations. While actions in the real world and their formalizations have little in common with one another, pictures can serve to bridge the gap. We develop this notion further, to a definition of semi-formal representations with formal and informal elements.

## 13.1 Pictures as Write-Only Data Structures

A picture presented on a computer screen is actually a visualization of a special kind of data structure. This data structure consists of a two-dimensional array of pixels, hence we shall refer to it as a "pixel structure". For example, each pixel may be represented by three bytes of data, leaving 8 bits for each of the red, green, and blue components, i.e., about 16 million possible different colors. Such a pixel structure is visualized by hardware within a terminal or workstation that continuously scans the pixel structure and refreshes the physical screen pixels.

The pixel structure is unique within computing systems. If the pixel structure's contents are *generated* by the computer, for example in a rendering process, it is one of the very few kinds of data structure that are written onto but almost never read again by application programs. Only the scan refresher and perhaps some utilities routinely read the data again. Only in rare cases is the output of a renderer read into an image-processing program (like Adobe Photoshop™) for post-processing. Thus to all intents and purposes, a pixel structure is in this case a *write-only* data structure.

The other side of the coin is, of course, that the pixel structure is designed almost exclusively for the user. It is one of only a few data structures presented to the user in such a "literal" way, i.e., where the mapping from the data structure to the visualization is so straightforward. Indeed, data structures that can be accessed in a sophisticated manner by machine can rarely be shown to a user in a format anything like their internal representation, while structures that are clumsy or inconvenient to access by application software are often visualized directly with ease.

Let us now examine the process by which pixel structures are created in the first place. We shall treat each of our three classes of pictures separately. Our aim will be to see how users will want to use the pictures in dialog systems and what ramifications this has for the data representations within the machine.

a) *Abstract-graphical pictures*

These pictures are most commonly produced by programs that use complex data structures as input. The rules for how to map a data structure onto a pixel structure are based on the experience of designers and have been well thought out. Usually there is a simple technique – such as to convert numeric values into distances in business graphics – which is applied with many variations. While innovative kinds of visualization are still emerging, the really new ones are few and far between. The inverse transformation – from coordinates obtained by the machine through the mouse to pointers into an underlying data structure – can often be accomplished easily because of the simplicity of the mapping function. We saw an example in Section 7.4.

b) *Pictograms*

Good pictograms are still being designed exclusively by designers; in Chapter 12 we studied some of the procedures which are followed. Rarely does an end-user want to know details about the appearance of objects shown in a pictogram. This is because, by definition, pictograms are designed to be viewed in their entirety and aim at evoking a single word or phrase in the viewer.

c) *Presentational pictures*

When images are generated with a renderer (recall Chapter 2.5), the model from which the pixel structure is generated and the pixel structure itself are in completely different formats. Furthermore, the inverse transformation – given a pixel of a rendered image, to establish the object in the model and part thereof to which it corresponds – is a very difficult one. It is so difficult, in fact, that it cannot feasibly be carried out.

These observations mean that if we are to draw presentational pictures into dialog systems, we must make more information about the picture available to the machine. What this amounts to is a formalization not only of the scene, but also of the visualization process and its effect.

Before studying this question in more detail, we shall briefly examine an example of a dialog system that makes a great deal of information available about a presentational picture.

Fischer, Lemke, and Schwab (1985) (see also Fischer 1993) developed a graphical interface for allowing users to design the layout of rooms, in their particular case kitchens (Figure 13.1). The point of their system is that the user is given feedback (called *criticism*) about the qualities of the design, from both a legal and standards-based point of view (e.g., drapes may not hang down over a stove) as well as from a practical point of view (e.g., the distance between the stove and the sink is too large). Although Fischer's system communicates via a presentational picture, practically every aspect of the picture has a well- defined meaning. In fact, the meaning may not even be fully

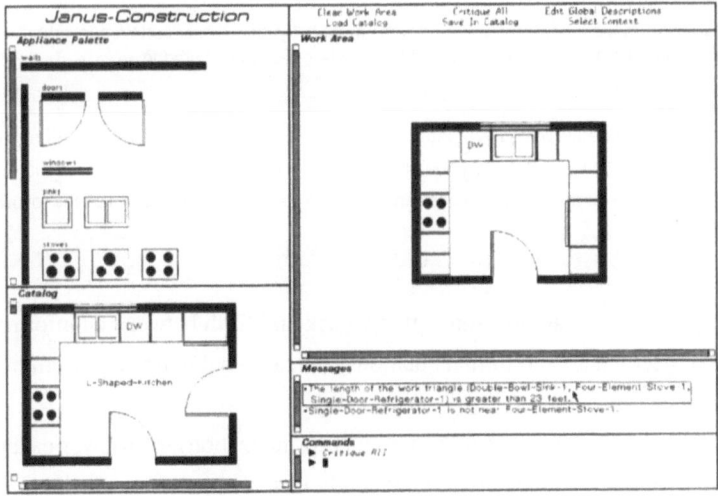

**Figure 13.1:** Presentational picture in the dialog with a critiquing system (Fischer 1993)

known to the user who constructed a design, whereas it is represented within the computer in an accessible manner.

We shall now turn to a deeper analysis of the underlying issues.

## 13.2 Formal and Less Formal Aspects of Human-Computer Interaction

One of the trends in academic computer science is toward more stringent formalization in all areas. This includes, among others, the specification of tasks, user interfaces, and domain-specific knowledge: in short, everything must be formalized for the results of research and development to be considered "solid".

What is meant by "formal"? Given the popular opinion that formality is highly desirable, a wide range of techniques and methods are claimed by their authors to have this attribute. For the present purposes, we define a formal notation as one with "expressions composed entirely of symbols giving a specialized meaning". An informal presentation is thus one without such symbols.

### 13.2.1 Formal Notations as Extensions to Informal Concepts

Naur (1982) argues that formal notations are merely extensions – not replacements – of informal notions. He cites as an example a proof presented by Gauss, which shows clearly that Gauss used a mathematical notation in the sense:

We can shorten the following discussion considerably by introducing certain convenient notations. Let the symbol $(k, p)$ represent the number of products among

$$k, 2k, 3k, ..., \frac{(p-1)}{2}k,$$

whose smallest positive residues modula $p$ exceed $p-2$. Further, if $x$ is a non-zero quantity we will express by the symbol $\lfloor x \rfloor$ the greatest integer less than $x$ so that $x - \lfloor x \rfloor$ is always a positive quantity between zero and one. We can then readily establish the following relation:

$$\lfloor x \rfloor + \lfloor -x \rfloor = -1.$$

Such passages, in which authors move freely back and forth between an informal discussion of the subject matter and formal notations, can be found in treatises from many areas of research in the sciences.

Naur uses such examples to demonstrate that formalizations themselves cannot suffice to describe a situation completely. He contends that it is precisely the intuitive understanding of the context of an expression in a formal mode that gives it its meaning. To drive his point home, Naur demonstrates that informal descriptions of ALGOL 68 were more precise, correct, and complete than a formalization attempted later; moreover, the attempted formalization left so many questions open that it could only be interpreted and understood after reading the original (informal) description!

Naur's observations have important implications for knowledge-based systems. Most importantly, the ability of Fregean structures (recall Section 10.3) to model situations adequately is put into question. Indeed, when one looks at some knowledge-based systems, it is surprising that they work as well as they do given the lack of an adequate representation of the context of the symbols used. Often it looks as if it is solely the human user who projects his or her knowledge of the context onto the presentation in a dialog system, giving the presentation its meaning.

This weakness of formalizations pointed out by Naur can in fact be exploited and made into a feature. If we accept that the informal context plays an important role, a Fregean structure can be used in several contexts. In each one, it will have its own meaning, since the user projects his or her expectations derived from the context onto the symbols used in the structure. If deployed correctly, this extra degree of freedom provides much of the flexibility needed for interactive systems.

### 13.2.2   Formalization in Knowledge-Based Systems

Much effort has been expended in computer applications research to define formal representations for diverse areas of human endeavor. While significant progress has certainly been made in such areas as formula manipulation (Maple 1985) and legal expert systems (Günther and Lehmann 1989), some very important areas have eluded successful formalization. For example, medical diagnosis systems still have difficulty in weighing between possible alternatives and have not gone beyond the experimental stages. Teaching systems that attempt to perform user modeling as a step in designing materials have yet to attain a high level of sophistication.

Some of the work in knowledge-based systems is spoiled by an overestimation of the underlying formalism. For example, it is possible to produce simple natural language sentences in response to users' questions in help systems. However, users are often fooled by such interfaces, because they have difficulty in assessing the system's actual potential. Indeed, natural language interfaces are a very good way of faking a competence in subject area that the computer does not really have. Thus it is the user who is led to understand a formal expression based on his or her own informal experience, rather than the formal expression having a meaning of its own.

This being so, it is absolutely legitimate to incorporate pictures into a knowledge base. Pictures have the potential to capture certain aspects of the subject matter of the domain of application – usually in fact, different ones from the Fregean structures. Even though pictures are often "write-only" data structures whose content has evaded general algorithmic analysis, using them is no less meaningful to a computer than using an isolated symbol of a LISP program as a word in natural language output. Both convey a meaning to the human recipient of a message making use of the picture or the symbol. In this sense, a "knowledge-based system" must include a user who has the ability to attach a deeper meaning to the output as a presentation, particularly when it contains pictures.

## 13.3  Semi-Formal Representations

From the preceding discussion, the value of informal aspects of a presentation, i.e., ones that evade formalization within the machine, should be clear. Of course this poses problems for the computational methods that rely on formalisms. In particular, Naur's claim that formal aspects serve merely to provide a shorthand for some informal aspects implies that a knowledge base should capture primarily informal notions and only resort to formal ones where necessary. Furthermore, if a human-computer dialog is to weave freely between formal and informal aspects – which appears appropriate from the example of Gauss' proof – the whole area of computer-based dialog systems appears to be at an impasse. As one possible solution, we will now turn our attention to hybrid forms of knowledge representation, combining formal and informal aspects. We refer to these as *semi-formal representations*.

### 13.3.1  Characteristics of Semi-Formal Representations

If it is to grasp informal and formal aspects, a semi-formal representation should have the following characteristics:

1. *Parts of the representation can be manipulated by formal means with respect to their meaning, while other parts are informal, i.e., cannot be fully manipulated by formal means.*

   That is to say, it must be possible to analyze and manipulate the representation syntactically to extract or determine part of its meaning. However, we shall relax the restriction imposed on knowledge representation in the past (see for example Dreyfus 1985) that they should exhibit *completeness* in their symbolic processing.

   We say that the representation must be able to be manipulated "with respect to its meaning" to exclude copying and other simple operations.

2. *The presentation when presented to a user leaves significant room for interpretation by a human viewer.*

That is to say, different viewers of the presentation may well have different verbalizations for what is being represented. These semi-formal representations are a clear departure from the goal of much work in knowledge-based systems, which aims at a complete formalization of all aspects of the application at hand. In a sense it is a kind of capitulation: Strength in the representation is to be attained by admitting that not everything can be formalized. On the other hand, it reflects the conjecture that not everything need be formalized.

### 13.3.2  The Trichotomy Informal – Semi-Formal – Formal

Symbolic structures attempt to model, in a formal manner, concepts of "reality", which we in turn consider to be an informal context. A pictorial representation (as a semi-formal representation) thus lies between a formal representation – which is intimately related to a linguistic representation – and its informal context, reality. We thus have the situation illustrated in Figure 13.2. The outermost circle represents the "world" to be modeled in the machine. Part of the world is modeled by semi-formal representations, while only a small core is actually modeled by the formal representation. The boundaries between the three aspects are flexible and depend on the specific application. Hence a formal representation captures only a small part of reality. A semi-formal representation captures part of the context and the formal representation itself.

If a piece of information to be presented to the user of a dialog system stems from information represented only formally, the user must deduce what aspect of the world is being referred to without any information as to the intuition behind it. It is here that semi-formal representations – and output stemming from them – can guide the user in his or her own concept formation by conveying information not captured in the formal

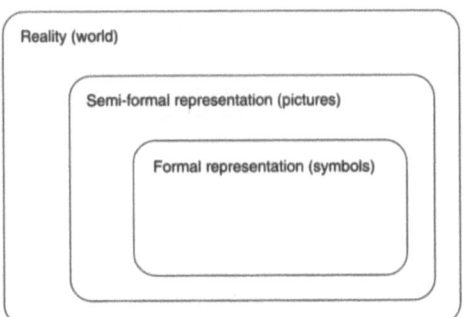

**Figure 13.2:** World, pictures, and symbols (Strothotte and Schmid 1990)

representation. Semi-formal representations serve as a bridge between formal representations and the world they aim to model.

This trichotomy allows us to view some phenomena and system designs in a new light and to see new interrelationships among them. We are not even limited to computer-related concepts. We shall review some of them in this section; a more detailed discussion of these and other examples may be found in Schmid (1989).

*Hieroglyphics and Modern Pictograms*

Hieroglyphics were an early form of writing. Symbols were pictorial in their appearance but combined sequentially for communication. Gradually they developed into symbols with a more precise meaning but a less recognizable appearance. The development of pictograms, as they are used in our society today, has been in the opposite direction: Linguistic symbols form the starting point, and pictograms are being developed to denote them.

In terms of the trichotomy, these two developments are illustrated in Figure 13.3. Hieroglyphics moved from being a semi-formal representation to a formal one, while pictograms have developed out of a formal representation. Pictograms today lie on the border between semi-formal and formal representations. By virtue of their pictorial nature they can be regarded as informal representations, but at the same time due to the precise meaning that members of our society associate with them they are considered to be formal representations. This borderline status is evident in the way a viewer ascertains the meaning of a pictogram that is new to him or her, which is the only time when a detailed analysis of the content of the pictogram is necessary or even desirable.

*Dialog Systems for Giving Instructions*

In many applications of dialog systems, a user obtains information from the system and then performs some manual operation. Examples can be found in teaching programs,

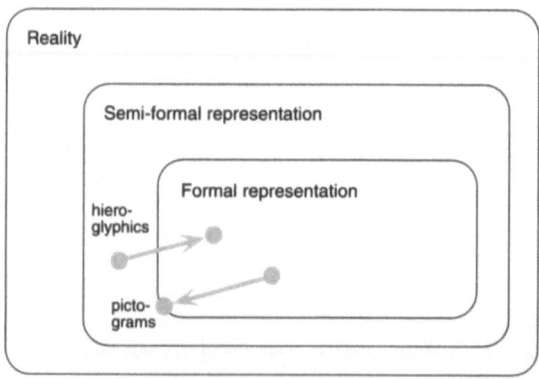

**Figure 13.3:** Analysis of hieroglyphics and modern pictograms (Schmid 1989)

where the user performs an exercise at the end of the session with the machine. Another example is a diagnostic system, where the user describes to the system a problem he or she is having with an electronic device and gets advice on what to do; after getting instructions, the user carries them out in an effort to solve the problem. MYCIN-like programs are sophisticated examples of this class of dialog systems.

In such systems, the goal is for the user to carry out some physical action in the real world, hence, in our terminology something *informal*. If the instruction is given verbally, the user must ascertain the details of the action by a translation of the linguistic form into a physical action. If the machine constructs a semi-formal representation (a picture) for presentation to the user, the transformation into a physical action that must be carried out by the user is often much less complex. The situation is illustrated in terms of the trichotomy in Figure 13.4, which shows how the semi-formal representation works as a bridge between a formal description and the informal reality.

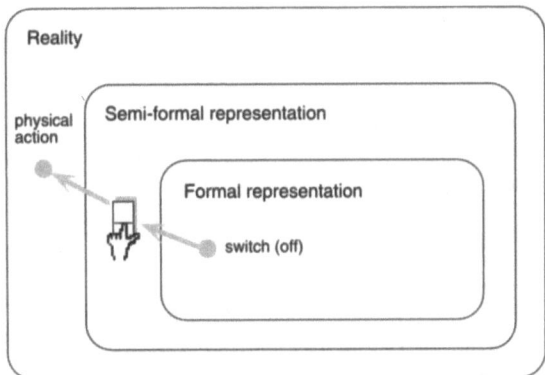

**Figure 13.4:** Analysis of pictorial versus linguistic instructions (Strothotte and Schmid 1990)

## 13.4 Discussion

In this chapter we have taken steps to reinforce the realization that computer representations of data pertaining to an application area need not all be *formal* in the sense of being composed entirely of symbols given a specialized meaning. We need this flexibility as we move away from abstract-graphical pictures and pictograms – where such formalizations are attempted and indeed realistic – to presentational pictures.

It may appear that the inability to provide a complete formalization of a picture is a disadvantage, but we put this concept to work in a constructive way. Semi-formal representations, as we have defined them in this chapter, have the potential to *transpute* a considerable amount of information to the user. The informal part often supplies the context that contributes to the meaning of the formal part. Indeed, we saw examples in Chapter 10 of pictograms whose meaning is relatively obvious in the intended context but which are difficult to decipher if taken out of context.

Another way of looking at the topic is that many – we even venture to say most – presentational pictures are in fact semi-formal representations. Regardless of how much information in a complex presentational picture can be formalized, some part of the image will elude any practical formalism. It is here that we once again meet the old cliché, "a picture is worth more than a thousand words". Making a complete formalization of a picture would entail collecting all the words which a picture says to all viewers, including the contradictions. This is obviously impossible.

As we now move to the part of this book dealing with presentational pictures, it will be important to keep in mind that in fact we are dealing generally with semi-formal representations. The question will be, how much formalization can we pack into a rendered image? The fact is, the output of a rendering process can lie anywhere on the scale ranging from language to presentational pictures.

# Presentational Pictures

*Worshipping Animals,*
Goll Ajuz, Nubic Desert (Africa)

# Image Generation

Presentational pictures can be characterized by the fact that they are generally produced well in advance of being exhibited to an end-user. For example, a painter's work is almost always first shown a long time after he or she has completed it, and the same is true for motion pictures. Computer with high-quality raster images have generally also followed this scheme of things, as the rendering has taken too long to be done while the user waits. Where rendering can be sped up to near real time, the computer itself must take on in this case the difficult task of deciding which piece of graphics will be presented next to the user, as there is no longer the opportunity for a human designer to be involved in every detail. Roughly speaking, it is this task that we refer to as *image generation*.

The context is typically a dialogue system. The machine has derived some information pertaining to what it should communicate next to the user; the semantics of what should be presented is represented as a Fregean structure. It is then the task of an image generator to compute the pictorial form of the presentation of these semantics. How difficult this can be is surely known to all persons who are not particularly talented at art: Most attempts at designing an illustration end up looking rather unprofessional, to say the least!

As we said in the introduction to this book, most people are much better at generating good texts than they are at generating good-looking pictures. This is probably also at the heart of the reason why computers today are also better at generating natural language than at generating pictures. Natural language generation has been a topic of interest since the late 1970s, when MacDonald first developed his text generator Mumble (see

MacDonald 1983, also Rösner 1986), and has received considerable attention since then. By contrast, only recently has work been carried out on algorithms for image generation. Such algorithms draw on the concepts of designers, although these usually have to be made more precise before they can be used as the basis for a computer's decisions.

In this chapter, we will survey the techniques developed to date on image generation. While no one thus far has claimed to have developed an image generator of any universal significance, the theoretical groundwork has been laid and will be discussed. Quite a number of isolated problems in image generation have been studied in detail, resulting in numerous heuristics governing successful solutions to the problems encountered.

## 14.1 Background

Image generation tackles in perhaps the most direct way possible the problem of determining the relationship between language and pictures. Computer representations of semantics, as they are used in today's dialogue systems, are all Fregean structures. An image generator has the task of taking such a Fregean structure as input and producing as output a description of graphics that can then be passed on to a conventional renderer and animation system for producing images. At the receiving end, users analyze the pictures and carry out their further tasks with the information gained through them. The graphics generated become the medium of the message, with all this medium's inherent degrees of freedom of expressive power (or stated in a more negative way, with all its ambiguities).

A user's analysis of pictorial presentations results indisputably in some sort of mental activity, though it is debatable how the pictures are encoded mentally. Users typically need to record the information transmitted or transputed to them: in some cases pointing or even drawing can be the method of choice for recording the results. More commonly, however, users will explicitly encode the results of their analysis in a linguistic form. In these situations a different level of abstraction is dictated by the expressive functionality available. For example, when a management report is required for decision making in a company, a verbal report tends to be required; this is certainly the case when the results must be telephoned to another person. Another example of this phenomenon (applied to abstract-graphical pictures) was developed in Chapter 9: A viewpoint description is a mainly linguistic description of the observations a user makes during a presentation.

A generator thus starts with a Fregean structure $s$ and consists of a function $G$ that produces a presentational picture $p = G(s)$. The user then analyses $p$ by applying an interpretation function $i = I(p)$ to compute $i$, which is what the presentation "says to him or her". Now what is the relationship between $i$ and $s$? We have five cases, shown in Table 14.1.

**Table 14.1:** Relations between a Fregean structure and the resultant image

| $i = s$ | This is the "ideal" case implicitly assumed by practically all image generators. But the further the presentation $p$ deviates from $s$ in form, the more difficult it gets to achieve this equality. It is not always even desirable, as it means the computer is not transputing but only transmitting information. |
|---|---|
| $i$ contains $s$ | The user has ascertained more than was initially represented. This additional information may be the result of additions to $s$ by the encoding function $G$ or, say, because the user discovered a pattern in the output $p$ that was not represented in $s$. The latter is transputed to the user, while the former is transmitted. |
| $i$ is contained in $s$ | The user has ascertained part of what was initially represented. For many applications this is very useful, since a graphic can often convey a great deal of information, of which the user may only require a small portion. |
| $i$ intersects $s$ | This case arises in many practical situations, and has the attributes of both "$i$ contains $s$" and "$i$ is contained in $s$". |
| $i$ does not intersect $s$ | The user ascertains something totally different than was represented. For example, when the user is a systems developer in debugging mode, the machine output may say something about the process of computing it that is irrelevant for the user. Then $i$ is generally transputed information. |

To be generally useful, a picture generator must be separate from the application, as illustrated in Figure 14.1. The application sends a description of what is to be encoded in the message to the image generator, which converts this into an appropriate graphic.

The problem of deriving heuristics for image generation is very difficult, since it encroaches on a domain of human expertise. While designers and artists can give some hints as to the tricks of their trade, the same problems are encountered as when carrying out knowledge acquisition for an expert system. Designers generally say they rely on their intuition and that their methods cannot be cast in algorithms. To a certain extent, this is in fact the case. Yet, a repertoire of techniques is necessary if we wish to endow a computer with the capability to generate images. We discuss these techniques in the following sections.

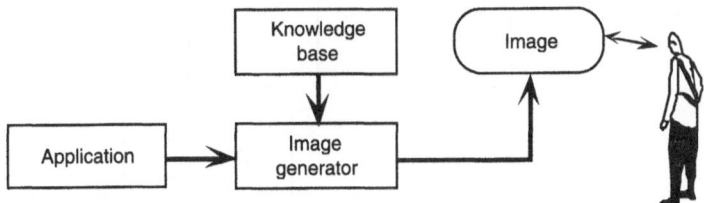

**Figure 14.1:** A picture generator separate from the application

## 14.2 Object Layout

It seems to be one of the simplest problems in image generation but in practice it is one of the hardest: deciding where to place the objects that are to appear in the presentation. In some applications, this can be hard-wired or determined once and for all by a human designer, but in general, for an arbitrary application, we have to assume that the generator begins by trying to solve this problem.

Because esthetic feelings depend strongly on the cultural environment (see Section 12.3), rules or recommendations for the design of pictures are only valid in a certain region. We will concentrate on the familiar Western world where a relatively uniform perception of pictures prevails.

The most important issue to address is where to place an object so that it is at the center of the viewer's attention. This depends on the assumptions made as to the order in which viewers examine an image. Researchers in the psychology of advertising have determined that viewers of a graphic begin in the upper left corner and work their way down to the lower right corner. The object intended to be at the center of interest can thus be placed in the upper left corner; alternatively it can be placed centrally and either enlarged or made a bright color.

Staufer (1987) underscores this finding by giving percentages for viewers' attention to different regions of a computer screen. As Figure 14.2 shows, the upper left quadrant is observed in 40 % of the time, while the upper right only gets 20 % of the observer's time. The lower left quadrant gets exactly a quarter of the whole time and the lower right just 15 % (see Erke 1975).

Furthermore, a graphic must appear well balanced, otherwise it will not have the esthetic appeal needed to keep the viewer interested in the topic. Even worse, an imbalanced image could distract and confuse the viewer. Several techniques have been developed and are now routinely applied in industrial design to achieve this effect.

An ancient rule for creating harmonious proportions may serve as an example. The golden ratio is a length proportion of 1 . 1.618. It has fascinated artists, architects, and

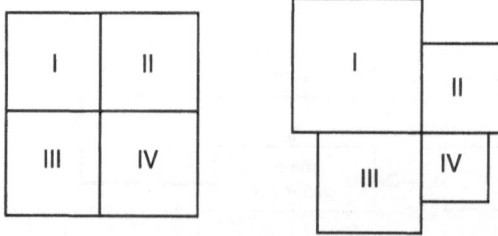

**Figure 14.2:** The distribution of viewers' attention on a computer screen (Staufer 1987)

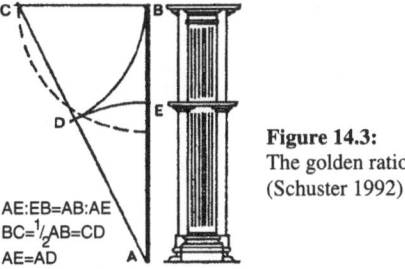

**Figure 14.3:**
The golden ratio
(Schuster 1992)

philosophers since the ancient Greeks, who named it and for whom it was the preferred standard, especially in architecture. Figure 14.3 shows the golden ratio on a pillar (Schuster 1992).

Recent work on automatic layout generation has emphasized constraint-based techniques. For example, the tool *LayLab* (see Graf 1995) is able to calculate positions at which graphical symbols may be placed in a rectangular space. A particularly interesting aspect of Graf's system is that it uses a hybrid approach for constraint satisfaction, a combination of problem-solving on constraints (searching for solutions) and constraint-based inference (problem-solving using constraints by modifying sub-solutions). The system offers users a language for formulating constraints. An application is to the placement of entries in a telephone book, in particular the yellow pages. This application has interesting characteristics. For example, the price for an advertisement is determined not only by its size but also by its placement on the page, and some companies require that their advertisement be the only one of its kind to appear on "their" page. *LayLab* is able to handle such constraints effectively. Figure 14.4 shows a screen dump of Graf's system.

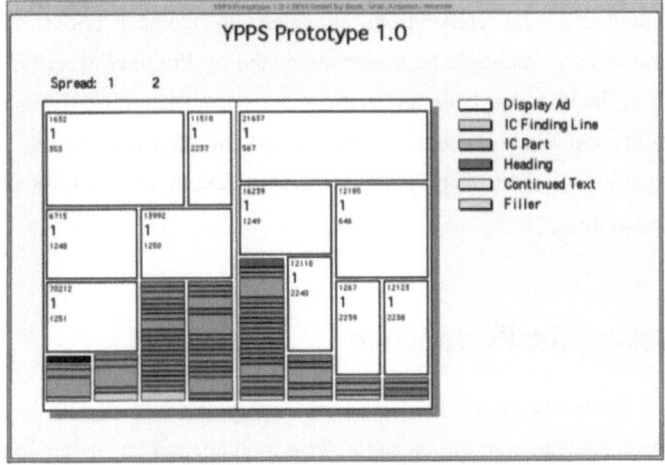

**Figure 14.4:** Screen dump of a system to calculate the layout of the yellow pages (Graf 1995)

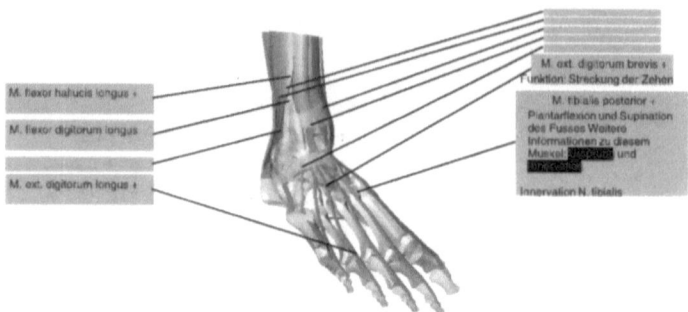

**Figure 14.5:** Dynamic layout of annotations in medical images (courtesy of Bernhard Preim)

While Graf's system is very good for computing a layout with fixed constraints, other work has emphasized dynamic reconfiguration of the screen layout in order to navigate in large information spaces. With the help of so-called fisheye techniques (Furnas 1986; Preim et al. 1995; Rüger, Preim, and Ritter 1996), objects are re-sized and moved about on the screen smoothly in real time. This work is based on animation techniques for dynamically changing the sizes of objects on the screen to respond the shifts in the degree of interest of the user. Making use of an idea of Bartram et al. (1994), Preim's system contains a continuous zoom algorithm that enables objects to get larger and smaller continuously, while other objects adjust not only their position but also their size to make good use of the screen space available. En route, the information displayed also adjusts to the screen space allotted to it: the more space, the more detailed the information presented.

These techniques are particularly useful in situations where not only the user expresses his wishes for the layout, but also the system is empowered to adjust the space depending on the data to be displayed. In one application, medical drawings are labeled and explained automatically, and conventions prevalent in medical books are followed. Figure 14.5 shows as an example an image annotated by Preim et al. (1995), where the level of detail in the texts has been adjusted by the system based on the space available (empty boxes are too small for text and merely indicate that information is available). Another application of their work is to the screen layout of windows in a window management system.

## 14.3  Choosing the Perspective

Once an object or objects have been chosen for display, the camera must be placed so as to view the scene from an appropriate angle. Two fundamental factors are important. The camera position must be chosen so that:

- the appropriate parts of the object are visible, and
- the orientation conforms with the viewer's expectation and supports his work.

Rist and André (1990) discuss criteria for selecting the camera position, which they then cast as rules for use in a knowledge-based system. Their criteria include:

1. *Functionality*
   Try to ensure that those parts of the object that are used most often are visible. For example, when displaying a radio, the front panel should normally be visible.

2. *Orientation*
   Make sure that if an unconventional viewpoint is required, the viewer knows how to get there. This can be done for example by showing the "normal" position and then moving the camera position as in an animation.

3. *Emphasize direction of movement*
   If it is important that an object can move, then the viewing angle should be chosen to be perpendicular or almost perpendicular to the direction of movement. For example, a car is often best visualized from the side. Van Sommers (1984) even contends that a wind instrument is best shown from the side so as to emphasize the direction of the sound wave.

4. *Emphasize the third dimension*
   Often a viewing angle is appropriate that allows the viewer to recognize the depth of the object. Looking precisely along a surface should thus be avoided. A viewing position that makes corners or edges meet coincidentally should also be avoided.

5. *Show characteristic shapes*
   The viewing angle should be biased toward large surfaces (for example, a pencil should be shown so that the side is visible, not top-down).

6. *Demonstrate importance*
   A rule of thumb is that to look down at an object gives it a lower status than looking up at it.

Liljefors (1988) (see also Strothotte 1989) studied the problem of the placement of an enlargement in order to show details that cannot otherwise be discerned. The following heuristics resulted from their study:

1. *Denoting the region to be enlarged*
   The region to be enlarged and the enlargement can be contained in geometric figures (call them A and B) of the same shape, usually a circle or ellipse.

2. *Associating the region to be enlarged with the enlargement*

A and B should be joined by two tangent lines. An aesthetically pleasing arrangement results when one of the lines is either horizontal or vertical.

3. *Covering up of detail*

Since B covers up part of the object that would otherwise be displayed, as little as possible of the detail relevant to the user's task should be covered up. This is easier said than done, but not impossible. For example, statistical methods can be used to determine the amount of information in parts of an image, and the region with the least amount of information can then be covered up.

Figure 14.6 shows an example of enlargement following these rules.

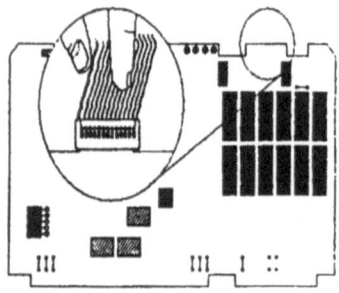

**Figure 14.6:** Example of an enlargement (courtesy of Karin Liljefors)

## 14.4 Choosing Light Sources

Most graphics systems that produce wire-frame-like output, as used in CAD, do not incorporate a thorough treatment of shadows. Renderers that produce photorealistic images, on the other hand, have traditionally been decidedly preoccupied with the effects of light sources. The reason for this difference is that shadows are cast on regions. Individual objects can be depicted well by drawing lines for their contours and edges, but overlapping shadows cast by several objects often have irregular shapes that would tend to confuse a wire-frame image. The pixel-based output of photorealistic renderers does not suffer this drawback, since collections of pixels represent regions rather than contours.

Shadows are nonetheless important even in wire-frame graphics for various reasons. The most obvious effect of shadows is to reinforce the viewer's perception of the three-dimensional nature of objects. Also, they provide the user with clues about the physical properties of the surfaces on which they are cast.

More subtly, shadows can enable a considerable amount of information to be transputed to the viewer with respect to emotions. This aspect of the information flow to the viewer is difficult to predict, since it depends on the larger context of the communication and is susceptible to a large variation based on individual differences. Nonetheless, artists like Parramón (1992) contend that there are indeed formalizable links between the direction of a light source and its effect; these are summarized in Table 14.2.

**Table 14.2:** Emotional reactions to light sources in graphics (Parramón 1992)

| Light source | Possible effect on viewer |
|---|---|
| front, diffuse light | purity, spirituality |
| side front | well balanced, upbeat |
| side | drama, power, depression |
| back | transparency, youth, freshness |
| top | the supernatural, celebration, timelessness, death |
| bottom | suffering, magic |

However, to nip any misconceptions in the bud, it cannot be overemphasized at this point that it would be premature and indeed dangerous to assume that an intended emotional effect on the part of a viewer could serve as the input to a renderer and that this could simply be translated into a position of the light sources, producing appropriate shadows to achieve the desired effect. We only wish to make the person fine-tuning the output aware of the possibilities and to provide him or her with the tools to use them.

## 14.5  Cutaways and Ghosting

In many graphics, the objects of interest in a particular application are not always visible from an arbitrary viewing angle. While numerous interesting visibility algorithms have been developed in computational geometry (see for example Sack and Toussaint 1989), guidelines for ensuring that the resultant image is understandable are more important than its formal visibility. Indeed, there may not be an external viewing angle from which the objects are visible, since they may be enclosed in other objects. An example is the interior of a car, which cannot be seen when viewing the car from a distance.

Artists and experts in technical drawing have developed various techniques for dealing with this situation. Besides the brute force method of removing the obscuring objects altogether, these can be cut away to reveal those behind them; this is referred to as a *cutaway*. Alternatively, obscuring parts can be rendered in a semi-transparent fashion, which is referred to as *ghosting*. Feiner and Seligmann (1992) developed algorithms for variations on these themes; we shall now survey these results.

Two steps are involved in computing cutaways. First, objects must be classified with respect to *occludability*. Constraints must be computed and maintained for unoccludable objects (these are ones whose visibility should not be obstructed by others in an illustration). In the second step, the scene must be *rendered* so that all objects are displayed appropriately.

Feiner and Seligmann devised several schemes for classifying the objects in a scene; here we will only survey one, the *viewpoint centered analytic* approach. A shadow is computed for every object in the scene, assuming there to be a point light source at the viewpoint. Each object **O** defines its own shadow volume: Any object **P** on which **O**'s shadow could fall (assuming no other objects are in the way) lies within this volume. Such an object **P** is thus at least partially obscured by **O**. Thus a list of all objects obscuring **P** can be computed easily.

Next the scene must be rendered. In general it would clearly be inappropriate to simply remove the obscuring objects, as the remaining ones would then be without their context. Instead, various strategies can be used to display the objects in question; Figure 14.7 shows some examples.

Figure 14.7a shows a radio as it would normally be rendered. Assuming that a battery within the radio is the unoccludable object, Figure 14.7b shows the result of making all objects obscuring the battery transparent. This has the potential disadvantage that the unoccludable object is not the only one that now becomes visible, which may distract the viewer. Figure 14.7c, d introduce a *cutaway mark*, here a jagged polygon shown opaque in Figure 14.7c and transparent in Figure 14.7d; everything outside this mark is rendered normally. Finally, Figure 14.7e shows a faded cutaway mark, which makes the transition from the unoccludable object to the others smoother with the disadvantage that the unoccludable one appears to rest on the others, instead of being behind them.

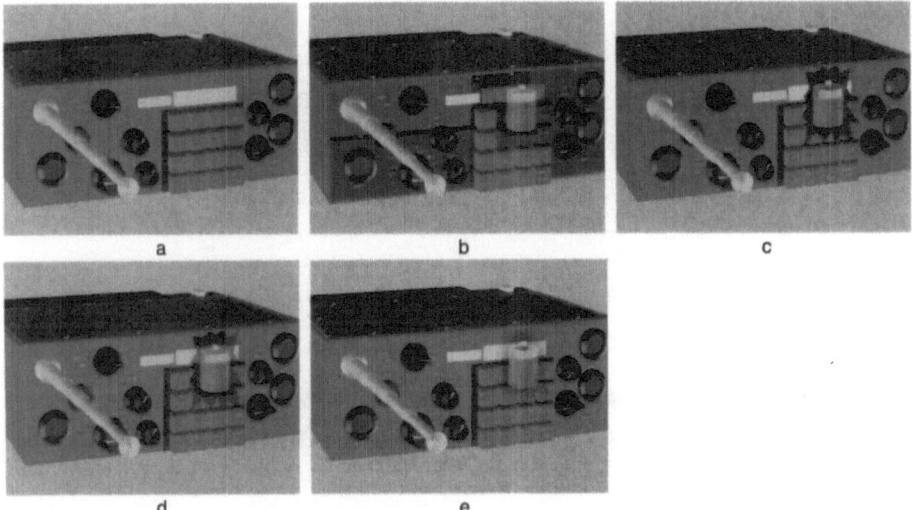

**Figure 14.7:** Examples of cutaways (Feiner and Seligmann 1992): radio with no visibility constraints (a); with objects occluding battery rendered as transparent (b), with a clear cutaway (c), with semitransparent cutaway (d), through a feathered cutaway (e)

## 14.6 Complex Communicative Goals

Perhaps the most thorough treatment of the generation of images with complex communicative goals was carried out by Rist (see Rist 1995, as well as Wahlster et al. 1994, and André 1995). The work is based on the "compositional hypothesis" that images can be composed of parts which are static pictorial symbols. This leads to processing with parallels to that of natural language generation, involving a great deal of the LISP programming typical of natural language processing (recall Section 1.2).

Rist develops an extensive repertoire of graphical design techniques that can be used by the system to express various phenomena. These techniques are encoded in a formal language, and can be assembled from parts and merged to form presentations. During the process of assembling a presentation, data structures are built up that describe the presentation. These structures can be interrogated when the application at hand involves adding more information to a presentation.

As a simple example, consider the case of an Espresso machine, the operation of which is to be conveyed in a pictorial form to a user. Depending on the context of the presentation, a single act may be better illustrated by emphasizing the starting state before the user performs the act or by emphasizing the final state upon completion of the act. Two possible images corresponding to the act "open lid" are shown in Figure 14.8.

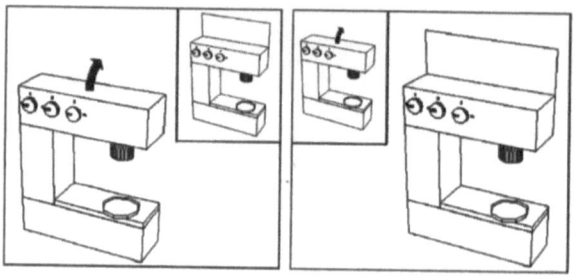

**Figure 14.8:** The act of opening the lid: the left image emphasizes the start,
the right the result (Rist 1995)

The formal notation used to describe these two possible aspects of the act of opening the lid is shown in Figure 14.9. The part under "description update" is the key to Rist's compositional hypothesis, as the description of the resultant image is updated according to the image generated.

---

[S42] **Header:**
    (SHOW-ACTION *action pic*)
**Applicability Condition:**
    ($\wedge$ (?resultative-action *action*)
        (!= $ws_s$ (@Action.Start-State *action*))
        (!= $ws_e$ (@Action.End-State *action*))
**Body:**
    (SHOW-STATE $ws_e$ *pic*)
    (!new-inset *inset pic*)
    (SHOW-STATE $ws_s$ *inset*)

    (!inset *inset pic* :LEFT-UPPER-CORNER)
**Description-Update:**
    ($\oplus$ (Encodes ($R^\theta_{Location}$ *inset pic* $loc_{inset}$) ($R^w_{Temp-After}$ $ws_e$ $ws_s$) *pic*)
    ($\oplus$ (SHOW-ACTION *action pic*) (@Description.Goals *pic*))

---

**Figure 14.9:** Formal description of design rule which led to Figure 14.8 (Rist 1995)

## 14.7 Animation

So far we have presented techniques for generating single, static pictures. These techniques can be used for generating the single frames of an animation, but there are a lot more problems to deal with when pictures begin to move. Assuming not every single picture of an animation is made by hand (as in the early Walt Disney films), the movement of objects for a number of pictures has to be defined so that the computer can generate the single frames representing this movement.

A number of specialized systems have been developed for automating the production of animations in particular application areas. An early example is the work of Khan (1979), who used an inference mechanism to plan the movements of characters based on a description of a story. But his system, ANI, emphasized symbolic (LISP) processing, hence it produced a 2D symbolic animation.

### 14.7.1 Cinematic Editing

The camera and its settings are an essential part of a computer animation, as they are for films generally. Even though the camera itself is not visible in a film or in an animation, its parameters influence strongly the impression viewers get from the scenes presented. In addition, animation producers have to arrange the transitions between scenes or shots to realize changes in place or time. Defining the camera model (including the camera movement as well as transitions) is a very time-consuming process and requires a high level of expertise.

Work has been done to support the processes involved in planning animations; these have drawn on techniques of film-making, which itself has evolved over its hundred-year history (Carrol 1980, Pasolini 1979). While it may seem at first glance that the methods and heuristics of film-makers could be automated relatively easily, in fact a great deal of creativity which is very difficult to express in algorithms is required for high-quality films. Nonetheless, some fundamentals can be incorporated into animation systems to make computer animations look more interesting and to ease the work of human animators.

Very interesting work in this area has been done by Karp and Feiner (1993). The "Expert System for PLANning Animation, Design and Editing" (ESPLANADE) is a presentation planner with a knowledge base of film-making techniques. It relies on an input specification of the communicative goals of the intended animation and draws on a domain database.

The architecture of the system is illustrated in Figure 14.10. The action goals specify what movements are to take place, and the action planner generates a presentation-independent plan of the action of the domain. The communicative goals specify which aspects of the animation are to be emphasized.

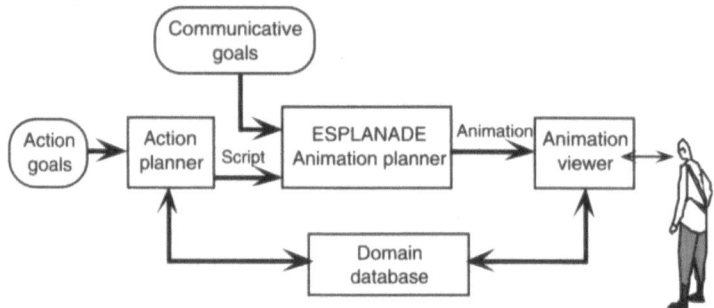

**Figure 14.10:** Architecture of ESPLANADE (Karp and Feiner 1993)

ESPLANADE's animation planner uses a hierarchical decomposition of the planning problem and solves it on three levels of abstraction in a breadth-first manner. The levels are:

- Sequence level
  A sequence is a set of actions that all occur at the same location.
- *Scene level*
  Here actions occurring during the same period of time in one sequence are grouped together. A variety of techniques can be made available for organizing scenes, including:
  - *Separation* (fragmentation of a scene into single images in alternation),
  - *Parallel action* (two or more independent narrative lines running simultaneously and presented by alternation between scenes),
  - *Slow disclosure* (the gradual introduction of context beginning with a close-up shot),
  - *Familiar image* (a stabilizing image periodically reintroduced without variation),
  - *Moving camera* (used as an alternative to a cut for changing viewpoint),
  - *Multi-angularity* (a series of shots with contrasting angles and compositions (including reverse and mirror images), and
  - *Master shot discipline* (beginning and ending with an establishing shot followed by closer shots).
- *Shot level*
  Scenes are broken down into shots, which illustrate one or more actions made with a single camera.

A particularly interesting aspect of ESPLANADE is the way transitions between shots are planned. To provide coherence, a series of rules govern the use of techniques to cut, fade in, wipe in, and dissolve a shot. The rules are shown in Figure 14.11.

```
(rule selective-dissolve
    if the goal is to find a transition
        and shot-2 follows shot-1
        and shot-2 is the first shot in scene-2
        and shot-1 is
            the last shot in scene-1
        and difference between the time period
            of the events in shot-1
        and the time period of the event in shot-2 is large
    then the starting transition for shot-2 is a dissolve
        and the ending transition for shot-1 is a dissolve)

(rule select-cut
    if the goal is to find a transition
        and shot-2 follows shot-1
        and shot-1 and shot-2 are part of the same scene
    then the starting transition for shot-2 is a cut
        and the ending transition for shot-1 is a cut)

(rule select-fade-in
    if the goal is to find a transition
        and there are not shots before shot-1
    then the starting transition is a fade-in)

(rule select-fadeout
    if the goal is to find a transition
        and there are not shots after shot-1
    then the ending transition is a fade-out)
```

**Figure 14.11:** Rules governing transitions between shots (Karp and Feiner 1993)

Figure 14.12 shows an example of the computational results. The domain relates to a material flow system in a warehouse (recall Chapter 8). The purpose is to illustrate the operation of a crane used to transport rolls of steel. The crane is operated by pushing buttons to move the crane up, down, left, right, to the front, or to the back, and to attach or detach the rolls.

The action goals are to move two rolls, No. 7 and No. 2, with the crane. The communicative goal is to show the moving rolls and the causal relationship between pressing the UP button and its effect (roll No. 7 lifting, and raising the crane's hoist).

Figure 14.12b shows how the first scene is expanded from the individual shots to a coordinated sequence of shots. Figure 14.13 shows a few shots as planned by ESPLANADE, illustrating the buttons ATTACH and UP being pushed and a sample frame from the application.

With the help of film-making techniques, ESPLANADE produces interesting and informative animations for special purposes, but it is restricted to the domain represented in the domain database. The construction of such knowledge bases is very time-consuming and does not work for complex domains. We deal with this topic next.

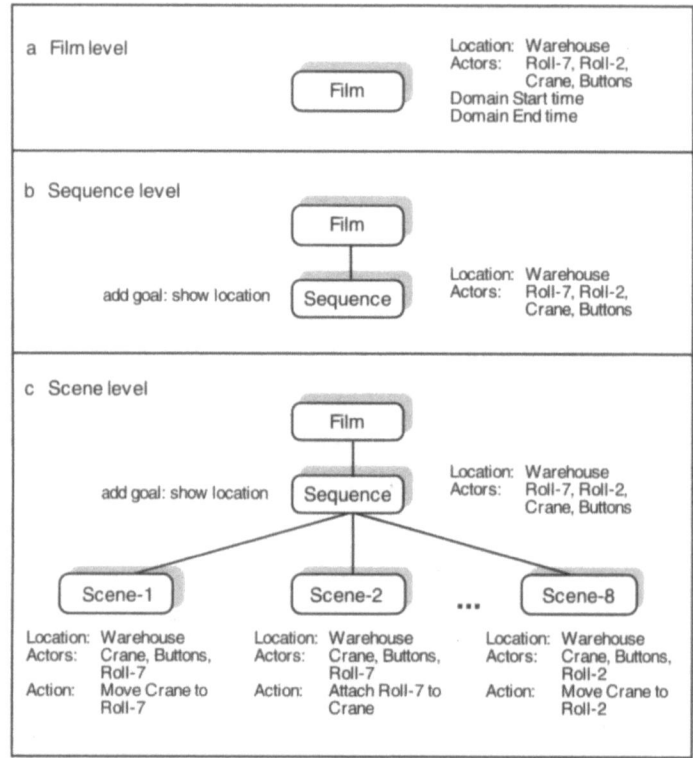

**Figure 14.12:** Example of the computation (Karp and Feiner 1993)

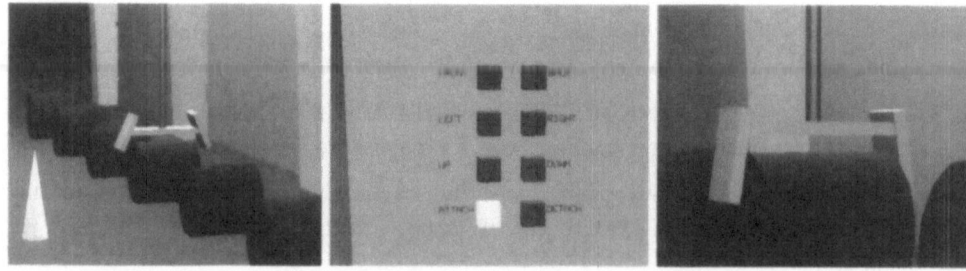

**Figure 14.13:** Sample frames generated by ESPLANADE (Karp and Feiner 1993)

### 14.7.2  Animation of Complex Processes

Producing animations for complex processes completely by hand does not work effectively. One alternative is simulating the complex process to reproduce its behavior over a period of time and taking the simulation results as input data for the animation (see also Chapter 8 for more on simulation and Chapter 9 on animation). The main problem is the interpretation of the simulation results and their automatic transformation into animation data, because no simulation user wants to invest a big effort to get the animation out of the simulation results.

One interesting approach to solving this problem is taken in the animation system AniPluS (see Helbing and Lorenz 1995, Kirchner and Helbing 1995). AniPLuS is a 3D post-simulation animation system with open interfaces to simulation software. Using the animator requires several steps, beginning with the definition of a scene made up of geometric objects representing the objects of the simulation model. These geometric objects are defined by their shape, location, size, orientation, and material properties. During an animation run, the geometric objects of a scene can carry out animation actions, like changing size, color, position, orientation, or visibility. An example of a scene used in AniPLuS was shown in Figure 2.17.

The key concept of combining simulation with AniPLuS is a set of *rules* for defining the translation of a single simulation event into a set of animation actions. These rules must be defined once for a simulator and may be modified for a specific simulation model. These rules can then be used for visualizing every simulation run for such a model. AniPLuS allows three ways for creating animations: automatically, semi-automatically, and user-defined. "Automatically" means that a pre-defined set of rules for a specific simulator is used and a default scene can be generated, while in the user-defined case all this has to be done by hand. Choosing one of these levels allows a trade-off between customization and effort. As a rule of thumb, the more automated the procedure, the more default files are required. Reusability of such default files makes it easier to handle similar models or multiple versions of the same model.

The architecture of AniPLuS shown in Figure 14.14 demonstrates a clear division between the animation and simulation modules. It is possible to couple several simulation interfaces with the remaining parts of AniPLuS. The simulation interface interprets simulation results with the help of corresponding rules for translating them and produces an animation script consisting of animation actions. If the simulator provides topological information the simulation interface can generate a default scene.

The AniPLuS kernel organizes the flow of the animation and co-ordinates the co-operation between the user interface, the simulation interface, and the graphics interface.

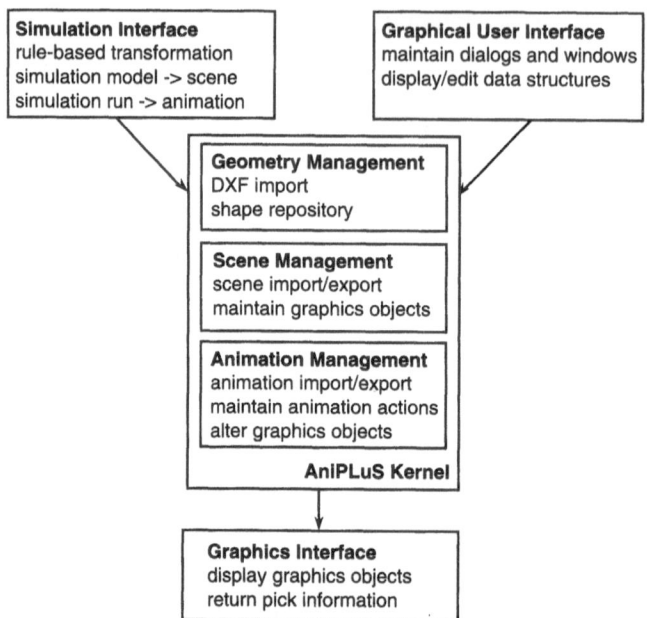

**Figure 14.14:** Architecture of AniPLuS (Helbing and Lorenz 1995)

While the geometric management provides geometric descriptions of animation objects as input for the scene management, the animation management combines a scene description with an animation script from the simulation interface for controlling the animation actions. The graphics interface is platform dependent and carries out the basic 3D graphic operations. The graphical user interface is responsible for all user interactions.

With this architecture, AniPLuS is an animation tool where a user can define rules for generating animations, but most of the specific information necessary for animating particular simulation results are then generated by the machine.

Although the automatic generation produces relatively good-looking animations of different simulation models, viewing these animations for longer than a few minutes can become tiresome. One (perhaps very important) reason for this is the static camera which can only be moved manually by the user. Looking at a scene from the same angle and distance quickly becomes boring. This may not be a problem for experts building simulation models, but it is a real problem for decision makers and people selling simulation studies to clients. As Law and Kelton (1991) state, a simulation model has to be not only valid but also *credible*. The credibility of a simulation model is influenced greatly by its presentation, i.e., by the quality of the animation.

```
FILM

Model
animationen/rraani_events.dat

Goals
Intro    20;        "drive in through shelves"
Intro    20;        "show warehouse"
Demo    30;        "drive cars in"
Demo    47.5;    "elevator brings a car down"
Demo    20;        "car leaves the elevator"
Demo    30;        "cars move forward"

Paths
Path (3000 160 700) (1400 160 735) (1260 110 790)
[...]
Path (800 5 924) (1417.24 26.8849 698.707)

Tech
CamMove fromgoal 1 Path 1 0 1  Path 2 0 1
CamMove fromgoal 2 Path 3 0 1  Path 4 0 1
CamMove fromgoal 3 Path 5 0 1  Path 7 0 1
CamMove fromgoal 4 Object "hebv11_platte" abs point (-90.9551 86.5048 55.18)
                            Object "hebv11_platte" abs point (3.24173 8.88487 -7.29276)
CamMove fromgoal 5 Path 6 0 1  Object "gol_3d_cyan N 21" abs point (0 0 0)
Sep fromgoal 6 Object "hubw2_121" Object "qu_1_99i_152"

Sequences
    Scenes
        Shots
                fromTech (1 ) eyepos (3000 170 700) lookat (1000 170 700)
                lookFromLink Path 1 0 1  lookAtLink Path 2 0 1 Medium 0 20 0;
                fromTech (2 ) eyepos (1600 240 800) lookat (-276 -456 807)
                lookFromLink Path 3 0 1  lookAtLink Path 4 0 1 Medium 0 20;
        Shots
                fromTech (3 ) eyepos (1124 193 673) lookat (800 5 924)
                lookFromLink Path 5 0 1  lookAtLink Path 7 0 1 Medium 20 40;
        Shots
                fromTech (4 ) eyepos (1279 60 750) lookat (1424.04 -48.5403 708.465)
                lookFromLink Object "hebv11_platte" abs point (-90.9551 86.5048 55.18) lookAtLink
                Object "hebv11_platte" abs point (3.24173 8.88487 -7.29276) Medium 323.822 47.5;
                fromTech (5 ) eyepos (803 104 803) lookat (1156.94 5 685.025) lookAtLink
                Object "gol_3d_cyan N 21" abs point (0 0 0) Medium 367.5 20 5;
        Shots
                fromTech (6 ) eyepos (1033.89 44.0309 1033.89) lookat (948.243 11.2507 948.265)
                lookAtLink Object "hubw2_121" abs point (-16.7566 10.2507 -36.735) Medium 467.5 5 5;
[...]
```

**Figure 14.15:** Part of a camera script (courtesy of Ralf Helbing)

Although fast animation in 3D is required, attention must be paid not only to *what* is presented, but to *how* is it presented. The movement of all geometric objects in a scene is computed during the simulation, but the *camera* does not have a corresponding object in the simulation model and therefore no movement of the camera can be derived. It is apparent that an *animation model* has to contain more information than only the transformed simulation events and the geometrical data of graphical objects (see Strothotte 1995). Camera data has to be integrated into the animation model (Helbing 1995).

Following the principle that every camera movement has to be well motivated, a concept for realizing the communicative goals of an animation designer was developed, influenced by the system ESPLANADE (see Section 14.7.1). The communicative goals were derived from the structure of viewpoint descriptions (see Chapter 9) and are:

- introduction
- explanation of
  - quality,
  - behavior,
  - causal dependencies, and
- relevance.

AniPLuS draws on film-making techniques similar to those of ESPLANADE for structuring the animation into scenes and arranging the camera. It uses a three-level hierarchy in which communicative goals represent the top level, film-making techniques represent the realization of the communicative goals, and the parameters of the film-making techniques form the lowest level. Film-making techniques use default parameters that can be modified by users, for example parameterizing the camera by direct manipulation.

Applying a film-making technique at some point in time in an animation leads to a camera script containing camera actions, i.e., camera shots describing exact data for the position, look-at, and focus (Figure 14.15 shows a part of such a camera script). This mechanism allows for the structuring of an animation into scenes and sequences on a much higher level than writing each camera action in a text editor by hand (which is often the only way to get an interesting animation of simulation results).

Figure 14.16 shows the extended architecture of AniPLuS using the concept of film-making techniques to produce structured animations realizing communicative goals.

Since ESPLANADE has access to an entire knowledge base about the concrete animation, it can choose the appropriate film-making techniques and parameters automatically. In the case of AniPLuS, the animation designer (a person) holds the knowledge about what is going on in the animation and is able to assess the contents with respect to the context of the animated simulation run. The interactive concept of AniPLuS, providing the user with utilities for interactively structuring the animation using film-making techniques, is an essential feature of the system.

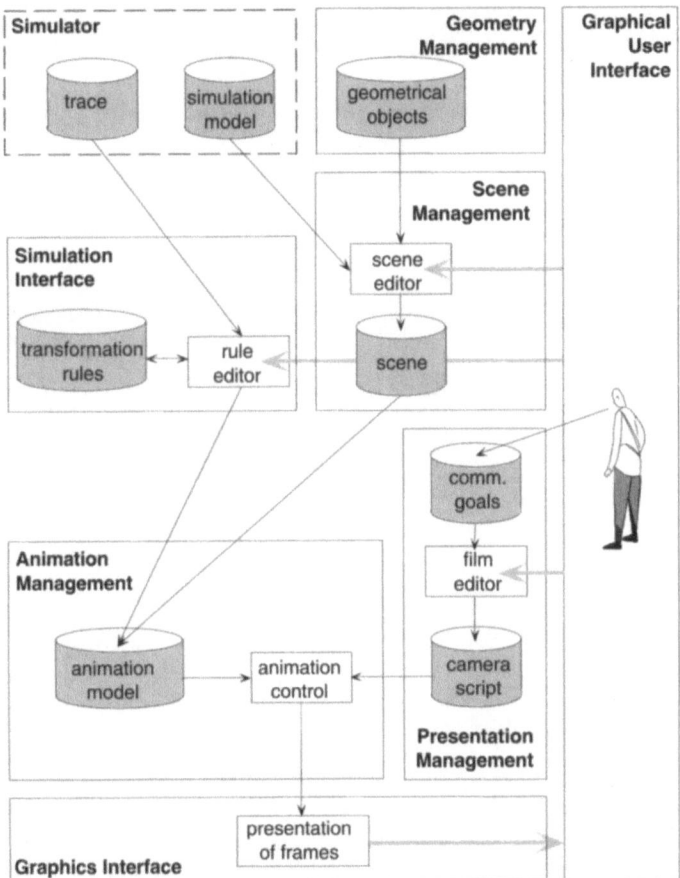

**Figure 14.16:** Extended architecture of AniPLuS

*Elephant*
In Habeter II, Fezzan, Central Sahara Desert, Africa

# Alternative Rendering of Images

Having studied systems which make use of various kinds of graphics, ranging from abstract-graphical to presentational pictures (in particular, photorealistic images), we now turn our attention to working situations in which graphics are actually used and examine the effect of the form of graphics on users. Our interest will be on the overall message users ascertain from viewing the graphics, particularly on the transputed information and how this can be affected.

## 15.1 Standardization

Standardization makes the co-ordination of industrial production efficient. For example, by allowing the windows of a house to be in only a small number of possible sizes, a contractor can choose among many suppliers, rather than having to arrange custom-made parts. This reduces the price while providing flexibility as to the choice of vendor.

Such standardization is not without cost, however, as it leads to a certain uniformity for users. A prime example is the modular design of Munich's new International Airport, where practically every waiting hall looks the same: some passengers regarded it as boring. Perhaps the most extreme examples can be found in the socialist countries before the collapse of communism, where only a small number of different types of a particular industrial product were produced. Thus most households in the German Democratic Republic had the same salt shakers and plastic cups, the same lamps in their living rooms and the same lawn mowers for their datschas. The effect of this uniformity on people can hardly be measured, although practice has shown that consumers long for a greater plurality.

Within computer science, standardization plays a central role. Interfaces, file formats, and programming languages must all be standardized if complex computing systems are to run reliably. When problems occur at run-time, it is often because of competing standards that are not all fully compatible with each other or not fully implemented. In user interfaces, the various systems running, for example, on Macintosh computers or IBM PCs hardly look different any more.

In text processing, LᴬTEX has evolved into a *de facto* standard. In this text formatting system, there are a small number of pre-defined styles from which the user can select. Once the style is fixed, the output is generated in the appropriate format. The output appears in a standardized form and the layout is consistent. LᴬTEX also has facilities for making overhead transparencies.

As with the standardisation of industrial products, LᴬTEX suffers from exactly what it was meant for: its widespread use. People who routinely read LᴬTEX documents can easily identify them and their style and fonts (see Figure 15.1). As in the case of the standardization of industrial products, the standardization of text output can leave readers bored with the format. A document that a user has formatted by hand can have a refreshing effect on readers, even if – or perhaps precisely because – some aspects of it are not perfectly designed.

In LᴬTEX users can in principle alter the layout by changing the parameters of the LᴬTEX macros or by adding TEX statements of their own. But such modifications are not feasible for the casual user of LᴬTEX : They are difficult to make, and risky, because

- the esthetic value of the layout may be destroyed,
- the changes may have side-effects that entail making further changes, and
- many users do not know how to make changes, perhaps even after consulting a manual.

Since customizing the output is so very difficult in LᴬTEX, most users are forced to stick to the standardized output format for most practical purposes.

By not being able to modify the output format with a reasonable amount of work, users are robbed of a significant degree of freedom. Users no longer determine details of *how* their final document appears, but only the *contents* of the document. This may be appealing at first glance. Users are freed from having to deal with the format of their output and can concentrate on their linguistic formulations. It has the drawback that users

**Figure 15.1:** Sample page from a L^AT_EX document (courtesy of Dietmar Rösner)

cannot influence their readers by the form of their output to the extent possible with traditional methods of compiling documents.

Consider the case where an author has produced the first of a document that is still incomplete and contains many typographical and other errors. If the document is produced with L^AT_EX, it looks just as professionally done as the final version. Other than by using explicit remarks like "first draft" in a heading, users today no longer have a way of communicating the tentativeness of the context of a document to the reader. This is a significant change over traditional methods of writing, where, for example, the handwriting reflected the degree of completeness of the document.

The form of a document is more than just cosmetics; we contend that it strongly influences the way readers perceive and work with its contents. A glossy brochure can generally be viewed as being more credible than typewritten output, L^AT_EX output more credible than handwriting with many corrections, and newspaper articles more credible than a simple flyer. High-quality output forms tend to convey the impression that the content is the author's final version.

The topic of explicitly representing information pertaining to the intended or probable perception of materials printed using modern computerized text processors is an open avenue of research. Indeed, it is a difficult topic since the perception of printed materials depends on many factors. Barring significant advances in the area of user modeling, adjusting output with the intention of influencing user perception of the content should not be carried out automatically. Users should be provided with tools and support and not left alone, the way many are when working with L^AT_EX.

## 15.2  Standardization in Computer Graphics

The goal of most work in computer graphics in the past 15 years has been to enable computers to produce synthetic images that can no longer be distinguished from high-quality photos taken with a camera. In tune with the goals of standardization, renderers take as input a model that describes the scene to be depicted and then compute the image automatically. The output is simply an RGB value for each pixel, typically 24 bits per pixel in one of a variety of formats.

In the present context, it is significant that individual renderers can basically be exchanged, resulting in only slightly different images for one and the same model. The differences are not intentional, but result only from the different algorithms used by the renderers to yield a more or less high quality of photorealism. A trained eye can often tell which of the popular standard renderers produced an image, though even these subtle differences may disappear in the coming years.

A question that arises when treating a topic like standardization in connection with computer graphics is the following: are such standardized graphics (i.e., photorealistic images) really more *interesting* than graphics the way they used to be drawn? Are they really more *pleasant* to work with? Are they more *appropriate* for helping users to carry out their tasks?

In Section 12.3, we discussed the point that the interpretation of pictures is culturally dependent. Figures 15.2 and 15.3 serve to demonstrate this point further. Figure 15.2 shows a photorealistic image of a bicycle that appeared in a journal as an example for computer graphics (IBM 1992). Figure 15.3, on the other hand, shows a diagram that appeared in a handbook on mechanical engineering at the beginning of the century (Georg 1912). While the quality of the photorealistic image is indisputably higher, very few renderers available today can produce an image like the one in the sketch. Indeed, we contend that the esthetic appeal of the photorealistic image can be considered to be lower, since this bicycle will always look basically the same when produced with a photorealistic renderer, an effect of the standardization. The sketch, on the other hand, is the product of an artist's interpretation. The artist made use of his freedom of expression, which today's software generally does not provide.

**Figure 15.2:** Photorealistic image of a bicycle (IBM 1992)

**Figure 15.3:** Sketch of a bicycle (Georg 1912)

We shall now study techniques for moving away from so-called photorealistic images as the output of renderers to other forms of images. We draw our inspiration from works of art and graphic design, moving away from photography as the underlying model for rendering.

**Figure 15.4:** Examples of faces drawn by humans
(courtesy of Petra Specht, Axel Hoppe, and Lucas Kirchner)

To remind us of the large variety of images that can be produced by a renderer, Figure 15.4 shows examples of faces drawn by humans. Such images are certainly atypical for computer graphics rendered from geometric models. Figure 15.5 shows an example of the state of what can still be considered to be the art in rendered faces (Magnenat Thalmann and Thalmann 1990).

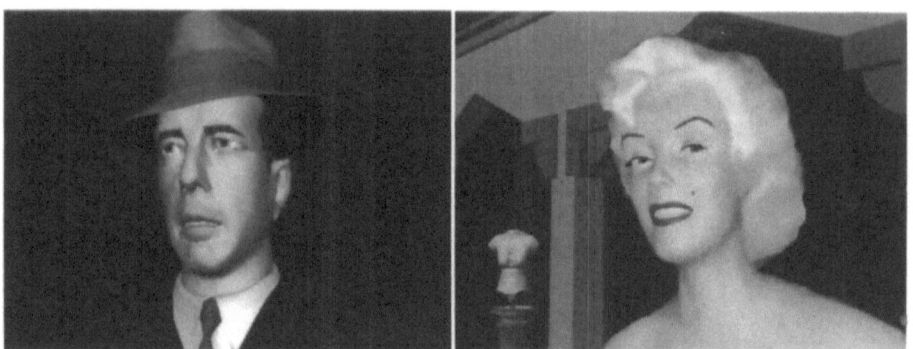

**Figure 15.5:** Examples of the state of the art in rendering faces.
Left: Humphrey Bogart, Right: Marilyn Monroe (Magnenat-Thalmann and Thalmann 1990)

In this chapter, we move toward the goal of being able to render specialized kinds of images, in particular ones resembling sketches done by hand. The goal is to be able to produce images that can be used in situations where line drawings with straight lines and smooth curves are inappropriate, but where ones resembling those produced by a person sketching with a pencil on paper are needed (see for example Figure 15.6). We choose the pencil-and-paper-model rather than the camera-model of photorealism because of its relative simplicity and because of its esthetic appeal.

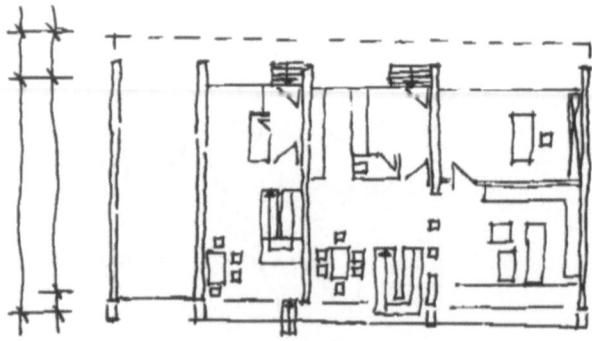

**Figure 15.6:** Example of the kind of image desired from a renderer (courtesy of Elke Faude)

# 15.3 Affecting the Effect of Rendered Images

### 15.3.1 Some Advanced Graphical Presentation Techniques

Alternative forms of graphical presentations have been of growing interest in recent years. Initially, considerable attention was paid to so-called paintbrush programs that allow a user to draw or paint using one of many line styles (see for example Strassmann 1986). In such systems, it is still the user who has full responsibility for the design of the image.

Recently, work has been done on modifying photorealistic images to give them a different appearance (for an overview, see Lansdown and Schofield 1995). Methods have been developed that take the pixel-based representation of such images and convert them into a style reminiscent of, for example, an impressionist painting (Haberli 1990, Hagerty 1991). Such algorithms are rather tricky in that they have no knowledge of the objects in the image. Pearson, Hanna, and Martinez (1990) took a similar approach, though for very different reasons. They developed methods of transmitting images over a telephone line by first analyzing and then simplifying them. The resultant images take on a different style, though this is a side-effect rather than the primary aim of their system.

A number of other authors have developed improvements to wire-frame renderers by adding special effects to the images produced. Dooley and Cohen (1990) showed how the three-dimensional effect of images can be reinforced by uniformly widening or thinning out curves or lines (see Figure 15.7a). Saito and Takahashi (1990) have shown how to add cross-hatches to curved objects, again to help viewers to understand the shape of their surfaces (Figure 15.7b).

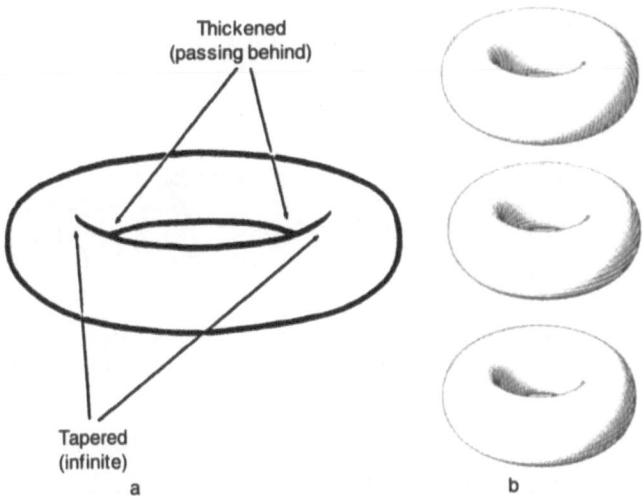

**Figure 15.7:** Enhancing the 3D effect of wire-frame images
(a) Dooley and Cohen (1990) and (b) Saito and Takahashi (1990)

A touch of imprecision has been introduced into rendering by working on the output device. To improve the output of CAD systems, Van Bakergem (1991) adjusted a plotter pen to wiggle when it moved, thereby achieving an effect similar to the wiggles of a human drawing hand. They also modified a PostScript driver to simulate the same effects. However, their system does not connect information about the underlying model with the resultant image.

Winkelbach and Salesin (1994) describe a system that focuses on mimicking the traditional "pen-and-ink" illustrations by a renderer. The system produces textures for surfaces and pays particular attention to adjusting the texture to the resolution of the output medium. Figure 15.8 shows an example of their work.

**Figure 15.8:** Example of a rendered pen-and-ink illustration (Winkelbach and Salesin 1994)

An interesting slant on alternative renderings is due to Burton (1995). His goal has been to model the process by which children construct line-drawings. In addition to modeling the cognitive process behind childrens' drawings, his system can produce interesting renditions (Figure 15.9).

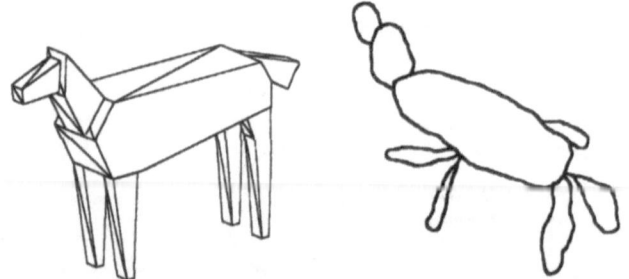

**Figure 15.9:** Renderings resembling childrens' drawings (Burton 1995).
On the left is a simple visualization of a geometric model, on the right a rendering.

Finally, systems for producing non-photorealistic images are beginning to appear on the market. An early example is the KATY system (see Figure 15.10). Such systems allow users to select the style of the drawing using global parameters. This system draws on techniques developed by Saito and Takahashi (see above).

**Figure 15.10:**
Example of an image
produced by KATY™

### 15.3.2  Information Flow

What is really happening when a graphic is shown to a user in an attempt to convey certain information to him or her? On the one hand, a rendered image displays *specific information* about the position, form, and appearance of the objects in the scene as well as some information about the lighting. This information is typically encoded in the scene description, which is the usual input to the renderer. On the other hand, the model of how to calculate the final appearance of the objects with respect to light sources (i.e., the physics) is encoded in the algorithm within the renderer itself. Only recently has there been work on explicitly representing such information (see for example Poulin 1993). Last to be considered is the *effect* the final image has on the viewer. This is a difficult issue, because perception varies between individuals and depends largely on the situation and upon the viewer's task. Yet we consider this issue to be of paramount importance for the success of information communicated through rendered images.

Traditionally, the designer of an image has had to modify the scene description directly to change the image. This is typically done "manually": the designer changes specific details of the model and then observes the effect on the image. The process is repeated until the user is happy with the resultant output. This is not only a very difficult task, but it also has two more fundamental drawbacks:

1. Since the method is rather *ad hoc* in the sense that the designer uses trial and error to fine-tune his or her image or animation, practically no tools are available to support the task (beyond what is normally available in modeling software).
2. Requiring changes to be made in the scene description makes it almost impossible to keep it consistent. Ideally, the scene description would be objective and invariant even though the effect of the image on the viewer is altered. For example, if the designer wished to change the color of an object in a scene slightly so as to focus the viewer's attention on it, he or she would actually change not the color of the object itself but only its appearance in the particular image to be generated. Such inconsistent use of a scene description makes it difficult to edit, maintain, and reuse it for other purposes.

We can use the terminology of Chapter 5 to describe what is going on when a designer attempts to modify the image to elicit a particular effect on a viewer. The objective part of a presentation tends to be the information transmitted. Here we take an object as a substitute for its name and the arrangement of objects in space to denote their interrelationships, assuming that the producer and recipient associate the same concepts with each word substitute. Transputed information, by contrast, tends to be much more subtle, since it usually relies on the ability of viewers to carry out a reasoning process, which varies.

An example will clarify this point. One important area of application of computer graphics is in architectural design. Architects use CAD systems to help them design and render images. However, images produced by conventional renderers are typically not appropriate for an architect to show clients at an early stage in the design process: Many architects will trace over the computer output with tracing paper and a pencil and redraw the image by hand because they feel that the computer output appears stale compared to the "more alive" presentation of hand-drawn images. Perhaps even more important is the message implicit in conventional computer output that a displayed object appears "complete" even if it is only a first draft. The architect has no way of adjusting the rendering to match his or her own level of confidence in the design, nor does the object reflect the amount of thought that has gone into it so far. Giving the client a photorealistic image and telling him or her that it represents a preliminary design simply does not have the same effect as giving the same client a sketch that is obviously in an early design stage. We will study these and other effects in detail in Section 15.7.

While there are tools for manipulating the information to be transmitted (e.g., the modeling software or, in the simplest case, the text-editor used to modify an ASCII representation of the model), graphics systems tend not to have enough methods, tools, and data structures to allow the designer to work explicitly with the information to be transputed to the user. The sketch-renderer described below provides the beginning of this capability.

## 15.4  The Sketch-Renderer

### 15.4.1  Software Organization

The basis of the ability to control the information transputed by an image without manipulating the scene description is the separation of content and form to allow independent editing of each. Thus we now have three persons involved in the production and use of an image: a *modeler*, who is responsible for constructing the scene description; a *designer*, who is responsible for determining the form of the final image; and a *viewer*, the end-user of the image who extracts information from it. The modeler is primarily concerned with the information to be transmitted to the user via the image, while the designer has the task of fine-tuning the image so that the correct information is transputed to the viewer.

Given this basis, the sketch-renderer of Strothotte et al. (1994)* is organized as in Figure 15.11.

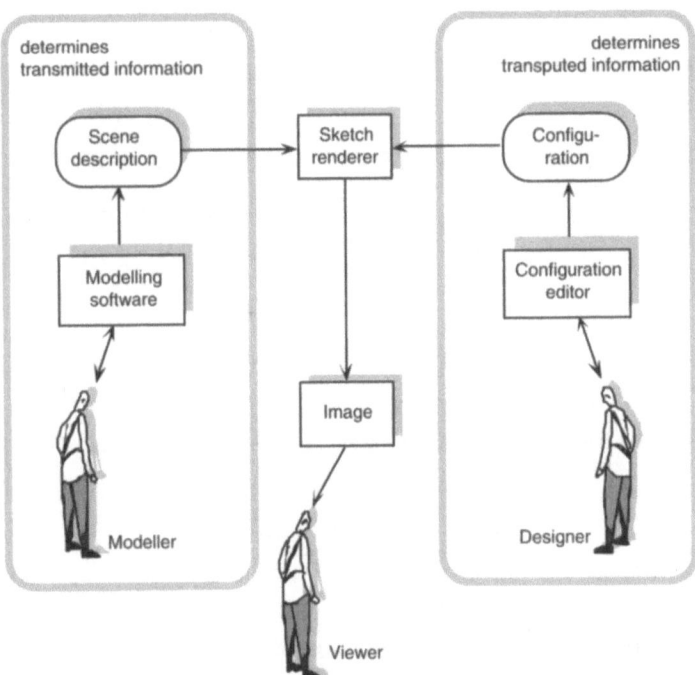

**Figure 15.11:** Architecture of the sketch-renderer

The modeler works with the system in the same way as with other graphics systems by using modeling software, and occasionally inspecting rendered images until the scene looks "right". The designer, on the other hand, tunes the image by interacting with a sketch-renderer to modify the so-called *configuration* of the image which along with the scene description completely defines the final image.

### 15.4.2 The User Interface

The sketch-renderer has a direct manipulative user interface which allows the user (designer) to modify the output of the renderer. The user is shown the rendering and can select lines, groups of lines, or objects to assign them specific lines styles. The changes

---

* See also Semmler (1992), Schumann (1993), Schumann and Godenschweger (1993), Godenschweger (1993), Preim (1994), and Raab (1994).

are made in real time. As a side-effect, the line-styles of the image are saved in the configuration referred to above, so that when the image is re-rendered, work to choose the line-style need not begin again from scratch. Figure 15.12 shows a screen dump of a session with the sketch-renderer.

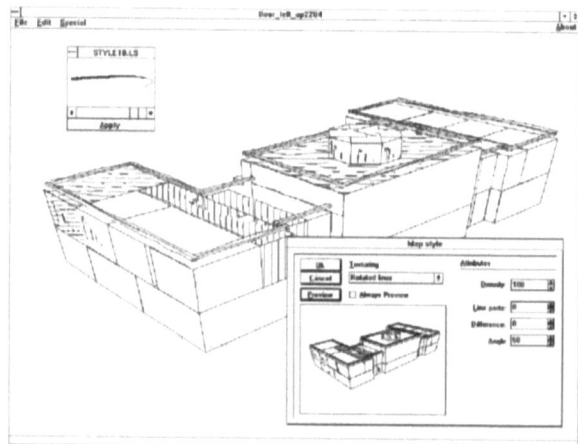

**Figure 15.12:** Screen dump of the interactive sketch-renderer (Schumann et al. 1996)

### 15.4.3 Examples

We now look at a number of examples of sketch renderings created with the sketch-renderer. An unbiased discussion of alternative renderings is rather difficult, since the point of the various kinds of sketches is the reasoning process of the viewer (here the reader of this chapter). By definition, this information cannot be dictated by the authors. Hence we will minimize our interpretative gloss.

Figure 15.13 shows two renderings of the scene description of a bicycle: Figure 15.13a shows a rendering with lines and circles, while Figure 15.13b was done with sketching techniques.

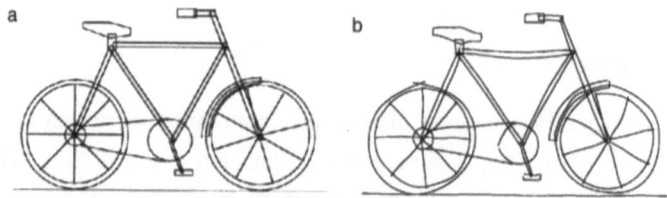

**Figure 15.13:** Graphics of a bicycle (a) and sketch of the same bicycle (b)
(Strothotte, Rojas, and Deconinck 1993)

Sketches allow their creators to add their personal touch, and this can be communicated to viewers. In particular, if a person edits a sketch to add the final touches, he or she is able to give the graphics certain human features, since the result is of a quality that could be produced by most persons. This is in contrast to the results of most "drawing" programs, which still convey to some extent the anonymity of a machine. The effect on recipients can indeed be positive. Asked in an informal test which of the two bicycles in Figure 15.13 they "liked better", several children between the ages of 3 and 6 expressed a clear preference for the more sketch-like bicycle. However, this observation should be put to a more systematic test.

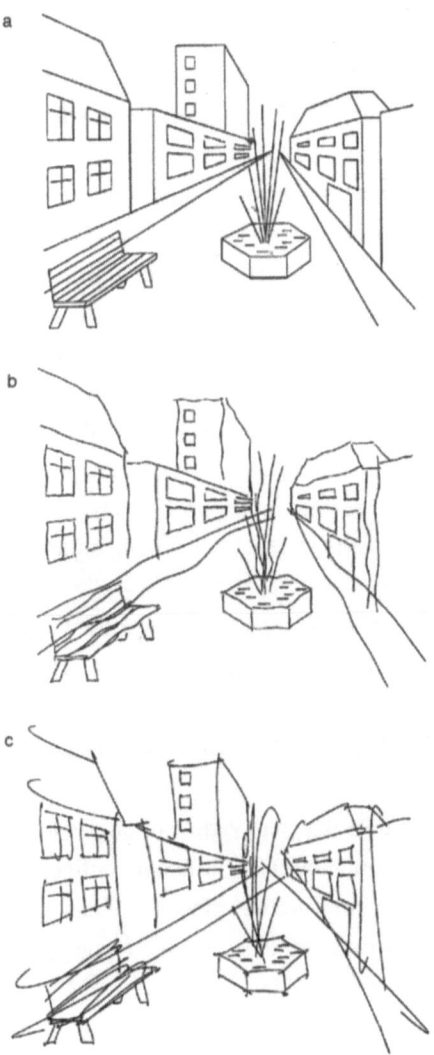

**Figure 15.14:** Three renderings of the same scene of a street (Schumann 1993)

We now turn to a more complex, three-dimensional example. Figure 15.14 shows three versions of a street scene. The first (a) appears to be a typical computer-generated scene. For Figure 15.14b and c, the line style has been altered by the user making changes that are recorded in the scene configuration. The effect is rather startling; the images are not necessarily associated immediately with computer output (see also McCorduck 1991).

It is particularly interesting to note the effect of the object in the foreground of the scenes. This represents a fountain where the water is squirted into the air. In Figure 15.14a the effect is all but lost through the presentation, but it is quite vivid in Figure 15.14b and c. Although the buildings are recognizable in all three images, the example shows that certain effects can be achieved using sketched lines that are difficult to achieve with straight lines.

The previous examples were of mere objects, without regard to light sources and their effects. The next example, Figure 15.15, illustrates these effects using one object with various different parameters. Figure 15.15a shows a wire-frame rendering of a chair on a carpet, the way one usually expects computer output to appear. Figure 15.15b shows a sketch-rendering of the scene, where the endpoints of the chair are of high precision, and those of the carpet are of low precision. The low-precision carpet is now interpreted as the floor, a single surface of arbitrary dimensions, rather than having a clearly bounded area.

In Figure 15.15c the chair has thicker lines, thus drawing the attention of the viewer towards the chair and away from the floor. Notice also the overshooting of the lines. Figure 15.15d in contrast has been sketched by adjusting individual line segments to have "short lengths"; the chair becomes rather weakly defined and when combined with other objects that are more clearly defined, its unique style will attract the viewer's attention.

Figures 15.15e–g show the effects of three different shadow types. Figure 15.15e has a weak light source, Figure 15.15f a strong one, and Figure 15.15g has only a diffuse light. Figures 15.15h–k demonstrate the effects of floor texture while Figures 15.15i and k also show the effects of a weak light source that makes the back and seat of the chair appear in a light shadow.

These images together illustrate the great variety of effects that can be produced from one and the same scene description but with different configurations. The designer has the freedom to choose a style to influence the effect it will have on the viewer.

As a further example to round off this section, Figure 15.16 shows the sketch-rendering of the model used to produce Figure 2.14.

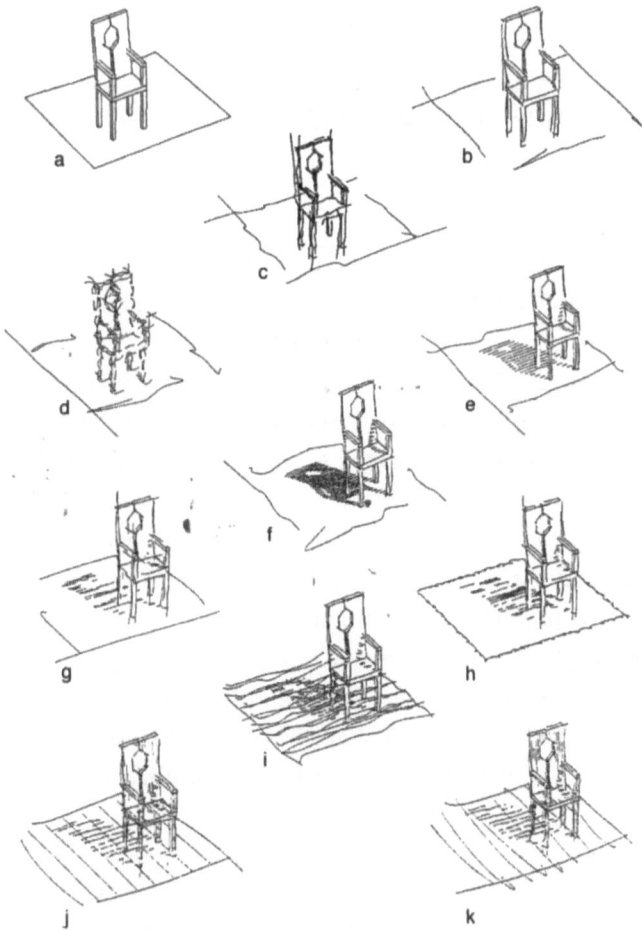

**Figure 15.15:** Various examples of images produced by the sketch-renderer (Godenschweger 1993)

**Figure 15.16:**
Sample sketch-rendering
(courtesy of Stefan Schlechtweg)

## 15.5 Algorithms for the Sketch-Renderer

In this section we treat the major steps carried out by the sketch-renderer so as to convey an intuitive understanding of how sketches are generated from geometric scene descriptions.

### 15.5.1 Rendering

Rendering line-drawings is quite different from the usual rendering of pixel-based (photorealistic) images. While users of modeling software are encouraged not to produce polygon-based models, such models are nonetheless very common. The major aim in photorealistic rendering is then to smooth ("smudge") edges of polygons so as to gloss over the fact that the polygons generally used to define models are only approximations of smooth surfaces. Rendering such images is accomplished in a pipeline with hidden-surface removal followed by shading (Figure 15.17a).

By contrast, sketch-rendering retains some of the edges of the underlying model, while completely discarding others. (This is actually an oversimplification: If one looks for example at comics, there will be lines drawn in places where one would not expect edges in the corresponding places in the underlying model. But how this can be accomplished with an algorithm is an open research problem, particularly for curved surfaces.) Hence it can also be performed in a pipeline, replacing the shading of photorealistic rendering by a process of line selection, followed by a (sketch-like) visualization of the selected lines (Figure 15.17b).

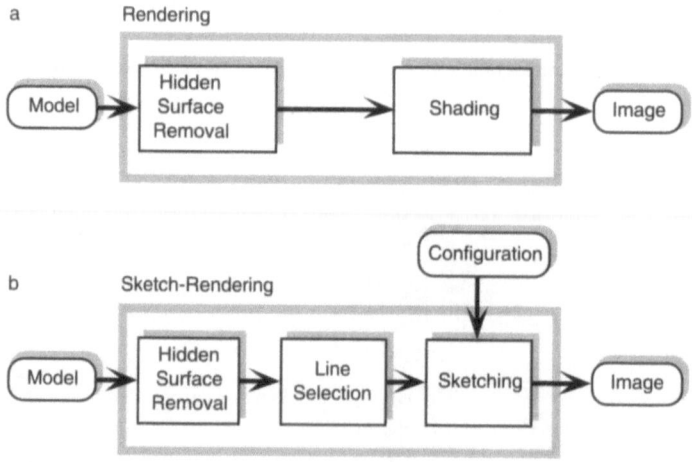

**Figure 15.17:** Steps in rendering (a) compared to steps in sketch-rendering (b) (Raab 1994b)

The key to the line selection algorithm lies in computing the so-called "image description". This data structure is a two-dimensional matrix the size of the image to be rendered (we will study it in more detail in Chapter 17). Each element of this scene-description matrix contains a pointer to the polygon visible at the corresponding pixel in the image. (Actually, the image description matrix need not be the same size as the pixel matrix of the image. Since the final image is an imprecise sketch anyway, a coarser image description suffices, saving run-time costs.) For each object in the scene, the contour lines are selected. In a final pass, these contour lines are examined and only such points on the lines retained that are actually visible (this is determined directly by examining the image description). Special care must be taken to account for rounding errors in the entries of the image description (see Raab 1994b for these details).

### 15.5.2  Sketching Shadows

Most graphics systems that produce wire-frame output do not generate shadows, while renderers that produce photorealistic images specifically deal with these and the other effects of light sources[*]. This is in part due to the fact that shadows are cast on regions, and while individual objects can be depicted well by drawing lines for their contours and edges, overlapping shadows cast by several objects often have irregular shapes that would tend to be confusing in a wire-frame image. For the pixel-based output of photorealistic renderers this is not a problem, since collections of pixels represent regions rather than contours.

This possible confusion of lines does not deter etchers and engravers from presenting scenes effectively. The most obvious effect of shadows is to reinforce the viewer's perception of the three-dimensional nature of objects. They also provide the user with clues about the physical properties of the surfaces on which they are cast. And in Section 14.4 we discussed the importance of shadows for transputing information pertaining to emotions. Not having shadows in a class of computer graphics means that the expressive power is severely restricted.

The sketch-renderer represents shadows by hatching and cross-hatching areas of an image using various kinds of line styles. At present, eight different patterns have been implemented (Figure 15.18). Although each of these appears rather monotonous out of context, when combined with the various kinds of line styles discussed in the previous section, the designer does indeed have a wide range of techniques at his or her disposal. Style No. 8 is effective, for example, for indicating the effect of a diffuse light source.

---

[*] An exception is the work of Appel (1968) (see for example Figure 16.52 in Foley et al. 1990).

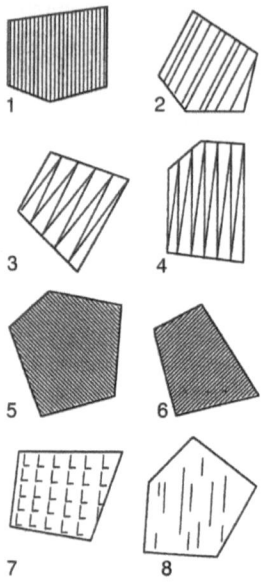

**Figure 15.18:**
Basic shadow types, each of which can be varied by statistical methods (courtesy of Frank Godenschweger)

Computationally the cross-hatching of a surface is implemented in a rather simple manner. As opposed to Winkelbach and Salesin (1994), who use a kind of gray-tone shading to select the density of hatches, the sketch-renderer simply overlays the desired texture over the region to be cross-hatched and performs clipping on each line. To ensure that the hatches do not "overshoot" the region they are to cover because of rounding errors, the hatches are clippped along the contour line of the object with the help of the image description (for details see Raab 1994b).

The designer can vary the appearance of each shadow separately, and shadows can even be produced in areas that would not actually be in a shadow given the scene description. Indeed, if traditional media restricted an artist to physical reality, then works such as Michelangelo's David, whose hands are proportionally far larger than those found on any human, could not be created.

### 15.5.3  Drawing Lines and Circles

*Attributes of Lines*
A wire-frame renderer takes a line or polygonal geometry defined in Cartesian coordinates, projects these into two dimensions, and connects them while possibly removing any hidden lines. The sketch-renderer produces images that appear similar to hand-drawn ones. Such drawings are characterized by non-uniformity in line quality due to irregular movements of the drawing hand as well as changes in the drawing instrument itself. In this case, the instrument is a pencil.

Each pair of end-points is joined up by one or more line segments. Each such segment has the following attributes (and values):

- width (thin to thick),
- basic saturation (weak to strong),
- saturation progression (variation of basic saturation as a function of line segment progression),
- edge quality,
- contour (crisp, blurred), and
- curvature.

Another feature of hand-drawn images is the length of each line segment and the accuracy with which they are joined. Thus the sketch-renderer also offers the following attributes:

- length of segments (relative to baseline or absolute),
- variation of sketch-line from baseline, and
- connection of segments (overlapping, open).

The endpoints of the lines require particular care, since the viewer's attention is often drawn to corners of objects. Thus we associate the following attributes with such endpoints:

- precision, and
- form (jagged, rounded, open).

Cubic curves are used to represent lines, and the deviation of each single control point can be modified to make a base-line into a more imprecise sketched line. Styles can be used in three different modes of abstraction affecting single objects or groups of objects. First, the most intuitive way is to choose a style via its visual appearance simply by scrolling through a list. The user selects a style by its name that is desired to be particularly descriptive. Second, it is possible to adjust all attributes interactively by appropriate control elements. Third, for those who know all the details, styles can be edited in a textual way. Within the interactive editor, the designer modifies the output of the renderer with respect to the line quality; the changes are then recorded in the configuration, so that a subsequent rendering will produce consistent results. The modeler thus makes changes in the scene description without the designer having to redo his or her work. Only when completely new objects or parts thereof are introduced by the modeler is the designer called upon to update the configuration.

*Methods*

Next, we see how a formal representation of a line drawing can be converted into a sketch-like form by relatively simple means, drawing on material presented originally in Strothotte, Rojas, and Deconinck (1993). The simple examples illustrated in this section were programmed in Mathematica (Wolfram 1991), though the full sketch-renderer was later implemented in C.

To render lines so that they resemble lines drawn by hand with a pencil on paper, three different approaches are possible. First, we can model the mechanics of a simulated hand-arm system to draw straight lines or curves. Second, straight lines and smooth curves can be modified stochastically to cause perturbations in the line quality. Finally, the modifications can be carried out with a neural network. Here we shall deal with the second of these alternatives, since it is implemented most directly.

Sketches are produced using only a small number of primitive objects: dots, lines, polygons, and simple curves. In real hand-drawn sketches, the line quality (e.g., thickness) also changes as a function of the position on the object, for example because the person presses the pencil harder on the paper.

A complex sketch is composed of several primitive objects. Two primitive elements are of particular interest (see also McCorduck 1991):

- **Line**$[\{x_1, y_1\}, \{x_2, y_2\}]$: draw a line from point $(x_1, y_1)$ to point $(x_2, y_2)$
- **Circle**$[\{x, y\}, r]$: draw a circle of radius $r$ around the center point $(x, y)$

Redefining these primitives is one of the simplest ways of modifying objects, in that individual points on the objects are specified explicitly, but lie somewhat off the original object, particularly when these individual points are joined by straight lines (Figure 15.19).

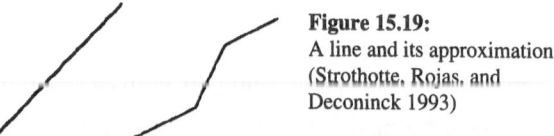

**Figure 15.19:**
A line and its approximation
(Strothotte, Rojas, and
Deconinck 1993)

To create the illusion of a hand-drawn sketch, an interpolation method can be used to smooth out the zigzag lines. For example, this can be done by using second or third order splines (Jain 1989). Figure 15.20 shows the result of interpolating such a zigzag by shifting four control points off the intended *xy*-diagonal using a third order spline. The reader may decide whether the result is more interesting or appealing.

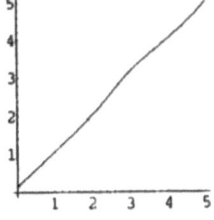

**Figure 15.20:**
Sketched line with four control points (Strothotte, Rojas, and Deconinck 1993)

Curves can be treated in the same manner: Figure 15.21 shows a circle and a sketched circle. The sketched circle was produced by altering the definition of the circle primitive in such a way that the radius was no longer a constant but varied as a function of the angle. The function $r(\theta) = 1$, for all $\theta$ in $[0, 2\pi]$, was plotted using a series of sketched lines in Figure 15.20. The sketched line was a function $r'$ of $\theta$ and is used as the radius of the sketched circle. For Figure 15.21b, nine angles in the interval $[0, 2\pi]$ were chosen at random and the radius was randomly enlarged or made smaller at these points. A subsequent interpolation produced the sketched circle. Allowing the angle through which the circle was drawn to exceed 360° made the ends overlap, further strengthening the sketch effect.

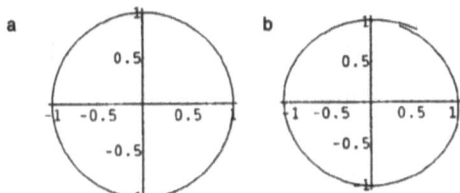

**Figure 15.21:** A circle (a) and a sketched circle (b) (Strothotte, Rojas, and Deconinck 1993)

Figure 15.22 demonstrates how the precision of the rendering is dependent on the order of the interpolation. Both objects were produced from the same nine perturbations of points on the underlying circle. However, the left object was rendered with a first-order interpolation, while the right one was rendered with a third order interpolation; the object on the right appears quite a bit smoother. In the sketch-renderer, the user can set this parameter so as to adjust the quality of the image produced.

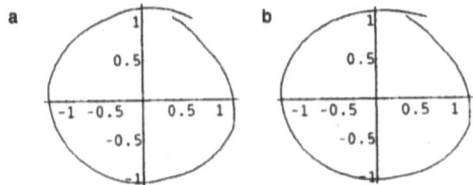

**Figure 15.22:** Sketched circles with orders of interpolation of 1 and 3
(Strothotte, Rojas, and Deconinck 1993)

Polygons can be processed in either of two ways, by sketch-rendering each individual line by itself or by first modifying the positions of the end-points and then interpolating over the lines. In the actual implementation, the user can choose between these methods, again affecting the quality of the image produced.

## 15.6 Special Effects in Line Drawings

### 15.6.1 Leaving Out Detail

Using sketches to visualize a scene has the advantage over photorealistic images that the laws of physics need not be followed, but can be broken to achieve a particular effect on the viewer, often without him or her particularly noticing the reason for the effect. Figure 15.23 shows four examples of output from our sketch-renderer, all of the same scene. The interested reader should study these images carefully before going on. What is the difference between them? Where is the attention drawn, how is this effect achieved?

The sketch-renderer allows the user to render each object in the scene with a different line style. There are many uses for this technique; in the present application, we use such differences in combination with a different level of detail and density of contours to direct the viewer's attention to a particular part of the picture. The sketch-renderer's editor is endowed with a function enabling users to point to a place (in 2D) in the rendered image to mark it as the *center of attention*. For each object in the scene, the algorithm then calculates the distance of the object from the center of attention and

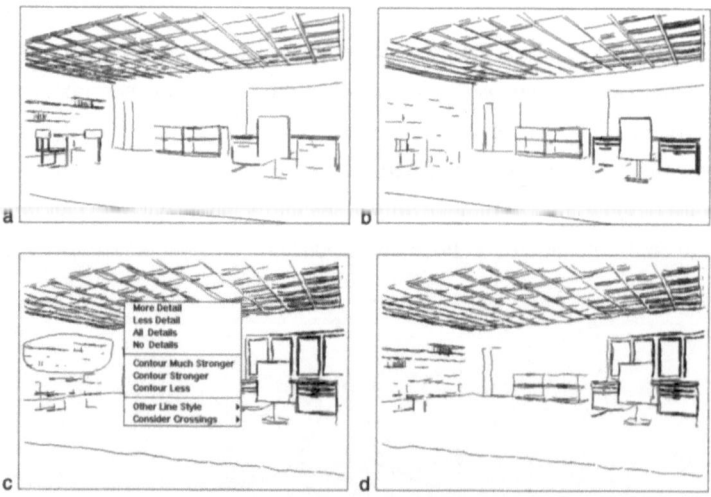

**Figure 15.23:** Sketch-renderings of the same scene. What is the difference between them? (Strothotte et al. 1994)

draws each single line corresponding to the chosen *focus style*, which can be a combination of the stylistic means, line style, level of detail, and hatching style (as shown in Figure 15.23a, b). In every case, the image that the computer generates according to the focus style is treated as a first suggestion, allowing the user to manipulate the image afterwards. Figure 15.23c demonstrates how the user can manipulate the style in a certain area of the picture, while 15.23d shows the effect of this operation. Details of this functionality are described in Preim and Strothotte (1995).

### 15.6.2 Representing Movements of Objects

Pictures differ from perceived reality in showing elements that produce a certain mental image of reality within the viewer. It is not the picture's actual resemblance to reality that is essential for the success of the communicative process, but its ability to produce mental images corresponding to the real world.

Sketches are a visual medium with almost no limits with respect to variety of line styles. Although sketches are a static medium (i.e., they can show only snapshots), they can be enhanced by stylistic elements that the viewer does not interpret as objects in their own right, but as elements of a meta-language to produce the visual impression of dynamics. The viewer's imagination is engaged to interpret these symbols and to change the meaning of the objects actually shown. The dynamic context of the picture will be completed in the viewer's mind (Steller 1994).

The meta-symbols that can be used to produce the impression of motion are easy to find in comic strips (see also Chang and Unger 1993). Three stylistic means are incorporated in the sketch-renderer:

- *Superimposition of moving objects*
  Moving objects are shown in past and future positions. Users can specify whether they wish the entire object or only the leading edge to be drawn.
- *Use of additional symbols*
  The sketch-renderer uses (sketched) lines whose thickness and length is proportional to the speed of the object.
- *Changes in the object geometry*
  The object is, for example, stretched at the start of a movement with a high acceleration.

Figure 15.24 presents two versions of a scene showing the effect of moving vehicles in front of motionless buildings. Motion is indicated by the repetition of parts of the contour and by speed lines, respectively. The techniques are a very direct way of showing the dynamic behavior of images. The user of the sketch-renderer simply indicates the direc-

**Figure 15.24:** Different renderings of the same scene, visualizing object movements
(courtesy of Jutta Schumann)

tion of movement in the image, which is then modified by the sketch-renderer according
to the defined motion style. Thus the user experiments with the system until the desired
effect is achieved.

## 15.7  Assessing the Effect of Rendered Images

Varying the form of the graphics so as to vary the effect the image has on the viewer is a
rather tricky task. The person (or indeed, program) responsible for choosing the style of
image to be produced has many degrees of freedom. A designer probably has a "feeling"
for which kind of image has which effect on a particular viewer. But it would clearly be
premature to claim that the process of influencing a viewer in a particular way could be
automated. On the other hand, there is no reason not to provide end-users with the means
to create these kinds of graphics, for there is more to rendering computer graphics than
photorealistic images.

Schumann et al. (1996) report on a study to assess the effect that specific kinds of
rendered non-photorealistic images have on their typical viewers. Of interest are questions about the tasks to be carried out with the various kinds of image that can be produced. However, this issue cannot be addressed in its full generality; instead, it must be
studied with respect to very specific examples, and care must be taken not to over-
generalize the results.

The study involves an empirical investigation of architects in Germany. A preliminary
study revealed that 70 % of the 54 architects interviewed said that they use CAD. Of
those not using CAD, 75 % indicated this was because of the quality of the presentations
that commercially available software is able to produce. They expressed the wish for
more individuality in the presentation, and the fear that the form of the output could deter
their clients.

One of the goals of the study was to determine in which situations an architect would use the various kinds of images. Since an architect's goal is in general to attract attention to the image, the authors hypothesized that

*H1 For presentations of early drafts of architectural designs, sketches are preferred over CAD plots and shaded images.*

The authors also hypothesized that there is a marked difference in the way the three images affect their viewers. To structure the hypothesis, the authors refer to the classification scheme of Peeck (1987), who divides the possible effects of an image into three groups (recall Section 4.2):

- a *cognitive* group, pertaining to aspects like the understandability, clarity, or spatiality of the image,
- an *affective* group, to assess emotional aspects, like how interesting or imaginative an image seems, and
- a *motivational* group, measuring to what extent users are encouraged to participate in the design process.

It was hypothesized that

*H2 Sketches perform better in the communication of affective and motivational aspects, while exact plots and shaded images perform better in cognitive aspects.*

Finally, it was expected that the exact plot would arouse more interest in the actual design of the object being visualized, which lead to the hypothesis that

*H3 Sketches stimulate viewers more than shaded images to discuss and actively participate in design development.*

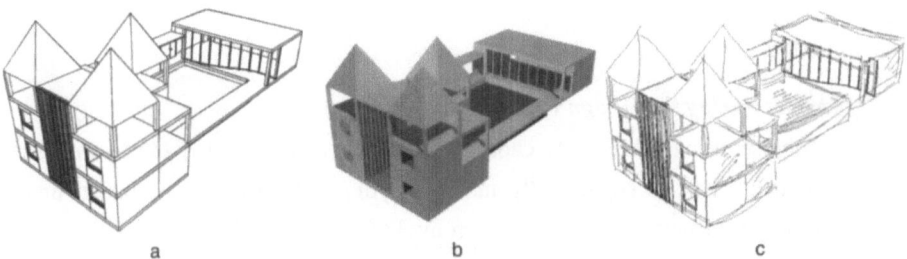

a                              b                              c

**Figure 15.25:** Three variants of renderings of a design: the CAD plot
(a) a wire frame produced with AutoCAD™, the shaded image (b) produced by a commercially available renderer (RenderMan™), and the sketch (c) generated by the sketch-renderer (Schumann et al. 1996)

### 15.7.1 Experiment

*Subjects.* A questionnaire was given to approximate 150 architects and architectural students in several cities in Germany. Of these, 54 (36 %) answered the questions and returned it. Of those returning it, 67 % said they regularly use CAD.

*Design.* Subjects where shown three different images, each portraying the same object (see Figure 15.25), which was designed by students of architecture as a term project. The CAD plot (ordinary wire-frame image with hidden-line removal) was produced with AutoCAD™, the image with constant shading was generated by the RenderMan™ renderer, while the sketch was produced with the sketch-renderer described above. Note that all three images were produced from the same geometric model in DXF format.

After being shown the three images, subjects were asked various questions. First, they were asked to say which image(s) they would want to use to show a first draft to a client and which image they would use for a final presentation. They were also asked to provide a verbal justification of their choice. Next, subjects were asked about a number of (possible) effects of the images, classified according to Peeck's scheme mentioned above. These were to be rated on a scale of 5 ("strongly disagree") to 1 ("strongly agree"). Subjects were also asked to give an additional verbal judgement of the images (not described here but a hint for further experiments).

To test the third hypothesis, subjects were asked to say how they would make changes to the design being visualized. They were given four options to choose from:

a)  using a verbal description,
b)  by gesturing or by pointing to the image,
c)  by drawing on another sheet of paper, or
d)  by drawing directly onto the image.

### 15.7.2 Results

#### *Use of Images during the Design Process*

Of those subjects using CAD, 53 % chose the sketch as a suitable way to present a first draft to a client. This is significantly more than those suggesting the shaded image (22 %), or the exact plot, which was chosen by 33 % of the subjects ($p < 0.05$). Those preferring the sketch generally argued that it best shows the preliminary character of the draft and does not focus on details that at this stage are not yet fixed. Many of those who chose the shaded image commented that they appreciated the ability to present the spatial concept of the design.

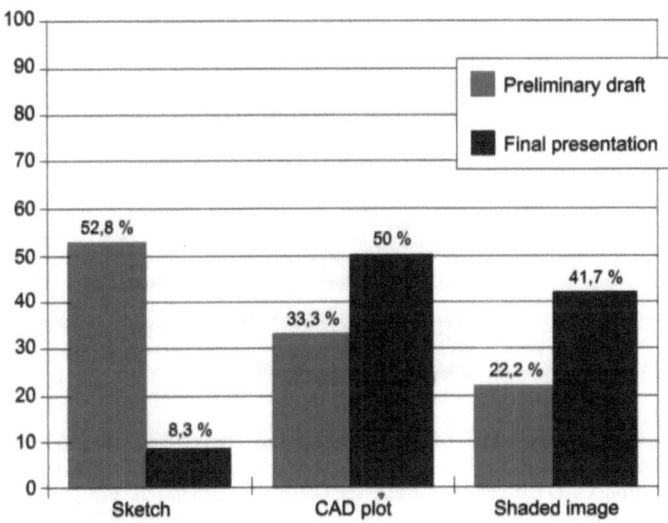

**Figure 15.26:** The use of sketches, CAD plots, and shaded images for the presentation of a first draft versus the presentation in a final presentation (Schumann et al. 1996)

By contrast, only 8 % chose the sketch to present a final result to a client, which is significantly less than those choosing the exact plot (50 %) or the shaded image (42 %) (p < 0.05). Subjects who chose the exact plot or the shaded image often argued that the selection committee "wants to see exact renditions", while those few who chose the sketch commented on its originality and the desire to stand out against competitors. Figure 15.26 summarizes the results.

### Impression Made by the Images

Subjects were asked to assess the impression made by the three images in more detail. The results are shown in Figure 15.27: The value on the far left of the x-axis scale (5.0) means complete disagreement, the value on the far right (1.0) means complete agreement with the statements made on the y-axis. The results show that sketches were found significantly more interesting, lively, imaginative, creative, and individual, and less artificial than both the other media (affective group). Furthermore, they were found to stimulate significantly more discussions and active changes, in which shaded images performed worst.

In sharp contrast to these affective criteria, the CAD plot performed significantly better in the cognitive group, being more comprehensible, more recognizable, and clearer than both the other media. The shaded image was found to support spatial concepts better, but differences were not significant.

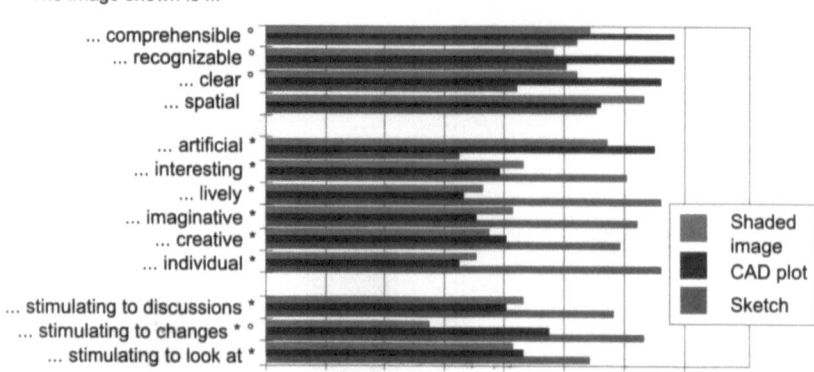

**Figure 15.27:** Mean values of the assessment of the effect of the media (CAD users) (Schumann et al. 1996). The symbol * denotes the items in which sketches differ significantly (p<0.05) from CAD plots and the shaded images, while ° denotes the items in which CAD plots differ significantly (p<0.05) from sketches and shaded images.

## *Expressing Changes in the Design*

The observations so far were concerned with assessing the impression architectural presentations make on viewers, but it is an important goal of the communication between architects and their clients to explain ideas mutually and to develop them further. A major criterion in the assessment of the effectiveness of a presentation medium is its ability to provoke the active participation of the partners within a discussion.

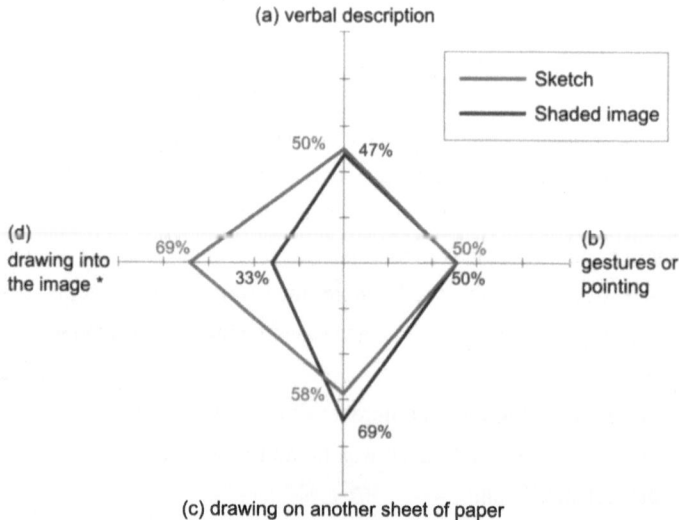

**Figure 15.28:** How subjects would realize changes in a sketch versus in a shaded image (CAD users) (Schumann et al. 1996). * means a significant (p < 0.05) difference between sketch and shaded image

The results in Figure 15.28 illustrate that in both the sketch and the shaded image, the methods (a), (b), and (c) (recall Section 15.7.1) were used almost equally often (the differences are not significant). However, drawing directly into the image was chosen significantly more often in sketches than in shaded images (69% versus 33%) ($p < 0.05$).

### 15.7.3 Interpretation of the Results

Evidence has been gathered in support of all three of the hypotheses by the experiments carried out. To explain the results, let us look at them from a more theoretical point of view. The cognitive effort required by viewers would be expected to be greater for sketches than for the other two kinds of images tested. This is because sketches are more irregular in their form, which means that they transpute more information to their viewers. This, in turn, increases the cognitive effort required to understand them (see Klix 1992).

Recall the discussion of Chapter 4 on *normalization demands* placed on a viewer deciphering an image. By the above reasoning, these are higher for sketches than CAD plots or shaded images. Applying the ideas of Berlyne's (1969) "collative variables", normalization demands lead to curiosity, which in turn is linked to interest and creativity, resulting in a high level of motivation (Klix 1992).

Going back now to the hypothesis H2, the less favorable score of the sketch in the cognitive group can be explained because of the difficulty involved in deciphering the irregular forms; the resultant ambiguities, however, are then responsible for the better scores in the affective and hence also motivational groups.

This reasoning also explains the results of H1. In a first draft, architects reported they want to arouse interest in their designs, which according to the above reasoning is higher with sketches. For a final draft, a good score in the cognitive group is more important, hence the shaded images and CAD plots are preferred.

To explain H3, a step to the theoretic background is necessary. Recall the discussion of Gombrich (1969) in Section 4.2, who speaks of the process of *projection* of our experience and expectations onto the phenomena seen. The empty spaces in the CAD plots and sketches can act as the required "projection screen". According to this argument, sketches and CAD plots provide more projection space than shaded images (because in these practically the whole area of the image is filled, and hence cannot act quite as well as a projection space). Sketches also provide more projection space than CAD plots, because in the latter there is no room for interpretation as to where and how lines (i.e., edges in the object visualized) meet. The larger projection space can thus explain the greater willingness of viewers of sketches to enter into a discussion about the design.

The results presented in this section are presently at the leading edge of research (Schumann et al. 1996) and will undoubtedly be scrutinized further in the years to come.

It is still unclear how far the results can be generalized to explain other observations. For example, Wong (1992) reported on differences in discussions about user interface design between handwritten and typeset versions of hypothetical screen dumps. The results may also have an effect on concepts of rapid prototyping.

## 15.8 Discussion

This chapter has made a case for more flexibility in computer output and has shown ways in which this can be achieved for computer graphics. We have argued that providing such flexibility can enhance computer graphics in certain communicative situations. While the information that is *transmitted* is encoded in the scene description and tends to be invariant over the output form, that form determines to a great extent the information *transputed* to the user.

From a technical point of view, rendering non-photorealistic images has interesting implications for the quality of the geometric models. Figure 15.29 shows two renderings of one and the same scene (Raab 1994; see also Strothotte et al. 1994). The model is an L-system, where the tree's branches are denoted by cylinders. The image on the left was rendered using a simple shader, while the one on the right was rendered using the sketch-renderer. Comparing the two images, it is apparent that a geometrically simple model may be visualized adequately using one particular style of rendering, whereas the result of rendering the same model using another style may produce an inadequate result. Inverting this relation, if a range of rendering styles is available, a geometric model should only be developed to the extent necessary for the style with which the user is happy. This can be an important economic factor, since it is often very expensive to develop a detailed geometric model that yields a good-looking photorealistic image, and a simpler model may suffice to produce an adequate-looking sketch-rendering. Especially in rendering natural scenes, described by fractals or graphtals (see Oppenheimer 1986, Smith 1984) this may be of particular significance.

Despite the seductive technical possibilities offered by computer graphics, the warning of Tufte (1983) is worth keeping in mind, that graphics should impress by the power of the data and not by the power of the technology used to produce them. However, it is unclear whether the viewer of sketch renderings will be more distracted from the image than the viewer of photorealistic images. The former may be enticed to try to discover how the imperfections were added, while the latter may search (perhaps in vain) for imperfections within the seemingly perfect image. We hypothesize that users without intensive training in computer science will be less distracted by sketch renderings, since these correspond to their expectations of man-made graphics.

**Figure 15.29:** Example renderings of a simple model for a tree using a shader (left) and the sketch-renderer (right) (courtesy of Andreas Raab)

Little explored thus far is the ability of non-photorealistic rendering to support the process of abstraction in visual expression. Figure 15.30 shows examples of comics drawn by hand in McCloud (1993). The simpler the shapes of the individual parts of the image, the abstracter the result. Computationally this would correspond to different approximations of the underlying geometric primitives, yielding successively simpler visualizations. The resultant abstraction can then be compared to the notion of abstraction in natural languages. An open question for further research is, can rendering be made as flexible for conveying information as natural language generation?

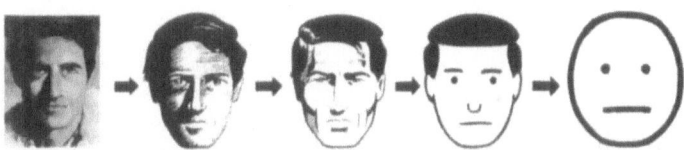

**Figure 15.30**: Stepwise abstraction in comics drawn by hand (McCloud 1993)

When working with photorealistic images, sketches, or any other alternative output form, it is important to remember the sociological context in which they are used. Habermas (1971) pointed out that every technological development is based on an ideological orientation in society. What is the orientation on which computer graphics are based? Examining the uses of computer graphics, such as in recent movies and advertising, it is clear that computer graphics are frequently used to display objects and phenomena that do not exist in reality. Indeed, the fact that the objects do not actually exist is often not conveyed to the viewer. Thus such graphics are used to fool viewers, to confuse their sense of reality. Sketches indicate by their format that the scene being represented is not the result of a camera snapshot. However, according to the philosopher Baudrillard (1991), viewers have trouble differentiating between reality and fantasy even if they are made aware of the fact that what they are seeing does not exist. We return to this point in the concluding chapter.

While this chapter has concentrated on providing more flexibility in graphics so as to get away from the strict standardization of output, it remains an open problem to what extent a compromise can be found between standardization and flexibility of form in other areas, such as text processing. Computer users at present have only very limited capabilities to determine the appearance of the materials they work with, and an individual touch is a desirable extra to make the work more interesting.

*Giraffes with symbolic circles*
In Habeter III, Fezzan, Central Sahara Desert, Africa

**Chapter**

# 16

# Tactile Computer Graphics

## 16.1 Introduction

The term "computer graphics" has traditionally been used to refer to images produced for visual inspection on computer screens, paper, or other media like celluloid and foils. In recent years, the computer graphics community has extended its scope to include richer interaction, such as in virtual reality systems. Of interest are no longer just visual impressions, but also sounds and users' movements to accompany interactive graphics.

One subproblem within this area is that of producing graphics. The goal is to be able to generate images that users can understand by running their fingers over them. Such images are well known from maps, where raised portions are used to denote mountains. However, relief images are only beginning to emerge in computer output.

Given the lack of general purpose solutions for tactile computer output, we will approach the topic from a more modest perspective. We wish to generate images that can be touched by blind users, for whom tactile output is the only feasible way to perceive forms. At first glance one may conclude that the problem is very simple: Raise the lines of conventional wire-frame output with suitable hardware, or raise the edges of objects visible in a photorealistic image. However, as we will show in this chapter, images intended to be touched and understood by blind people must be designed differently from images to be understood by visual inspection alone. This means that graphics systems require a new functionality if the output is to be in a tactile form.

A natural question to ask is, are there enough blind people around to warrant widespread attention being paid to this problem within the computer graphics community? The number of people affected is (fortunately) only approximately 0.2 % of the population in developed countries. However, a deeper understanding of this problem can serve as a basis for the use of tactile elements in images for sighted users; we will return to this point in the discussion at the end of the chapter. Also, demographic statistics show that in the Western world, there are even more blind and visually impaired people than university graduates of computer science! Only about 5 % of blind people in Western countries are proficient in Braille, since many are elderly or have other handicaps which make it difficult for them to learn Braille, hence the ability to feel forms is an important element of their communicative repertoire.

## 16.2  Tactile Output

The easiest way to produce tactile graphics is with a strong dot-matrix printer and a thick kind of paper. The printer's pins make small dents in the paper. If one turns the page over, corresponding to the dents are raised dots which can be felt. Using this method, one can easily produce dotted lines and textures on paper. However, it is not possible to produce full lines or even different styles of lines.

Another quite simple way is the use of so-called swell-paper (also termed microcapsule or Minolta paper): The pictures are drawn (or printed) on normal paper. A copy of the drawing is then made by a photocopier onto swell-paper. Swell-paper contains a layer of encapsulated resin particles which swell under the influence of heat. The copy on swell-paper is heated in an appropriate device. The heat is absorbed by the (black) ink on the swell-paper and the resin micro-capsules directly under the ink layer swell, thereby creating the relief on the paper, i.e., the page has a tactile dimension when one runs one's fingers over the graphics.

Yet another method involves a somewhat more elaborate procedure, requiring special equipment. This procedure, called thermography, is also used to produce fancy business cards. The areas to be drawn on are covered with wax. Resin particles are blown over the printing ink when it has just been printed and is still wet, and the particles stick to the ink. The surplus of particles is removed by aspiration, and the page with the wet ink and resin is then heated. The ink dries and the resin swells.

In a totally different approach, a prototype device was built to plot line drawings onto paper using a plotter enhanced with a special pen and a heating system. The pen plots the drawing onto paper using so called puff-ink, then the heating system is moved over the paper and ink, causing the ink to "puff", or to swell (see Rathgeber 1990).

Finally, Minsky et al. (1990) developed a device for displaying tactile graphics using force feedback (Brooks et al. 1990). The user moves a ping-pong-like ball around on a surface. The ball is attached to devices beneath the surface and the user has the sensation that the surface has a texture.

## 16.3  Blind Computer Users

With the widespread introduction of computers in the 1980s, new office jobs for blind people were created (several thousand in Germany alone). These blind employees gained access to conventional text-based programs running on a PC or terminal by using technical aids. More specifically, these are devices that convert the text displayed on the screen into acoustic or tactile signals. The area of memory that contains the screen contents (in ASCII format) is read, and the letters found are presented via speech synthesis (acoustic output) or using a Braille display (tactile output). Programs providing such services are called *screen-readers*.

The increasing use of graphical user interfaces (GUIs) poses problems to blind people (see Emiliani 1993, Gill 1993; see also Jansson 1993, Petrie et al. 1993). Conventional screen-readers can read and present only text-based screen contents, whereas GUIs  are based not on text but on graphical information stored as a bitmap. Even in places where text is displayed on the screen, usually only the shape of the letters is stored in the screen memory, not an ASCII representation. This results in a number of problems for visually disabled users, both for input into the computer and output from it. Indeed, blind people risk losing many of the jobs they gained in the 1980s because of the technological advance in user interfaces.

Research and development is underway to provide blind people with access to GUIs. Hardware has recently been constructed that gives blind users the capability to develop a feeling for the two-dimensional nature of the computer screen. This is done by providing both a horizontal and a vertical tactile display. A small pressure-sensitive pad is provided as a replacement for the mouse, in addition to routing keys associated with the tactile output positions (see Figure 16.1).

Blind users can work with GUIs with the help of this hardware. The idea is that an "off-screen" model is constructed by the system, which describes in a symbolic fashion what is on the screen. The blind user can interrogate this model to obtain the necessary information. It is a time-consuming process, but it works for all screen contents with the exception of pictures.

To display computer graphics to blind users, a "pin matrix" device was constructed at the University of Stuttgart (Figure 16.2; see also Schweikhardt 1985, Schweikhardt 1993). This device has a rectangular array of about 7,000 pins which can be raised and lowered individually. Graphics are displayed via dialogues, in which a blind user can obtain information about such attributes of the pixels as their colors. For example, the user can ask the machine to raise all pins corresponding to pixels colored red or green on the screen, while leaving all other pins lowered. The device was initially used for displaying videotext pages to blind users. However, in its current form it is not suitable for widespread use because of its high cost (about 50 000 ECU).

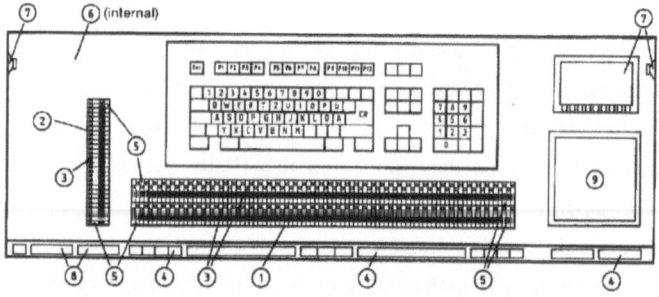

**Figure 16.1:** The GUIDE display produced by FH Papenmeier (Schwerte, Germany). The terminal integrates (1) two horizontal Braille displays (80 cells), (2) a vertical tactile display (46x4 dot lines), (3) keys for routing input (2x80 for horizontal routing and 23 for vertical routing), (4) keys for exploration as well as mouse button substitutes, (5) touch-sensitive sensors along the horizontal Braille display and the vertical tactile display, (6) a multi-lingual speech synthesizer, (7) stereo loudspeakers and a cordless headphone, (8) a stereo mixer for internal and external acoustic signals, (9) a pressure-sensitive touch pad

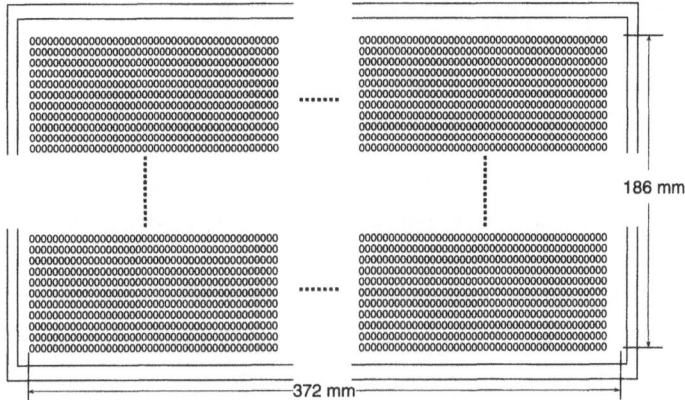

**Figure 16.2:** The pin-matrix device (adapted from Schweikhardt 1993)

## 16.4  Visual and Tactile Graphics: A Comparison

Starting with the assumption that visual and tactile graphics should convey about the same information, we have to look more carefully at the way a tactile graphic is perceived in comparison to a visual one. First, both kinds of graphics have several characteristics in common:

- Graphics consist mainly of dots (points), lines, and (textured) areas.
- Objects that are physically close to each other in the real world are (usually) close together in the corresponding graphics as well.
- Graphics can express their producers' *intention* directly or subtly.
- *Pleasure* can be one of the most important effects of graphics. Thus blind people often have tactile images hanging on their walls the way sighted people have visual ones.

Then again the way visual and tactile graphics are perceived is different:

| | |
|---|---|
| • Visual graphics are looked at and understood in a very short time. The eye usually finds the most important features of the image very quickly. The perception is two-dimensional. | • Tactile graphics are scanned linearly, line by line and dot by dot. This is a time-consuming process. It is not guaranteed that the "viewer" will find the most important area at all. The perception is largely one-dimensional. |
| • The eye is capable of recognizing very small details. | • The human sense of touch is limited to a minimum distance between touched points of about 1.5 to 2 mm. |
| • Color and patterns are additional dimensions seen in visual graphics. | • Texture and temperature have similar meaning for tactile graphics. |
| • Visual graphics are two-dimensional in space. | • Tactile graphics are three-dimensional in space, although the extent to which the third dimension is used can vary. |

Figure 16.3 shows an example of a visual graphic (a) and a reproduction of a tactile one (b), taken from a children's book (Vincent and Germeau 1991). The setting is that a sighted adult tells the story to a blind child. This example will help discover important differences between these kinds of pictures:

- Most objects are drawn in *less detail* (for example the stove).
- Some *redundant* or unnecessary objects can be *removed* (some of the vegetables, the back wall).
- Objects *partially hidden* by others are removed (the right leg of the bear).
- *Graphical effects*, such as shadows, are removed; others may be added to enhance tactile recognition (for example the calendar on the wall).
- Some (important) lines are drawn *thicker* to draw attention to them (texture on the bear's shirt).
- Some lines may be *added* to the graphic to make spatial relations between objects clear.
- Some objects may be *moved* to a different place (the pans hanging on the wall).
- Objects in the visual graphic may be *replaced* by different objects in the tactile form to help the viewer distinguish them from others.
- The *point of view* of the whole scene or just for some objects may be different in the tactile form to make recognition easier (for example the chair).

This enumeration shows that graphics designed to be viewed by sighted people ought not simply to be scanned and converted into a tactile form for tactile perception (see Edman 1992). Instead, the pictures must be transformed into a new form, paying attention in particular to

- details that might be redundant/unnecessary or too vague or complex,
- the characteristic feature of a tactile graphic that it is a two-dimensional representation of a three-dimensional scene and is perceived in a one-dimensional fashion.
- additional details to ease the recognition of graphic items via tactile perception.

In summary, tactile graphics must be rendered in a different manner than visual graphics.

**Figure 16.3:** Sample images from a children's book (Vincent and Germeau 1991):
An image produced for a sighted person (a), a tactile image, reproduced in black and white, of the same
scene, produced for a blind person (b). ERNEST ET CELESTINE LE PATCHWORK, by G. Vincent.
© Casterman, Belgium 1991

## 16.5 Constructing 2D/3D Models

The vast majority of pictures that are generally available and of potential interest to blind persons are printed on paper and not – as computer scientists would like – accessible in the form of computer models. However, the kinds of manipulation required on visual graphics to turn them into a form that can be understood as tactile images clearly require an underlying model. It is not reasonable in any practical setting to expect a sighted person to construct a 3D model using conventional modeling tools for every scene that may be needed by a blind person. This means that if "only" rendering software is written to produce tactile images, a purely academic problem of little or no practical relevance is being solved. Kugas (1993) (see also Kurze, Strothotte, and Kugas 1994) thus designed and implemented modeling software for a particular class of pictures.

The modeling software allows a sighted user to construct a model, assuming he has at his disposal a picture on paper. The model is to be 3D for those objects or parts thereof for which manipulation is later necessary to produce a tactile image; for the rest, 2D models suffice. Such models are referred to as 2D/3D models. The study restricted itself to the class of pictures found in the DUDEN/OXFORD picture dictionary: accurate line drawings primarily of objects, augmented by numeric labels and a legend giving the name of the objects and parts thereof (Figure 7.5 showed an example).

The procedure for interactively constructing a 2D/3D model is as follows:

1. The picture is analyzed using the method of Section 7.2 to separate graphical symbols from the presentational parts of the picture. The result is that the graphical symbols, including textual labels, are removed and the presentational part is vectorized. The user is given the opportunity to edit the vectorization to remove possible errors. Figure 16.4 shows the result of the application of this procedure to the first example in Figure 7.5.

**Figure 16.4:**
Object without extra symbols
(Kurze, Strothotte, and Kugas
1994)

2. The system constructs a series of equations describing possible 3D interpretations of the 2D vectorization. These equations contain unknowns (variables) to account for the third dimension.
3. The user carries out simple manipulation to work out the unknowns in the equations of Step 2, thereby converting parts of the 2D vectorization into a 3D model.

Step 1 was described in detail in Section 7.2, Steps 2 and 3 require more detailed explanation. Consider the perspective view of a house as illustrated in Figure 16.4. Since the machine has no *a priori* knowledge about the object, it is not possible to construct any data structure but the 2D vectorization. And yet to a human viewer, a great deal of information is obvious, for example which surfaces are at 90° to one another and which are not, and which lines that appear not to be parallel to one another are in fact parallel.

The software provides the user with a simple set of manipulation primitives and predicates to specify information about the third dimension. The user can select two or more lines and give them one of the following attributes:

- are parallel to one another,
- define a plane, or
- are perpendicular to one another.

Furthermore, the user can select

a) points, lines or planes, and
b) a plane

and combine them with the predicate "a) lies in b)".

The user can also select two planes and specify the angle between them, most often 90 or 180 degrees. Finally, the user can identify pairs of lines and specify that they are analogous, thereby enabling the construction of a 3D model of hidden parts based on symmetry assumptions.

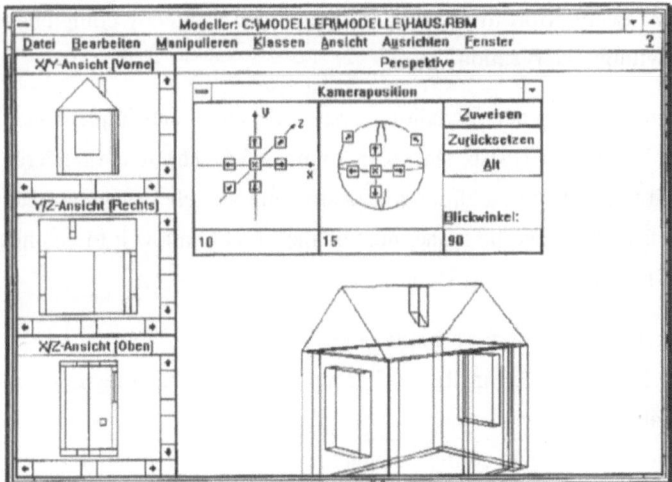

**Figure 16.5:** Screen dump of the modeler (Kurze, Strothotte, and Kugas 1994, see also Raab 1993)

An essential feature of the modeler is that the user can choose to leave parts of his or her image unmodeled in 3D, i.e., can simply use the 2D representation where desired. These will then be treated by the system as two-dimensional drawings on a clear glass plate within the 3D model. This is particularly useful for parts of the image that require no transformation into another form for the tactile output, or where the modeling would require an unreasonable amount of effort and the user is prepared to accept a certain loss in quality of the tactile output.

At any time, the user can switch to a conventional 3D modeler written for the purpose. The user can view the current state of the model as he or she has constructed it and update parts with the usual features of rotation, copying, etc. (see Figure 16.5); details may be found in Raab (1993).

## 16.6   A Rendering/Editing System for Tactile Graphics

Given a 2D/3D model for the scene to be rendered, the system is responsible for producing tactile images, paying particular attention to the points addressed in Section 16.4. Two approaches are possible:

1. We can assume that a sighted user (to avoid confusing him or her with the blind viewer, we shall say the "designer") is responsible for making sure that the output is in a form that can be understood by a blind user touching the output. In this case the system should point out possible problems to the designer and provide him or her with the means to fix them.
2. Alternatively, we may assume that the blind user is working alone, so that the system should make every effort to produce an image that is directly comprehensible to the blind user without intervention.

The architecture of the rendering/editing system designed and implemented by Kurze, Strothotte, and Kugas (1994) is shown in Figure 16.6. The touch-renderer accepts as input the usual model, but in addition a data structure we refer to as the "tactile configuration". This describes how the scene must be modified to allow it to be understood in a tactile form. These modifications include:

- change of camera position for a single object,
- removing visible surfaces in the background to make the foreground more clearly distinguishable,
- removing detail that would confuse the tactile image or be too small to recognize, and
- changing the size of objects and moving them around to make the overall image more comprehensible.

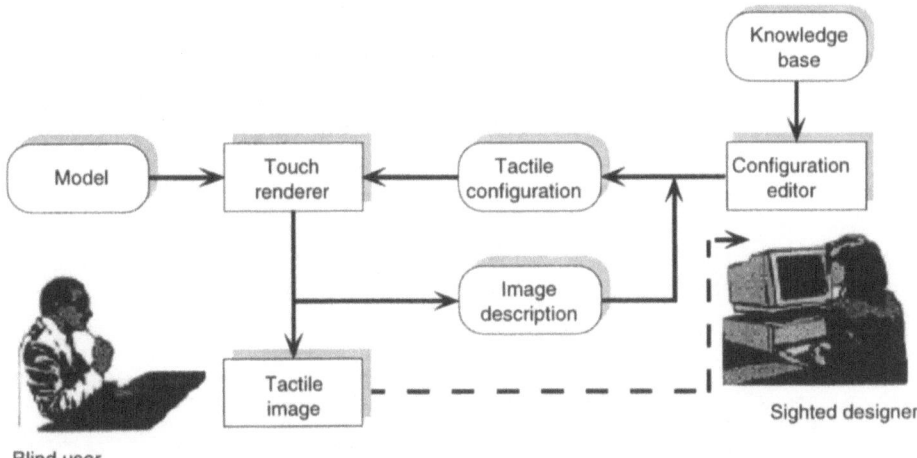

**Figure 16.6:** Architecture of the tactile rendering/editing system
(see Kurze, Strothotte, and Kugas 1994)

The knowledge base contains heuristics for recognizing the problematic aspects of an image, which, if there is no sighted designer, determine the tactile configuration autonomously. In the case that there is a sighted designer available, the configuration editor points out its observations to him or her and provides facilities to modify the image appropriately.

The system works in a cyclic fashion. Initially the tactile renderer produces a first image with an empty tactile configuration. This corresponds to the usual wire-frame-like image with hidden line removal. Besides this first image, the renderer also produces an "image description" that contains a symbolic description of what is represented in the output. This in turn is read into the configuration editor, which analyzes this representation of the image and, with the help of the knowledge base and perhaps the sighted designer, produces a new tactile configuration. This process is repeated until the images can no longer be tuned further. Finally, the line drawing on the screen is output onto paper and transferred to swell paper so it can actually be touched by the user.

Figure 16.7a shows a sample scene as it was produced initially and 16.7b shows the image after the designer finished editing it. It may appear odd to a sighted person, but it corresponds to the principles derived in Section 16.3. Blind people do not think of the combination of different camera positions in one image as a contradiction.

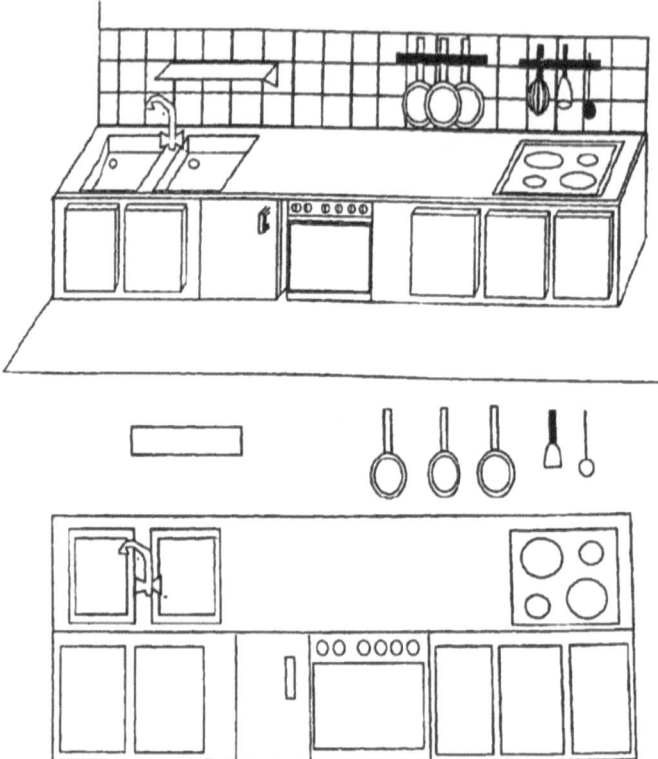

**Figure 16.7:** Original wire-frame and tactile output produced for the blind user
(Kurze, Strothotte, and Kugas 1994)

## 16.7 Discussion

In this chapter we have identified key features of tactile graphics intended for blind people and discussed ways to make tactile graphics for them.

The key point is that tactile graphics for blind people are very different in form from visual graphics. Care must be taken to avoid such features as overlapping regions, perspective, and small items. Ideally, a human designer should be involved in the editing process and supported by a knowledge base. If the blind user wishes to work autonomously, the system implemented will make the design decisions itself.

This work is to be seen in the larger context of tactile output in multimedia and virtual reality systems. Whereas force feedback can be used to provide a small amount of information pertaining to the values of selected variables, tactile output similar to that we suggest in this chapter can be used for more complex forms. Ideally we would like to have more interactive tactile graphics, but it is still an open problem to design such hardware technology. We envision the use of material that can be formed and deformed quickly by the computer.

Sighted users need not be restricted to touching tactile graphics. The questions of superimposing color images on top of tactile portions quickly arise. How can colors and raised surfaces augment one another in computer output? Such effects are only used today in some hand-made maps, in which for example mountains are actually represented by raised portions of material. Having such facilities in computer output could further enhance for example the display of statistical data, the results of scientific computing, and handbooks for technical devices.

Having gained experience in generating tactile graphics for blind users, a next step is to generate images that are both visual and tactile for sighted persons. This would not only enable a user to gain more information by touch about the scene or data being displayed, but could also serve to enhance the visual effect of the image. Light projected onto such images would cast shadows that provide another dimension to their interpretation.

*Pregnancy*
Coso Range, California

# Immersive Systems

In recent years, a great deal of hype has been generated around the term "virtual reality". The news media jumped onto the bandwagon and raised the expectations of the general public, and even members of the scientific community, well beyond reason. Despite the fact that this area of endeavor has failed to deliver what was projected after the initial advances, some interesting concepts have been developed which show promise. Thus a book on pictures in human-computer interaction would not be complete without at least a brief look into this area. We will do so without claiming any kind of completeness; for a detailed analysis, books devoted entirely to the subject are recommended (for example, Rheingold 1991; Bryson 1992; and Earnshaw, Gigante, and Jones 1993). We will survey aspects we consider particularly relevant to the part of the interaction pertaining to pictures and language, following and extending the nomenclature of Henry and Furness (1993). We will argue for a certain amount of language to augment pictures in immersive systems.

## 17.1 Reality and Immersion

Immersive systems aim at *apparently* removing human-computer interfaces altogether. Instead of a user working on a specialized machine, he or she is allowed to carry out actions like head or hand movements, in a simulated environment. The simulative aspect of the interaction pertains to the reactions of the system, which are primarily in the form of visualizations, but also of acoustic signals and force feedback. The goal is to allow users to focus on the task they wish to perform, rather than on the operation of a computer (Nielsen 1993). To reflect this difference, the literature often refers to the person involved as the *participant* rather than the *user*. We will use this term throughout this chapter.

Which aspects of the environment being simulated should be selected when designing an immersive system? We should remember that we are once again constructing a *system*, in which certain objects and relationships between them are selected for presentation, while others are not. Which ones are chosen is very technology driven. Various usable solutions have been developed more or less successfully for simulating visual experience, hence immersive systems tend to concentrate on this aspect. The generation of sound is also an issue (see for example Takala and Hahn 1992) but will not be treated here.

Another aspect of the simulated environment to be considered is the movement of the participant, either by his or her own will or following commands from the machine (force feedback). Participants' movements tend only to make sense if they are monitored by the computer. To realize this, a number of hardware solutions have been developed, for example the VPL Data Glove data gloveand the VPL Data Suit data suitand more recent similar products. But such systems are still either unreliable or too expensive for everyday applications. Force feedback is still at a stage where specialized solutions are being developed and a general methodology has not yet emerged.

### 17.1.1  The Role Model

Figure 17.1 demonstrates the kind of situation to be simulated in immersive systems. A real person is illustrated in a real room, ready for action. The goal of many applications developed to date is to simulate precisely such a real environment (Sutherland 1965 was the first to formulate this as a goal for interactive systems). For example, in architecture, participants can "tour" a building or site that may not yet exist, and in flight simulators trainee pilots can experience the feeling of flying an aircraft without any risk to themselves, other people, or the real world.

Immersive systems are intended to go a step further. Assuming that the computer generates the visual and acoustic signals necessary to simulate reality (neglect for now the technologically difficult aspect of force feedback), the computer could in principle enhance these effects, allowing objects to do desirable things they do not do in reality. For example, a technological gadget could itself demonstrate how it works; or an object on display in a museum could automatically provide a verbal explanation of itself as soon as the viewer comes within range and looks in its direction. Immersive systems have diverse goals, but the world in which the participant is to be immersed must be – or, more positively put, can be – designed by software engineers. This design is an immense challenge.

**Figure 17.1:**
A real person in a real room:
the ultimate immersion
(Henry and Furness 1993.
© IEEE 1993)

### 17.1.2  Augmented Reality

Augmented reality systems attempt to harness some of the attributes of immersive systems that go beyond simulating reality. These are applied to reality itself, rather than to a simulated environment, as illustrated in Figure 17.2.

Sutherland (1968) presented the first system for augmented reality. Feiner, Macintyre, and Seligmann (1993) built what is perhaps the most interesting hardware to date for supporting this kind of information. The participant wears a headset with a clear glass plate mounted in front of his or her eyes. The objects about which information is to be made available to the participant and his or her headset are equipped with receivers for ultrasonic signals; the emitters are stationary in the environment.

Reality is now augmented by having the computer project abstract-graphical pictures onto the display of the headset. This additional information is intended to answer the participant's queries or otherwise give him or her instructions.

**Figure 17.2:**
Augmented reality: better
than the real thing?!

**Figure 17.3:**
Example of the participant's view
(Feiner, Macintyre, and
Seligmann 1993)

Figure 17.3 shows an example of the system developed in Steve Feiner's lab. The participant wishes to add paper to a laser printer and has asked for assistance. The image shows what the participant sees when looking at the printer; an abstract-graphical picture is overlaid onto his or her view of the real printer, giving information about parts of the device not visible from the outside, and saying what he or she should do next.

It is interesting to see the nature of the abstract-graphical pictures Feiner, Macintyre, and Seligmann use to augment reality. On the one hand, a wire-frame image of the real object to be worked on is displayed: this is to confirm the participant's orientation, to improve his or her confidence in the dialogue system, and to draw his or her attention to the object in question. Otherwise, this wire-frame image does not provide any further information. The more abstract symbols that are added, by contrast, are closely related to language, as they are generally substitutes for specific words or short linguistic formulations. Hence, even though the display is graphical, the information being conveyed is primarily linguistic; the system can also display preformulated texts. We come back to this point later in the chapter.

One of the fundamental problems associated with augmented reality, which Feiner, Macintyre, and Seligmann's system solves only in a rudimentary way, is the perception of the state of reality by the computer, so that it can be augmented correctly. It is a pity that image processing algorithms are not more advanced, otherwise a camera could be mounted on the headset to assess the image seen by the viewer. Such systems hold a great deal of promise for assisting users in carrying out difficult tasks with well-defined solutions, particularly for people who do so only rarely.

## 17.2  Degrees of Immersion

### 17.2.1  Low Level of Immersion

Various technical approaches have been taken to achieve visual immersion in a simulated environment. Perhaps the simplest, the "monitor solution", is illustrated in Figure 17.4. A participant views a computer screen and carries out actions, like moving the camera position (taken to be his or her own viewing position) by manipulating a space ball or other multi-dimensional input device. Such systems, which correspond to the usual computer graphics configuration (albeit with real-time rendering), rely on the participant's concentration to achieve immersion. Even then, it is only a low level of immersion for the following reasons. Firstly, the monitor takes up only a small portion of the participant's field of view, while his or her peripheral vision perceives the surrounding environment (usually an office or a laboratory). Second, the participant's head movements do not change the parallax of the image on the screen, but do change everything perceived by the participant's peripheral vision (e.g., the monitor and the wall behind it). This discontinuity tends to impede the feeling of immersion.

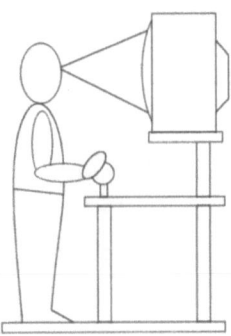

**Figure 17.4:**
The "monitor solution" for achieving immersion (Henry and Furness 1993. © IEEE 1993)

### 17.2.2  Head-Tracking and Parallax to Improve Immersion

Depth viewing can be improved considerably when the image changes with any head movements. Figure 17.5 shows the monitor solution augmented by facilities to track the participant's head position. We refer to this as the "parallax monitor solution".

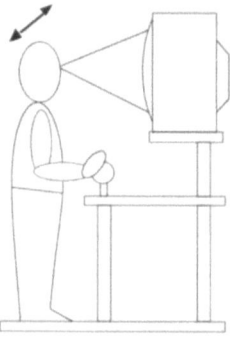

**Figure 17.5:**
The "parallax monitor solution"
with facilities to track the head
position

For some images, the apparent shift of one object with respect to another due to head movements may not be sufficient to give clues about the 3D nature of the scene. Ware, Arthur, and Booth (1993) suggest that scenes be given what they refer to as a "vection background". They successfully used a background consisting of a random field of objects computed as though they were at infinity with respect to the observer (see Figure 17.6 as an example). Objects in the foreground can then be located by means of the shift relative to the background.

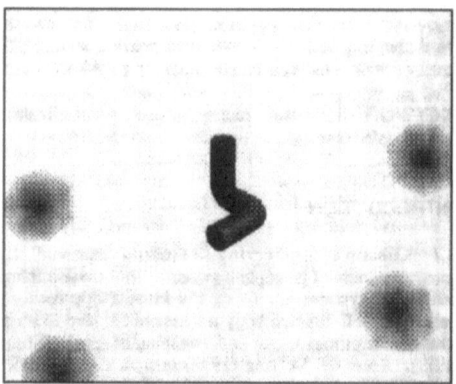

**Figure 17.6:** Vection background with a simple object in front of it
(Ware, Arthur, and Booth 1993)

Ware, Arthur, and Booth carried out experiments to assess the usefulness of head tracking to produce parallax. To further enhance the parallax monitor solution, they introduced stereo vision (using the StereoGraphics CristalEyes system). They compared the subjective viewing quality for simple scenes with respect to the variables (1) whether or not parallax (i.e., head tracking) was used and (2) whether stereo, monocular, or binocular viewing was used. Subjects were asked to toggle between each pair of possible viewing conditions and state which of these gave them the better perception of 3D space. Their results are summarized in Table 17.1.

**Table 17.1:** Subjective comparison of viewing conditions for 3D perception (Ware, Arthur, and Booth 1993). The percentages indicate subjects' preferences of the row's viewing condition over the column's viewing condition.

|  | Picture | Non-Parallax | Parallax Monocular | Parallax Binocular | Parallax Stereo | All |
|---|---|---|---|---|---|---|
| Picture | — | 43% | 4% | 0% | 7% | 13% |
| Non-Parallax | 57% | — | 7% | 11% | 0% | 19% |
| Parallax Monocular | 96% | 93% | — | 29% | 61% | 70% |
| Parallax Binocular | 100% | 89% | 71% | — | 68% | 82% |
| Parallax Stereo | 93% | 100% | 39% | 32% | — | 68% |

The results show that the conditions with parallax were considered more effective, while stereo viewing did not enhance 3D perception over binocular viewing.

To verify the results with a specific task, Ware, Arthur, and Booth asked subjects to examine pairs of overlapping trees drawn on the screen, and shown a leaf, to report to which of the trees it belongs. The time to complete the tasks and the error rate were measured. An example of the trees used for the experiment is shown in Figure 17.7; Table 17.2 summarizes the results.

The results demonstrate further the value of parallax visualization, as well as the superiority of parallax stereo vision over monocular and binocular vision for the particular task chosen by the authors.

In summary, parallax visualizations have been demonstrated to be decisive for the participant's performance in certain tasks and should be seriously considered by designers of graphics systems.

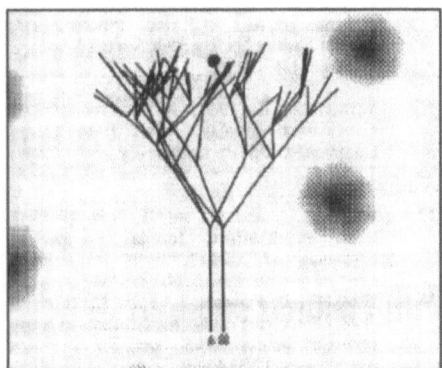

**Figure 17.7:** Example of graphics used by Ware, Arthur, and Booth (1993)

**Table 17.2:** Results of carrying out recognition task under various conditions (Ware, Arther, and Booth 1993)

| Condition | time (sec) | % errors |
|---|---|---|
| Picture | 7.50 | 21.8 |
| Stereo | 8.09 | 14.7 |
| Parallax Monocular | 8.66 | 3.7 |
| Parallax Binocular | 9.12 | 2.7 |
| Parallax Stereo | 6.83 | 1.3 |

### 17.2.3  Head-Mounted Displays in Immersive Systems

State-of-the-art technological solutions for immersive systems use head-mounted displays (Figure 17.8). Quite a number of these systems have been built and commercialized, the most notorious being the VPL eyephones. The horizontal view in such systems varies greatly but is, for example, 75 ° per eye with a 60 ° overlap, yielding 90 ° for both eyes combined. Compared to the monitor solutions discussed above, the HMD has the decided advantage that the entire peripheral vision is eliminated, much like when wearing goggles in real life. The disadvantage is that the resolution of inexpensive devices is often much lower. For example, a few hundred pixels maybe spread over 90° of the view horizontally, compared to over 1K pixels for about 30° on a monitor. HMD's are often coupled with head-tracking mechanisms that record the position and rotations of the participant's head (Figure 17.9).

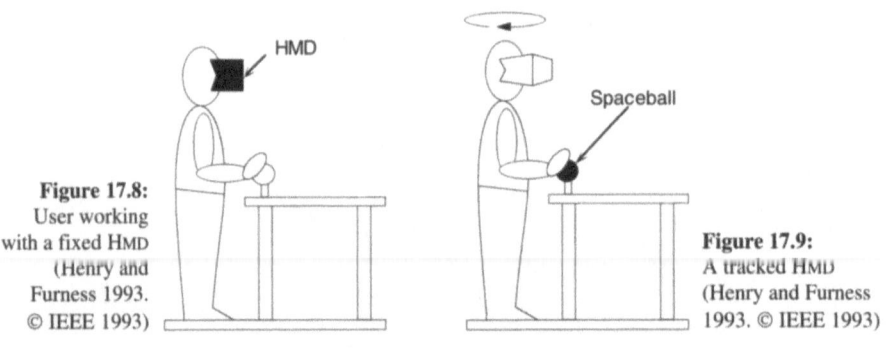

**Figure 17.8:**
User working
with a fixed HMD
(Henry and
Furness 1993.
© IEEE 1993)

**Figure 17.9:**
A tracked HMD
(Henry and Furness
1993. © IEEE 1993)

## 17.3  How Much Immersion Is Enough?

Having looked at various degrees of immersion, we shall discuss various aspects of the interaction to weigh their pros and cons.

### 17.3.1  Monitors Versus Head-Mounted Displays

While HMDs are just beginning to offer a quality sufficient for complex, even photo-realistic images, monitors still offer a number of other advantages (Ware, Arthur, and Booth 1993):

- they can easily be used in offices and laboratories without disrupting normal routines,
- it is easier to share experiences with co-workers or clients when working with a monitor,
- with the HMD it is difficult for participants to appreciate the difference between objects in the foreground and those in the background.

Hence for the time being, for all but specialized tasks, there is no real alternative to the monitor for high-quality pictures.

### 17.3.2  Spatial Perception of Architects

The various kinds of immersion must be compared with regard to the task being undertaken by the user. In this section we discuss one such representative study.

When participants are to work with immersive systems to carry out real tasks, individual differences show up among the different degrees of immersion. One area in which such differences have been observed is in architecture, which is certainly one of the best thought out applications of immersive systems technology. Henry and Furness (1993) set out to compare several levels of immersion with respect to how well architects carried out certain routine tasks and how they assessed their own experience. We will briefly survey their results.

Architects were placed into one of four groups, each of which toured an art gallery under one of the conditions of immersion discussed in Section 17.2. These were the monitor solution, the fixed HMD, the tracked HMD, and the real situation. The tasks were to

1. estimate the size of the rooms, and
2. comment on their feelings about the attributes pertaining to lighting, color, and mood.

The results showed that the horizontal dimensions were significantly underestimated in the simulated conditions compared to the real situation, while the vertical dimensions were estimated with a high degree of accuracy. The precision of the vertical estimates is attributed to standards in the building codes which restrict the number of possible choices. The inaccuracy of the horizontal estimates is attributed by the authors essentially to the lack of peripheral vision in the simulated environments. Further, subjects with the tracked HMD underestimated distances significantly more than participants with the fixed HMD. This can be explained by the way the subjects carried out their tasks: those with the tracked HMD were assumed to move their eyes more in anticipation of objects moving into the field of view when moving their heads. The HMD used for the experiment has a higher distortion at its perimeter, explaining the results.

Finally, participants were asked to comment on their experiences using a bipolar checklist of adjectives. The real situation was then compared to the simulated conditions. The regression values were as follows: real and monitor 0.88, real and fixed HMD 0.79, real and tracked HMD 0.91; the higher the value the closer the result of the test condition to the real situation, assumed to be optimal. These values reflect the degree to which participants felt comfortable with the simulated experience. The results offer evidence of the superiority of the tracked HMD over the single monitor for the tasks specified.

### 17.3.3 Degree of Presence

To what extent can participants actually *be fooled* or *fool themselves* about the simulated environment? This question most certainly has an effect on the usefulness of immersive systems. We refer to the extent to which users feel their virtual environment is actually a real one as the degree of presence. This is difficult to measure, since it is highly dependent on the actual system and the task at hand, but it is important.

Though results in the literature on this question are few and far between, there are indirect indications that extremely high-end immersive systems are successful in conveying a a feeling of presence, to the extent that a danger is perceived that participants will confuse the simulated and the real environment after working in the immersive system. This is why pilots in the US military are not permitted to fly a plane within 24 hours of a session with a flight simulator. However, this regulation says little about more modest applications for a larger target group of participants.

Slater and Usoh (1993) describe an interesting way to measure the degree of presence. Subjects are given a questionnaire to complete, Part A immediately after the session in the immersive system, Part B twenty-four hours later. Part A consists of the following questions:

**To what extent did you experience a sense of being "really there" inside the virtual environment?**

(1) not at all really there, (2) there to a small extent, (3) there to some extent, (4) a definite sense of being there, (5) a strong experience of being there, (6) totally there

**Were there any circumstances that especially increased your sense of being "really there"?**

(1) being able to move around, (2) interacting with objects/doing a task, (3) great concentration, (4) mention of body, (5) fear reaction, (6) being upside down

**Were there any circumstances that especially decreased your sense of being "really there"?**

(1) outside events (including instructor), (2) screen/up-dates/lag/resolution, (3) things don't behave naturally (laws of physics are violated), (4) things aren't done naturally, (5) body doesn't behave naturally.

Part B consists of an essay reporting on the sense of presence. Specifically, subjects answered the following question:

Write as much as you want about your overall experiences in the virtual environment. Pay attention to your sense of being there or not, your physical sensations, your mental experiences, your thoughts about what happened – in fact about anything that occurs to you about what you experienced.

To analyze the essays, they suggest drawing on a therapeutic model known as neuro-linguistic processing (NLP) (see also Dilts et al. 1979). The model uses an analysis of the linguistic account of a participant to determine the degree of presence. Each sentence is analyzed to determine whether it falls into the visual, auditory, or kinesthetic category, as well as the so-called *position* from which the subject reports (1st person singular, 2nd person singular, or 3rd person singular). For example, the sentence "I saw the car" is classified as (visual, 1st person), while "you felt the surface of the board" is classified as (kinesthetic, 2nd person). The statistical spread of the uses of the persons in relation to the senses they refer to gives clues as to the sense of presence with respect to the techniques used to create it. The results of the specific experiment of Slater and Usoh go beyond the scope of this book, as they are highly dependent on the details of the specific immersive system used for the experiment. Of interest in the present context is their method of experimentation.

# 17.4  Support for Richer Interaction in Immersive Systems

So far, immersive systems technology has penetrated only very few application areas. We contend that part of the reason for this is the lack of rich interaction possibilities for participants of immersive systems. Let us study this hypothesis in more detail.

Notoriously lacking in many immersive systems developed to date are images of other people. Exceptions are systems for computer supported co-operative work (CSCW), where other workers are involved in the same simulated environment (Shaw 1993). To be realistic, and maybe even help participants carry out certain tasks, these (simulated) people should react to what the participant is doing. An egocentric world in which the viewer is the only person around is not particularly exciting for communication-loving participants who are supposedly immersed in another, better world.

In most applications, the participant can do little more than move about and perform simple functions. The input is typically carried out by pointing with his or her finger, which causes a simulated laser beam to hit objects, or by manipulating a hand-held input device. This in turn results in selection of the object hit, which causes a chain reaction of other actions to be carried out, depending on which object has been selected. The procedure is analogous to clicking on an item on the screen when using a desktop metaphor, although selection in immersive systems tends to be a unary function with only rudimentary parameterization of the selection. In systems using gesture input a richer repertoire of commands is in principle available, but in practice it is very difficult to recognize gestures accurately enough for this to be really useful.

Perhaps the most significant attribute missing from immersive systems, however, is highly reliable speech input. Clearly such input is not really necessary from an objective point of view, since there are seldom people (simulated or real) around in the world in which the participant is immersed who could hear the speech and understand it. Nonetheless, such input could, in principle, be parsed by the system and processed appropriately, for example to parameterize a selection as mentioned above. This could then result in some sort of response by the system.

The reason for this lack of speech is twofold. First, speech recognition technology is not advanced enough to recognize speaker-independent input in real time with an accuracy high enough to produce reasonable results (Fellbaum 1993, Mehnert, Fellbaum, and Hoffmann 1993). Also, linguistic methods of analyzing natural language utterances are not good enough yet to process unrestricted input by participants. Applying restrictions of any kind, the way it is usually done in experimental natural-language dialogue systems, could defeat in many situations the purpose of immersive systems and be unacceptable in this context. Thus the first reason is a technological one with little hope of a viable solution in the near future.

The second reason is more profound. Even if, say, a participant's utterance could be reduced to an equivalent expression in a formal language, the machine would still have to process it in some sophisticated manner. Presumably the utterance would refer to objects in the scene at hand, and in particular to the image currently viewed by the participant, information which is not represented explicitly in today's graphics systems (recall Section 2.5).

We have now arrived at one of the important cross-roads of pictures and language. Pictures are generated by renderers from scene descriptions describing the geometry of objects; a participant responding to a perceived image might well do so in a linguistic utterance, using words referring to the objects, relationships among them, and his or her intentions for altering the state of affairs. This gap is typical of the interface between language and pictures and must be addressed if we hope to develop truly interactive systems.

How can this gap be bridged? Participants have no problems seeing and understanding a picture first and then speaking about the picture in a language. How this is done is of no concern here; indeed, we swept this issue under the carpet with our language-oriented definition of transmitted and transputed information (recall Chapter 5). To enable a computer to react appropriately, however, we must now construct algorithms that can access both the geometric information encoded in pictures and the ASCII representations of language. The key is to structure each of these information sources in a sophisticated manner. A great deal of work has been done on the textual side of this issue, for example, with symbol-manipulation languages and knowledge bases; in the following we report progress on the graphical side.

### 17.4.1 Requirements

In order to enrich immersive systems and facilitate a stronger link with language-based dialogue systems, two prerequisites must be fulfilled:

1. *Scene descriptions must be extended to allow more uses than just producing images.*
   Scene descriptions, as they are generally realized, are used exclusively as input to renderers, which in turn do nothing but produce images. This implies a pragmatic isolation of a scene description from all other software components. Either the scene description languages must be extended to enable deductions, or they must be made compatible with knowledge representation formalisms.
2. *Images must be integrated with the other software components.*
   Images today are designed to satisfy the viewing pleasure and communicative need of participants. A renderer produces an image as a pixel matrix, in such a way that the semantics of the image are no longer accessible by the machine, only by the participant. This isolation too must be overcome, if images are to be used more extensively.

To move toward realizing these goals and to provide a platform for studying the crossroads of language and pictures, Emhardt and Strothotte (1992) developed an application-independent system for processing images. The goal is that as a by-product of the rendering process, the computer produces information it can benefit from.

### 17.4.2 Hyper-Rendering

The utility of graphics systems can be greatly enhanced by making information about the rendering process explicitly available to other programs. This process of deriving such information is referred to as *hyper-rendering* (Emhardt and Strothotte 1992; see also Emhardt 1995). Hyper-rendering produces a formal description of the scene as viewed by the participant and can be carried out either within a renderer or in a separate program. The latter approach has the advantage that separate algorithms can be used for rendering and hyper-rendering of the same image, especially when hardware facilities are used for rendering. Indeed, when an image is to be produced with ray-tracing, it may suffice to carry out the hyper-rendering with a fast $z$-buffer algorithm. In certain applications it may even suffice initially just to carry out hyper-rendering and only later to perform the more time-consuming rendering.

An example of the software architecture for a graphics systems with hyper-rendering is shown in Figure 17.10.

The architecture contains the modules of a traditional graphics system (a model, also referred to as a scene description; a renderer; and an image; recall Section 2.5) as well as a number of other modules. Conceptually, hyper-rendering software is built around the renderer. It computes various pieces of information about both the rendering process and the rendered picture, which conventional renderers either throw away or do not bother computing in the first place. This information is stored in a data structure called the "image description".

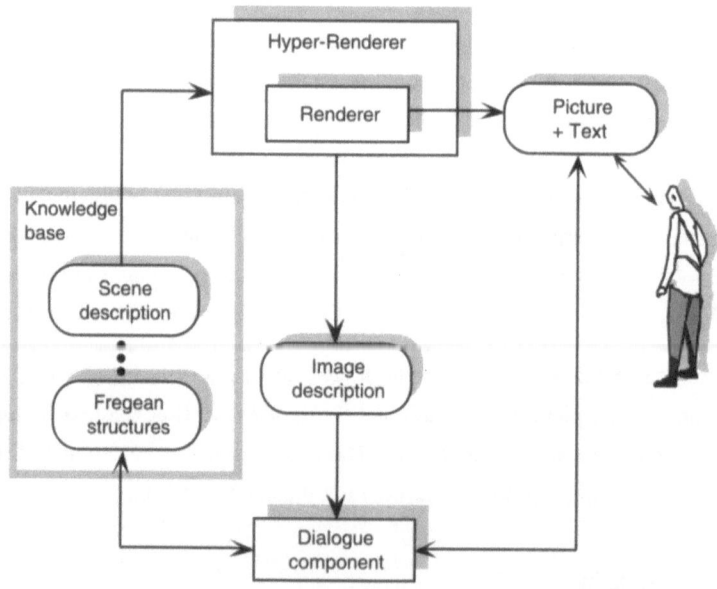

**Figure 17.10:** Architecture of a hyper-rendering-based system

The primary purpose of hyper-rendering is to allow participants to do more with the rendered pictures than just look at them; this is facilitated by various kinds of applications that take as input the image description. Depending on the application, the scene description may also be integrated or modified. Thus an application has information about what the participant can see in the picture that it can use to conduct a dialogue with the participant about the picture, to evaluate the picture under certain criteria, or even to modify it so as to change the visibility of the objects.

The scene description is an integral part of the knowledge base, as is a component for recording the linguistic information needed to conduct a dialogue with the participant. How well these complement one another depends on how carefully they are constructed. In particular, the same identifiers must be chosen for objects in the Fregean structures and those in the scene description. Also, the scene description must be designed so that

1. the physical organization of the objects is encoded in a hierarchical manner, and
2. a systems designer can update (edit) it reasonably easily.

### 17.4.3  Notes on the Implementation of a Hyper-Renderer

Rather than integrating a hyper-rendering facility into an existing renderer, Emhardt and Strothotte chose to work with a commercially available renderer (in this case Pixar's RenderMan™) and build a hyper-rendering facility as an extra program. This has the disadvantage that certain codes must be duplicated, but it also allows the use of different algorithms for rendering and hyper-rendering.

The hyper-renderer is written in about 5K lines of C code on an IRIS 4D35 TG. Input is the scene description file in the format used by RenderMan™. To support the maintainability of the scene description file and to facilitate dialogues about the graphics produced by the renderer, its format is extended to include the symbolic names of the objects as well as the grouping of objects into compound objects.

The hyper-renderer contains typical rendering algorithms which have been enhanced to record information symbolically about the graphics. In particular, an extended $z$-buffer algorithm is implemented for hidden-surface removal, but in contrast to conventional $z$-buffers, information about hidden surfaces is stored, not thrown away. The implementation is related to Atherton's (1981) implementation of an object-buffer, but whereas Atherton's three-dimensional display buffer was implemented as a solid object description, the hyper-renderer approximates quadric surfaces using polygons. Finally, a $z$-buffer is used to generate shadows caused by opaque objects, as proposed by Atherton (see also Bouknight and Kelley 1970).

The resolution of the hyper-rendering algorithms need not be the same as the resolution of the picture actually rendered; their resolution is determined dynamically by the application program. A coarser hyper-renderer suffices for many applications and means that the results of hyper-rendering can be made available significantly before the rendered picture becomes available.

By default, the hyper-renderer carries out a fast $z$-buffer-algorithm in a first pass. By recording which objects are in the line of sight of each pixel, and with information about which surfaces cause specular reflection or refraction, for example, those parts of the scene that require ray tracing are determined. Thus, the ray tracer is "selective" and restricts itself to the parts of the picture it deems necessary. The visibility information supplied by the $z$-buffer-algorithm can be used for hidden surface removal, which makes the ray tracer itself much more efficient (this concept is related to that of an "item-buffer" as described by Weghorst, Hooper, and Greenberg 1984). However, the application program that calls it can override these "fancy" features and force the use of particular hyper-rendering algorithms.

The output of the hyper-renderer is an image description. It is implemented as an object-oriented file. The names of the objects in the scene description file are associated with various pieces of information, including low-level data on pixels affected by the object and colors as well as high-level information about the visibility (and invisibility) of objects, their interior, the intersection with each other, certain prepositional attributes (e.g., in front of, behind, on, under), and a description of which objects lie in shadows. The data produced by the hyper-renderer can be summarized as follows:

- shadows
- materials
- reflection properties
- light sources
- prepositional information (in front of, behind, ...)
- intersection of objects
- interior, exterior of objects
- visibility information

As output for each object and its parts, the hyper-renderer produces a semantic net that contains information about visibility and invisibility, shadows, the interior of the object, other objects intersecting it, prepositional information, information about the position of light sources relative to the object, its reflection properties, and its material properties.

### 17.4.4   Applications of Hyper-Rendering

*Participant Control*

There are two broad categories of application for hyper-rendering. The first includes applications in which the participant leads a dialogue in the immersive system. If a participant is to engage in a dialogue with the machine about the contents of the graphics, it is an absolute prerequisite that the application has at its disposal detailed information about what the participant can see. This is particularly important in systems where the participant is to be able to ask for information and explanations about certain objects in the scene, such as in teaching applications. It should be particularly clear here that the scene description itself is not sufficient to enable the machine to lead such a dialogue, since a participant's input must be interpreted with respect to *what he or she can see* (or in some cases, more importantly, what he or she *cannot* see) rather than only with respect to the *model* of the scene.

To demonstrate the capabilities of hyper-rendering, a simple dialogue system was developed for navigating in a scene. Since a low level of immersion suffices to demonstrate the techniques, the monitor solution of Figure 17.4 was used. The dialogue is conducted in a restricted natural language that allows a participant to specify the kind of graphics to be displayed (wire-frame or full-surface rendering). The most significant feature of the application is that it allows the participant to formulate a constraint on the view, upon which the application computes a change in the scene description file and initiates re-rendering and re-hyper-rendering of the graphics.

As an example, we shall now explore the IKEA cupboard displayed in Figure 17.11. A description of the cupboard and its contents was designed with a modeler and stored in a RenderMan™ ".rib-file".

**Figure 17.11:**
Rendered image of an IKEA cupboard (originally in Emhardt and Strothotte 1992; redrawn courtesy of Stefan Schlechtweg)

The participant obtains the image of Figure 17.11 by typing an appropriate command:

Application:        Please enter command.
Participant:        Draw cupboard.

The participant now wishes to see more of the object in the picture and decides to switch to a wire-frame image.

Application:        Please enter command.
Participant:        Draw wires.

The RenderMan™ is invoked again and produces Figure 17.12.

**Figure 17.12:**
The rendered wire-frame image of the cupboard. All objects are visible, though largely indiscernible (originally in Emhardt and Strothotte 1992; redrawn courtesy of Stefan Schlechtweg)

The participant realizes that neither of the images shown alone provides convincing information as to what is in the cupboard. Referring now back to the rendered image, he or she asks for information on what cannot be seen:

Application:        Please enter command.
Participant:        What can I not see?
Application:        Ball, box, safe.

In this response, the application has made use of the hyper-renderer. The image description contains information about the visibility of objects and from this it is easy to compute which objects are *not* visible.

The participant now wishes to look at a particular object, the safe. By looking at the wire-frame image, he or she recognises that there are *two* candidate objects that could be a safe (one is at the bottom and another is below the top on the left side). So he or she enters the following command:

Application:        Please enter command.
Participant:        Show safe through glass.

The application responds by showing Figure 17.13.

**Figure 17.13:**
The modified image showing the
inside of the cupboard (originally
in Emhardt and Strothotte 1992;
redrawn courtesy of Stefan
Schlechtweg)

The application used the information in the image description file to determine that it was the cupboard itself which blocked the participant's view of the safe. It then changed the material of the upper left part of the cupboard to "glass" in the scene description and drew the resulting picture.

It must be noted that the way the system is designed, the user is not given a high "sense of presence", since the dialogue he or she leads involves the keyboard. Even if the participant could speak the commands in a natural language, the situation would still be "unnatural", since it is presently not normal to speak to a machine\*, and there exists no well-defined person with whom this dialogue is being held. This, in turn, goes against the grain of immersive systems and their preoccupation with the "sense of presence". However, by sacrificing some of this sense, the participant can take advantage of the capability of the computer to visualize situations that are physically impossible.

As another example of this kind of interaction, Strothotte et al. (1993) developed a dialogue system for providing blind people with at least rudimentary access to rendered images. Their system, called the "image description machine", is integrated in a working environment for blind persons based on graphical user interfaces. It enables the participant to lead a language-like dialogue, in which he or she can ask which objects can be found in the image or certain parts thereof. Geometric data is displayed on the horizontal and vertical Braille displays of an output device for blind persons (recall Figure 16.1). The rendered image is taken to be as wide as the horizontal display and as high as the vertical one. Thus the blind person can ask where a certain object is: the answer is given by raising the appropriate pins on the two Braille displays, thereby giving him or her the $x$ and $y$ positions of the objects in question. A blind participant also has at his or her disposal a small window that can be maneuvered over the image using the cursor keys. Whenever the window leaves an object or reaches a new one, an appropriate message is generated using synthetic speech output.

---

\* The social acceptability of actually speaking to machines may indeed change over time.

The image description machine provides blind persons with the fundamental functionality to explore a rendered image. It is implemented as a simple application, following the architecture of Figure 17.10. The description produced with the help of the hyper-renderer is drawn upon by the dialogue system to provide information as to what is in the picture. However, it is still difficult for users to "picture" the image being described to them. Perhaps more fundamentally, such a system is mainly limited to conveying the information normally *transmitted* to sighted users. The information that is generally *transputed* to sighted users through subtle features in the image, on the other hand, is very difficult to convey to blind users. This information cannot be captured by the hyper-renderer.

### *Design in Immersive Systems*

The second broad application of hyper-rendering is in situations whereas a picture shown to the participant (or intended for display) must be evaluated for appropriateness by the machine. Linking an application program to a renderer without modifying the latter is not possible without storing the information the renderer calculates. With the architecture described above, it is possible to build knowledge-based systems that analyze the modeling of a scene with respect to given constraints, generate improvements, and prepare explanations for the participant. For example, Fischer, Lemke, and Mastaglio (1990) discuss the critiquing approach to building knowledge-based interactive systems and describe a system for developing specialized architectural designs. Hyper-rendering can be used to enable the application of critiquing to rendered images.

On the basis of the hyper-renderer, Emhardt, Semmler, and Strothotte (1993) (see also Preininger 1993, Emhardt 1995) developed a critiquing system for designing overhead transparencies and slides in an immersive system. The problem in this area is that it is difficult for a person preparing visual materials for a presentation, a lecture at a conference for instance, to know what the effect of a particular overhead transparency will actually be when it is shown in the lecture hall. Are the letters legible from the back of the room? Does the picture appear well-balanced, with an emphasis on the intended part? Will the viewers at the front of the room be overwhelmed by the headers and footers? Should the lights be dimmed to show a slide with a photorealistic image or can all the details be seen from everywhere in the hall, even under normal lighting conditions? These are typical questions that go through the mind of a speaker while preparing his or her overheads.

The participant chooses a lecture hall from a set modeled on actual rooms, and chooses the lighting and the place from which he or she wants to look at the overheads. Using the "monitor solution", the participant is shown what the slides look like when they are projected onto a screen (see Figure 17.14).

**Figure 17.14:** An overhead transparency projected onto a screen and viewed by the participant as though he or she were in the lecture hall (Emhardt, Semmler and Strothotte 1993. © IEEE 1993)

The system also computes the areas of legibility for the texts displayed on the screen and informs the participant of the results. For example, Figure 17.15 shows a lecture hall viewed from the ceiling down; the circles indicate the areas in which the text is legible. The participant now modifies the text on his or her workstation or asks the system to adjust the sizes so that the text will be legible in the regions of the room he or she indicates. The participant then re-examines what the new slides look like. The procedure continues until he or she is happy with the result.

The hyper-renderer certainly cannot be used to design good (or even appropriate) presentations *automatically*. It can be used to evaluate a particular graphic with respect to communicative goals. If the evaluation is negative, other means must be found to correct

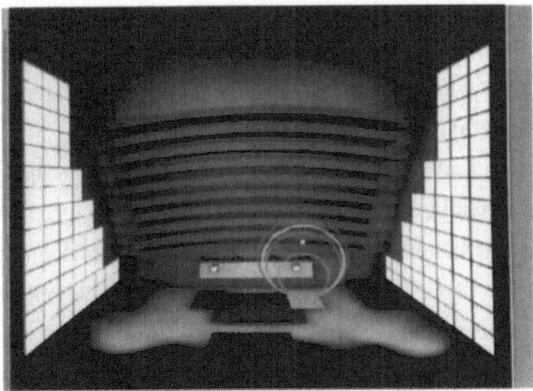

**Figure 17.15:** Legibility regions in a lecture hall viewed from the ceiling
(Emhardt, Semmler, and Strothotte 1993. © IEEE 1993)

the situation. Either an appropriate knowledge base (Fregean structures in the architecture of Figure 17.10) is drawn upon, or the user makes the improvements him- or herself. Thereafter the participant is given an evaluation of the modified result.

## 17.5 Discussion

An overriding concern in the analysis of immersive systems has been the lack of language for participants to communicate with the machine. As a basis for the discussion, we once again return to the *system* aspect of the design of presentations. Immersive systems in general, and specifically the visible portion of presentations, concentrate on certain objects and relations between these objects. The emphasis is on heightening the "sense of presence", by making the simulated environment behave more and more according to the laws of physics, having the participant's body take effect on the image, and ensuring that things behave naturally (recall Section 17.3).

If these are to be attributes of an immersive system, then the visual portion may deal only with *visible* objects and relations. It must consist purely of presentational pictures. If, by contrast, the participant is to see *invisible* objects, the sense of presence will certainly suffer. As soon as we compromise the sense of presence and set as our goal to provide participants with information about visible objects, but also about invisible portions of the overall system, we must use means other than presentational pictures. According to our definitions, these will be abstract-graphical pictures.

Time and time again in this book we have seen that the use of abstract-graphical pictures means we need linguistic information, or equivalently stated, Fregean structures. Drawing on the methods and tools developed for such structures enables us to carry out a dialogue, even in immersive systems, where the emphasis is on the visible. This is of paramount importance, since many methods, tools, and applications developed within computer science deal with matters that are invisible, and the results should be made available and put to use in immersive systems.

The hyper-rendering tool we discussed in this chapter bridges the gap between purely geometric data and symbolic knowledge representation in the usual (Fregean) sense, and enables participant interaction with elements that are generally not visible. The tool bridges this gap on the part of the machine; the participant's cognitive capabilities do so for his or her part. This phenomenon is revealed in the architectural diagram of Figure 17.10, and Figure 17.16 provides an alternative view that demonstrates the effect more clearly. Within the computer there is a cycle leading from the knowledge base, the hyper-renderer, the image description, and the application, back to the knowledge base. The other cycle involves the user, leading from the knowledge base, the renderer, the participant, the application, and back to the knowledge base.

The hyper-renderer takes on certain image analysis tasks within the machine in the inner circle which the participant carries out in the outer circle, but the two cycles are by no means equivalent. The difference lies primarily in the amount of information that can be *transputed*. While the hyper-renderer can compute and store much of the information to be transmitted in the image description, the machine lacks the basis for a reasoning process. Only the user has complete information about why he or she is looking at the image and what his or her goals are. These are the starting points for the participant's reasoning process. It would be very tricky for the machine to try to second-guess these intentions and attempt to compute the information transputed by the computer to the participant.

In summary, our emphasis on interaction with pictures in this chapter has underlined the importance of an integration of linguistic representations with pictures. Whatever the implementation technique, be it with hyper-rendering or another process, the gap between linguistic representations and pictures must be bridged. This way the lack of language in immersive systems can be compensated for at least to some extent.

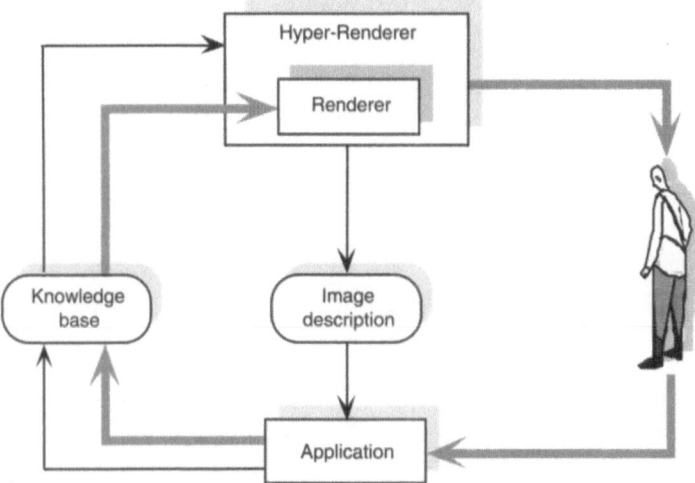

**Figure 17.16:** Cycles in the flow of information

Part
**VI**

**Epilogue**

*Magician spears kangoroo*
Cave painting on bark
Arnhem Land, North Australia

**Chapter**

# 18

# Pictures and Language

In this chapter, we return to some of the more fundamental issues surrounding pictures. We draw on the terms we have developed to look back at the material we have studied. The goal is to shed more light on the relationship between pictures and language.

## 18.1   A Comparison Between Pictures and Language

Throughout this book we have seen that it is difficult to differentiate between pictures and language. Indeed, this may be another symptom of the difficulties already encountered in Chapter 1, where we were not even able to give a precise definition of what a picture really is. To remind us of the difficulties, Figure 18.1 shows a collection of pictures that can be used as linguistic symbols.

The problem of differentiating between pictures and language becomes acute when we recall the old proverb alluding to the thousand words in the context of information transmitted and transputed. Language plays an important role in the latter terms, since they both refer to "words or their substitutes" (recall Chapter 5) and are elements in the hypothesis of a language-like reasoning process that generates new information for the recipient. Since we also speak of information being transmitted and transputed via pictures, we implicitly assume that a picture does indeed say something linguistic to the viewer.

**Figure 18.1:** Letters as pictures (left Brügelmann and Balhorn 1990, right Hetzger 1981)

The examples of pictures in Figure 18.1 are surely exceptions to any rule we could construct, hence in the following we will concentrate our comparison between pictures and language on more practical mainstream examples. Perhaps the most important component of a comparison between pictures and language is the realization that both describe a *system.* In both, selected objects are described with selected attributes. The producer of a sentence can leave many attributes unspecified, since many words are vague. This in turn leaves the recipient many *degrees of freedom* for his or her interpretation of the utterance. Indeed, it is not a rare occurrence that the recipient of a message will interpret a sentence differently from what was intended by the producer. The same is true for pictorial formulations, although the point is that different degrees of freedom exist.

At the same time, both linguistic and pictorial presentations are governed by certain *constraints* that must be satisfied: certain pieces of information may not be left unspecified if the presentation is to be complete. Here completeness could mean that a sentence is grammatically correct or that a picture represents a physically possible scene, though these constraints and freedoms are different from language to language and from picture style to picture style. Figure 18.2 illustrates these points.

| Utterance | Example of constraints | Example of freedoms |
|---|---|---|
| Language:<br><br>He is speaking to her. | there is no apparent disagreement bet-ween the persons | "speaking" action may be taking place on the phone or in person |
| Presentational picture: | • type of clothing<br><br>• approximate distance between the speakers | • which language is being spoken<br><br>• tone of voice |

**Figure 18.2:** Constraints and freedoms of language and presentational pictures

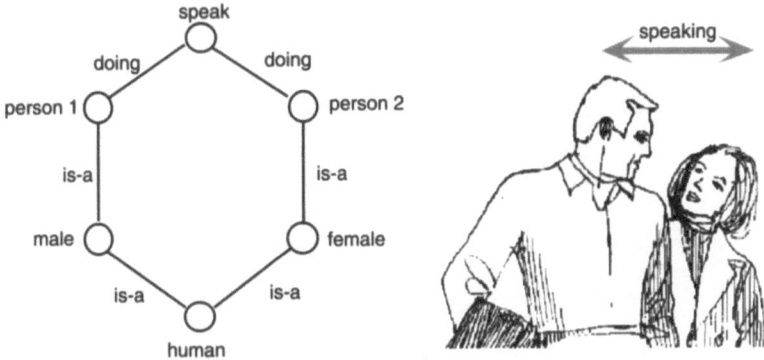

**Figure 18.3:** Two abstract-graphical pictures for the utterance of Figure 18.2

In general, abstract-graphical pictures can span the spectrum of constraints and freedoms between language and pictures. On the one extreme, an abstract-graphical picture can, for example, visualize a semantic network describing the utterance (Figure 18.3 left) (see for example Barr and Feigenbaum 1981); on the other hand, it can be a presentational picture, for example with a small amount of additional information which itself may or may not be redundant (Figure 18.3 right). Here the constraints and freedoms either of presentational pictures or of language apply, depending on the visualization chosen.

For this reason, there is only a basis for comparing pictures and language in the case of presentational pictures. Some of the deficits of such pictures can be made up for in some cases, for example by adding symbols or even adding a linguistic caption. We mention some of the advantages and disadvantages of pictures as compared to language in the following sections, paying particular attention to the special usage of these kinds of communication in human-computer interaction.

### 18.1.1 Disadvantages of Presentational Pictures Compared to Language

* *The author of a picture has difficulty referring to him- or herself.*
  This is a very important characteristic of pictures. The first person singular ("I") in a text refers to the author of the text insofar as it is not contained within quotation marks. The producer of a picture, on the other hand, has no means of drawing him- or herself in the picture. It is an unwritten law that a picture represents the opinion and view of its producer, who implicitly expresses the notion "This is how I see the subject matter" (see Weidenmann 1988). Schneider confirms this when he says "The reproduction excludes the first person" (see Schneider 1984). M.C. Escher picked up on this notion in his sketch of two hands drawing themselves, see Figure 18.4.

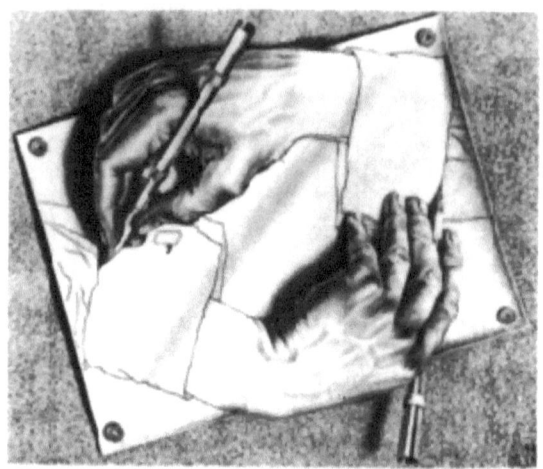

**Figure 18.4:** M.C. Escher's "Drawing Hands"

In a sense, this disadvantage can become an advantage for some dialogue systems. Whereas it is often considered somewhat poor style for a computer to refer to itself in the first person during a dialogue, this possibility does not even arise when the computer shows the user a presentational picture.

- *A presentational picture is neither true nor false.*

Pictures do not have the power to represent the negation of a fact. They can only say: "It is this way" or "It was like that". An assertion may be true or false, but a presentational picture does not consist of a single assertion (indeed, it can express many different, perhaps even contradictory assertions). Hence a presentational picture cannot be assigned the value true or false.

This implies that it would not make sense to store presentational pictures like facts in a Prolog database. Instead, if logical values must be extracted from a presentational picture, geometric primitives can be applied to its internal representation, which in turn results in a Boolean value.

- *Presentational pictures are studied less sequentially than texts.*

A text is usually studied from front to back, even when just scanning it. A reader who studies a text in a non-linear fashion will at least be aware of the fact that the order of perception is not as intended by the author. In a picture, on the other hand, the artist can only attempt to influence the way the picture is perceived by the viewer. In learning materials about painting and drawing, the students will find directions on how to organize objects in a picture to structure and direct the viewer's attention (see Astin et al. 1981). Psychologists studying advertising have determined typical eye movements that an untrained viewer will perform unconsciously (see Bernhard 1978).

- *Language is produced more directly and more quickly by a speaker than presentational pictures by an artist.*

  The physiology of humans allow us to produce language directly. To produce presentational pictures, prepared media, such as a pencil and a sheet of paper, are necessary. The result is that such pictures cannot be used as dynamically as language. However, with the advent of better user interfaces for drawing programs, this deficit may be overcome.

  In the context of human-computer interaction, this restricts users' input possibilities. They can make changes in pictures, but this entails a time-consuming dialogue.

- *Meta-information is difficult to communicate in a presentational picture.*

  A well-structured text contains information as to the goals of the text, its form, and its conclusions. Such information is very difficult to encode in a presentational picture, or even in a sequence of such pictures. Structural information, such as the description of the chapters in this book (Section 1.5), forms a culturally accepted and even necessary part of the text. Some books, such as Law and Kelton (1991), point out at the beginning of each chapter which sections are necessary for a first reading (Figure 18.5).

---

Recommended parts for a first reading: 3.1 through 3.3

---

**Figure 18.5:** Example of meta-information in texts (Law and Kelton 1991)

Attempts to include such information in presentational pictures would be disruptive at best.

- *Verbs are awkward to express in presentational pictures.*

  In general, presentational pictures lack an equivalent to the verb in a language. The inherent problem that a presentational picture represents a snapshot, whereas a sentence can describe a time span, can be bridged in a number of ways. For example, to indicate movement, symbols can be added to the presentational picture, making it into an abstract-graphical picture (see also Feiner 1987, Seligmann 1993). Figure 18.6 illustrates three ways of indicating movement:

i)   adding symbols,

ii)  superimposing several presentational pictures one on top of the other, and

iii) producing a sequence of presentational pictures.

For many applications, such as technical handbooks, these techniques are definitely satisfactory (see also Figure 15.24).

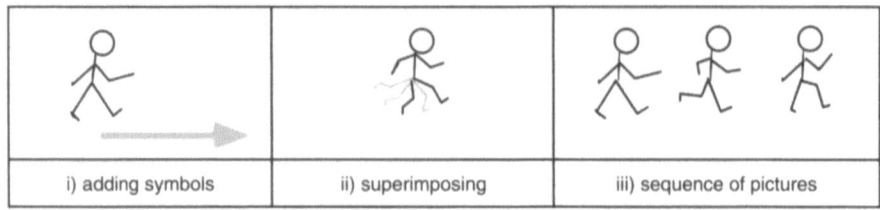

| i) adding symbols | ii) superimposing | iii) sequence of pictures |

**Figure 18.6:** Indicating movement in a picture

### 18.1.2  Advantages of Presentational Pictures over Language

In some ways, presentational pictures are much superior to language. Indeed, each of the above-mentioned points cited drawbacks of presentational pictures, can be seen as plus points in a different context. For example, the fact that an artist has great difficulties referring to himself in a picture means that he does not have to do so and cannot be forced to.

In general, some of the important advantages of presentational pictures over language are:

- *Presentational pictures are good for communicating the visible.*
  It is not a coincidence that tourists typically have a camera with them, but not a tape-recorder. This is because of the iconicity of pictures. Language as a description of visual facts is not unique, since to define a visible scene there are an infinite number of linguistic descriptions.
  In the context of dialogue systems, verbalizations of physical phenomena tend to be clumsy and difficult to produce.

- *2D or even 3D pattern recognition can be invoked on the part of the viewer of a presentational picture.*
  The human eye can recognize a great many patterns in 2D presentations with a higher degree of accuracy than any computer algorithm known today. This ability is harnessed in pictures, but not in language. On another level of granularity, the skilled layout of a text can help guide the reader, though in this case the reader treats the image of the layout as a presentational picture, rather than a language composed of words.

- *Presentational pictures are good for communicating structural information.*
  This point is a kind of corollary to the previous one. Presentational pictures tend to illustrate very well relationships between components of a structure, since viewers can use their pattern recognition capabilities. Gestalt psychology investigates the rules for human perception of object structures. Examples of gestalt rules are the law of proximity (Figure 18.7a), the law of good continuation (Figure 18.7b), and the law of virtual lines and subjective contours (Figure 18.7c).

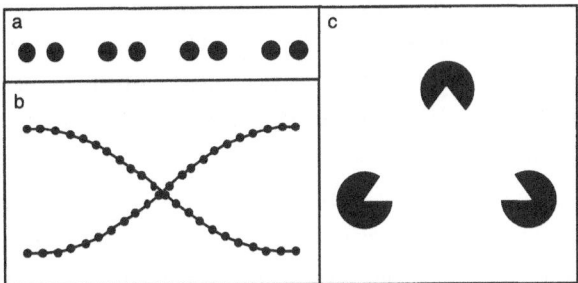

**Figure 18.7:** Examples for gestalt rules

- *Pictures are good at eliciting emotions quickly.*
  The direct and complex perception of pictures facilitates involvement of the observer. But not only the objects in the picture elicit emotions; the colors, lines, and light effects can also influence them, as we saw in Chapter 14. Language can involve the reader emotionally, too, but not so quickly (see Weidenmann 1988). This is particularly true for pictures in immersive systems (recall the feeling of fear created in subjects by Usoh and Slater, discussed in Section 17.3.3).

### 18.1.3 Common Strengths of Presentational Pictures and Language

In a variety of situations, presentational pictures tend to be just as good as language for communicating certain kinds of information. Among these are:

- *Answers to "who", "where", and "how" questions*
  Answers to such questions can typically be given very well with an appropriate presentational picture. The viewer must be familiar with the context of the picture, but this restriction applies analogously to language, where the vocabulary and the names of the persons, places, or objects must be known for the communication to be successful. In teaching materials especially, pictures are an important medium. It is often the case that a pupil is acquainted with physical objects being discussed but not with their names. In a high school power mechanics class, for example, a motor can be illustrated along with the vocabulary for working with it (recall Section 7.3).

- *Expressing metaphors*
  Both language and pictures are good at expressing an idea using different objects from the ones actually being referred to. This is commonly exploited for the presentational pictures in cartoons, where analogies are usually easy to see, even for an untrained eye. Language metaphors tend to be more explicit, such as in the sentence "He works *like a horse*" or "He's a great bear of a man".

- *Directing the attention of the viewer or reader/listener*

  Both in presentational pictures and language, the author has techniques at his or her disposal for directing the attention of the viewer to certain parts of the presentation. For
  example, items placed early on in a written sentence tend to receive more attention,
  whereas intonation can be used to highlight certain parts of a spoken sentence. Psychologists studying advertising have determined certain positions in a representation that
  are more readily perceived by viewers than others. Colors and lighting effects can also
  be used to advantage in influencing a viewer's perception or representation.

- *Portraying interrelationships between objects*

  Pictures can be used to bind symbols or objects together in groups, for example by
  representing them physically close to one another. Similarly, relationships between
  objects can be described in a text. Conjunctions of ideas can readily be represented
  both pictorially and linguistically.

## 18.2  Languages for Non-verbal Communication
### Does a Language for Pictures Exist?

In the literature, the term "language of pictures" is used very often (see for example
Weidenmann 1986). But it is not always clear what is meant by this term, since often
neither "picture" nor "language" are well defined.

For our present purpose, it suffices to consider language in a broad sense to be charac-
terised as a system of semantic elements and rules for combining them in a correct and
meaningful manner, forming a code in the semiotic sense. To find out whether a language of pictures exists analogous to natural language, we have to ask whether there is a
pictorial code that defines the production and perception of pictures.

Before addressing this question, let us briefly discuss Pasolini's theory about a language of cinema (see Pasolini 1979) as opposed to natural language. Pasolini postulated
the existence of the smallest components of the cinematographic language, the so-called
*cinems*. The coordination of cinems builds a picture, but this coordination is not a special
technique like a grammar. To create a picture, one needs only a stylistic system, not defined by linguistic rules. Pasolini argued against the existence of a language of pictures,
and concluded that pictures have a meaning beyond any prior definition of the meanings
of their basic components.

Eco (1991) develops this idea further when he characterizes contemporary art works.
For him, pieces of art justify their own individual code, which is contained in the work.
In semiotics, the *metalanguage* or *metacoordination* is the basis for individual codes. To

understand contemporary pictures one must find the rules for these individual codes, the metalanguage. If these are unknown, the artist must explain the work. For such art, every observer or interpreter has to find out the code of the work.

The languages of cinema and contemporary works of art make it clear that the iconic code of pictures is really a weak one (recall Chapter 4). The qualities of the iconic code of pictures, and the lack of exact basic components and of rules for combining them, imply that the term "language of pictures" makes little sense.

Examples of languages whose symbols are actually pictures can be found in various areas of application. To get a feeling for the issues involved, we cite several examples from just one area, dance. Figure 18.8 shows several notations that have been used in the last few centuries (see Tufte 1990). Nowadays computer animation is used as the language to express movement (Calvert et al. 1993; see Figure 18.9).

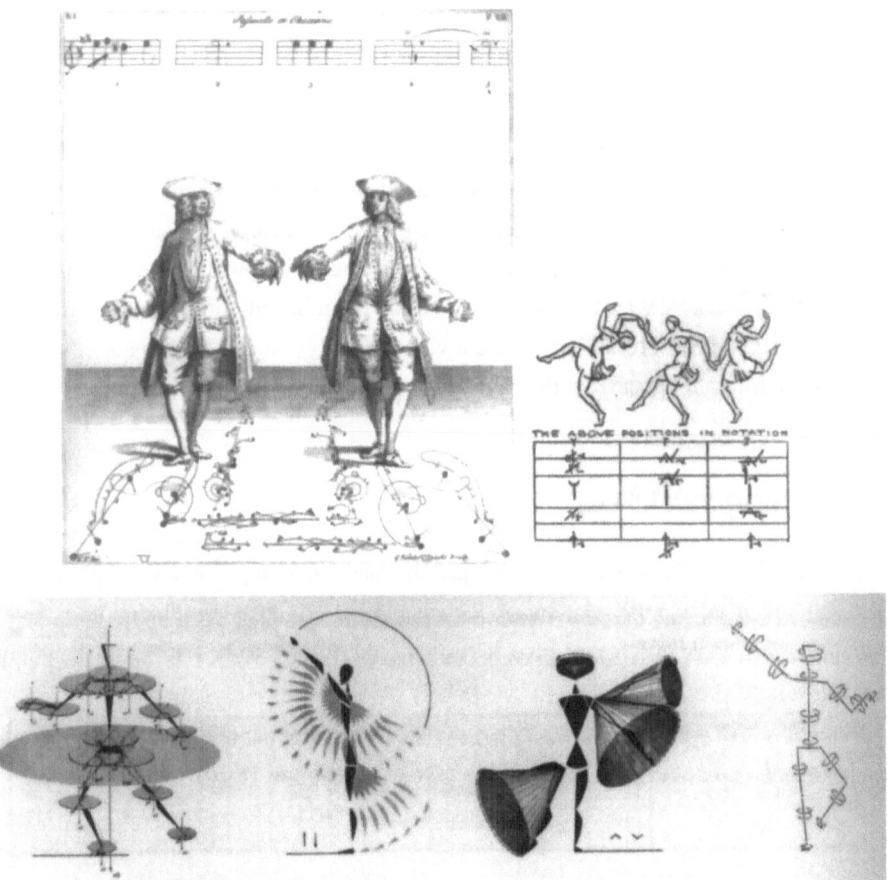

**Figure 18.8:** Examples of languages of pictures for dance (Tufte 1990)

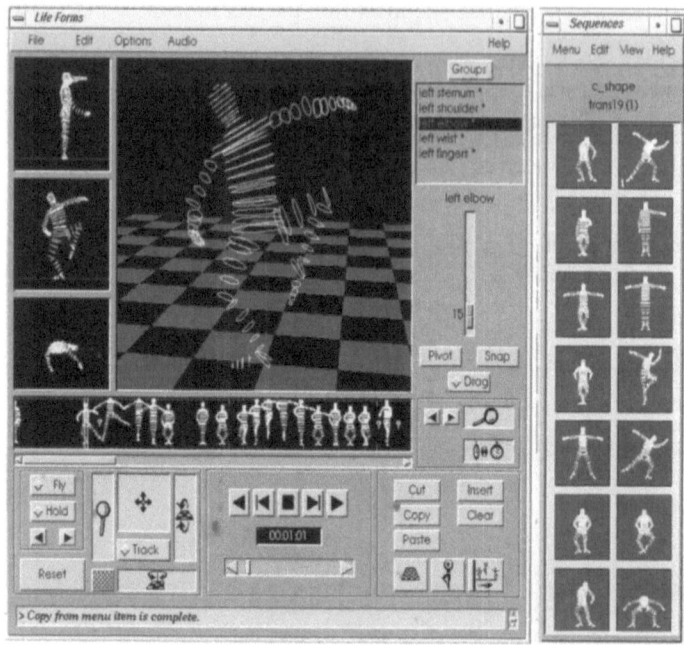

**Figure 18.9:** Computer animation used as a language of pictures for dance (Calvert et al. 1993)

Our conclusion is that there do exist languages of pictures, in our sense, but there is not *one* language. Expressions in the dance languages are pictures because of the visual nature of the individual elements. However, a language of pictures can be of a more modest nature, too. A well laid out text, such as is produced automatically by LATEX, gives the page the aura of a picture, and a viewer can get valuable clues about where to search for information just from the page layout and fonts.

## 18.3  Going Full Circle

Computer scientists in modern times are just the latest in a long chain of people to study pictures, language, and the relationship between them. To recall the long tradition and to put our current work into perspective, let us go to the Bible*, JOHN 1:1: "In the beginning was the word".

What does the Apostle John really mean? Wolfgang Goethe (1749–1832) studied this question and expressed his thoughts in his play *Faust* (Figure 18.10).

---

* King James translation

**Figure 18.10:** Speech from Goethe's *Faust* (Goethe 1958)

We provide two translations of this text (Table 18.1), both written for English-speaking stages, and leave a further interpretation of these thoughts to the reader as an exercise.

**Table 18.1:** Translations of the above excerpt from Goethe's *Faust*

| Translation by J. Prudhoe Goethe (1974), pp. 40-41: | Translation by R.D. MacDonald Goethe (1988), p. 51: |
|---|---|
| 'In the beginning was the word' he said. And there I stick! Where shall I look for aid? I cannot give the Word such adulation. So! We must make a new translation, And if my intuition is correct, 'In the beginning' he said 'Was Intellect'. Wait, though! You will need more time For thought before you phrase that opening line. Does Intellect inform creation's course? One should say 'In the beginning was the Force'. Yet even as I write it down I see I'll come to change that too, eventually. All at once the spirit meets my need— I'll put 'In the beginning was the deed'. | St. John: "In the Beginning was the Word." Can words be as powerful as here inferred? Words are by Intelligence designed; it must mean – in the beginning was the Mind. No! Mind or Thought are not the source of Life. In the beginning was the Force. But even as I say it, I'm aware it's not enough to leave the matter there. At last, the spirit gives me the exact translation: In the beginning was the Act! |

The final morsel of food for thought we present also stems from the Bible. We quote a translation by Juli Gudehus (1992) of the creation story, translated into a language with presentational pictures as its symbols. We present it not for its entertainment value, but as an exercise for the reader to classify the symbols used and appreciate the expressive power of the pictures.

In the beginning, God created the heaven and the earth.

And the earth was without form, and void;

and darkness was upon the face of the deep.

And the spirit of God moved upon the face of the waters.

And God said, let there be light:

And there was light.

And God saw the light, that it was good:

and God divided the light from the darkness.

And God called the light Day,

and the darkness he called Night.

And the evening and the morning were the first day.

And God said, Let there be a firmament in the midst of the waters,

And let it divide the waters from the waters.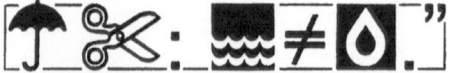

And it was so.

And God called the firmament Heaven.

And the evening and the morning were the second day.

And God said,

Let the waters under the heaven be gathered together into one place

and let the dry land appear;

and it was so

And God called the dry land Earth

and the gathering together of the waters he called Sea;

and God saw it was good.

And God said, Let the earth bring forth grass,

the herb yield seed,

and the fruit tree

yielding fruit after its kind,

with a seed in it.

And the earth brought forth grass and herbs and trees

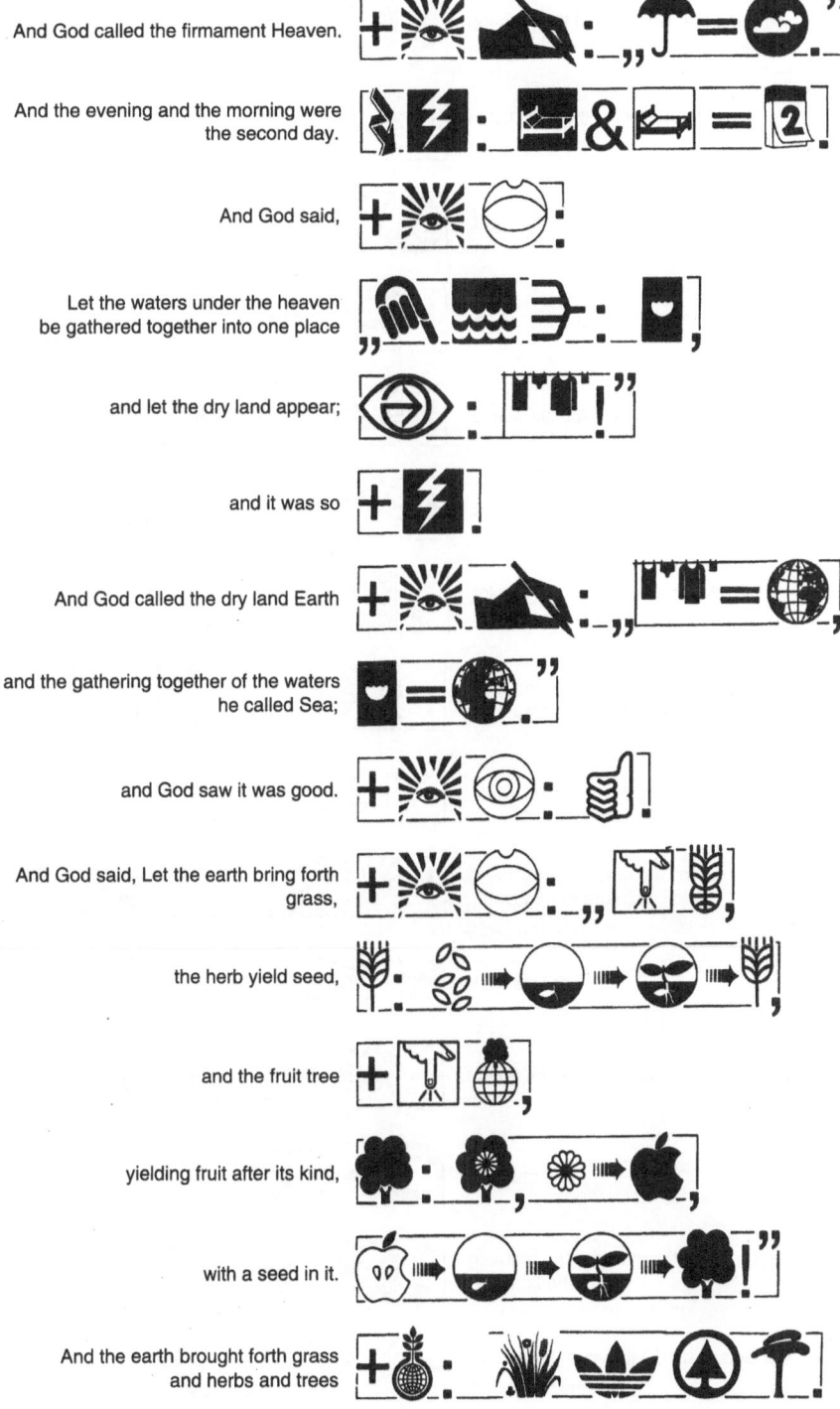

and the evening and the morning were the third day.

And God said, let there be lights in the heavens

to divide the day from the night.

And God created the sun and the moon,

he made the stars also.

And God saw, that it was good.

And the evening and morning were the fourth day.

And God said, let the waters bring forth abundantly the moving creatures

and fowl that may fly above the earth.

And God created every living creature that moveth,

each after his kind.

And God said, be fruitful

and multiply!

And the evening and morning were the fifth day.

And God said: Let the earth bring forth living creatures!

And God made the beasts of the earth,

And God saw that it was good.

And God said:  Let us create men

after our likeness.

And God created man

and woman.

And God blessed them

and God said to them:  Be fruitful

and multiply!

And God saw it was very good.

And the evening and the morning
were the sixth day.

And on the seventh day, God rested
from all his work.

And God blessed the seventh
day and sanctified it.

These are the generations of the heaven
and the earth when they were created.

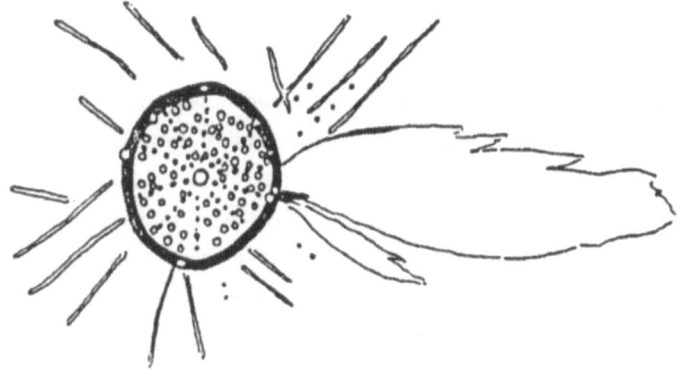

## Chapter
# 19

*Comet*
Burro Flats, California

# Quo vadis?

Generally we assume that pictures represent the *truth* in some sense. Even though we have already determined that a picture has no truth value *per se*, it is only natural to trust photos to reproduce scenes in the same way as our eyes perceive the real scene. The aura of photography gives pictures a great deal of credibility.

Compared to photos, printed text is often judged more critically with respect to its correctness. A statement in a text is regarded (by default) as the opinion of the author, unless otherwise stated. In contrast to pictures, a text can quote an authority to lend further credibility to a statement. This is done with quotation marks or indentation; no such techniques exist for purely presentational pictures, be they photos or photorealistic computer renderings. Indeed, a picture generally reproduces a single view, an image with one eye or camera position. Imagery is thus like a language restricted to the first person singular.

We shall briefly look into the social aspects of using pictures in interactive systems and end with some concluding remarks.

## 19.1 Falsification of Pictures

The falsification of statistical data – be it intentional or unintentional – is common practice, even though such falsification has been the topic of many studies. Nonetheless, it is shocking how reputable magazines routinely manipulate their readers; recall that of the 12 business graphics in an issue of DER SPIEGEL (recall Chapter 7), two were simply incorrect.

The falsification of pictures is not new, either. For example, the image of American soldiers missing in action (so-called MIAs) turn up from time to time to document their supposed presence in POW camps (Mitchell 1992), but they generally turn out to be falsifications. While the casual observer can easily be fooled, a close examination of details such as shadows cast by objects reveals inconsistencies that are obvious giveaways.

Whereas in the past, a photolab and considerable skill were needed to modify images, modern tools available on PCs make it easy for anyone to falsify images. Applications such as Corel Draw™ can be used for serious purposes, such as many of the illustrations in this book, but they can be used just as easily for ulterior motives. The widespread availability and ease of use of such tools give cause for concern.

**Figure 19.1:** Cover pictures of various tabloid magazines showing Stephanie of Monaco holding her newborn baby. Each of these images was taken prior to the birth of the child!

Figure 19.1 shows an example of the consequences of easy falsification of pictures. During the Fall of 1992, many German tabloid magazines discussed the birth of Louis Robert, the son of Princess Stephanie of Monaco. The child was born on November 26th, 1992, yet pictures of Stephanie and her child already began appearing on the covers of magazines in June 1992! Some of the covers showed real pictures of Stephanie, while others used similar-looking models. In all cases, the image of another child was merged with the supposed mother.

More serious magazines, like NATIONAL GEOGRAPHIC, include relevant information in the caption of a picture if it has been altered or computer-generated (Matthews 1993). However, this policy was adopted by the magazine only after the furor caused by the picture on the cover of a 1992 issue in which the Egyptian pyramids had been moved closer together to improve the esthetics.

While the pictures in Figure 19.1 clearly go too far, it is generally judged to be acceptable to touch up a photo, for example to remove facial blemishes of the person shown or to remove errors caused during electronic transmission of a document or scanning. However, the line between good and evil is thin and is difficult to draw.

To what extent is the use of image processing software for such purposes as these legally or ethically wrong? The Association for Computing Machinery (ACM), like some other professional organizations, provides a Code of Ethics to guide the conduct of its members. An examination of this code (Anderson et al. 1993) shows that it is in fact too weak to affect such harmful falsification. The relevant articles are:

1.2   **Avoid harm to others.**
      "Harm" implies injury or negative consequences ...
1.3   **Be honest and trustworthy.**
      ... The honest computing professional will not make deliberately false or deceptive
      claims about a system or systems design ...
1.7   **Respect the privacy of others.**
      ... It is the responsibility of professionals to maintain the privacy and integrity of data
      describing individuals. This includes taking precautions to ensure the accuracy of
      data ...

It is clearly against the code of ethics for an ACM member to construct any one of the cover pictures in Figure 19.1, because

- it can be argued that false information harms the individual it pertains to, and
- the pictorial data is changed to the point where it is no longer accurate.

However, the difficulty arises when computer professionals create tools which in themselves are meant for honest purposes, but are misused by certain individuals.

The Associated Press in the United States, the largest supplier of news photos around the world, has written a code of ethics to assure its customer newspapers that the pictures it provides have been altered only to improve the images' quality. The code stipulates that

"The content of a photograph will NEVER be changed or manipulated in any way" (Matthews 1993). This makes sense if one considers the "content" to be only that which is encoded explicitly in a picture. However, in the light of the model of information flow introduced in Chapter 5, *any* change in the image may change the content of the image, since the content is in part computed by the recipient (transputed information). Hence this code of ethics is also not strong enough to exclude subtle, even unintentional changes in the "content" of a picture and is thus of questionable value.

Legal issues have also arisen. For example in Germany, § 823 BGB[*] protects the rights of an individual. The first case involving pictures came up in 1958 in the so-called *Herrenritterurteil*: A picture showing an athlete who was well known at the time was used in an advertisement for a product that shed a poor light on the athlete. He had not given his consent for the use of the picture. The court ruled that the use of the picture of a person falls under the article mentioned and is therefore protected by law. Similarly, in the UK someone misusing a photograph of another person can be sued for libel. While in Germany the damage claims are still relatively small, in the UK the sums can easily be considerable (over 50,000 ECU).

In this context, a somewhat different but rather interesting line has been taken in a case which has arisen in Germany with respect to photographs of the "Wrapped Reichstag" (recall Figure 1.8). The artists responsible for the wrapping, Christo and Jeanne-Claude, have taken steps to hinder publication of such pictures without explicit permission – and presumably a fee. This is because the relevant German law permits photographs of works of art to be copied and published only if the work of art is permanently situated in a public place (taz[**] , January 13/14, 1996, p. 3). Since the wrapping was removed soon after being installed, the work of art is not considered to be permanent.

Should a computer scientist refuse to construct image processing software that is capable of falsifying such images as those of Stephanie above? Clearly this would be going too far. After all, the programmers of text-processing software cannot be held responsible for any lies written with their software, any more than the inventors of the alphabet. Indeed, Hine (1980) has commented that "while photographs may not lie, liars may photograph", and the same is at least as true for modeling and rendering. While the consequences for humanity are not nearly as dramatic as, for example, splitting the atom was in the 1940s, we must not forget that pictures are one of the important elements of our cultural heritage (Belting 1991). Falsification of pictures is a step toward destroying that heritage.

---

[*] *Bürgerliches Gesetzbuch* (German Civil Code)
[**] German daily newspaper, *die tageszeitung,* Postfach 610229, 10923 Berlin

## 19.2 The Grey Area Between Enhancement and Falsification

Every bit of free interpretation of a model during a rendering process can be construed as a falsification. Yet one of the fundamental tasks of computer science is to convert data from one representation into another. In such a process, some data may get lost, while other data must be added, particularly when the representations are radically different as pictures on the one hand and formal languages on the other.

A simple example illustrates the point. In computer graphics, polygons are often used to model an object – such as a basketball – in a scene. Such a model is only an approximation, but it is much easier to handle this than a more accurate mathematical function. Shading algorithms aim at simulating the more accurate model by interpolating around the crisp edges of the polygons. But is this not a falsification of the underlying model, carried out simply because it is too crude for comfort? With what right does the renderer approximate the model in the first place? In any case, this is an example of data in the original scene description being lost and the rendering process yielding new data.

Further examples are abundant in the literature. Gershon (1993) asserts that objects with shapes that are familiar to the visual system can create false impressions of data. Coggins (1993) points out that the hard-edged surfaces of discrete objects make beautiful visualizations, but hide the often arbitrary criteria used to form the surfaces. Edholm (1993) adds that a two-dimensional image of a three-dimensional object forces the eye to select the "right" interpretation from the many possible ones.

It is clear that the process of enabling the user to understand an image must be supported by the computer, even if the methods of support have little to do with the physics of the scene. This is where the gray area between enhancement and falsification becomes important. The case where our drawing techniques influence the viewer of computer-generated sketches is an even more pertinent example in this gray area. Coggins (1993) goes so far as to say that to convey a feeling for data to a user is so difficult that half-truths or even outright fabrications are necessary mechanisms to *sneak up* on the truth.

The work on producing sketches from models goes another step further, as there is an explicit attempt to influence the user in a number of different ways. For one, he or she is to get the impression that the image represents an object in an early stage in its design, which may or may not be correct. Next, techniques are used to attract and direct the attention of the user in a subtle manner. Is this still within the bounds of the reasonable, even though the user is being affected without his or her knowledge?

We feel that each design engineer must ask him- or herself this question every time a technique is programmed and used. We must keep reminding ourselves that there is no full objectivity, either in pictures or in language. The object of a dialogue should be to exchange data in the one or the other direction, or in both directions. The person programming the user interface is responsible for furthering this process and should use whatever means are at his or her disposal to achieve this goal.

## 19.3  The Bottom Line

We have studied many facets of the topic of integrating pictures of various kinds in interactive systems. While graphics already appear on computer screens in abundance today, we feel there is still a great deal of progress to be made in the thoughtful use of pictures for conveying information through pictures.

The results of our studies can be summarized in three points, which we consider to be of central importance for the successful integration of pictures into interactive systems. Our recommendations to engineers designing user interfaces are:

1. *There is more to pictures than just pixels and their underlying geometric models.*
   A picture generated by a computer should not be represented as a collection of pixels only. A variety of sources are available, such as rendering processes and origin of the underlying model. Care must be taken to collect and structure this data.
   The process of modeling should be extended to include such additional information. Viewers are an excellent source of information about a picture. A user's interpretation can often provide insights into the underlying model, which can be used to the advantage of both dialogue partners. The expressive resources for a dialogue about those insights should be available, as should facilities for the reconciliation of the different views of multiple users.

2. *Formulate pictures carefully.*
   Pictures must be held in high esteem if they are to succeed in conveying information to users. Engineers should be aware of the fact that pictures are not objective mirrors of reality, but also represent a point of view. This means not only that they entail a camera position but also that many other factors affect how the objects in the picture and the relationships between them are perceived by viewers. Pictures leave many questions open, and a great deal of information simply cannot be encoded in a presentational picture. Language, on the other hand, has other strengths and weaknesses with respect to its expressive power and ability to elicit reactions in listeners and readers.
   The strengths and weaknesses of pictures (compared with language) must be analyzed and the expressive possibilities of each one exploited in the application at hand. Pictures must be *formulated*, not just drawn.

3. *Elicit normalization demands carefully.*

Normalization demands can be elicited to achieve specific effects with respect to information flow. Design engineers should be aware of the intended normalization demands of an application, as well as be prepared to deal with the consequences, if their expectations are not met.

The expected normalization demands should form the basis of the dialogue design with respect to issues like the initiative and responsibility of the dialogue partners. In particular, high normalization demands result in cognitive activities on the part of the user, which are responsible for information being transputed from the computer to the user. The results of this information flow in one direction should allow for feedback in the other. The user should be given the means to transpute information back to the computer in response to pictures presented to him or her.

In this book, we have retracted some steps that have been taken in the direction of binding pictures more firmly in human-computer interaction and have explored some features of this process. Our approach has stayed within the realm of computer science, where representations of data and conversions between these form the fundamental repertoire of methods available for the study of the subject matter. We feel that pictures used in the sense of the recommendations outlined above can play a significant role in binding together users and computers for the more effective solution of important problems.

# List of Figures, Tables, and Credits

Figure 3.1:    Examples of "typical" pictures

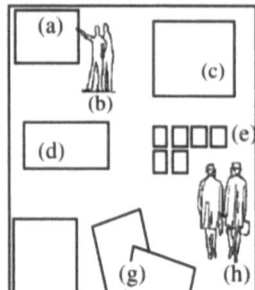

(a)    "The city of cupboards" Salvador Dali (taken from Schuster 1992, p. 61, © VG Bild-
       Kunst, Bonn 1995/lDemart pro arte B. Reprinted with permission)
(b)    Taken from Evans 1987, p. 87
(c)    Map of the campus of the University of Magdeburg
(d)    Comic (courtesy of Frank Godenschweger, © Frank Godenschweger 1996. Reprinted
       with permission)
(e)    Pictograms (taken from Stiebner and Urban 1988, p. 316, © Schweizerische
       Bundesbahn 1988. Reprinted with permission)
(f)    Lily Lacey (adapted from Heaton 1986, p. 24, © Longman Group Ltd. 1986. Reprinted
       with permission)
(g)    Self-made holiday photos
(h)    Taken from Evans 1987, p. 126

Figure 3.2:    Presentational pictures of a real object ((b) is taken from Ching 1985, p. 113, © Van
               Nostrand Reinhold 1985; (c) © Kreuter Foto Kalender 1990. Reprinted with permission)
Figure 3.3:    Virtual reality snapshot (courtesy of Matthias Kunze and Heiko Dorwarth, © Matthias Kunze
               and Heiko Dorwarth 1995. Reprinted with permission)
Figure 3.4:    Graphical symbols
Figure 3.5:    Vorticity in the North Atlantic (taken from Earnshaw and Wiseman 1992, p. 23, © Springer-
               Verlag 1990. Reprinted with permission)
Figure 3.6:    Different user icons appearing in the literature

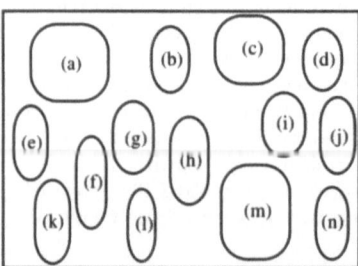

(a)    Taken from Charles P. Pfleeger, Security in Computing, © 1989, p. 133. Reprinted by
       permission of Prentice Hall, Upper Saddle River, New Jersey
(b)    Taken from Redmiles (1992), p. 25, © David F. Redmiles 1992. Reprinted with
       permission
(c)    Taken from Fehrle (1993), p. 92, © Springer-Verlag 1992. Reprinted with permission
(d)    Taken from Fehrle, Strothotte, and Szardenings (1990), p. 29, © Springer-Verlag 1992.
       Reprinted with permission

# List of Petroglyphs

# Bibliography

Alesandrini K.L. (1987): Computer graphics in learning and instruction. In: H.A. Houghton, D.M. Willows (eds.), *The psychology of illustration.* Volume 2: *Instructional issues*, Springer-Verlag, Berlin, pp. 159–188.

Ali A.T., Dagless E.L. (1992): Alternative practical methods for moving object detection, *Proc. 4th International Conference on Image Processing and its Applications*, Publication No. 354, Maastricht

Anderson J.R. (1989): *Cognitive psychology and its implications,* 2nd edition, W.H. Freeman and Company, New York, NY

Anderson R.E., Johnson D.G., Gotterbarn D., Perrolle J. (1993): Using the ACM code of ethics in decision making, *Communications of the ACM 36* (2), February, pp. 98–107

André E. (1995): *Ein planbasierter Ansatz zur Generierung multimedialer Präsentationen.* PhD Thesis, Technical Faculty, University of the Saarland, Saarbrücken

Appel A. (1968): Some techiques for shading machine renderings of solids, *Proc. SICC*, AFIPS Press, Reston, VA, pp. 37–45

Arend U., Muthig K.P., Wandmacher J. (1986): *Evidence for global feature superiority in menu selection by icons*, Technical Report, Department of Psychology, Technical University of Darmstadt

Arnheim R. (1966): *Toward a psychology of art*, University of California Press, Berkeley, CA

Arnheim R. (1969): *Visual thinking*, University of California Press, Berkeley, CA

Arnheim R. (1974): *Art and visual perception: A psychology of the creative eye*, University of California Press, Berkeley, CA

Arnheim R. (1978): *Kunst und Sehen*, Walter de Gruyter, Berlin

Astin D., Daniels A., Liddle B., Marshall S. (1981): *Learn to paint & draw*, Victoria House Publishing, London

Atherton P.R. (1981): A method of interactive visualisation of CAD surface models on a colour video display, *Computer Graphics 15* (3), pp. 279–287

Atkinson M.D., Sack J.-R., Santoro N., Strothotte T. (1986): MinMax heaps and generalized priority queues, *Communications of the ACM 29* (10), October, pp. 996–1000

Atkinson R.C., Shiffrin R.M. (1968): Human memory: A proposed system and its control processes. In: K.W. Spence, J.T. Spence (eds.), *The psychology of learning and motivation: Advances in research and theory 2*, Academic Press, London, pp. 89–195

Baer H.-W. (ed.) (1981): *Biologie: Anatomie, Physiologie und Hygiene des Menschen*, Volk und Wissen Volkseigener Verlag, Berlin

Baird H.S., Bunke H., Yamamoto K. (eds.) (1992): *Structured document image analysis*, Springer-Verlag, Berlin

Ballard D.H., Brown C.M. (1982): *Computer vision*, Prentice-Hall, Englewood Cliffs, NJ

Barnes A.C. (1993): *Great french paintings from the Barnes foundation*, Alfred A. Knopf, New York, NY, in association with Lincoln University Press, National Gallery of Art Edition

Barr A., Feigenbaum E.A. (eds.) (1981): *Handbook of artificial intelligence*, William Kaufmann, Los Altos, CA

Barthes R. (1964): Eléments de sémiologie, *Communications 4*, pp. 91–135

Bartlett F.C. (1932): *Remembering*, Cambridge University Press, Cambridge

Bartram L. Ovans R., Dill J., Dyck M., Ho A., Havens W.S. (1994): Contextual assistance in user interfaces to complex, time-critical systems: The intelligent zoom, *Proc. Graphics Interface '94*, May, Banff, pp. 216–224

Baudrillard J. (1991): Der Feind ist verschwunden, Interview in *DER SPIEGEL 6*, pp. 200–201

Belting H. (1991): *Bild und Kunst. Eine Geschichte des Bildes vor dem Zeitalter der Kunst*, 2nd edition, Verlag C. H. Beck, Munich

Berlyne D.E. (1969): *Conflict, arousal and curiosity*, McGraw-Hill, New York, NY

Bernhard U. (1978): *Blickverhalten und Gedächtnisleistung beim visuellen Werbekontakt unter Berücksichtigung von Plazierungseinflüssen*, Haag & Herchen, Frankfurt a.M.

Bernhauser J. (1979): *Wandbilder im Anschauungsunterricht. Studien zur Theorie und Praxis der Medien in der Volksschule des 19. Jahrhunderts*, Lang Verlag, Frankfurt a.M.

Bewley W.L., Roberts T.L., Schroit D., Verplank W.L. (1983): Human factors testing in the design of Xerox's "Star" office workstation, *Proc. CHI '83, Human Factors in Computing Systems*, New York, NY, pp. 72–77

Böcke D., Strothotte T. (1988): Technical diagrams in knowledge-based systems, *Proc. 8ème Journées Internationales sur les Systèmes Experts et leurs Applications*, Avignon, France, June, Volume 1, pp. 79–93

Boehm G. (ed.) (1994): *Was ist ein Bild?* Wilhelm Fink Verlag, Munich

Bouatouch K., Bouville C. (eds.) (1992): *Photorealism in computer graphics*, Springer-Verlag, Berlin

Bouknight W.J., Kelley K. (1970): An algorithm for producing half-tone computer graphics presentations with shadows and movable light sources, *Proc. SICC*, AFIPS Press, Reston, VA, pp. 1–10

Bove T., Rhodes C., Thomas W. (1986): *The art of desktop publishing*, Bantam Books, New York, NY

Bower G., Karlin M., Dueck A. (1975): Comprehension and memory for pictures, *Memory & Cognition 3*, pp. 216–220

Brander S., Kompa A., Peltzer U. (1989): *Denken und Problemlösen. Einführung in die kognitive Psychologie*, Westdeutscher Verlag, Opladen

Braun G. (1993): *Grundlagen der visuellen Kommunikation*, Bruckmann, Munich

Brooks F.P. Jr., Ouh-Young M., Batter J.J., Kilpatrick P.J. (1990) : Project GROPE – Haptic displays for scientific visualization, *Computer Graphics 24* (2), April, pp. 177–185

Brown D.I. (1978): Dual task methods of assessing workload, *Ergonomics 21* (3), pp. 221–224

Brown G., Yule G. (1983): *Discourse analysis*, Cambridge University Press, Cambridge

Brunner D.T., Earle N.J., Henriksen J.O. (1991): Proof animation: The general purpose animator. In: B.L. Nelson, W.D. Kelton, G.M. Clark (eds.), *Proc. 1991 Winter Simulation Conference*, pp. 81–85

Brügelmann H., Balhorn H. (eds.) (1990): *Das Gehirn, sein Alfabet und andere Geschichten*, Faude Verlag, Constance

Bryson S. (1992): *Virtual reality*, ACM Siggraph '92 Course No. 9 Notes

Buhr R.J.A. (1984): *System design with Ada*, Prentice-Hall, Englewood Cliffs, NJ

Buhr R.J.A. (1990): *Practical visual techniques in system design*, Prentice-Hall, Englewood Cliffs, NJ

Burger P., Gillies D. (1989): *Interactive computer graphics*, Addison-Wesley, Wokingham, UK

Burton E. (1995): Thoughtful drawings: A computational model of the cognitive nature of childrens' drawings, *Eurographics '95*, Maastricht, September, pp. 159–170

Calvert T.W., Bruderlin A., Mah S., Schiphorst T., Welman C. (1993): The evolution of an interface for choreographers, *Proc. INTERCHI '93, Human Factors in Computing Systems*, Amsterdam, April, pp. 115–122

Carrie A. (1988): *Simulation of manufacturing systems*, John Wiley & Sons, Chichester, UK

Carrol J.M. (1980): *Toward a structural psychology of cinema*, Mouton Publishers, The Hague

Carroll J.M., Mack R.L. (1985): Metaphor, computing systems, and active learning, *International Journal of Man-Machine Studies 22*, pp. 111–119

Chang D.-W., Unger D. (1993): Animation: From cartoons to the user interface, *Proc. ACM Conference on User Interface Software Technology*, pp. 45–55

Chang S.-K. (1989): *Principles of pictoral information systems design*, Prentice-Hall, Englewood Cliffs, NJ

Ching F. (1985): *Architectural graphics*, 2nd edition, Van Nostrand Reinhold, New York, NY

Coggins J.M. (1993): Contribution in Gershon N.D., Coggins J.M., Edholm P.R., Globus A., Ramachandran V.S. (1993), How to lie and confuse with visualization, *Computer Graphics, Proc. SIGGRAPH '93*, pp. 387–388

Copi I.M. (1958): Objects, properties and relations in the tractatus, *Mind 67*, pp. 145–165

Cox S. (1987): Interactive graphics in GPSS/PC, *Simulation 49* (3), pp. 117–122

Daitz E. (1953): The picture theory of meaning, *Mind 62*, pp. 184–201

Dale E. (1946): *Audio-visual methods in teaching*, 2nd edition 1954, 3rd edition 1969, Dryden Press, New York, NY

Damnjanovic L., Duce D., Robinson S. (1993): *GKS-9x: Some implementation considerations*, Technical Report ERCIM-93-R017, Rutherford Appleton Laboratory, Chilton, Didcot, Oxon, UK

Deering M. (1992): High resolution virtual reality, *Computer Graphics 26* (2), pp. 195–202

Dilts R. Grinder J., Bandler R., DeLozier J., Cameran-Bandler L. (1979): *Neuro-linguistic programming I*, Meta Publications, Cupertino, CA

DIN 66261: *Deutsche Norm. Sinnbilder für Struktogramme nach Nassi-Shneiderman*, November, 1985, Beuth Verlag

Dooley D., Cohen M.F. (1990): Automatic illustration of 3D geometric models: Lines, *Computer Graphics 24* (2), pp. 77–82

Drevna D.R., Kasales C.J. (1994): Introduction to Arena™. In: J.D. Tew, S. Manivannan, D.A. Sadowski, and A.F. Seila (eds.), *Proc. 1994 Winter Simulation Conference*, pp. 431–436

Dreyfus H. (1985): From micro-worlds to knowledge representation – AI at an impasse. In: R. Brachman, H. Levesque (eds.), *Readings in knowledge representation*, Morgan Kaufmann, Los Altos, CA

Duden (1977): *Bildwörterbuch der deutschen Sprache*, Volume 3, Bibliographisches Institut, Mannheim

Dwyer F.M. (1972): *A guide to improving visualized instruction*, State College, Pennsylvania State University, University Park, PA

Earle N.J., Henriksen J.O. (1995): Power and performance of Proof animation. In: C. Alexopoulous, K. Kang, W.R. Lilegdon, D. Goldsman (eds.), *Proc. 1995 Winter Simulation Conference*, Arlington, VA, pp. 775–780

Earnshaw R.A., Gigante M.A., Jones H. (1993): *Virtual reality systems*, Academic Press, London

Earnshaw R.A., Wiseman N. (1992): *An introductory guide to scientific visualization*, Springer-Verlag, Berlin

Easterby R.S., Zwaga H.J.G. (1976): Evaluation of public information symbols, *International Organization for Standardization Tests, Report No. 60*, Applied Psychology Department, University of Aston, Birmingham, UK

Eco U. (1972): *Einführung in die Semiotik*, Fink, Munich

Eco U. (1991): *The limits of interpretation*, Indiana University Press, Bloomington, IN

Edelmann W. (1986): *Lernpsychologie*, Urban & Schwarzenberg Psychologie Verlags Union, Munich

Edholm P.R. (1993): Contribution in Gershon N.D., Coggins J.M., Edholm P.R., Globus A., Ramachandran V.S. (1993), How to lie and confuse with visualization, *Computer Graphics, Proc. SIGGRAPH '93*, pp. 387–388

Edman P.K. (1992): *Tactile graphics*, American Foundation for the Blind, New York, NY

Emhardt J. (1995): *Agentenunterstützte Erkundung von virtuellen Welten*, PhD Thesis, Faculty of Mathematics and Computer Science, Free University of Berlin

Emhardt J., Strothotte T. (1992): Hyper-Rendering, *Proc. Graphics Interface '92*, Vancouver, May, pp. 37–42

Emhardt J., Semmler J., Strothotte T. (1993): Hyper-navigation in virtual buildings, *Proc. IEEE Virtual Reality Annual International Symposium*, Seattle, WA, September, pp. 342–248

Emiliani P.L. (1993): Graphical user interfaces for blind people, *Proc. ECART 2*, Stockholm, pp. 2.2

Erke H. (1975): *Psychologische Grundlagen der visuellen Kommunikation*, Technical University of Braunschweig, Department of Applied Psychology

Erpel F. (1989): *Vincent van Gogh. Lebensbilder Lebenszeichen*, Henschel Verlag, Berlin

Evans L. (1987): *Bildvorlagen-Atlas*, Bauverlag, Wiesbaden

Fehrle T. (1993): Empirische Evaluation von Benutzungsschnittstellen. In: H.-D. Böcker, W. Glatthaar, T. Strothotte (eds.), *Mensch-Computer-Kommunikation. Benutzergerechte Systeme auf dem Weg in die Praxis*, Springer-Verlag, Berlin, pp. 91–99

Fehrle T., Strothotte T., Szardenings M. (1990): Generating pictorial presentations for advice-giving dialog systems. In: P. Gorny, M.J. Tauber (eds.), *Visualization in human-computer interaction*, Lecture Notes in Computer Science 439, Springer-Verlag, Berlin, pp. 27–36

Feiner S.K. (1987): *Computer generation of pictorial explanations*, PhD Thesis, Department of Computer Science, Brown University, Providence, RI

Feiner S.K., Macintyre B., Seligmann D.D. (1993): Knowledge-based augmented reality, *Communications of the ACM 36* (7), July, pp. 52–62

Feiner S.K. and Seligmann D.D. (1992): Cutaway and ghosting: satisfying visibility constraints in dynamic 3D illustrations, *The Visual Computer*, (8), pp. 292–302

Fellbaum K. (ed.) (1993): *Proc. Eurospeech*, Berlin

Fischer G. (1986): Menschengerechte Computersysteme – mehr als ein Schlagwort. In: G. Fischer, R. Gunzenhäuser (eds.), *Methoden und Werkzeuge zur Gestaltung benutzergerechter Computersysteme*, Walter de Gruyter, Berlin, pp. 17–44

Fischer G. (1993): Beyond human-computer interaction. In: H.-D. Boecker, W. Glatthaar, T. Strothotte (eds.), *Mensch-Computer-Kommunikation. Benutzergerechte Systeme auf dem Weg in die Praxis*, Springer-Verlag, Berlin, pp. 274–287

Fischer G., Lemke A.C., Mastaglio T. (1990): Using critics to empower users, *Proc. CHI '90, Human Factors in Computing Systems*, New York, NY, pp. 337–347

Fischer G. Lemke A.C., Schwab Th. (1985): Knowledge-based help systems. In: L. Borman, B. Curtis (eds.), *Proc. CHI '85, Human Factors in Computing Systems*, New York, NY, pp. 161–167

Foley J., van Dam A., Feiner S.K., Hughes J. (1990): *Computer graphics, principles and practice*, 2nd edition, Addison-Wesley, Reading, MA

Frege G. (1973): *Schriften zur Logik*, Akademie-Verlag, Berlin

Frege G. (1986): *Funktion, Begriff, Bedeutung*, Vandenhoeck & Ruprecht, Göttingen

Friedman A. (1979): Framing pictures: The role of knowledge in automized encoding and memory for gist, *Journal of Experimental Psychology: General 108*, pp. 316–355

Frobenius L. (1993): *Kulturgeschichte Afrikas: Prolegomena zu einer historischen Gestaltlehre*, Peter Hammer, Wuppertal

Funt B.V. (1980): Problem-solving with diagrammatic representations, *Artificial Intelligence 13* (3), pp. 201–230

Furnas G.W. (1986): Generalized fisheye views, *Proc. CHI '86, Human Factors in Computing Systems*, pp. 16–23

Gass S.I. (1984): Documenting a computer-based model, *Interfaces 14* (3), pp. 84–93

Georg R. (1912): *Der Maschinenbau*, Verlag J.J.Arnd, Leipzig

Gershon N.D. (1993): Contribution in Gershon N.D., Coggins J.M., Edholm P.R., Globus A., Ramachandran V.S. (1993), How to lie and confuse with visualization, *Computer Graphics, Proc. SIGGRAPH '93*, pp. 387–388

Gibson J.J. (1971): The information available in pictures, *Leonardo 4*, pp. 27–35

Gibson J.J. (1982): *Wahrnehmung und Umwelt*, Urban & Schwarzenberg, Munich

Gill J. (1993): *Access to graphical interfaces by blind people*. Royal National Institute for the Blind, London

Gloor P.A. (1990): *Hypermedia Anwendungsentwicklung, Leitfäden der Angewandten Informatik*, Teubner-Verlag, Stuttgart

Goble J. (1991): Introduction to SIMFACTORY II.5. In: B.L. Nelson, W.D. Kelton, G.M. Clark (eds.), *Proc. 1991 Winter Simulation Conference*, Piscataway, NJ, pp. 77–80

Godenschweger F. (1993): *Varianten des Schattierens und des Schattenwurfs zur dreidimensionalen Darstellung von skizzenhaften Computerausgaben*. Diplomarbeit, Faculty of Computer Science, Technical University of Magdeburg

Goethe J.W. (1974): *Faust, the tragedy part one*, Translated by J. Prudhoe, Barnes & Noble, New York, NY

Goethe J.W. (1988): *Faust, a tragedy, parts one and two*, Translated by R.D. MacDonald, Oberon, Birmingham, AL

Goethe J.W. (1958): *Faust, Der Tragödie Erster Teil*, Verlag der Nation, Berlin

Goffman E. (1959): *Wir alle spielen Theater*, R. Piper, Munich

Gombrich E.H. (1967): *Kunst und Illusion*, Kiepenheuer & Witsch, Cologne

Gombrich E.H. (1969): *Art and illusion: a study in the psychology of pictorial representation*, Princeton University Press, Princeton, NJ

Goodman N. (1968): *Languages of art: an approach to a theory of symbols*, Hackett Publishing Co., Indianapolis, IN

Graf W. (1995): The constraint-based layout framework LayLab and its applications, *Electronic Proc. ACM Multimedia '95*, San Francisco, CA

Groß M. (1994): *Visual Computing*, Springer-Verlag, Berlin

Grünert H. (1982): *Geschichte der Urgesellschaft*, Deutscher Verlag der Wissenschaften, Berlin

Gudehus J. (1992): Die Schöpfungsgeschichte, *Die Zeit 1*, January 1, pp. 38–39

Günther F., Lehmann H. (1989): Discourse analysis for a legal expert system, *Computers and the Humanities*

Gunzenhäuser R. (1962): *Ästhetisches Maß und ästhetische Information. Einführung in die Theorie G.D. Birkhoffs und die Redundanztheorie ästhetischer Prozesse*, Stuttgart

Haber R.N. (1970): How we remember what we see, *Scientific American 222*, pp. 104–112

Haberäcker P. (1991): *Digitale Bildverarbeitung*, Carl Hanser, Munich

Haberli P. (1990): Paint by numbers: Abstract image representations, *Computer Graphics 24* (4), pp. 207–214

Habermas J. (1971): *Towards a rational society*, Beacon Press, Boston, MA

Hädrich G. (1994): *Tanzstunde: Das Welttanzprogramm leicht gelernt*, Falken Verlag, Niedernhausen

Haggerty M. (1991): Almost automatic computer painting, *IEEE Computer Graphics & Applications*, pp. 11–12

Handford M. (1987): *Where's Waldo?* Grolier, Canada

Heaton J.B. (1986): *Writing through pictures*, Longman Group, Harlow, UK

Heaton J.B. (1990): *Composition through pictures*, Longman Group, Harlow, UK

Hebb D.O. (1949): *The organization of behavior*, Wiley, New York, NY

Helbing R. (1995): *Filmische Gestaltungsmittel in der technischen Animation*, Diplomarbeit, Faculty of Computer Science, Otto-von-Guericke University of Magdeburg

Helbing R., Lorenz P. (1995): *Simulation and animation*, Tutorial EuroSim '95, Vienna

Helms C. (1994): *Sichtbeschreibungen für die Mensch-Computer Interaktion am Beispiel der Computersimulation*, PhD Thesis, Faculty of Computer Science, Otto-von-Guericke University of Magdeburg

Hemenway K. (1982): Psychological issues in the use of icons in command menus, *Proc. CHI '82, Human Factors in Computing Systems*, Gaithersburg, MD, pp. 20–24

Henry D., Furness T. (1993): Spatial perception in virtual environments: Evaluating an architectural application, *Proc. IEEE Virtual Reality Annual International Symposium*, Seattle, WA, September, pp. 33–40

Herczeg M. (1986): Modulare anwendungsneutrale Benutzerschnittstellen. In: G. Fischer, R. Gunzenhäuser (eds.), *Methoden und Werkzeuge zur Gestaltung benutzergerechter Computersysteme*, Walter de Gruyter, Berlin

Hemenway K. (1982): Psychological issues in the use of icons in command menus, *Proc. CHI '82, Human Factors in Computing Systems*, Gaithersburg, MD, pp. 20–24

Hetzger W. (1981): *Fidibus – kleines deutsches Wörterbuch 1/2*, Ernst Klett Verlag, Stuttgart

Hine L. (1980): Social photography. In: A. Trachtenberg (ed.), *Classical essays on photography*, Leete's Island Books, New Haven, CT, pp. 111

Hollocks B. (1992): A well-kept secret? Simulation in manufacturing industry reviewed, *OR INSIGHT 5* (4), October, pp. 12–17; see also *EUROSIM – Simulation News Europe 5*

Horton W. (1994): *The icon book. Visual symbols for computer systems and documentation*, John Wiley & Sons, New York, NY

Hoppe U., Kirchner H., Rüger M. (1990): Objektorientierte Modellierung von Bausteinen innerhalb der Simulatorentwicklungsumgebung Create!, F. Breitenecker, I. Troch, P. Kopacek (eds.), *Fortschritte in der Simulationstechnik 1*, Vieweg, Braunschweig, pp. 140–144

Houghton H.A., Willows D.M. (eds.) (1987): *The psychology of illustration*. Volume 2: *Instructional issues*, Springer-Verlag, Berlin

Howell W.C., Fuchs A.F. (1968): Population stereotype in code design, *Organizational Behaviour and Human Performance 3*, pp. 310–339

Hupka W. (1983): Wort und Bild. Die Illustration in einsprachigen französischen Wörterbüchern

Hübner W. (1990): *Entwurf Graphischer Benutzerschnittstellen*, Beiträge zur Graphischen Datenverarbeitung, Springer-Verlag, Berlin

Hudson T., Lee G. (1984): Function and symbolism in Chumash rock art, *Journal of New World Archaeology*, Vol. VI (3)

Hutchins E.L., Hollan J.D., Norman D.A. (1986): Direct manipulation interfaces. In: D.A. Norman, S.W. Draper (eds.), *User centered system design*, Lawrence Erlbaum, Hillsdale, NJ

IBM (1992): *Zeitschrift der IBM Deutschland GmbH*, June

IJCAI (1995): *Proc. International Joint Conference on Artificial Intelligence*, Montréal, August

Jackson P. (1990): *Introduction to expert systems*, Addison-Wesley, Reading, MA

Jacobs C.E., Finkelstein A., Salesin D.H. (1995): Fast multiresolution image query, *Computer Graphics, Proc. SIGGRAPH '95*, pp. 277–286

Jain A. (1989): *Fundamentals of digital image processing*, Prentice-Hall, Englewood Cliffs, NJ

Janson H.W., Janson D.J. (1987): *Malerei unserer Welt*, Vol. 2, DuMont Kunst Taschenbücher, Cologne

Jansson G. (1993): In what ways can the psychology of perception contribute to the development of rehabilitation technology? In: E. Ballabio, I. Placencia Porrero, R. Puig de la Bellacasa (eds.), *Studies in Health Technology and Interfaces 9*, IOS Press, Amsterdam, pp. 216–219

Jaroslavski L.P. (1990): *Einführung in die digitale Bildverarbeitung*, VEB Deutscher Verlag der Wissenschaften, Berlin

Jastrow J. (1900): Fact and fable in psychology, Houghton, Mifflin, and Co., Boston. Reprinted in Selected Bibliographies Reprint Series, Ayer Company Publishers, North Statford, 1977

Jones Sh. (1983): Stereotypy in pictograms of abstract concepts, *Ergonomics 26*, pp. 605–611

Jünemann R. (1989): *Materialfluß und Logistik*, Springer-Verlag, Berlin

Kahn K.M. (1979): *Creation of computer animation from story descriptions*, PhD thesis, AI Lab, Massachusetts Institute of Technology, Cambridge, MA

Kalasky D.R., Davis D.A. (1991): Computer animation with cinema. In: B.L. Nelson, W.D. Kelton, G.M. Clark (eds.), *Proc. 1991 Winter Simulation Conference*, pp. 122–127

Karp P., Feiner S.K. (1993): Automated presentation planning of animation using task decomposition with heuristic reasoning, *Proc. Graphics Interface '93*, Toronto, pp. 118–127

Kehnscherper G. (1983): *Hünengrab und Bannkreis*, Urania, Leipzig

Kirchner H., Helbing R. (1995): A scalable 3D animator with open interfaces. In: F. Breitenecker, I. Husinsky (eds.), *Proc. EuroSim '95*, Vienna, Session Software Tools and Products, pp. 65–68

Klaver P. (1990): *Das Motorrad und seine Technik*, Motorbuch Verlag, Stuttgart

Klinger H. (1991): Prozeßsimulation für die Aus- und Weiterbildung in der Automatisierung unter Einsatz neuer didaktischer Medien – Konzepte und Erfahrungen, *Proc. ASIM Tagung Simulation und Verstehen*, pp. 229–240

Klix F. (1980): *Information und Verhalten*, Deutscher Verlag der Wissenschaften, Berlin

Klix F. (1992): *Die Natur des Verstandes*, Hogrefe, Göttingen

Klöditz C. (1995): Sehen mit Multi-Resolution, *Proc. Integration von Bild, Modell und Text '95*, Otto-von-Guericke University of Magdeburg, March, pp. 91–102

Knowlton J.Q. (1966): On the definition of 'Picture', *AV Communication Review 14* (2), Summer 1966

Kobsa A., Wahlster W. (eds.) (1991): *User models in dialog systems*, Springer-Verlag, Berlin

Koffka K. (1935): *Principles of gestalt psychology*, Routledge & Kegan Paul, London

Korfhage R.R., Korfhage M.A. (1986): Criteria for iconic languages. In: S.-K. Chang, T. Ichikawa, P.A. Ligonenides (eds.), *Visual languages*, Plenum Press, New York, NY

Kosslyn S. (1980): *Image and mind*, Harvard University Press, Cambridge, MA

Krahl D. (1994): An Introduction to Extend™. In: J. D. Tew, S. Mannivannan, D.A. Sadowski, A. F. Seila (eds.), *Proc. 1994 Winter Simulation Conference*, Lake Buena Vista, FL, December, pp. 538–545

Krampen M. (1986): Geschichte und Struktur von Pictogrammsystemen. In: H. Espe (ed.), *Visuelle Kommunikation: Empirische Analyse*, Georg Ohms Verlag, Hildesheim

Kreutzer W. (1986): *System simulation: Programming styles and languages*, Addison-Wesley, Reading, MA

Kreutzer W. (1992): Model presentation and process visualization in Tim: A programming environment for model construction animation. In: V. Hinz, P. Lorenz, T. Strothotte (eds.), *Proc. 1st Workshop on Visualisation and Presentation of Models and Results of Simulation*, Otto-von-Guericke University of Magdeburg, March, pp. 91–100

Krömker D. (1992): *Visualisierungssysteme*, Springer-Verlag, Berlin

Krueger M. (1991): *Artificial reality II*, Addison-Wesley, Reading, MA

Kugas D. (1993): *Benutzerunterstützte Modellierung von Szenen auf der Basis gescannter Bilder*, Diplomarbeit, Faculty of Computer Science, Technical University of Magdeburg

Kuhlen R. (1990): Zum Stand pragmatischer Forschung in der Informationswissenschaft. In: J. Herget, R. Kuhlen (eds.), *Proc. 1st International Symposium on Information Science*, Konstanzer Schriften zur Informationswissenschaft Bd. 1, University of Constance, Germany, October, pp. 13–18

Kuhlen R. (1991): *Hypertext. Ein nichtlineares Medium zwischen Buch und Wissensbank*, Springer-Verlag, Berlin

Kunen S., Green D., Waterman D. (1979): Spread of encoding effects within the nonverbal visual domain, *Journal of Experimental Psychology: Human Learning and Development 5*, pp. 574–584

Kunkel K., Strothotte T. (1990): Visualizations and direct manipulation in user interfaces: Are we overdoing it? In: P. Gorny, M.J. Tauber (eds.), *Visualization in Human-Computer Interaction*, Lecture Notes in Computer Science 439, Springer-Verlag, Berlin, pp. 183–193

Kurlander D., Feiner S.K. (1992): Interactive constraint-based search and replace, *Proc. CHI '92, Human Factors in Computing Systems*, Monterey, CA, pp. 609–618

Kurze M., Petrie H., Morley S., Deconinck F., Strothotte T. (1995): New approaches for accessing different classes of graphics by blind people. In: I. Placencia Porrero, R. Puig de la Bellacasa (eds.), *The european context for assistive technology*, IOS Press, Amsterdam, pp. 268–271

Kurze M., Strothotte T., Kugas D. (1994): Tactile computer graphics, *Proc. Graphics Interface '94*, May, Banff, pp. 101–111

Lansdown J., Schofield S. (1995): Expressive rendering: A review of nonphotorealistic techniques, *Computer Graphics and Applications*, May, pp. 29–37

Larkin J.H., Simon H.A. (1987): Why a diagram is (sometimes) worth ten thousand words, *Cognitive Science 11*, pp 65–100

Law A.M., Kelton W.D. (1991): *Simulation modeling and analysis*, McGraw-Hill, New York, NY

Leeson M. (1981): *Systems analysis and design*, Science Research Associates, Chicago, IL

Leggett J., Williams G. (1984): An empirical investigation of voice as an input modality for computer programming, *International Journal of Man-Machine Studies 21* (6), pp. 493–520

Lichtner W. (1983): Computerunterstützte Verzerrung von Kartenbildern bei der Herstellung thematischer Karten, *Internationales Jahrbuch für Kartographie 23*, Kirchbaum Verlag, Bonn, pp. 83–96

Liljefors K. (1988): *Techniken zur dynamischen Erzeugung bildhafter Darstellungen in wissensbasierten Systemen*, Studienarbeit, Department of Computer Science, University of Stuttgart, August

Lorenz P. (1991): Simulation und Animation: Konvergenz oder Divergenz? In: R. Möller (ed.), *Proc. Workshop Sichtsysteme, Visualisierung in der Simulationstechnik*, Bremen, November, Springer-Verlag, Berlin, pp. 1–15

Loubertin C. (1992): *Steinzeitmenschen. Vom Nomaden zum Bauern*, Otto Maier, Ravensburg

MacDonald D.D. (1983): Natural language generation as a computational problem: An introduction, *Proc. International Joint Conference on Artificial Intelligence*, Karlsruhe

Magnenat-Thalmann N., Thalmann D. (1990): *Synthetic actors in computer-generated 3D films*, Springer-Verlag, Berlin

Mandler J., Ritchey G. (1977): Long-term memory for pictures, *Experimental psychology: Human learning and memory 3*, pp. 386–396

Maple (1985): *Maple user's guide*, Technical Report, University of Waterloo, ON

Marcus A. (1992): Graphic design for electronic documents and user interfaces, ACM Press, New York, NY

Märkisch A. (1973): *Konkordanz zu Goethes Werken*, Akademie-Verlag, Berlin

Matthews R. (1993): When seeing is not believing, *The New Scientist 1895* (16 October), pp. 13–15

McCloud S. (1993): *Understanding comics – The invisible art*, Kitchen Sink Press, Northampton, MA

McCorduck P. (1991): *Aaron's code: Meta-art, artificial intelligence, and the work of Harold Cohen*, W.H. Freeman and Co., New York, NY

McKeown K.R., Feiner S.K., Robin J., Seligmann D.D., Tanenblatt M. (1992): Generating cross-references for multimedia explanation, *Proc. AAAI-92*, San Diego, CA, July, pp. 9–16

Mehnert D., Fellbaum K. Hoffmann R. (eds.) (1993): *Elektronische Sprachsignalverarbeitung in der Rehabilitationstechnik, Studientexte zur Sprachkommunikation 10*, Gesellschaft für Signalverarbeitung und Mustererkennung, Dresden

Metzger W. (1953): *Gesetze des Sehens*, Kramer, Frankfurt a.M.

Miller G.A. (1956): The magical number seven, plus or minus two: Some limits on our capacity for processing information, *Psychological Review 63*, pp. 81–97

Miller R.A., Masarie F.E. (1990): The demise of the greek oracle model for medical diagnostic systems, *Methods of Information in Medicine 29*, pp. 1–2

Minsky M. (1975): A framework for representing knowledge. In: P.H. Winston (ed.): *The Psychology of Computer Vision*, McGraw-Hill, New York, NY, pp. 421–452

Minsky M., Ouh-Young M., Steele O., Brooks F.P. Jr., Behensky M. (1990): Feeling and seeing: Issues in force display, *Computer Graphics 24* (2), April, pp. 235–243

Mitchell W.J. (1992): *The reconfigured eye. Visual truth in the post-photographic era*, MIT Press, Cambridge, MA

Morris C. (1946): *Signs, language and behaviour*, Prentice-Hall, Englewood Cliffs, NJ

Morrison D.L., Green T.R.G., Shaw A.C., Payne S.J. (1984): Speech-controlled text-editing: Effects of input modality and of command structure, *International Journal of Man-Machine Studies 21* (1), pp. 49–63

Naß T. (1993): *Regeln für die Objektfluß-Diagnose in Materialflußsystemen*, Diplomarbeit, Faculty of Mechanical Engineering, Otto-von-Guericke University of Magdeburg

Naur P. (1982): Formalisation in program development, *BIT 22*, pp. 437–453

NDFCI (1980): *Noveau dictionnaire du français contemporain illustré*, Paris

Nelson T.O., Metzler J., Reed D.A. (1974): Role of details in long-term recognition of pictures and verbal descriptions, *Journal of Experimental Psychology 102* (1), pp. 184–186

New Encyclopedia Britannica (1991): *New Encyclopedia Britannica*, Vol. 8, Chicago, IL

Newell A., Simon H.A. (1972): *Human problem solving*, Prentice-Hall, Englewood Cliffs, NJ

Nielsen J. (1993): Noncommand user interfaces, *Communications of the ACM 36* (4), April, pp. 83–99

Noche B., Wenzel S. (1991): *Marktspiegel Simulationstechnik in Produktion und Logistik*, TÜV Rheinland, Cologne

Norman D.A. (1983): Some observations on mental models. In: A.L. Stevens, D. Gentner (eds.), *Mental models*, Lawrence Erlbaum, Hillsdale, NJ, pp. 7–14

Norman D.A. (1984): Stages and levels in human-machine interaction, *International Journal of Man-Machine Studies 21*, pp. 365–375

Norman V.B. (1992): AutoMod. In: J.J. Swain, D. Goldsman, R.C. Crain, J.R. Wilson (eds.), *Proc. 1992 Winter Simulation Conference*, Arlington, VA, pp. 328–331

Nyhuis A. (1994): Ein Trace in ISO-Normformat zur instrumentenunabhängigen Unterstützung objektbezogener Auswertungen. In: H. Graeßner, P. Lorenz, E. Blümel (eds.), *Proc. Simulation und Integration' 94*, Magdeburg, March, pp. 26–34

Oleson L.R., Doescher S.W., Holm T.M. (1991): Image brouse in the global land information system, *Proc. 1991 ACSM-ASPRS Annual Convention 3: Remote Sensing*, Baltimore, MD, pp. 294–30

Oppenheimer P.E.(1986): Real time design and animation of fractal plants and trees. D.C. Evans and R.J. Athay (eds.), *Computer Graphics, Proc. SIGGRAPH '86*, pp. 55–64

O'Reilly J.J, Ryan N.K (1992): Introduction to SLAM II and SLAMSYSTEM, J.J. Swain, D. Goldsman, R.C. Crain, J.R. Wilson (eds.), *Proc. 1992 Winter Simulation Conference*, Arlington, VA, pp. 352–356

Oxford Cyclopedic Concordance (undated): *The Oxford bible reader's dictionary and concordance*, Oxford University Press, London

Oxford/Duden Picture Dictionary (1989): *Oxford/Duden picture dictionary*, Oxford University Press, Oxford

Paivio A. (1971): *Imagery and verbal processes,* Holt, Rinehart & Winston, New York, NY

Parramón J.M. (1992): *Wie male ich Licht und Schatten*, Edition Michael Fischer, Stuttgart

Pasolini P. (1979): *Ketzererfahrung: Schriften zu Sprache, Literatur und Film*, Carl Hanser, Munich

Patterson A. (1992): *A field guide to rock art symbols of the greater southwest*, Johnson Printing Company, Boulder, CO

Patzig G. (1981): *Sprache und Logik*, 2nd edition, Vandenhoeck & Ruprecht, Göttingen

Pavlidis T. (1982): *Algorithms for graphics and image processing*, Computer Science Press, Rockville, MD

Pavlidis T., Van Wyk C.J. (1985): An automatic beautifier for drawings & illustrations, *Computer Graphics 19* (3), July, pp. 225–234

Pearson D., Hanna E., Martinez K. (1990): Computer-generated cartoons, *Images and understanding*, Cambridge University Press, Cambridge, pp. 46–60

Peeck J. (1987): The role of illustrations in processing and remembering illustrated text, D.M. Willows, H.A. Houghton (eds.), *The psychology of illustration*. Volume 1: *Basic research*, Springer-Verlag, Berlin, pp. 115–151

Pegden C.D., Shannon R.E., Sadowski R.P. (1990): *Introduction to simulation using SIMAN*, McGraw-Hill, New York, NY

Peirce C.S. (1935): *Collected papers*. In: C.H. Hartshorne, P. Weiss (eds.), Harvard University Press, Cambridge, MA

Pejtersen A.M., Goodstein L.P. (1988): *The book house: Modelling user's needs and search strategies as a basis for system design*, Technical Report Risø-M-2794, Risø National Laboratory, Denmark

Peschl M.F. (1990): *Cognitive modelling*, Deutscher Universitäts-Verlag, Wiesbaden

Petit Larousse (1971): *Petit Larousse*, Paris

Petit Robert (1985) . *Petit Robert*, Paris

Petrie H., Strothotte T., Weber G., Deconinck F. (1993): The design and evaluation of rehabilitative technology for blind people: The need for a multi-disciplinary approach. In: E. Ballabio, I. Placencia Porrero, R. Puig de la Bellacasa (eds.), *Studies in Health Technology and Interfaces 9*, IOS Press, Amsterdam, pp. 220–224

Pfleeger C.P. (1989): *Security in computing*, Prentice-Hall, Englewood Cliffs, NJ

Pflieger H. (1987): *Entwurf und Implementierung eines Diktatsystems für Pascal*, Diplomarbeit, Department of Computer Science, University of Stuttgart, January

Placencia Porrero I., Puig de la Bellacasa R. (eds.) (1995): *The European context for assistive technology*, IOS Press, Amsterdam

Poulin P. (1993): *Shading and inverse shading from direct illumination*, PhD Thesis, Department of Computer Science, University of British Columbia, Vancouver, BC

PONS (1992): *Bildwörterbuch*, Klett, Stuttgart

Preim B. (1994): *Umsetzung kommunikativer Absichten in computergenerierten Skizzen*, Diplomarbeit, Faculty of Computer Science, Otto-von-Guericke University of Magdeburg

Preim B., Strothotte T. (1995): Tuning rendered line-drawings, *3rd International Conference in Central Europe on Computer Graphics and Visualisation*, Plzen, February, Volume 2, pp. 227–237

Preim B., Ritter A., Strothotte T., Pohle T., Forsey D.R., Bartram L. (1995): Consistency of rendered images and their textual labels, *Proc. CompuGraphics '95*, December, Alvor, Portugal, pp. 201–210

Preininger R. (1993): *Präsentationen in virtuellen Räumen*, Diplomarbeit, Faculty of Computer Science, Technical University of Magdeburg

Preuss J. (1979): *Von der archäologischen Quelle zur historischen Aussage*, Akademie-Verlag, Berlin

Prusinkiewicz P., Lindenmayer A. (1990): *The algorithmic beauty of plants*, Springer-Verlag, Berlin

Raab A. (1992): *Documentation for the Prolog interpreter in Smalltalk-80*, Faculty of Computer Science, Technical University of Magdeburg

Raab A. (1993): *An object oriented modeler*, User's Reference Manual, Department of Computer Science, Free University of Berlin

Raab A. (1994): *Skizzenhafte Darstellung natürlicher Wuchsformen*, Diplomarbeit, Faculty of Computer Science, Otto-von-Guericke University of Magdeburg

Raab A. (1994b): *Aufbau und Funktionsweise eines Skizzen-Renderers*, Faculty of Computer Science, Otto-von-Guericke University of Magdeburg

Rand H. (1993): *Hundertwasser*, Benedikt Taschen Verlag, Cologne

Rathgeber M. (1990): *Tactile computer-prints for blind people*, Studienarbeit, Department of Computer Science, University of Stuttgart

Redmiles D. (1992): From programming tasks to solutions – bridging the gap through the explanation of examples, Technical Report CU-CS-629-92, Department of Computer Science, University of Colorado at Boulder

Reischuk K. (1990) : *Einführung in die Komplexitätstheorie. Leitfäden und Monographien der Informatik*, Teubner Verlag, Stuttgart

Reisig W. (1985): *Systementwurf mit Netzen*, Springer-Verlag, Berlin

Rheingold H. (1991): *Virtual reality*, Summit Books, New York, NY

Rist T. (1995): *Wissensbasierte Verfahren für den automatischen Entwurf von Gebrauchsgraphik in der technischen Dokumentation*. PhD Thesis, Technical Faculty, University of the Saarland, Saarbrücken

Rist T., André E. (1990): Wissensbasierte Perspektivenwahl für die automatische Erzeugung von 3D-Objektdarstellungen, *German Computer Society Workshop on Graphics and AI*, Bonn, April 2-3. In: K. Kansy, P. Wißkirchen (eds.), *Informatik-Fachberichte 239*, Springer-Verlag, Berlin, pp. 48–57

Robertson G.G., Card S.K., Mackinlay J.D. (1993): Information visualization using 3D interactive animation, *Communications of the ACM 36* (4), pp. 56–71

Rösner D. (1986): *Ein System zur Generierung von deutschen Texten aus semantischen Repräsentationen*, PhD Thesis, Department of Computer Science, University of Stuttgart

Rohr G. (1984): Understanding visual symbols, *Proc. IEEE Workshop on Visual Languages*, Hiroshima, December, pp. 184–191

Rohr G. (1986): Using visual concepts. In: S.-K. Chang, T. Ichikawa, P.A. Ligonenides (eds.), *Visual languages*, Plenum Press, New York, NY, pp. 325–348

Rohr G. (1988): Grundlagen menschlicher Informationsverarbeitung. In: H. Balzert (ed.), *Einführung in die Softwareergonomie*, Walter de Gruyter, Berlin, pp. 27–48

Rosenfeld A., Kak A.C. (1982): *Digial picture processing*, Vol. 1 and 2, Academic Press, London

Rüger M., Preim B., Ritter A. (1996): Zoom navigation: Exploring large information and application spaces. *Proc. Advanced Visual Interfaces '96*, Gubbio, Italy, May, pp. 40–48

Rüger M., Behlau T. (1995): Create!: An object-oriented ide for descrete event simulation. In: C. Alexopoulous, K. Kang, W.R. Lilegdon, D. Goldsman (eds.), *Proc. 1995 Winter Simulation Conference*, Arlington, VA, pp. 775–780

Russo P., Boor S. (1993): How fluent is your interface? Designing for international users, *Proc. INTERCHI '93, Human Factors in Computing Systems*, Amsterdam, April, pp. 342–347

Sachs-Hombach K. (ed.) (1995): *Bilder im Geiste. Zur kognitiven und erkenntnistheoretischen Funktion piktorialer Repräsentationen*, Rodopi, Amsterdam

Sachs-Hombach K. (1995b): Der Mensch als homo pictor. In: H. Kämpf, R. Schott (eds.), *Zeitschrift für Ästhetik und allgemeine Kunstwissenschaft*, Beiheft 1, Bonvier, Bonn

Sack J.-R., Toussaint G. (1987): Separability of pairs of polygons through single translations, *Robotica 5*, pp. 55–63

Saito T., Takahashi T. (1990): Comprehensible rendering of 3-D shapes, *Computer Graphics 24* (4), Siggraph '90, pp. 197–206

Saussure F. de (1967): *Grundfragen der allgemeinen Sprachwissenschaft*, 2nd edition, Berlin

Schleich R., Dürst R. (1994): Beyond WYSIWYG: Display of hidden information in graphics editors, *Computer Graphics Forum 13* (3), pp. 185-194

Schmid C. (1989): *Grenzen sprachlicher Darstellungen in der Informationsverarbeitung*, Diplomarbeit, Department of Comptuer Science, University of Stuttgart

Schmidt J. (1992): Simulationseinsatz gegen das Planungsrisiko, *Fördern und Heben 42* (4), pp. 220–222

Schneider P. (1984): *Matisse*, Prestel, Munich

Scholz O.R. (1991): *Bild, Darstellung, Zeichen. Philosophische Theorien bildhafter Darstellung*, Verlag Karl Alber, Freiburg i.Br.

Scholz O.R. (1993): When is a picture? *Synthese 95*, pp. 95–106

Schriber T.J. (1991): *An introduction to simulation using GPSS/H*, John Wiley & Sons, New York, NY

Schriber T.J. (1992): Perspectives on simulation using GPSS. In: J.J. Swain, D. Goldsman, R.C. Crain, J.R. Wilson (eds.), *Proc. 1992 Winter Simulation Conference*, Arlington, VA, pp. 338–342

Schumann J. (1993): *Linienqualität in ungenauen Graphiken*, Diplomarbeit, Faculty of Computer Science, Technical University of Magdeburg

Schumann J., Godenschweger F. (1993): *Sketch-Rendering von 3D-Modellen*, Technical Report B-93-15, Department of Computer Science, Free University of Berlin

Schumann J., Strothotte T., Raab A., Laser S. (1996): Assessing the effect of non-photorealistic rendered images in computer-aided design, *Proc. CHI '96, Human Factors in Computing Systems*, April, Vancouver, BC, pp. 35–41

Schürholz A. (1991): Create! – Entwicklungsstand und Funktionsumfang einer objektorientierten Simulatorenentwicklungsumgebung, *Fortschritte in der Simulationstechnik, ASIM Symposium Simulationstechnik*, Hagen, September, pp. 10–14

Schuster M. (1992): *Wodurch Bilder wirken*. Psychologie der Kunst, DuMont Buchverlag, Cologne

Schweikhardt W. (1985): Interaktives Erkunden von Graphiken durch Blinde, *Proc. Software-Ergonomie '85*, Stuttgart, March; *German Chapter of the ACM*, Teubner-Verlag, Stuttgart, pp. 366–375

Schweikhardt W. (1993): Beiträge der Informatik zur Integration Blinder. In: H.-D. Boecker, W. Glatthaar, Th. Strothotte (eds.), *Mensch-Computer-Kommunikation. Benutzergerechte Systeme auf dem Weg in die Praxis*, Springer-Verlag, Berlin, pp. 179–189

Shneiderman B. (1992): *Designing the user interface. Strategies for effective human-computer interaction*, 2nd edition, Addison-Wesley, Reading, MA

Shu N.C. (1989): *Visual Programming*, Van Nostrand Reinhold, New York, NY

Sedgewick R. (1988): *Algorithms*, 2nd edition, Addison-Wesley, Reading, MA

Seligmann D.D. (1993): *Interactive intend-based illustration: A visual language for 3D worlds*, PhD Thesis, Department of Computer Science, Columbia University, New York, NY

Semmler J. (1992): *Verfahren zur maschinellen Erzeugung von Skizzen aus formalen Szenenbeschreibungen*, Studienarbeit, Faculty of Electrical Engineering, Technical University of Berlin

Shannon C.E., Weaver W. (1969): *The mathematical theory of communication*, University of Illinois Press, Urbana, IL

Shaw C. (1993): The MR toolkit peers package and experiment, *Skigraph '93*, Vernon, BC, March

Shiffrin R.M. (1977): Capacity limitations in information processing, attention, and memory. In: W.K. Estes (eds.), *Handbook of learning and cognitive processes 4*, Lawrence Erlbaum, Hillsdale, NJ, pp. 177–236

Slater M., Usoh M. (1993): Presence in immersive virtual environments, *Proc. IEEE Virtual Reality Annual International Symposium*, Seattle, WA, September, pp. 33–40.

Smith A.R. (1984): Plants, fractals and formal languages. In: Hank Christiansen (ed.), *Computer Graphics 18*, pp. 1–10

Smith D.C. (1977): *Pygmalion. A computer program to model and stimulate creative thought*, Birkhäuser, Stuttgart

Smith J.B., Weiss S.F. (1988): Hypertext, *Communications of the ACM 31* (7), pp. 816–819

Sowa J.F. (1984): *Conceptual structures – Information processing in mind and machine*, Addison-Wesley, Reading, MA

Spada H. (1990): *Allgemeine Psychologie*, Verlag Hans Huber, Bern

Sperber D., Wilson D. (1986): *Relevance: Communication and cognition*, Blackwell, Oxford

Stading L., Conezio J., Haber R.N. (1970): Perception and memory for pictures: Single-trial learning of 2560 visual stimuli, *Psychonomic Science 19*, pp. 73–74

Staufer M.J. (1987): *Piktogramme für Computer: Kognitive Verarbeitung, Methoden zur Produktion und Evaluation*, Walter de Gruyter, Berlin

Steller E. (1994): *Computer und Kunst*, BI-Wissenschaftsverlag, Mannheim

Stiebner E.D., Urban D. (1988): *Zeichen + Signets 1*, F. Bruckmann KG, Munich

Stiebner E.D., Urban D. (1989): *Zeichen + Signets 2*, F. Bruckmann KG, Munich

Strassmann S. (1986): Hairy brushes, *Computer Graphics 20* (4), pp. 225–232

Strombach W. (1992): Die verschiedenen Aspekte von Information, *Grundlagenstudien aus Kybernetik und Geisteswissenschaft/Humankybernetik 33* (3), September, pp. 99–112

Strothotte C. (1995): Viewpoint descriptions influencing animation models, *Proc. Modelling and Simulation*, Prague, pp. 225–229

Strothotte T. (1989) : *Interaktive und wissensbasierte Methoden zur Integrierten Bild- und Sprachkommunikation*, Habilitationsschrift, Faculty of Computer Science, University of Stuttgart

Strothotte T. (1989b): Pictures in advice-giving systems: From knowledge representation to the user interface, *Proc. Graphics Interface '89*, June, London, ON, pp. 94–99

Strothotte T. Böcke D. (1989): Informationsvermittlung in interaktiven wissensbasierten Systemen durch bildhafte Darstellungen, *Proc. Software-Ergonomie '89*, Hamburg, *Berichte des German Chapter des ACM 32*, Teubner-Verlag, Stuttgart, pp. 345–354

Strothotte T., Kurze M., Fellbaum K., Krause M., Crispien K. (1993): Multimedia interfaces for blind computer users. In: E. Ballabio, I. Placencia Porrero, R. Puig de la Bellacasa (eds.), *Studies in health technology and interfaces 9*, IOS Press, Amsterdam, pp. 30–34

Strothotte T., Preim B., Raab A., Schumann J., Forsey D.R. (1994): How to render frames and influence people, *Computer Graphics Forum 13* (3), September, pp. 455–466

Strothotte T., Rojas R., Deconinck F. (1993): Anti-Perfektionismus in Computerausgaben am Beispiel von ungenauen Graphiken, *Software-Ergonomie '93*, Bremen, March; *Berichte des German Chapter of the ACM*, Teubner-Verlag, Stuttgart, pp. 111–122

Strothotte T., Schmid C. (1990): Semiformale Darstellungen in wissensbasierten Systemen, *German Computer Society Workshop on Graphics and AI*, Bonn, April. In: K. Kansy, P. Wißkirchen (eds.), *Informatik-Fachberichte 239*, Springer-Verlag, Berlin, pp. 1–9

Sutherland I.E. (1965): The ultimate display, *Proc. IFIP Congress*, 2, pp. 506–508

Sutherland I.E. (1968): A head-mounted three dimensional display, *Proc. FJCC*, Thompson Books, Washington, DC, pp. 757–764

Takala T., Hahn J. (1992): Sound rendering, *Computer Graphics 26* (2), pp. 211–220

Thimbleby H. (1990): *User interface design*, ACM Press, New York, NY

Travers R.M.W. (1964): The transmission of communication to human receivers, *AV Communication Review 12*, pp. 373–385

Tsal Y., Kolbet L. (1985): Disambiguating ambigious figures by selective attention, *The Quarterly Journal of Experimental Psychology*, 37 A, p. 28

Tufte E.R. (1983): *The visual display of quantitative information*, Graphics Press, Cheshire, CN

Tufte E.R. (1990): *Envisioning information*, Graphics Press, Cheshire, CN

Van Bakergem O. (1991): Free hand plotting: Is it live or is it digital?, *CAAD-Futures '91*, Verlag Schmitt/Vieweg, pp. 567–582

Van Sommers P. (1984) : *Drawing and cognition*, Cambridge University Press, Cambridge

Varela F.J. (1990): *Kognitionswissenschaft, Kognitionstechnik: eine Skizze aktueller Perspektiven*, Suhrkamp Verlag, Frankfurt a.M.

VDI (1992): Verein Deutscher Ingenieure, VDI-Richtlinie 3633: *Anwendung der Simulationstechnik zur Materialflußplanung*, VDI Verlag, Düsseldorf

Vernon D. (1991): *Machine vision*, Prentice-Hall, Englewood Cliffs, NJ

Viewpoint Datalabs (1995): *Viewpoint datalabs int'l catalogue*, 625 South State Street, Orem, UT 84058, USA

Vincent G., Germeau E. (1991): *Ernest et Célestine – Le patchwork*, Feeling, Brussels, (Adaptation of the book published by: Editions Duclot, Paris 1982)

von Bertalanffy L. (1969): *General systems theory*, George Braziller, New York, NY

von der Herberg H. (1988): X INSPECTOR Ein Navigationswerkzeug zur Untersuchung von Objektstrukturen. In: R. Gunzenhäuser, H.-D. Böcker (eds.), *Prototypen benutzergerechter Systeme*, Walter de Gruyter, Berlin

Wahlster W., André E., Finkler W., Profitlich H.J., Rist T. (1994): Plan-based integration of natural language and graphics generation. In: F.C.N. Pereira., B.J. Grosz (eds.), *Natural Language Processing*, MIT/Elsevier, Cambridge, MA, pp. 387–427; see also *Articicial Intelligence 63*, pp. 387–427.

Waldeyer A., Mayet A. (1987): *Anatomie des Menschen 1*, Walter de Gruyter, Berlin

Ware C., Arthur K.W., Booth K.S. (1993): Fish tank virtual reality, *Proc. INTERCHI '93, Human Factors in Computing Systems*, Amsterdam, April, pp. 37–42

Waters F. (1963): *Book of the Hopi*, Penguin Books, New York, NY

Watt A., Watt M. (1993): *Advanced animation and rendering techniques*, ACM Press, New York, NY; Addison-Wesley, Wokingham, UK

Weber G., Kochanek D., Stephanidis C., Homatas G. (1993): Access by blind people to interaction objects in MS Windows, *Proc. ECART 2*, Stockholm, pp. 2.1

Webster (1986): *Webster's third new international dictionary*, Encyclopedia Britannica, Chicago, IL

Webster (1990): *Webster's ninth new collegiate dictionary*, Merriam-Webster, Springfield, MA

Weghorst H., Hooper G., Greenberg D.P. (1984): Improved computational methods for ray tracing, *ACM Transactions on Graphics 3* (1), pp. 52–69

Weidenmann B. (1986): Psychologie des Lernens mit Medien. In: B. Weidenmann, A. Krapp (eds.), *Pädagogische Psychologie*, Urban & Schwarzenberg, Munich, pp. 493–554

Weidenmann B. (1988): *Psychische Prozesse beim Verstehen von Bildern*, Verlag Hans Huber, Bern

Wertheimer M. (1923): Untersuchungen zur Lehre von der Gestalt, *Psychologische Forschung 4*, pp. 301–351

Willows D.M., Houghton H.A. (eds.) (1987): *The psychology of illustration*. Volume 1: *Basic research*, Springer-Verlag, Berlin

Winkelbach G., Salesin D.H. (1994): Computer-generated pen-and-ink illustrations, *Computer Graphics 28* (4), pp. 91–100

Winograd T., Flores F. (1992): *Erkenntnis Maschinen Verstehen*, Rotbuch Verlag, Berlin; *Understanding computers and cognition: A new foundation for design*, Ablex, Norwood, NJ, 1986, paperback by Addison-Wesley, Reading, MA, 1987

Winston P.H. (1975): *The psychology computer vision*, McGraw-Hill, New York, NY

Winston P.H. (1992): *Artificial intelligence*, 3rd edition, Addison-Wesley, Reading, MA

Wittek M. (1993): *Entwicklung und Anwendungen einer Sichtbeschreibung für Create!*, Diplomarbeit, Faculty of Computer Science, Technical University of Magdeburg

Wolfram S. (1991): *Mathematica – A system for doing mathematics by computer*, Addison-Wesley, Reading, MA

Wong Y.Y. (1992): Rough and ready prototypes: Lessons from graphics design, *Proc. CHI '92 Human Factors in Computing Systems*, Monterey, CA, short talk, pp. 83–84

Yourdon E. (1989): *Modern structured analysis*, Prentice-Hall, Englewood Cliffs, NJ

Zelazny G. (1985): *Say it with charts*, Dow Jones-Irwin, Homewood, IL

Zell M., Scheer A.W. (1991): Graphikunterstützte Simulation in der dezentralen Fertigungssteuerung, *Proc. Operations Research*, Springer-Verlag, Berlin, pp. 243–252

# Subject Index

3D computer graphics 25; 36; 42
3D model 36; 37

abstract symbols 192
abstract-graphical picture 46; 47; 55; 57; 58; 60;
    109; 110; 111; 114; 115; 127; 128; 173; 177;
    216; 223; 249; 297; 298; 316; 323
    analysis 116
    availability 116
    characterisation 101; 102
    focus on behaviour 105
    focus on functionality 104
    focus on properties of elements 107
    focus on relations 102
    for instruction 113; 115
acoustic output 283
active help 93
AdOculos™ 117
ALGOL 68 218
animation 148; 149; 228; 239; 329
    criticism 134; 138
    observation of 147; 160
    planning 239
    role of 133; 170
    underestimation 133
animation model 245
AniPLuS 148; 243; 246
architectural
    design 258
    picture 103
Arena™ 148
attention 230
augmented reality 298
AutoMod 39

blind users 313
Braille 282
    display 283
bubble chart 104
business graphics 107; 121; 122; 123; 124; 216
    interpretation 121

CAD 59; 258
camera 290; 299
    position 232; 233
cave-paintings 43
CINEMA 132
cinematic editing 239
cinematographic language 328
cinems 328
code of ethics 339
cognitive
    activity 110
    capacity 199
    overhead 95
    processes 70; 177
    processing 198
    psychology 154
    skills 94
    stress 198
    workload 201
cognitivism 70
color
    cultural associations 212
comics 59
communication 97
    high-level language 97
    low-level language 97
    theory 175
communicative
    goals 239
    intent 10
    theory 72
complexity theory 135; 136
    data structures 88; 103
computational geometry 235
computer 258
computer assisted instruction 184
computer graphics 227; 278; 284
    expressive power 265
    uses of 279
computer supported co-operative work 305
concordance 32
configuration 259; 262
connectionism 70
constraints 231

# Author Index